Market and Society

Karl Polanyi's 1944 book *The Great Transformation* offered a radical critique of how the market system has affected society and humanity since the industrial revolution. This volume brings together contributions from distinguished scholars in economic anthropology, sociology, and political economy to consider Polanyi's theories in the light of circumstances today, when the relationship between market and society has again become a focus of intense political and scientific debate. It demonstrates the relevance of Polanyi's ideas to various theoretical traditions in the social sciences and provides new perspectives on topics such as money, risk, work, and the family. The case studies present materials from around the world, including Britain, China, India, Jamaica, and Nigeria. Like Polanyi's original work, the critical engagement of these essays will be of interest to a wide readership.

CHRIS HANN is a director of the Max Planck Institute for Social Anthropology in Halle, Germany.

KEITH HART is Professor of Anthropology Emeritus at Goldsmiths College, University of London.

Market and Society: *The Great Transformation* Today

Edited by

Chris Hann

and

Keith Hart

CAMBRIDGE
UNIVERSITY PRESS

CAMBRIDGE UNIVERSITY PRESS
Cambridge, New York, Melbourne, Madrid, Cape Town,
Singapore, São Paulo, Delhi, Tokyo, Mexico City

Cambridge University Press
The Edinburgh Building, Cambridge CB2 8RU, UK

Published in the United States of America by Cambridge University Press, New York

www.cambridge.org
Information on this title: www.cambridge.org/9780521295086

First published 2009
First paperback edition 2011

A catalogue record for this publication is available from the British Library

ISBN 978-0-521-51965-6 Hardback
ISBN 978-0-521-29508-6 Paperback

Cambridge University Press has no responsibility for the persistence or
accuracy of URLs for external or third-party internet websites referred to in
this publication, and does not guarantee that any content on such websites is,
or will remain, accurate or appropriate.

Contents

List of figures and table   *page* vii
List of contributors   ix

1   Introduction: Learning from Polanyi 1   1
    KEITH HART AND CHRIS HANN

2   Necessity or contingency: Mutuality and market   17
    STEPHEN GUDEMAN

3   The great transformation of embeddedness: Karl Polanyi
    and the new economic sociology   38
    JENS BECKERT

4   The critique of the economic point of view: Karl Polanyi
    and the Durkheimians   56
    PHILIPPE STEINER

5   Toward an alternative economy: Reconsidering the market,
    money, and value   72
    JEAN-MICHEL SERVET

6   Money in the making of world society   91
    KEITH HART

7   Debt, violence, and impersonal markets: Polanyian meditations   106
    DAVID GRAEBER

8   Whatever happened to householding?   133
    CHRIS GREGORY

9   Contesting *The Great Transformation*: Work in
    comparative perspective   160
    GERD SPITTLER

10 "Sociological Marxism" in Central India: Polanyi, Gramsci,
    and the case of the unions   175
    JONATHAN PARRY

11 Composites, fictions, and risk: toward an ethnography of price   203
    JANE I. GUYER

12 Illusions of freedom: Polanyi and the third sector   221
    CATHERINE ALEXANDER

13 Market and economy in environmental conservation
    in Jamaica   240
    JAMES G. CARRIER

14 Embedded socialism? Land, labour, and money
    in eastern Xinjiang   256
    CHRIS HANN

15 Afterword: Learning from Polanyi 2   272
    DON ROBOTHAM

Bibliography   284
Index   313

Figures and Table

Figures

8.1 A "Porphyrian tree" illustrating the key distinctions in
     Polanyi's (1944) concepts   *page* 137
8.2 A Venn diagram to illustrate Polanyi's (1944) interpretation
     of Aristotle's distinction between production for use and
     production for gain   137
8.3 The relationship between Marx's central concepts: slave-,
     serf-, and wage-labor.   140
8.4 "Householding" may be either autarkic or non-autarkic,
     or both – a modification of Polanyi's (1944) basic framework   143
8.5 A new concept: householding of the non-autarkic kind   147

Table

8.1 A tabular presentation of Polanyi's first
     conceptual toolbox   136

Contributors

CATHERINE ALEXANDER is reader in anthropology at Goldsmiths College, University of London. She is working on the third sector and a series of projects related to waste in Britain and Kazakhstan. She has published on the processes and effects of privatization in Turkey (*Personal States: Making Connections Between People and Bureaucracy in Turkey* [2002]) and also in Kazakhstan and Britain. She is writing a book, *Mercurial Cities*, on changes to Almaty in Kazakhstan since 1991.

JENS BECKERT is managing director of the Max Planck Institute for the Study of Societies in Cologne. His research focuses on the role of the economy in society, with particular reference to studies of markets, organizational sociology, sociology of inheritance, and sociological theory. His recent books are *Beyond the Market: The Social Foundations of Economic Efficiency* (2002), (edited with Milan Zafirovski) *International Encyclopedia of Economic Sociology* (2005), and *Inherited Wealth* (2007).

JAMES G. CARRIER has done research and taught in Papua New Guinea, the United States, and Great Britain, and has research affiliations in anthropology at Oxford Brookes University and at the University of Indiana. His current research is on the economic anthropology and political economy of environmental conservation in Jamaica. His publications in economic anthropology include *Gifts and Commodities* (1995) and the edited collections *Meanings of the Market* (1997), *Virtualism* (1998, co-editor with Daniel Miller), and *A Handbook of Economic Anthropology* (2005).

DAVID GRAEBER is reader in anthropology at Goldsmiths College, University of London. Apart from continuing work on value theory, he has a long term research project on direct action and direct democracy within global social movements. He is the author of *Toward an Anthropological Theory of Value* (2001), as well as *Lost People: Magic and the Legacy of Slavery in Madagascar* (2007) and a collection of essays, *Possibilities* (2007).

CHRIS GREGORY is reader in anthropology at the Australian National University, Canberra. His current research interests are the political economy and culture of rice-growing in middle India, and Halbi kinship in comparative context. He is the author of *Savage Money: The Anthropology and Politics of Commodity Exchange* (1997) and (with Harihar Vaishnav) *Lachmi Jagar: Gurumai Sukdai's Story of the Rice Goddess of Bastar* (2003) (in Halbi, Hindi and English).

STEPHEN GUDEMAN is professor of anthropology at the University of Minnesota. He has undertaken fieldwork in Panama, Colombia, Guatemala, and Cuba. His interests include social, symbolic, and material life. In many of his writings, he approaches economics through the lens of anthropology and in reverse. He is currently editing a book, *Economic Persuasions*, and he recently completed *Economy's Tension* (2008). Previous publications include *The Anthropology of Economy* (2001), *Conversations in Colombia* (with Alberto Rivera) (1990), and *The Demise of a Rural Economy* (1978).

JANE I. GUYER is professor of anthropology at Johns Hopkins University. Her research has been primarily in Nigeria and Cameroon, being first devoted to production dynamics and later to money as well. Her most recent books are *Marginal Gains: Monetary Transactions in Atlantic Africa* (2004) and an edited collection (with LaRay Denzer and Adigun Agbaje) on the Nigerian popular economy under structural adjustment and military rule, *Money Struggles and City Life: Devaluation in Ibadan and Other Urban Areas in Southern Nigeria, 1986–96* (2004).

CHRIS HANN is a director of the Max Planck Institute for Social Anthropology in Halle, where he leads the "Socialist and Postsocialist Eurasia" program. Recent books, all in the series *Halle Studies in the Anthropology of Eurasia*, have been *The Postsocialist Agrarian Question; Property Relations and the Rural Condition* (2003, with the "Property Relations" Group), *"Not the Horse We Wanted!": Postsocialism, Neoliberalism and Eurasia* (2006), and *The Postsocialist Religious Question; Faith and Power in Central Asia and East-Central Europe* (2006, with the "Civil Religion" Group).

KEITH HART is professor of anthropology emeritus at Goldsmiths College, University of London. His work in economic anthropology has focused recently on money, informal economy, and the Internet. He is the author of *The Memory Bank: Money in an Unequal World* (2000), *The Hit Man's Dilemma: Or Business, Personal and Impersonal* (2005), and *The African Revolution: Africa in the 21st Century World* (forthcoming).

JONATHAN PARRY is professor of anthropology emeritus at the London School of Economics and Political Science. He has done field research in various parts of north and central India on different topics, most recently on industrial labor. His publications include *Caste and Kinship in Kangra* (1979),

Death in Banaras (1994), and edited volumes on *Money and the Morality of Exchange* (with M. Bloch, 1989) and *The Worlds of Indian Industrial Labour* (with J. Breman and K. Kapadia, 1999).

DON ROBOTHAM is professor of anthropology at the Graduate Center, City University of New York, where he specializes in the Caribbean and West Africa (Ghana). His interests are in political economy, development, and social and cultural theory. His most recent work is *Culture, Society and Economy: Bringing Production Back In* (2005).

JEAN-MICHEL SERVET is professor of economics and finance at the Graduate Institute of Development Studies (Geneva) and Associate Research Director at the Institut d'Études du Développement (Paris). He founded the "Microfinance and Socially Sustainable Development Programme" at the French Institute of Pondicherry (India). He is the author of *Banquiers aux pieds nus: la microfinance* (2006), co-editor of *Microfinance en Asie: entre traditions et innovations* (2006), and a contributor to the *Dictionnaire de l'autre économie* (2006).

GERD SPITTLER is professor emeritus of social anthropology at Bayreuth University. His current research concerns the anthropology of work and a comparative study of consumption in African societies and Germany. His recent books include: *Founders of the Anthropology of Work* (2008), *Heinrich Barth et l'Afrique* (2006, co-edited with Mamadou Diawara and Paulo Fernando de Farias), *Between Resistance and Expansion: Explorations of Local Vitality in Africa* (2004, co-edited with Peter Probst).

PHILIPPE STEINER is professor of sociology at the University of Paris IV-Sorbonne, and co-director of the research group "Économie et sociologie" of the CNRS. His interests include the intellectual history of political economy and the social sciences, and the economic sociology of markets. His current field research is on organ transplantation and the limits to the market. He is the author of *La sociologie économique* (2005), *L'école durkheimienne et l'économie: sociologie, réligion et connaissance* (2005), and editor of *Traité de sociologie économique* (forthcoming).

1   Introduction: Learning from Polanyi 1

Keith Hart and Chris Hann

Market and society

Markets are networks constituted by acts of buying and selling, usually through the medium of money. For most of history they were kept marginal to the mainstream institutions on which societies were built. But not long ago, and at first only in some parts of the world, markets came to be accepted as central to society, leading to a vigorous political debate, which is ongoing, about the appropriate relationship between the two. It is widely acknowledged that the publication of Adam Smith's *The Wealth of Nations* in 1776 provided a charter for "the market" (now often singular) to assume its place as the dominant institution of modern societies. The idea of economy, which started out as a principle of rural household management, now became closely identified with markets, as did the profession of economics which grew up to study them. One man, however, made the modern history of the relationship between market and society his special concern: Karl Polanyi (1886–1964), whose *The Great Transformation*, published during the Second World War, remains the most powerful indictment of what he considered to be the utopian and ultimately destructive attempt to build society on the basis of self-regulating markets. Our authors therefore consider the relevance of this Central European polymath for their work.

All the agrarian civilizations of Eurasia tried to keep markets and money in check, since power came from the landed property of an aristocratic military caste who were afraid that markets might undermine their control over society. This opposition was expressed in medieval Europe as one between the "natural economy" of the countryside and the commerce of the city. Earlier, Aristotle, as tutor to Alexander the Great when the Macedonian cavalry overran the Greek cities, preferred to found society on the self-sufficiency of manorial estates, declaring that markets geared to profit-making were antisocial. This view of economy (*oikonomia*, literally "household management") prevailed until the dawn of the modern era, when Jane Austen could describe one of her characters as a poor "economist" for her inability to handle the servants. When Marx and Engels claimed that history had been a struggle between town and countryside, they had this conflict between landed power and urban commerce in mind.

In stateless societies, too, markets were usually kept marginal and subject to regulation by the agents of dominant social institutions. Thus, according to the contributors to *Markets in Africa* (Bohannan and Dalton 1962), a volume put together by Polanyi's followers, markets there were traditionally restricted to specific times and places, leaving the bulk of production and consumption to be organized by kinship ties. Colonial demand for export crops and wage labor meant that the market principle became more pervasive, undermining the existing authorities. Why are markets supposed to be subversive of traditional social arrangements? Because commerce knows no bounds – all markets are in a sense world markets – and this threatens local systems of control. They offer a potential means of escape to the dominated classes: women, young people, serfs and slaves, ethnic minorities. The power of long-distance merchants often modified the autonomy of local rulers; and markets have not always been peripheral. Rather, a dialectic of local and global economy defined the struggle between these competing interests long before they became prominent features of the way we perceive the modern world. Traditional societies have varied in the methods they adopted to tackle the problem of markets. But one common ploy was restriction of mercantile activities to excluded ethnic groups, thereby ensuring that local citizens had no access to money and that those who did lacked political power. The most famous example was the pariah status of Jews in medieval Europe. Another method was to prevent merchants from investing in production, with the same ultimate intention of protecting local monopolies of power from the disruptive influence of markets and money.

So Adam Smith knew what he was taking on when he proposed that society had nothing to fear from markets and indeed much to gain. As a moral philosopher, Smith was not prone to celebrate the narrow pursuit of self-interest in market transactions; but he found it preferable to indulge this trait en masse than to concentrate economic power in the hands of an ostensibly high-minded elite. He stood conventional wisdom on its head by asserting that a "propensity to truck and barter" was part of human nature and that markets had a better chance than any other means of increasing "the wealth of nations." He stopped short of claiming that society's interests as a whole were best served by markets left to their own devices; but these reservations have largely been forgotten.

The last two centuries have seen a strident debate between capitalist and socialist camps insisting that markets are either good or bad for society. The latter draws implicitly on the pre-industrial apologists for landed rule, whose line was, broadly speaking, Aristotle's. Karl Marx himself considered money to be indispensable to any complex economy and was radically opposed to the state in any form. However, many of his socialist and communist followers, when they did not try to outlaw markets and money altogether, preferred to return them to the marginal position they occupied under agrarian civilization and were less hostile to the state, pre-industrial society's enduring legacy for our world. Polanyi falls within this camp in that he acknowledged Aristotle as his master and considered "the self-regulating market" to have been the principal cause of the twentieth-century's horrors.

A less apocalyptic version of socialism in the tradition of Saint-Simon acknowledges the social damage done by unfettered markets (what Joseph Schumpeter (1948) called "creative destruction"), but would not wish to do away with the wealth they produce. Indeed, the leading capitalist societies at one stage all signed up for Hegel's (1821) idea that states should try to contain the inequality and ameliorate the social misery generated by markets. Within this framework, the emphasis has shifted over time between reliance on states and on markets for managing national economy, between social and liberal democracy of various hues. The general economic breakdown of the 1930s turned a large number of American economists away from celebrating the logic of markets toward contemplating their repair. This "institutional economics" persists as the notion that markets need self-conscious social intervention if they are to serve the public interest. John Maynard Keynes (1936) produced the most impressive synthesis of liberalism and social democracy in the last century. Much recent writing on Polanyi would place him more squarely in this category rather than as a card-carrying antimarketeer. Indeed, in *The Great Transformation* he did recognize that markets and the principle of barter associated with them coexisted with reciprocity, redistribution, and householding, which he viewed as the primary "principles of economic behavior" (2001: 59).

The market's apologists likewise divide between some for whom it is a transhistorical machine for economic improvement best left to itself and those who acknowledge a role for enlightened public management of commerce. Classical liberals promoted markets as a means toward greater individual freedom as a corrective to the arbitrary social inequality of the Old Regime. But the industrial revolution brought about a shift to urban commerce that made vast new populations of wage labourers rely on markets for food, housing, and all their basic needs. Under these circumstances, in Britain in particular, society itself seemed to retreat from view, being replaced by an "economy" characterized this time by market contracts instead of domestic self-sufficiency. Indeed, Margaret Thatcher, one of the architects of the contemporary revival of market fundamentalism, once said "There is no such thing as society." Others hold that society's remaining defenses are simply too weak to hold out against the rising tide of global money: you can't buck "the markets." Unregulated markets are engines of inequality, so this notion of markets as a natural force beyond social regulation serves also to legitimize wealth and even to make poverty seem deserved.

The founders of modern social theory all considered markets to be progressive in that they broke up the insularity of traditional rural society and brought humanity into wider circles of discourse and interaction. But the founders also differed over the consequences of this move. Karl Marx and Friedrich Engels considered that the power of private money ("capital") was too fragmented to organize the urban societies brought into being by machine-production of commodities; so they looked to the enhanced social potential of large concentrations of workers for a truly collective remedy. Max Weber recognized that the formal rationality of capitalist bureaucracy led to the substantive deterioration of livelihood for many. But, as a liberal, he considered wholesale state intervention in markets to be a recipe for economic disaster. Émile Durkheim and Marcel Mauss were both socialists who wanted to emphasize the human interdependence entailed in an expanded social role for markets and money, while rejecting the Social Darwinist claim that an unfettered capitalism ensures the "survival of the fittest."

Karl Polanyi's position in relation to these founders was distinctive. In what follows we will introduce the argument of his greatest book and explain its continuing relevance. In the process we hope to indicate why Polanyi's stock as a social thinker is rising and how we can learn from his work.

The Great Transformation

Karl Polanyi lived for most of his life in Central Europe, but he wrote the bulk of *The Great Transformation: The Political and Economic Origins of Our Times* ([1944] 2001) in a small New England college near the Canadian border at the height of the Second World War. He wrote it in the spirit of an Old Testament prophet, but his prophecy turned out to be wrong. The world was coming to the end of a period of unparalleled human disasters – two world wars, the Great Depression, Fascism, Stalinism, and a lot of ugly conflicts like the Spanish Civil War. He believed that only social planning could meet human needs and repair the disaster of committing society to a market framework. Even after 1945, many people thought civilization would not soon recover; and it took the Korean War to bump-start the economic recovery of the 1950s and 1960s. But the world liberal economy did recover under American leadership, thereby refuting Polanyi's claim that the market was finished as the prime vehicle for organizing society.

His historical analysis went as follows. The nineteenth century – 1815 (the end of the Napoleonic wars) to 1914 – was a period of peace and prosperity, at least for the major European nations. It rested on the self-regulating market, the gold standard, the liberal state, and the balance of power. But the whole exercise was utopian and misguided, and in the first half of the twentieth century the chickens came home to roost. Following Aristotle, Polanyi believed that society was a natural form designed to provide material sustenance for its members. In time various distribution measures had evolved to secure this: householding, reciprocity, and redistribution, with the market restricted to a peripheral role. The new apostles of political economy held that market economy could be self-regulating as long as everything was bought and sold without restriction. This led to what Polanyi called "the fictitious commodities." Nature, Society, and Humanity entered the market as land, money, and labor; and the traditions that ensured material provisioning for everyone were swept aside. In a "double movement," the rise of the market provoked various classes to act as the vehicles of protest on society's behalf, but the market was unswayed. The so-called "nightwatchman state" of liberal theory, a minimal state concerned only with regulating property, was a sham. Political power was used to ensure that capital was free to move where it wanted, but many other freedoms, such as the right to work, were sacrificed in order to achieve this. The gold standard made participation in international trade contingent on abandoning politically managed currencies (of the sort that Keynes reintroduced in order to cope with the 1930s' collapse of the market economy). And this economic interdependence underwrote a fragile peace, with only two minor wars being fought between the leading countries in the whole century.

It couldn't last and it didn't. The balance of power broke down in the First World War, the gold standard had to be abandoned, countries turned to authoritarian governments, and the market economy was ruined. The "freedom" of liberal theory was false because we must accept society as necessary in its natural form before we can exercise any other freedoms. Modern societies should be built on the ancient mechanisms evolved for managing distribution in primitive societies and agrarian civilizations, with the market relegated to a supplementary and marginal role.

Polanyi's interpretation of world history was deceptively simple. He presented the emergence of "market society" in the nineteenth century as a radical break. In this he resembles another child of Central Europe. Ernest Gellner (1983) contrasted *Industria* with *Agraria* and maintained that the modern nation-state was demarcated by a "Great Ditch" from all previous social formations. By contrast, Jack Goody links the rise of capitalism to the spread of markets and "merchant cultures" over millennia in various regions of Eurasia (Goody 2004; see also Graeber, in Chapter 7). From Goody's point of view, to focus on the advantage gained by Western Europe in the nineteenth century (or in Polanyi's case just one country, Britain) is to distort the broader picture. Polanyi was certainly aware of the *longue durée* stressed by Goody, and, indeed, he taught courses in general economic history (Fusfeld 1994). Nonetheless, he insisted that we should acknowledge the qualitative change that took place when "market society" first became dominant. This moment was epitomized by the repeal of the Speenhamland law in 1834 and the consequent reduction of human labor itself to the status of a "fictitious commodity."

Polanyi's characterization of this new institutional form as "the market" misses some important features of the bureaucratic capitalism that built up in the late nineteenth century, leading to the denouement of 1914–1945 or "the second thirty years war," as Winston Churchill called it. The modern synthesis of the nation-state and industrial capitalism may be termed "national capitalism:" the institutional attempt to manage money, markets, and accumulation through central bureaucracy. It is linked to the rise of large corporations as the dominant form of capitalist organization and is, in essence, Hegel's recipe in *The Philosophy of Right* (1821), namely, that only state power could contain the excesses of capitalism, while markets could in turn limit the excesses of political power. Society should be managed by an educated bureaucratic elite in the national interest. Marx certainly didn't envisage anything of this sort, but Weber recognized in it Germany's historical experience of the alliance between Rhineland capitalism and Prussian bureaucracy. "National capitalism" is still the dominant social form in our world, even if the transnational aspects of neoliberalism obscure that fact.

Polanyi's challenge to organize an industrial economy without the dehumanization of society was met in a very different manner by the socialist regimes that held power until the last decade of the twentieth century. Yet, despite the obvious affinity between his critique of market society and Marx's critique of capitalism, Polanyi was unsympathetic to Marxist economic determinism; although his wife Ilona Duczynska was active in several communist parties, he himself never joined. He was influenced by Christian socialists, especially during his years in Britain, but he never joined a church either. His sympathy for guild socialism reveals an affinity with Durkheim and Mauss (Hart 2007a). Polanyi interpreted the Hungarian revolution of 1956 as an effort to reform socialism rather than to reject it, and he was clearly attracted by some notions of a "third way" (McRobbie 1994a). He devoted his last years to the literary works of "populist" writers in the land where he grew up. Soon after his death, in 1964, the introduction of the New Economic Mechanism promoted a form of "market socialism" in Hungary. The debates of those years would surely have reminded Polanyi of his work on "socialist accounting" in the Vienna of the 1920s, when he stressed the need to counter the market sphere with principles of redistribution.

Hungary's socialist mixed economy was transformed as a result of the collapse of the Soviet bloc in 1990, though the changes here were less radical than elsewhere in the region. In recent years its government has again been led by a party that calls itself socialist. Although this is a socialism that seems closer to Tony Blair's "third way" in Britain (see Alexander, in Chapter 12) than to any Marxist legacy, the continued widespread sympathy for socialist welfare policies is unmistakeable. The debates about "market socialism" are of more than antiquarian interest, if only because China has been pursuing comparable "mixed" policies for several decades now. Would Polanyi be repelled by the increasing dominance of the profit motive in contemporary China, which has led to enormous social inequality without the freedoms of bourgeois democracy? Or would he impressed by how the expansion of markets has undoubtedly been associated with a reduction in poverty (see Hann, Robotham below)?

In 1957 Polanyi, with two colleagues from a Ford Foundation interdisciplinary project designed to keep him employed after retirement (Conrad Arensberg and Harry Pearson), produced a collection of essays, *Trade and Market in the Early Empires: Economies in History and Theory*. Polanyi (1957a) himself revisited the Aristotelian roots of his approach in one chapter, but it was the other that shaped post-war economic anthropology (see also Polanyi 1977). In "The economy as instituted process," Polanyi (1957b) says there are two meanings of the word "economic" that have been conflated: the substantive and the formal. He attributed this distinction to Carl Menger (1871). The first refers to the provisioning of material wants, whereas the second is a means–end relationship, the mental process of economizing. Most preindustrial societies are ruled by institutions that guarantee collective survival; but industrial societies have a delocalized economy, "the market," in which individual decision-making rules. This proposal that anthropologists and historians should focus on noncapitalist economies, leaving modern capitalism to the economists, proved to be congenial at the time and led to what became known as "the formalist–substantivist debate" (Frankenberg 1967). But this division of academic labor never had much intellectual credibility and the present collection therefore pays more attention to his great war-time polemic.

Polanyi's relevance to changing times

Karl Polanyi was a maverick public intellectual who spent more years working as a journalist than as a tenured academic. He was fundamentally an historian, while a keen appreciation of literature lent his best writing a memorable vivacity (McRobbie 2000). He was more interested in substantive historical change than in speculating about an abstract, formal rationality. A distinctive vision of what makes us all human underpins his work; but, as Gregory points out below, he sought general patterns rather than universal laws. It is easy to argue that his contribution to the modern understanding of society is relatively unsystematic and imprecise. Yet, far from fading into obscurity, his influence seems greater now than ever. Polanyi's life and texts have, in recent decades, been intensively scrutinized by scholars of various disciplines.[1] We do not seek to replicate this effort in this section or to add to it in any significant way but only to note the major factors which have influenced the historical reception of his ideas.

In *The Great Transformation,* Polanyi brought a radical critique of modern capitalism to bear on his moment in history. His recommendations seemed to be contradicted by the postwar boom, which rested on a combination of world markets and political management of the economy in the leading industrial nations. In the real world of economic policymaking his dramatic vision was effectively refuted from the 1940s onward, initially by British liberals such as Keynes and Beveridge and later by many capitalist governments espousing more or less the principles of social democracy, from post-New Deal USA to Nehruvian India (see Parry, in Chapter 10). Polanyi never engaged in any detail with the impact of Keynesianism, the new welfare states and the dangers which lurked in new forms of corporatism. In the context of a Cold War that formed the backcloth to his last years, he never saw any need to renounce his radical diagnosis.

Ours is a very different world from when Polanyi so confidently predicted the demise of the market model of economy (see Hart, in Chapter 6). Yet the revival of market capitalism and dismantling of state provision since the 1980s furnish plentiful material for Polanyi's thesis that the neglect of social interests must eventually generate a political backlash and a retreat from market fundamentalism. The last three decades have seen the reintroduction of something more like Victorian capitalism, with a much reduced role for the state, at least in the organization of economy. It may be that we are due for another round of disasters such as those Polanyi attributed to reliance on "free" markets for social organization. Cracks are already appearing in the façade of neoliberal hegemony; and the ongoing globalization of capital – its spread to Japan, China, India, Brazil, Russia, and elsewhere after centuries of Western monopoly – is also bound to affect our understanding of economy. The absolute dominance of market logic is less plausible today than it was not long ago; the recent surge of interest in Polanyi's ideas is therefore not surprising.

---

[1] An important new collection of essays on Polanyi in French was published just when our volume was being submitted for publication: "Avec Karl Polanyi, contre la société tout-marchand," *Revue du MAUSS Semestrielle,* No. 29, Premier Semestre 2007. Paris: La Découverte and MAUSS. For rich personal materials see Polanyi Levitt (1990); McRobbie (1994b); Polanyi Levitt and McRobbie (2000). There is still no comprehensive intellectual biography, but this gap will shortly be filled by Gareth Dale, who is completing two complementary studies to be published by Polity Press and The University of Michigan Press. Meanwhile Stanfield (1986) and Baum (1996) explore key philosophical and economic aspects of his thought. See also Halperin (1984) for Polanyi's debt to Marx and Hann (1992) for comparisons with Malinowski. Isaac (2005) offers a balanced assessment of Polanyi's oeuvre and its current standing inside and outside anthropology. For a recent collection on Polanyi's relevance to the twenty-first century, see Bugra and Agartan (2007). See also the HomePage of the Karl Polanyi Institute of Political Economy: http://artsandscience1.concordia.ca/polanyi.

Polanyi never denied the utility of markets for the allocation of some goods and services. What he condemned was the elevation of the "self-regulating market" to a position of dominance and the high price the British working classes paid for this. Laissez-faire liberalism was not the necessary, "natural" concomitant of industrialism: the "self-regulating market" is to some extent a misnomer, an illusion even, since this regime could only emerge and reproduce itself thanks to specific interventions by the state. At the same time many new enterprises depended on exploiting "unfree" forms of labor in family and kin networks. The dominance of the new order was challenged by countermovements within society, as the victims of the new liberalism sought to defend themselves against its consequences. The Chartists were the first mass movement through which workers sought to protect themselves from the new market mechanisms. The market thus remained thoroughly "embedded" in two distinct senses: first, in its dependence on the state, and, second, because, like other forms of exchange, it was associated with a range of domestic and social institutions, including some new ones explicitly formed to counter allegedly impersonal and "natural" market forces. Polanyi sometimes played down these tendencies, characterizing laissez-faire liberalism as a society that was "disembedded." This concept of market society is perhaps best viewed as an overdrawn ideal type, the rhetorical encapsulation of a lifelong anti-capitalism. His real objection was to "market fundamentalism" (see Servet, in Chapter 5).

Since the 1980s both Keynesian and traditional socialist techniques of economic management have been discredited and swept aside. The neoliberal ideology that has taken their place far exceeds the original liberal prototype in the claims it makes for the virtues of the market. This is why so many scholars in different fields now find inspiration in Polanyi's work. For example, the political economist Helleiner (2000) has argued that there are historical precedents for the dramatic expansion of finance capital in recent decades, and that a Polanyian critique is timely as a result (see Graeber, in Chapter 7). Analogous to Polanyi's "double movement," the current globalization of market capitalism has been accompanied by a comparable tendency in social movements. Society is now protecting itself not through the formation of trades unions within nation-states but through transnational networks of activists protesting against the power of the G8 states. Polanyi would probably sympathize with all those currently seeking to develop new and more radical forms of democracy. These constellations of forces may mitigate the continuing damage inflicted by "the market" on people and the natural environment. Global markets and "global civil society" implicate each other (Keane 2003); our task is to understand more closely the changing institutional forms of this interdependence.

Polanyi sometimes referred to the "human economy". What might this mean? In the remaining parts of this introduction we outline our aim to develop a more humane approach to economy and the role of economic anthropology in this undertaking.

The human economy

The days are long gone when politicians could concern themselves with affairs of state and profess ignorance of the livelihoods of the masses. Hence Bill Clinton's famous memo, "It's the economy, stupid!" For millennia, as we have seen, economy was conceived of in domestic terms. Then, when markets, money, and machines began their modern rise to social dominance, a new discipline of political economy was born, concerned with the public conse-quences of economic actions. For over a century now, this discipline has called itself economics and its subject matter has been the economic decisions made by individuals, not primarily in their domestic capacity, but as participants in markets of many kinds. People as such play almost no part in the calculations of economists and they find no particular reflection of themselves in the quan-titative analyses published by the media.

The founders of neoclassical economics, such as Alfred Marshall (1890), started out with the same broad style of questioning as their classical predeces-sors, but their speculations on human nature and society subsequently dropped out of the modern discipline, leaving it to anthropologists and others to pick up on these questions. Anthropologists aim to produce an understanding of the economy that has people in it, in two senses. First, we are concerned with what people do and think, as workers or consumers, in economies that are domi-nated by large-scale organizations, but in which they nonetheless retain some freedom to organize themselves – as farmers, traders, managers of households, or givers of gifts. Second, our interest is in the universal history of humanity, in its past, present, and future; and our examples are drawn from all over the world. Somehow we have to find meaningful ways of bridging the gap between the two. There are, of course, many economies at every level from the domestic to the global and they are not the same, but economics is itself universal in pretension and so we, too, in giving priority to people's lives and purposes, aspire to a degree of intellectual unity. At the very least, an anthropological critique will show that claims for the inevitability of currently dominant eco-nomic institutions are false.

In *Capital*, Marx (1867) expressed humanity's estrangement from the mod-ern economy by making abstract value (money) organize production, with the industrial revolution (machines) as its instrument and people reduced to the passive anonymity of their labor power. He aimed at reversing this order and that remains our priority today. The last two centuries saw a universal experi-ment in impersonal society. Humanity was everywhere organized by remote abstractions – states, capitalist markets, science. For most people it has become impossible to make a meaningful connection with these anonymous institutions, and this has been reflected in intellectual disciplines whose structures of thought had no room for human beings in them. Whereas formerly anthropologists had studied stateless peoples for lessons about how to construct better forms of society, scientific ethnography no longer sought to change a world where ordinary citizens for the most part felt disempowered. Of course, people everywhere continued to express themselves where they could – in domestic life and informal economic practices. But the three most important components of modern economic life – people, machines, and money – were not properly addressed by the academic discipline devoted to its study.

What might be meant by the term "economy?" English dictionaries reveal that the word and its derivatives have a number of separate, but overlapping referents:

1 order
2 efficient conservation of resources
3 practical affairs
4 money, wealth
5 the circulation of goods and services
6 involving a wide range of social units.

The Greek word *oikonomia* referred to the imposition of order on the practical affairs of a house, usually a large manor house in the countryside with its slaves, animals, fields, and orchards. Economic theory then aimed at self-sufficiency through careful budgeting and the avoidance of trade, where possible. The market, with its rootless individuals specialized in money-making, was the very antithesis of an economy that aimed to conserve both society and nature. So in origin "economy" emphasized the first three items on the above list while focusing on the house as its location. But the economy has moved on in the last 2,500 years and especially in the last two centuries. Adam Smith's intellectual revolution switched attention from domestic order to "political economy" and especially to the functioning of markets using money. Two things happened next. First, the market was soon dominated by large firms, a system of making money with money eventually named as "capitalism" (Sombart 1902). Second, states claimed the right to manage money, markets, and accumulation in the national interest; this is why the prime referent of "the economy" today tends to be the country we live in, even though the question of world economy has begun to encroach on public consciousness. In the process, "economy" is often used to denote the money nexus of market exchange, even though we retain the old meaning of efficient conservation of resources.

Part of the confusion with the word "economy" lies in the historical shift from the self-sufficiency of rural households to complex dependence on urban, national, and world markets. It is by no means clear whether the word is primarily subjective or objective. Does it refer to an attitude of mind or to something out there? Is it ideal or material? Does it refer to individuals or to collectivities? Perhaps to all of these – in which case, we need to explore the links between them. Economists may argue that economy is principally a way of reasoning (Robbins 1932, Schumpeter 1954), but we can hardly say that all those people who talk of economies as social objects are wrong. If the factory revolution shifted the weight of economy from agriculture to industry, mainstream economic life now takes the form of electronic digits whizzing around cyberspace at the speed of light. The idea of economy as provision of material necessities is still an urgent priority for the world's poor; but for a growing section of humanity it no longer makes sense to focus on economic survival. The confusion at the heart of "economy" reflects not only in an unfinished history but also in the enormous inequalities of contemporary economic experience.

Economic anthropology

Economic anthropology is the product of a juxtaposition of two academic disciplines in the twentieth century. It would be wrong to speak of the relationship between economics and anthropology as a dialogue. Economists in the dominant neoclassical tradition have rarely expressed any interest in anthropology and none at all during the last half-century, when their discipline became the ideological and practical arm of global capitalism. Anthropologists, on the other hand, when they have been concerned with "the economy," have usually felt obliged to address the perspective of mainstream economists, sometimes applying the ideas and methods of the latter to exotic societies, more often being critical of the discipline's claim to base itself in universally valid assumptions of scarcity and rational choice.

The purpose of economic anthropology, when still known as "the economics of primitive man," was to test the claim that a world economic order must be founded on capitalist principles. The search was on for alternatives that might support a more just economy, whether liberal, anarchist, or socialist/communist. Hence the interest in origins and evolution, since society was understood to be in movement and had not yet reached its final form. Anthropology was the most inclusive way of thinking about economic formation; only secondarily was it a critique of capitalist inequality. The First World War marked a new stage in the convergence between capitalism and highly centralized state bureaucracies. With the expansion of the universities, knowledge was compartmentalized as so many impersonal disciplines modeled on the natural sciences. Anthropology eventually found itself pigeonholed as the study of those parts of humanity that the others could not reach, with a bias to their ideas or "cultures" rather than to their material conditions. The concentration of social power in immense anonymous institutions discouraged people from trying to make a better world by themselves. So, from being at one time a constructive economic enterprise of universal intent, anthropology came to be driven by the passive aim to accumulate an objectified data bank on "other cultures," largely for internal consumption. The profession became fixed in a cultural relativist paradigm, by definition opposed to the universalism of economics. Anthropologists based their intellectual authority on extended sojourns in remote areas ("fieldwork") and their ability to address the world's economic trajectory was much impaired as a result.

The development of economic anthropology needs to be viewed in this wider context. Until the 1940s, ethnographers sought to engage the more general propositions of neoclassical economics with their particular findings about "primitive societies." They failed, mainly because they misunderstood the economists' epistemological premises. From the 1950s to the 1970s, coinciding roughly with the West's experiment in social democracy at the height of the Cold War, economic anthropologists argued among themselves about whether or not special theories and methods were needed to study their preserve, tribal and peasant economies. The "formalist–substantivist debate" launched by Karl Polanyi petered out in the late 1960s, thereby opening the way for Marxists to exercise a temporary dominance, while still mainly referring to the traditional objects of ethnography. In the phase of neoliberal globalization from the 1980s to the present day anthropologists have explored the full range of human economic organization from a great variety of perspectives. Many now study the innermost workings of capitalism at its core and in its global spread, together with the privatization of the former Second World economies ("post-socialist transition") and the plight of poor people in what we used to call the Third World ("development").

While some anthropologists have generated a critical commentary on capitalist civilization at a time when the market economy became truly global, few have launched a direct challenge to the economists on their home territory of national and global economic analysis. Perhaps the time is ripe to address the world economy as a whole as well as its parts; engaging with the historical sweep of *The Great Transformation* might be one means to that end. The fundamental issue remains whether or not capitalist economy rests on human principles of universal validity. Anthropologists can be proud of our discipline's commitment to joining the people where they live in order to find out what they think and do. But fieldwork-based ethnography needs to resume engagement with this theoretical debate and with new perspectives on world history.

Among the abiding questions at the intersection of economics and anthropology are the following: Is the economists' aspiration to place human affairs on a rational footing an agenda worthy of anthropologists' participation or just a bad dream? Since economics is a product of Western civilization – and of the English-speaking peoples in particular – is any claim to universality bound to be ethnocentric? If capitalism is an economic configuration of recent origin, are markets and money nonetheless human universals? Can markets be made more effectively democratic and the unequal voting power of big money somehow neutralized? Can private and public interests be reconciled in economic organization or will the individualism of *Homo economicus* inevitably prevail? Should the economy be isolated as an object of study or is it better to stress how economic relations are embedded in society and culture in general? None of these questions is exclusive to economic anthropology: they have been taken up by many scholars, including economic sociologists, political economists, and historians. We are not arguing here to draw the boundaries between disciplines more tightly, quite the opposite. That is why we invited economic sociologists and political economists to join us in this exercise. Today the boundaries between the disciplines have become fuzzier than ever; and that is a good thing. Agreeing on a common label for humanizing the study of the economy matters less than identifying clear questions for collaborative inquiry. This volume is the fruit of such a coalition; but it is also an effort to rejuvenate the study of economy and world history within academic anthropology at a time when they have been neglected by a fragmented discipline.

The chapters

The book opens with four chapters of broad theoretical scope. For Stephen Gudeman (Chapter 2) the prime task of the economic anthropologist is to understand the remarkable diversity of economic life in human societies, which is manifested in local models of the economy that owe little to the generalizations and universalist aspirations of economists. Here he takes Polanyi's "double movement" and strips it of its historicity to generate a universal dialectic of mutuality and market, which he then explores comparatively across a wide range of societies. Gudeman's chapter is followed by two reviews of the burgeoning field of economic sociology, one arguing how recent work has to a large extent taken Polanyi's name in vain, the other juxtaposing Polanyi with the field's modern founders. Jens Beckert (Chapter 3) draws attention to how economic sociology of late has adopted Polanyi's concept of "embeddedness" to the point that it has become almost a universal mantra. However, embeddedness for Polanyi clearly did not mean network analysis from the point of view of maximizing economic efficiency. This largely American subdiscipline shares nothing of Polanyi's reformist critique and as a result the concept has lost its edge. As an alternative starting point, Beckert suggests examining three basic problems of "coordination" common to all societies. Philippe Steiner (Chapter 4) argues that Polanyi had similar preoccupations to those of the Durkheimians. Both were concerned with how economics shapes the terms through which we experience markets and both turned from history to anthropology as their work matured. Steiner finds Durkheim intellectually more rigorous and the reasons he gives will sharpen the debate about Polanyi's proper place in the history of social thought. Jean-Michel Servet's contribution (Chapter 5) illustrates a flourishing French tradition in institutional economics (see also Laville and Cattani 2006), which since the fall of the Berlin Wall is more likely to cite Mauss and Polanyi than Marx. He argues that Polanyi's contribution is too often misconstrued as a romantic critique of commodification. Only if we recognize the originality of his critique of the very concept of economy as a separate sphere of human activity will we be in a position to develop new economic institutions, such as alternative currency systems.

The remaining chapters are all by economic anthropologists. The first group offer wide-ranging syntheses of the historical and ethnographic literature. Keith Hart (Chapter 6) considers the relevance of Polanyi's account of the rise and fall of nineteenth-century civilization to the renewed experiment with "the self-regulating market" in recent decades. His specific focus is on the part played by money in the making (and unmaking) of world society then and now. David Graeber (Chapter 7) draws on Polanyi to speculate about the origins of market ideology. He offers an original periodization of world history in terms of money's oscillation between being an abstract value generated in markets and a social construction founded on debt. He also identifies a transhistorical affinity between market expansion and violence. Chris Gregory (Chapter 8) asks why the principle of household autarky introduced in *The Great Transformation* subsequently dropped out of Polanyi's conceptual toolkit. Drawing on the contemporary ethnography of India, Africa, and elsewhere, he suggests that the deinstitutionalization (or informalization) of economy has rendered Polanyi's earlier focus on domestic organization pertinent once more. Gerd Spittler (Chapter 9) calls attention to an undeservedly neglected German tradition of studies of work, a surprising blind spot for Polanyi. Unfortunately this spilled over into his influence on anthropologists: with the brief exception of the Marxist interlude of the 1970s, labor was never a prominent focus of Anglo-French economic anthropology, where exchange has always occupied a privileged position.

The last five substantive chapters develop theoretical arguments through ethnographic analysis. On the basis of long-term fieldwork in and around an Indian steel plant, Joanathan Parry (Chapter 10) invokes Michael Burawoy's comparison of Polanyi with Antonio Gramsci on the relationship between state and market. If the latter emphasized how state hegemony can co-opt the working class, Polanyi was more optimistic concerning the possibilities for societal resistance against the predations of the market. Nonetheless Parry doubts that the "double movement" is alive and well in contemporary India. Jane Guyer (Chapter 11) provides an experimental ethnography of the commodity form and price, extending her monumental research on Nigeria (especially in the 1990s) to a more speculative concern with conditions in the USA and Britain since the Second World War. She raises the intriguing possibility that Polanyi's list of "fictitious commodities" may have been augmented of late, notably through the addition of "risk." Catherine Alexander's (Chapter 12) ethnography of recycling schemes in London examines state promotion of the market as a rhetoric of redistribution. This offers a lens on Polanyi's version of the formation of the wage labor system in the nineteenth century, while opening up critical reflections on Tony Blair's Britain. James Carrier (Chapter 13) asks whether *The Great Transformation* supplies helpful concepts for the ethnographic analysis of environmental conservation schemes in Jamaica. He concludes that Polanyi is less useful for that purpose than Marx and Weber. Chris Hann (Chapter 14) suggests an adaptation of Polanyi's conceptual toolkit that would allow us to approach Marxist–Leninist–Maoist socialism as a distinctive variant of disembedding. "Reform socialism" as pioneered in Hungary after 1968 and further developed in China and Vietnam over the last three decades, may then be understood as a form of re-embedding in which the market principle is no longer the radical antithesis of the moral economy, but is rather encompassed by it.

Finally, in a trenchant Afterword, Robotham (Chapter 15) notes that many of the authors distance themselves from Karl Polanyi to some degree, though, as academic intellectuals, most share his basic hostility to "the market." Yet to focus on the market draws attention away from the evolution of production on a world scale. Perhaps most damning is our collective failure to consider the liberal argument that market expansion can still be emancipatory for a large portion of humanity. Robotham helps us to understand why Polanyi's *chef d'oeuvre* has never had much direct influence on economic anthropology; nevertheless, its unique historical scope and literary achievement have inspired the present volume.

Acknowledgements

This volume has developed from a workshop which we convened in June 2006 at the Max Planck Institute for Social Anthropology. We thank Bettina Mann and Anke Meyer for their help in organizing that meeting, and Anke Meyer for her patience and efficiency in processing several versions of the manuscript.

2   Necessity or contingency: Mutuality and market[1]

Stephen Gudeman

Karl Polanyi bequeathed to anthropology the concept of the embedded economy. First developed in his book, *The Great Transformation* (1944), to describe the transition from "pre-industrial" to industrial life, Polanyi subsequently used the idea of embeddedness to understand ethnographic ("primitive") and historical ("archaic") economies. In the ethnographic cases, reciprocity is the predominant transaction mode; in the historical contexts, redistribution primarily governs the transaction types. In modern societies, however, disembedded markets dominate transactions. Despite his earlier historical presentation, Polanyi offered a static typology of economies that has usually been set within a binary opposition: either material life is embedded within social relationships or it is disembedded as anonymous exchanges. For Polanyi, the historical reversal of the necessary (society) and the contingent (the market), which occurred with the emergence of industrial society, was a one-time event that was accomplished at great human cost. Granovetter (1985) modified the stark opposition by observing that many economies are more embedded than economists perceive, whereas material life is more disembedded than anthropologists allow. But neither he nor Polanyi developed the theme that the embedded/disembedded pair or mutuality and market, make up the dialectic in economy.

In contrast to Polanyi, a neoclassical economist might argue that real markets sometimes include mutual commitments, but these ties are imperfections in an ideal model. To the extent that personal relationships, misperceptions, emotions, and imperfect information influence price-setting, markets are less efficient than they might be and mutuality ought to be eliminated. Becker (1993, 1996) surmounts this problem by including mutuality as a preference or taste of the rational actor. For him, mutuality is a contingent variable, which he "endogenizes" (or accounts for) by including it in a utility function. Closely related to the neoclassical perspective is the older formalist view in economic anthropology by which culture and social obligations are sometimes seen as constraints on optimal production. These formal constructions conceal economy's dialectic.

---

[1] This chapter is a revised version of Chapter 5 in Gudeman (2008).

New institutional economists offer a different perspective. Drawing in part on the work of Coase (1998) concerning transaction costs, the new institutionalism has developed in recent years and expanded its reach to the realm of public choice, history, and governance among other topics. Like neoclassical economics, it starts with the idea of rational choice but employs it to explain the emergence and form of economic institutions. New institutionalists try to show how social relationships, norms, and their changes can be modeled as outcomes of calculative reason (Gudeman 2005, 2006). Social bonds, on this view, are not always frictions or inefficiencies to be eliminated in modernization, because these ties can be efficient in an historical context. Instead of calling social bonds *altruism*, and inscribing them as one among other preferences in the self-interested actor as does Becker, new institutionalists argue that social relationships are conscious or unconscious calculations in the drive to be efficient. Institutions can stabilize markets (sometimes as oligopolies), reduce risks, lower transaction costs, and make markets more efficient in an historical context. But there is an elision in their model, for new institutionalists are explaining only the uses, predications, or spillovers of existent mutuality. By presuming that individuals are self-interested, which leads to contextually efficient institutions, new institutionalists fail to account for the prior, necessary presence of relationships that constitutes these "persons-in–community" (Gudeman 1992).

My picture of economy is different. I hold that all economies are both embedded and disembedded. Economy contains two value realms, mutuality and market, or community and impersonal trade. In part, individuals live from the trade of goods and services that are separated or alienated from enduring relationships. I term this mode, "competitive trade or market." For example, trade in which goods are parted from their holders and impersonally and competitively exchanged occurs in all historical and ethnographic situations, though varying in importance. People also live from goods and services that mediate and maintain social relationships. I term this mode "mutuality or community in which goods are secured and allocated through continuing ties." The difference between these two realms might be characterized as the distinction between a commitment and a contract, or the difference between an activity undertaken "for its own sake" and one done "for the sake of" something else.

In formal discourse a market is usually associated with the central value of efficiency in the allocation of resources. Efficient trade is the trump card in this story because it leads to the optimal use of resources in production and consumption. In contrast, in the mutual realm of economy, goods are secured and allocated through continuing ties: by means of taxation and redistribution within associations, kinship groups, and households; through bride wealth, indenture, and reciprocity; and by self-sufficient activities such as agriculture, pastoralism, foraging, and keeping house. I name these allocation modes, "allotment" and "apportionment" (Gudeman 2001). Guided by social values, such as merit, age, gender, or need, these locally established customs exhibit diversity, and they are contested, negotiated, individually interpreted, and changed.

In markets, the substance of trade is private property or capital. Alienated in exchange, it neither mediates relationships nor connects people over time unless by contract, which is part of the trade. By way of contrast, for the mutual realm of economy, I use the term "base" to designate the shared interests and holdings of a people. The word covers a heterogeneous collection of things and intangibles that makes and mediates relationships between people. Always in the making, a base is specified by situation and varies in prominence across cultures. It may be very important in an economy (as in the case of lineage land), ephemeral (as in the case of shared information in an ethnic group), or relatively minimal (as in the case of a household group that shares stocks of food). A base consists of both produced things and non-produced parts of the environment; for example, it can be valued forests, lakes, or mountains. Some parts of a base, such as tools, monuments, or a cave drawing, emerge from intentional acts, and some are unintentional outcomes, as in the case of a footprint, the remaking of the landscape when a plant species is domesticated, or the serendipitous discovery of a drug. But a base is more than the material objects which establish and continue relationships. It is a heritage that lies outside the person as resources, tools, information and symbols, and within as sediments from others that help establish identity. Through a base, a person is the product of others from the past and in the present.

But what is the relation between these two different value realms? I argue that they are dialectically connected. Polanyi revealed one agonizing historical moment when market "economy" was disembedded from society. In contrast, I suggest that disembedded economies do not exist apart from embedded ones, and the reverse. But the mutual domain provides the transcendent and necessary conditions for the emergence of trade, although communal allocations are not the whole of material life, for a degree of impersonal trade is always encountered. This dialectic varies across economies and over time, but it is not without direction. Competitive trade reverberates in markets and usually cascades into new spaces leading to the expansion of the competitive arena and the increased use of calculative reason in practices and discourse (Gudeman 2006). As the market realm expands, it *colonizes* and *debases* the mutual one on which it also relies.

This dialectic emerges not only in the shifting practices of a state, civil society and economy, which was Polanyi's concern, but also in everyday behavior, in ethnographic contexts, and in mentalities. Today, the dominance of competitive trade has led to extreme wealth differences within and between nations, to environmental devastation, to large and small discords over political economy, and to divided subjectivities in ways not anticipated by Polanyi.

My purpose is to explore comparatively a part of this alternative picture of economy. I begin with some of the ways that mutuality sustains markets and then turn to examples of the ambiguities, mystifications, and erasures that occur through the interplay of the two realms. I close with a look at a contemporary discourse that reduces one realm to the other so that the ever-present dialectic is veiled and everything appears to be for the best in the best of all worlds.

Framing markets: the precariousness of trust

In recent years trust as mutuality has drawn the attention of various scholars, because relying on another person's words or actions is a necessary component of market relations.[2] Ties of trust may play several roles in markets, such as ensuring that information provided between traders is reliable, that debts will be paid, or that open-ended contracts may be formed so adjustments can be made over time. But trust can be an ambiguous relation, for it would seem to deny the exclusive presence of the self-interested actor in the market. Does trust provide a framework of mutuality in which competitive trade and calculative reason may be exercised, or is trust a calculated bond that reflects self-interest? If trust is a calculation, it cannot be a shared commitment and offers an unstable framework for traders; conversely, if trust is a commitment, can it be insulated from the expression of self-interest that it nourishes? A leading economist, Kenneth Arrow (1990: 137), states the problem for standard economics and in effect observes that mutuality must precede trade:

In a rational type of analysis it will be said that it is profitable to be trustworthy. So I will be trustworthy because it is profitable to me. But you can't very easily establish trust on a basis like that. If your basis is rational decision and your underlying motive is self-interest, then you can betray your trust at any point when it is profitable and in your interest to do so. Therefore other people can't trust you. For there to be trust, there has to be a social structure which is based on motives different from immediate opportunism. Or perhaps based on something for which your social status is a guarantee and which functions as a kind of commitment. How all this works is not explainable in Becker-type terms.

How is it formed? The Frafra migrants from north-east Ghana who moved to a shantytown in Accra provide one example of the way trust bonds are forged in an informal market. Lacking resources, Hart (1988) reports, the Frafra became very small traders who engaged in both licit and illicit activities. Because they had little access to currency, traders often relied on loans and the extension of credit among themselves, but default was an ever-present reality. The shantytown traders existed at the margins of state control and enforcement, so legal contracts to ensure trade could not be used, while resort to violence

---

[2] See, for example, Fukuyama (1995), Gambetta (1988b), and Hollis (1998).

or public shaming were not long-term solutions to the enforcement problem. In the rural area, the Frafra traders had belonged to large kinship groups, but this traditional ethic of sharing did not fit with the self-interested exchanges in which the traders engaged: "separate interests" could not be expressed through the idiom of kinship (Hart 1988:90). Also, most of these ties dissolved when people from different clans mixed together in the urban context: kinship morality that connoted identity, sameness, and a collective self no longer had a strong claim. How did the migrants solve the risk problem? Eventually, through trial and error, and at the cost of time and monetary losses, individual trust relationships began to emerge, and credit was offered only to these partners. Loans were never provided to strangers, with whom transactions were made on the basis of immediate cash payments. Ultimately, within the market a loosely structured arena that depended on personal networks of debits and credits emerged. The relationships were instigated by the need and desire to have market trade, and they could be broken. Market trust, I suggest, is a projection from prior mutual experience, but this communality is tenuous because it is caught between calculation and commitment. With their slowly emerging trust bonds and failures, the Frafra migrants exemplify the ambiguous seam between the mutual and moral basis that trade requires and the calculated transactions that it sustains (see also Beckert, Chapter 3 in this volume).

Making markets

Mutuality establishes markets by specifying the arena in which trade takes place. Referring to market agreements, Hayek (1960: 106) states, "It is the acceptance of such common principles that makes a collection of people a community." The ways of defining a space for trade include formal and informal laws, norms, and rules. Markets have shared expectations; they may be contained within social agreements, such as a peace pact, a threatening fetish, or legal organizations through which expectations about the conduct of others can be assured. Personal ties also frame market exchange, as in the Frafra example. Other ethnographic studies reveal that people may inherit trade partners or project kinship bonds to stabilize an exchange and create a zone of peace. When trades take place in a local marketplace, the norms may be customary, with an agreement sealed by a handshake. When markets are large, with anonymous participants, the rules usually are explicit and the agreements specified or written; shunning and personal sanctions work in a small market but not a large one. Markets also may be thickly or thinly regulated, ranging from the minimal specification of a peaceful space for interaction to a tightly controlled drug or food market. The varying agreements may be assured by a government, by kinship, by the participants, or by cultural expectations, and they are reformulated over time and contested; even if "silent trade" between noncommunicating strangers, outside any social framework, might occasionally have occurred, it soon developed a set of market agreements.[3]

Market agreements also specify who may enter and what can and cannot be brought to the bar of exchange. The Chicago Board of Trade was literally an arena or pit reserved for traders (and their assistants) who exchanged commodity futures by shouting and hand signals.[4] In many cases, a trader may be required to purchase a license or a seat in the arena as on the New York Stock Exchange. But informal markets arise without legal permission, although their marginal space is usually limited to an alley or sidewalk. A market may have rules about the order of entry for buyers and sellers (through rationing and quotas), and about its physical layout (Gell 1982). Mutual accords frame rules of exchange and the obligations of traders, such as agreements to use fair weights and measures. Such concords include laws of ownership and contract, rules about product quality and disclosure, as well as controls on oligopolies and the mode of trade (such as one-to-one bargaining, set prices with add-ons and discounts, or auctions). Markets also have rules about what can and cannot be traded, as in the case of automobile emissions and regulations on the use of a natural resource. But entry stipulations, that enhance mutual wellbeing via exclusions, often are contested and subverted: there are black markets in babies, drugs, and many other "goods."

Consider an ethnographic example of the way mutuality helps determine the contents, participants, and space of a market. In Arnhem Land (Australia) the Gunwinggu held a "ceremonial exchange" (called *dzamalag*) with neighboring groups.[5] In one exchange, that took place on a dancing ground or designated space, the mutual festivities included music-making, singing, dancing, joking, and sharing food. The two groups also circulated tobacco, beads, and sexual favors between their opposite moieties that regulated marriage. These shared and reciprocal transactions created and expressed communality between the

---

[3] In a recent work Callon (1998a:19–20) focuses on market framing, "which allows for calculation and consequently makes possible the emergence of calculative agencies." In the case of a strawberry market that was established in France, he speaks of the "existence of a perfectly qualified product, existence of a clearly constituted supply and demand, [and] organization of transactions allowing for the establishment of an equilibrium price." To account for framing, he draws on Bourdieu's recounting of the Maussian notion of the gift along with the concepts of externalities and Coasian transaction costs. But Callon (1998b) also says that framing is imperfect and speaks of market overflows that may either be measured as externalities or made objective through social science knowledge and brought to the bar of negotiation. My concept of the market arena is similar to his idea of framing, but I do not think Callon sees the "inside" and the "outside" or the internalization of externalities in a sufficiently dialectical manner. He constitutes the outside as remainders from the inside and not as local models. In effect, Callon pictures economy through the lens of the market.

[4] It has now merged with the Chicago Mercantile Exchange, and both are converting to electronic trading.

[5] This material is drawn from Berndt (1951), which I have discussed at greater length elsewhere (Gudeman 2001).

groups, and they provided the frame for trade, for as these forms of sharing took place cloth and blankets were offered by the Gunwinggu to the other group; upon completion of this exchange, the visitors presented spears but in a threatening manner. As a result, spears were traded for cloth and blankets; however, all the other goods and services went in a circle from a moiety in one group to its opposite moiety in the other and then back! The ethnographic report provides no information about the trade rate for the blankets plus cloths in relation to the spears, but we may suppose that it could vary even if "prices" were sticky in the short term. In this exchange, mutuality between groups provided a structure for market trade by specifying the locale, rules of exchange, and contents of the trade. Communal bonds of reciprocity within a group were extended through the tobacco, beads, and sex to the opposite group so that trade could occur. Yet, the ceremony expressed the tension between the discrepant practices of doing something for its own sake and doing something for the sake of something else.

Mutuality inside markets: the house and house-business

Communal agreements not only set a space for trade, they may be inside the market arena. Market traders often incorporate the dialectics of mutuality and market. A house-business and even a house often combine the two projects because they place communal commitments on their market participants and their returns. For example, one Sunday I saw a range of house-business combinations in a town market held high in the southern Andes of Colombia.[6] At one extreme, an older man, who lived a few blocks from the marketplace, sat on a stool next to a wheelbarrow filled with blocks of partially refined brown sugar. His sales were minimal and earnings negligible, but he had no household commitments: he came to visit with people who browsed, and he used the proceeds to replace his stock so he could return the next week. He was trading to create mutuality in the marketplace. Near him, two adults with three young children were selling a small range of agricultural goods, which they had grown and had purchased for cash. Their goal was to maintain their household. On the one hand, they were trading some homegrown goods for cash to buy other necessities. On the other, with the purchased items they bought for resale, the couple tried to recover their monetary costs and to have some goods left over, which they could take home for consumption during the week. Neither transaction was directed toward monetary profit (which would have been difficult to calculate since their own productive labor was unpaid). By contrast, a number of transporters sold food from the backs of their trucks. They were buying and selling to make a profit but were assisted by their offspring and other young

---

[6] The fieldwork was carried out with Dr. Alberto Rivera.

kin who were learning the skills of transporting and trading. These youngsters earned a small wage and were provided with cooked food as they learned the skills of trading and transporting. Finally, in a different area of the plaza, a woman was selling small hardware items (knives, locks, and nails) that she purchased from wholesalers. She sold in three different markets each week, and rented space for her inventories in each market town so she would have no cartage costs. Her aim was to make a money profit but she used this return to purchase food and clothes for her children. She was trading for domestic maintenance. Overall, these market participants displayed shifting combinations of mutuality and trade.

A house-business that draws on family relationships can be filled with disagreement about the use of the returns. Do family laborers deserve a market wage or are they providing communal support that is returned in disparate ways? Who deserves what when offspring may be expected to perform chores such as washing dishes or working in the fields? I once recorded the suicide of a young man in rural Panama who thought he was being denied the monetary returns that his brother received for driving a truck for their father, which is an extreme example of the dialectic as played out in everyday life.

When individual traders participate in a market as representatives of a community, mutual obligations link their trading resources and returns to others. These traders exchange with commitments on what they offer and receive, for the purpose of the trade is to maintain the community on which they and others depend. Because their trades are impersonal, calculated, and bargained, the traders continuously shift between the contradictory roles of being an "individual" and a "person-in-community" (Gudeman 1992). For example, in the interior of Panama, agriculturalists bartered their homegrown rice and maize for salt that was needed at home, and the exchange rates shifted over the years. But agriculturalists did not barter chickens or other household belongings for salt; their authority to trade was limited to agricultural products, and they were trading to meet the needs of the house. Their offerings and takings were structured by domestic mutuality, although this communality was maintained by competitive exchange.

This transformation of the person-in-community into the individual trader leads to tension between the two identities. For example, in Guanajuato, Mexico miners collect their pay on Saturday afternoon. Sometimes they spend some or even all of their returns meeting other men and drinking, with the result that their wives accuse them of seeing prostitutes and being worthless (Ferry 2005: 130, 134). One man justified his actions by explaining, "I deserve a little 'motherlessness'" (Ferry 2005: 44): he was denying his mutual commitments. Elsewhere in rural Latin America when men sell a household animal or crop, they may use part of the return for private use. In Panama, the private sugar mills paid their cane suppliers on Saturdays. The cash return was gained in place of using the land for subsistence farming; however, men often used a portion of the receipts for drink and amusements. In contrast, some of the women sewed clothes or wove straw hats for sale, and they used this return to buy food for the house. This gender difference between the strength of communal commitments often led to quarrels within the household.

But a household also provides a zone of resistance to market principles when market earnings become part of a base. Carsten (1989) tells how this transformation takes place in households on the island of Langkawi, off the coast of Malaysia. Men principally fish for a living; they bring their cash earnings home but immediately pass them to women who use the returns for domestic expenses. Women are at the center of the Malay house: they prepare the shared rice meal that is the symbol of domestic and kin unity, and is cooked over the hearth that makes up the center of the home. Through this transfer from men to women and into the house for domestic uses, the values of the individual and the market are transformed to those of the person-in-community and family unity. The market return becomes a part of the base and is used as needed to sustain the home. As Carsten remarks, the women "cook" the money and so transform it from market to home.

Similar dialectics are found in market economies, but often without the careful "washing" that the return in Langkawi undergoes. What does the exchange of work for a wage mean? Is it a private return and the property of the wage earner or does it have elements of a base trade for a community? For example, who controls a salary-earner's return and has rights to the flow? At one extreme the return might be distributed on the basis of contributions. Alternatively, does the income-earner have special rights to the flow and dole out an intermittent return to his partner or do spouses share a joint account that receives all household income? High wages allow for more mutual uses and greater household welfare but also the separation of the return among base, personal uses, and new investment. High market wages also allow for communal subcontracting. Domestic workers can be hired to supplement the work of maintaining a base, as in the case of caregivers, such as nannies and domestic workers. But does purchased care create an enlarged set of mutual relationships between householders and caregivers who become family-like; is it a pure trade relation, is it a dialectic combination of both, or is it a market tie mystified as mutuality? (And does this sale of care have a cascading effect on the base of the caregiver who must divert attention from her own domestic work and sustain it with cash?)

In the United States, the top end of the individual wealth scale has exploded upward, especially in relation to the lower and middle classes, not to speak of less industrialized nations. Some accumulators pass their money to offspring through an inheritance, which is allocation within mutuality: the moral principles vary. The money may be allocated per capita, per stirpes, by need, by gender, by age, or by personal relationships. Similarly, some wealthy capitalists – through social pressure – establish charitable foundations or give to philanthropic organizations and universities, and then explain their gifts by saying that they owe something to the larger community that supported them. But do these acts cleanse the money of its separatist value? The moral commitments, enabled through market success, vary in amount, timing, and direction according to the giver's choice. Are the acts calculated selections, commitments, or ambiguous? The dialectic of market and mutual values reaches through every domain of economy.

Mutuality inside markets: oligopolies

Mutual ties within markets often burst the expectations of perfect competition. These relations seem to be like the communal agreements that set a market arena. But there is a difference: they are used by a community within a market often to the detriment of other market participants. In these cases, calculative reason cascades into and appropriates mutuality to become a means of individual profit-making and accumulation.

At times, mutual relationships create cooperation among competitors and help frame production arrangements. Cooperatives can unite competitors to bolster their individual purchasing or selling power (or to serve social welfare purposes), as in the case of the Mondragan cooperatives in Spain.[7] Social ties also may structure trade through longer-term exchanges between production firms which adjust their output and techniques in relation to one another. White (2002) shows how upstream and downstream commitments between firms help frame production markets and reduce uncertainty for individual firms. Networks of intermediate products and services, he argues, belie simplistic views of markets as containing isolated firms that form spot contracts with each other. Likewise, a number of studies, from areas such as northern Italy, France, and Germany, show how cooperation among small-scale producers and some larger firms emerges to form industrial districts.[8]

Mutual ties also occlude competition when information is withheld from others to be circulated only among a few, as in attempts to rig the initial public offering of a stock, and they can be used to send false information. Diasporic traders, who are linked by kinship or ethnicity, may pass information across large distances, provide special prices and unsecured loans to each other, offer spaces for private trade or reach agreements informally (Greif 1993, 1994; Middleton 2003). The Rothschild brothers used family ties to send secret information between national markets and accumulate profits. Today, antique furniture

---

[7] See, for example, Kasmir (1996), Community Economies Collective (2001), Whyte (1999), and Whyte and Whyte (1988).

[8] For one comparative study of regions, see Bagnasco and Sabel (1995). On France, see Lorenz (1988).

dealers or rare book sellers sometimes buy and sell among themselves, to keep up their listed prices, share information, and have temporary control and use of the circulating goods: they project similarity of interests on otherwise competitive ties. Similarly, barter clubs that include competitors and buyers and sellers help members to sustain a business in lean times, to evade taxes on financial profits, and to form new connections. In a competitive market as well, a buyer and seller may form a semipermanent tie that promises better product information, assures favors when trading, or modulates risk.[9]

Because market agreements about proper comportment may be quasi-formal or tacit, such as providing "transparent" accounting, new and shared regulations may be needed to limit practices. When the Enron Corporation and the Arthur Anderson accounting firm took part of the corporation's debt off its balance sheet and out of footnotes, in order to increase the company's profit and credit rating, and when these techniques were shown to be used by others, investors were shocked.[10] The participants composed an inside community that shared alternative accounting practices. Enron investors lost money, but the larger market tremors had to do with the broken trust and the revelation that a non-transparent community was secreted within the market. As a result, the larger community insisted that some accounting practices be made more explicit and enforceable, and their regulation was formalized and shifted, to a degree, from market participants to an oversight board. New laws also were passed, and the principals were convicted. The Enron case offers a different example of the ever-present dialectic: a small community within a larger shared arena may subvert it, or a market made possible by a community may be debased by a smaller community of calculating actors within it.

On the consumer side as well, information gained through mutuality may influence market choices. Individuals seeking work, whether in industrial markets or on plantations, may find jobs through social connections.[11] People often select lawyers, doctors, dentists, mental health professionals, insurance agents, accountants, restaurants, college professors, and car dealers by information gathered through social relationships. Stock tips, too, often pass between acquaintances. Economists may argue that such social connections lower the cost of securing market information, but often this knowledge arrives serendipitously through relationships maintained for other purposes. In these

---

[9] Mintz (1961) provides a classic example from Haiti.

[10] According to *Business Week*, the goal of "hundreds of respected U.S. companies ... is to skirt the rules of consolidation, the bedrock of the American financial reporting system and the source of much of its credibility." (January 28, 2002). For discussion of the Enron case, see also Henwood (2003) and Toobin (2003).

[11] On the place of social networks in markets, the role of labor markets, and a broader discussion critical of many neoclassical and neo-institutional models, see Granovetter (1985). Missing from his critique of the concept of the atomic individual, and his use of the idea of networks is the realization that networks involve overlapping interests or values.

cases, community provides a costless spillover of information for trading purposes. But how is this "free gift" reciprocated? Or is it? Economists claim there is no free lunch, and anthropologists say there is no free gift. But is this spillover a gift from mutuality to market, a case of debasement, or a strengthening of communal ties? Should one offer a friend payment for advice? If so, what does that say about the friendship or about reciprocity that is measured? In one case a businessman offered his cousin valuable market information and was repaid with an expensive piece of art. Was the object a gift that represented strengthening of their kinship bond or a repayment? Was profit-making being mystified under the cover of mutuality?

Everyday mystification: the appropriation of features

Trade and mutuality mystify each other. Sometimes, market contracts may be veiled as mutuality to enhance individual efforts and commitment. For example, corporations may represent themselves as a community by taking employees on retreats and subsidizing lunchrooms to promote loyalty and increase profits. The production team on an automobile assembly line may speak of "its" cars – even in advertising. Construction workers refer to the building they helped create as "theirs" just as a carpenter may sign and hide a piece of wood within a house he helped to construct. Individuals in a corporation identify with corporate property as if it had been allocated like a base in a community: a worker speaks of his shovel, tractor, chair, office, or desk.[12] Assertions of communal possession and identity arise with respect to intellectual property. At a computer institute in Paris, where research groups develop software, sociality emerges among workers and provides "social gratification" (Born 1996: 108). As the software product develops and the sense of group possession grows, information needed by others at the institute is increasingly withheld. This assertion of a shared holding may be a protest against the contractual setting in which their work is performed, but it intensifies their commitment, efforts of innovation, and profits for the larger organization. Are these commitments mystifications of contractual relations, are they communal relations, or are they a contradictory combination of the two?

The contingency of these mutual relationships is revealed at the poignant moment of downsizing when a person is asked to clean out his desk, his

---

[12] Humphrey (2002) offers a similar observation about property in markets but also provides an example from socialist Mongolia (in the 1970s) where an individual claimed a horse, that was brigade property, as a kind of personal possession. When against his will the horse was presented to someone outside the brigade, the man refused to drive horse carts until it was returned. She interprets his claim to the horse as the realization of "person-thing" relations that emerge through use, but the man's assertion might also be seen as his way of connecting to objectified property as if it were an apportionment of base and of asserting a place in the local brigade; alienating the horse severed his community position.

computer passwords are frozen, and he is escorted from the building. The moment epitomizes the severing of salary, work, and relationships, or a place in a corporate community. During the 1990s in the United States, an interesting self-critique emerged when many corporations began to use "downsizing" to increase productivity. Several years into this movement articles began to appear questioning the tactic because it was said to lead to decreased productivity, loyalty, and morale among the remaining employees; the "best" would seek work elsewhere, leaving a corporation with the least productive and motivated workers. A corporation could fall victim to its attempts at increasing efficiency by destroying the communities on which its success depended. In fact, three economists have analyzed the effects of downsizing. Downsizing did not increase corporate competitiveness or productivity, although that was the stated goal; instead, it decreased unit labor costs. They concluded that downsizing is an effective strategy for holding down wages, raising profits, and transferring income from labor to management, which "is the dirty little secret of downsizing" (Baumol, Blinder and Wolff 2003: 262). Led by the pull of calculation and colonization by the financial realm, downsizing undermines the mutuality on which corporations depend, while increasing the financial wellbeing of high management.

If corporations mystify themselves as communities while contradicting this pose by downsizing, their external presentation is much the same. Companies often reach out to consumers by representing their trade relation as mutuality. Frequent flyer offers, credit card points, and supermarket clubs are part of market trades that offer the persistent buyer a discount. Participants are called "members," and the rhetoric of mutuality is used when inviting participation and communicating with customers. The ideology of community becomes a calculated means for market ends rather than an end itself. Is it an assertion of community or its mystification?

It may be that we are seized by the "culture industry" and persuaded to purchase through advertising, product labeling, and public display of goods (Horkheimer and Adorno 2002), but corporate advertising does offer personal identity through belonging to "new" communities.[13] Through our choices do

---

[13] The connecting process occurs in many ways. For example, through the division of labor, one corporation purchases its resources from another: in the classic arm's-length case, the butcher purchases animals from the cattleman; the baker procures flour from the miller who bought his resource from the farmer. But today, products may be presented as threads linking one producer to another, and offered to the consumer as a conglomerate community. These "communities" of corporations are advertised: an Apple computer contains an Intel chip; synthetic products from 3M, Dupont or Gore-tex are advertised as components in clothes and shoes that are branded as products of another manufacturer. NutraSweet™ is advertised as a constituent of diet drinks that are competitors. Automobiles embody branded radios, speakers, or tires that are advertised with the vehicle. Conversely, sometimes the connections between corporations are silenced. Dashboards of different brand cars may be produced by the same supplier but not labeled; different brands in the General Motors "family" of cars may use the same engines (an occurrence

we take on the communal "properties" that we purchase in the market? Is the owner of a Ford automobile connected to the car that he displays, to other owners, to the human being Henry Ford (but to which one – the ancestor or his descendants in the company)? Branding suggests that we are linked to what we buy and who made the product, and this connection helps formulate our identity through physical or metonymic interaction with that product.[14] This assertion of a connection between corporation and consumer holds even for wrappings, such as labeled shopping bags or paper seals that are placed on new purchases, although in some countries people still bring their own carrying bags to the grocery store.

Slogans may summon mutuality as a reason to purchase. A large department store used to advertise, "The customer is always right," as if the company had a give-and-take relationship with its shoppers. Other slogans of mutuality are metaphorical, such as General Electric's motto: "We Bring Good Things to Life." "We" apparently refers to the corporation that creates things just as parents bring children to life, and are connected to what they have produced. But the word "life" also refers to the consumer (as in your life) to whom General Electric brings good things, like a gift. The exchange takes place in the market through the competitive trade of property rights but is represented as a communal tie that connects producer, product, and consumer in a family. Which is the "reality" – the market trade or the happy family?

But the dialectics of mutuality and trade are not confined to formal markets and corporations. Garage sales in the United States combine mutuality and profit-making in shifting, sometimes tension-filled practices.[15] Held at a home, a garage sale is a domestic event in that goods come from the house, have been used by a community, and are sold by the homemaker who is usually female. The owner "gives" the sale, and the charges are low – at "give-away" amounts – but the items are priced and sold as if to deny that the sale is charity. The low charges convert what might otherwise be interpreted as a free gift or as an impersonal trade into a moment of give-and-take. People attend garage sales for different reasons – from being thrifty to making money. Purchasers are acquiring some of the tastes and remainders of another, just as sellers are giving something of themselves. But buyer and seller may have conflicting readings of the event: a seller may feel that the object sold is almost a gift,

that caused a minor scandal some years ago). What does cross-branding mean? Do the products present the consumer with a cooperative community or do they represent impersonal market trades embedded one within another?

[14] Even when an article, such as a shoe or blouse, is made in a light assembly plant by "anonymous laborers" from abroad, its origin is discretely noted on the label. In contrast, some expensive, hand-knit products, such as a sweater, may bear a signed label (usually by a woman who works at home). These markers convey the mutuality of a home, almost as if the item were a personal gift.

[15] I draw some of this material from Herrmann (1997).

while the buyer may read it as a fair price. Precisely, a garage sale can be nearly pure trade, an expression of mutuality, or an ambiguous combination.

The dialectics of reason

In consumption calculated trade reaches limits because it is countered by a different practice and mode of reason – being thrifty or making savings. Thrift, which often starts in the communal domain, marks the boundaries of competitive trade, even as it is slowly colonized. By thrift, I mean making savings, economizing, and being parsimonious, frugal, or sparing. The thrifty person is careful when expending and stands opposed to the spendthrift. Making savings is not the same as making money. Both practices are means to ends directed, but making money focuses on the relation between means and ends (or the profit obtained), whereas making savings focuses on preserving the means to have an unused remainder as a precaution for the future. Making savings is a changing collection of practices. We can make savings by eating less, reusing building materials, repairing a sandal, preserving string, reusing a nail, or finding new uses for discarded materials.

Because making savings often is connected to meeting communal needs, it can be opposed to indulging in wants that are provided through markets. I have found that households in Latin America frequently distinguish between needs they require for maintenance and wants – from alcohol to clothes – that are not required. Similarly, in a recent study of shopping, Miller (1998) finds that most shoppers in North London are neither profligate nor extravagant but concerned with being thrifty. Of course, they are bound by the budget constraints of their households, but thrifty buyers also indulge in "treats," such as stopping for a cup of coffee or eating out. The distinction between needs and wants, however, does not capture the way that making money can draw on making savings for the house. In market production, thrift is often practiced as an adjunct to rational calculations, such as downsizing a corporation. Small-scale agriculture in Colombia offers a transparent case: a rural household may raise potatoes for domestic consumption and onions for market sale. If it purchases the inputs for the onions (seed, fertilizer, labor, pesticides), the monetary costs will exceed the revenue for the onions. But if the potatoes are sold to purchase the inputs and fed to the laborers, the onions can make money. As the people say, "If you can't make savings with potatoes, you can't make money with a crop for sale." The second practice colonizes and debases the first, just as downsizing can debase a corporation.

Market advertising mystifies this dialectic of communal thrift and calculated gain when it represents purchasing as thrift and a means to build mutuality. Today we are inundated by "sales" that have many forms: sometimes they are held on a particular day; sometimes they consist of remainders or unsold seasonal goods; sometimes they are special offers. But why are they appealing, since anything on sale costs money? Perhaps the buyer can think of himself as a fine trader in the market and so achieve this identity; at the same time, he is a proper communal member because he is economizing and saving for the household reservoir, like keeping a car one more year, or soaking off and using uncanceled postage stamps. In these cases, economizing is recruited by calculative reason to conform to the market project.

Effective advertisements often capture this contradiction between consumer saving and corporate profit, or the need to appeal to mutuality while making money. Consider a failed retailer. In its grandest days, when Sears Roebuck and Company was the world's largest store, it advertised, "Shop at Sears and Save." In this memorable phrase that combined the embedded and disembedded realms of economy, the merchant linked its purpose of making money ("Shop at Sears") with the consumer's project of economizing money ("and Save"). (I used to wonder if Sears really wanted its customers to walk away with unspent cash or to disburse the savings in a different part of the store.) Once Sears deviated from this corporate mission, and began to sell paintings and upscale goods (or wants), its fortunes lagged: KMart (with whom it later merged) surpassed it, and the two were overtaken by Wal-Mart. Market projects need to draw on local models, even as they appropriate them for their own purposes.

Cascading and mystification in discourse: disembedding the embedded

If cascading, mystification, veiling, and debasement are found in everyday practices, they also are encountered in formal models, because economists have added a new bolt to their locker. New institutionalists focus on market associations, which seemingly brings them closer to including mutuality as part of economy. The institutions explained include clubs, guilds, ethnic groups, and other communities. But most of these models presume the self-interested person.

The concept of institution usually refers to formal or written rules, such as property rights and laws, as well as informal or unwritten rules, such as shared norms and beliefs. New institutionalists seek to explain such shared norms principally as ways of coping with economic uncertainty, and as solutions to local economic problems. The idea of "transaction cost" is central, because every exchange has costs of formation, information, monitoring, and completion; contracts do not cover every contingency. For example, can a trading partner be trusted to deliver the promised quantity and quality of goods on time? How can compliance be enforced, and what can be done about shirking at work or withholding information? Given such problems between contracting parties, argue the new institutionalists, institutions develop to mitigate risk and minimize costs, and market competition helps to sort for the more efficient solutions. On this view, institutions are a means within the project of achieving market efficiency. They may yield some inefficiencies but lasting ones lower transaction costs in an historical context; and when formal laws arise to structure markets or when other conditions change, these institutions usually wither or disappear. Like neoclassical economists, new institutionalists assume individual economizing with the difference that they try to show how social forms, values, and relationships rather than prices are shaped in accord with the decisions of the rational actor. Institutions exist for the sake of something else rather than for their own sake.

Some institutional economists have turned their attention to communities. For example, Aoki and Hayami (2001) argue that communities often stand between the market and the state. They are not rivals of the market but can enhance development in the early stages of market formation. Although community regulations may offer inferior market equilibriums, they do provide low-cost enforcement of contracts through personal relationships among traders. For example, Greif (2001) has offered a number of studies to show that contract enforcement between traders from different communities can be achieved by mechanisms within a community, such as shunning or avoiding outside traders who do not meet their obligations. He calls this the "Community Responsibility System" which embeds an otherwise spot trade. Greif (2001: 35) suggests that communities in pre-modern Europe provided an important complement to the market through such means:

A Community Responsibility System enabled exchange that was impersonal up to one's community affiliation in late medieval Europe. It took advantage of the existing social context, namely, the existence of communities.

With population growth, heightened mobility, and the strengthening of political orders, these systems slowly faded.

Greif tends to use game theory in support of his explanations, but other authors provide different derivations.[16] Aoki (2001), for example, assumes that traders have preference rankings for both economic outcomes and for social standing, such as reputation, esteem, or higher status. These two preference scales are exchangeable so that what one loses in one may be compensated by a gain in the other. For example, an actor who breaches market obligations may be excluded from festivals and ceremonies (Aoki 2001: 108). These

[16] Greif, unlike some other new institutionalists who focus only on social relationships, presumes that cultural beliefs influence social organization and that social organization reflects cultural beliefs. For example, he argues that societies may be divided into collectivist and individualist forms. "In collectivist societies everyone is expected to respond to whatever has transpired between any specific merchant and agent, whereas the opposite holds for individualist societies" (Greif 1994: 919). But shared cultural beliefs express mutuality, which means that both the collectivist and individualist forms of trade require sociality.

are linked games, and the key idea is that sociality is not only subjected to a measuring rod but that this measuring rod is part of a larger utility function that includes economic events and outcomes. In both examples, according to the theorists, the calculating actor is everywhere and there is no tension or contradiction between mutuality and market; if the cost of maintaining a community is higher than the benefits, it disappears.

Goodbye to *pensée sauvage*

Inevitably, given the tendency to cascade a market model into the realm of mutuality, one new institutionalist, Janet Tai Landa, has applied the approach to ethnography in order to demonstrate its power, expand the reach of economics, and claim that a new institutionalist approach can lead to the "unification of the social sciences" (Landa 1994: 38). Goodbye to one hundred years of anthropology, and to Malinowski and Mauss.

Landa starts her tale when Mr. Rational Chooser meets another maximizer: "Imagine a world," she says, "in which there are no clubs and in which the state affords no protection of contracts" (Landa 1994: 117). Traders are opportunistic, so breach of contract is always a possibility. This moment of uncertainty marks Landa's entry point. Drawing on the concepts of rational choice, property rights, and transaction costs, she tries to explain the emergence or origin of trade institutions, such as ethnic trader organizations and gift exchange as responses to contract uncertainty. In the language of economists, she argues that rules of trade are generated endogenously rather than exogenously, or that rational choosers generate the social institutions within which they can carry out rational choice.

For Landa, institutions are rules that specify roles and expectations. Like other new institutionalists, she inserts a new level in the model. Operating between individuals as rational choosers and pricing outcomes, institutions are a means to the end of acquisition because they function to assure regularities of trade and economize on its costs (Landa 1994: 23). Landa attacks traditional functionalist theory in sociology because it does not explain how norms emerge; however, she continuously evokes the notion of function in her story (Landa 1994: 5, 13, 29, 116, 134, 155). But this reliance on a functionalist account is hardly surprising because, in her model, institutions or valued social relationships are not satisfying ends. They are instruments in the toolkit of the maximizing actor. Landa (1994: 28) explains:

From a comparative institutional perspective, contract law, ethnic trading networks, and gift-exchange can be viewed as alternative governance structures or economic organization in different historical contexts that function to constrain traders from acting opportunistically by breach of contract. The existence of exchange externalities arising from breach and the transaction costs involved in internalizing the externalities are crucial for the emergence of constraints – formal legal norms or informal social norms – against opportunism

Landa continues that institutions and trading groups are "clubs," which function as alternatives to legal contracts backed by law. She assumes that the costs of belonging to such a club are lower than the benefits (Landa 1994: 126), although she presents no calculations to support the argument.

Landa then brings this argument to the heart of anthropology when she applies her model to the realm of kinship. Drawing on the language of Meyer Fortes, she claims that "Kinship relations are the irreducible jural and moral relations, and kinsmen are thus the most reliable people with whom to trade" (Landa 1994: 109), which is not what Fortes intended. Next, she invokes Fortes's phrase – the "calculus of relations" – which referred to the realm of kinship (Fortes 1969: 50, 107) to argue that locating these social positions, with their rights and obligations, is an ingenious strategy or efficient screening device that enables traders to pick up nonprice signals for predicting the behavior of a potential partner (Landa 1994: 109). By employing her pick-anything-out-of-context strategy, Landa avoids mentioning Fortes's central argument that kinship and descent relations embody what he called the "axiom of amity," which might also be glossed as the principle of mutuality. Fortes even surmised that amity might be imbibed with "mother's milk."[17] He was arguing that a calculus of kin relations helped individuals determine their degree of social amity rather than trade relationships. Here Landa's misreading of Fortes is especially disingenuous, because he always vigorously distinguished between moral ties and voluntary contracts, and claimed that kin must share "without putting a price on what they give" (Fortes 1969: 238). Fortes urged that economic processes "have never been incontrovertibly shown to be the ultimate *raison d'être* of such [kinship] institutions, norms, and relationships regarded as an internal system" (Fortes 1969: 229). Landa misconstrues and turns his argument inside out to legitimate her own, that kinship functions to provide a screening device for trade.[18] Then, generalizing on this misrepresentation, Landa claims that all clubs, including kin organizations and ethnic groups, have signaling devices so that members can identify themselves and know whom they can trust. Such signals include flags, totems, clothing (such as Scottish tartans), and the dietary laws of Jews. (Landa adds that the *chai*, worn about the neck, has replaced the Star of David as the emblem of religious identity and information device for Jews.) Such signals reduce a trader's search and information (or transaction) costs. Anything and everything is grist for her derivational mill – including the *kula*.

The Trobriand Islands' *kula* provides Landa's principal illustration of institutional growth "where the legal framework ... is not well developed" (Landa

---

[17] "It is conceivable – and I for one would accept – that the axiom of amity reflects biological and psychological parameters of human social existence. Maybe there is sucked in with the mother's milk, as Montaigne opined, the orientation on which it ultimately rests" (Fortes 1969:231).

[18] Her new institutionalist argument oddly repeats the more Marxist argument of Worsley (1956) which was countered by Fortes (1969); see also Sahlins (1976).

1994: 28). As every anthropology student knows, the *kula* consists of two opposite circuits of exchange: armshells are passed in one direction against a flow of necklaces from the other. The original work dates to Malinowski (1922) who showed that these open-ended, delayed exchanges involve chains of debts and credits, are surrounded by ceremonies, spells, and rituals, and are connected to gender relations, productive activities, canoe-building, kinship obligations, and the achievement of rank and prestige. Through his analysis of the *kula*, Malinowski firmly established the importance of context or meaning in use, and of social give-and-take or reciprocity. Since Malinowski, the *kula* has been extensively discussed in the anthropological literature, and it was used by Mauss (as well as Polanyi) to exemplify the role of the gift or reciprocity, which he sharply distinguished from market trade (as did Fortes).[19] But Landa follows a different trail: for her, "the Kula Ring is an institutional arrangement that emerged primarily in order to economize on transactions costs of intertribal commercial exchange in stateless societies" (Landa 1994: 143). She claims that the *kula* functions to cover the costs of transport, set-up, search, contract negotiation, and enforcement for the Trobriand Islanders who engage in ordinary trade (*gimwali*). According to Landa, the entire *kula* network, which links the Trobriands and other islands, emerged through the action of self-interested traders (even though the relationships are built on reciprocity). Landa adds that the ring pattern of the *kula* is an efficient two-market system because it economizes on traders' costs of acquiring goods in other markets; the opposed exchange cycles make up an efficient way to barter valuables across group boundaries, because each *kula* participant, as a middleman, participates in only two adjacent markets, which is more efficient than attending several markets on different islands or a central marketplace. The ring pattern also allows sanctions to work chain-like throughout the entire region: word about unreliable participants will circulate efficiently. Finally, the associated magical rites and mortuary rituals of the *kula* are efficient signaling devices for identifying people who are or can be members of this exclusive trading club (Landa 1994: xii). The entire system of social relationships, magical rites, myths, and expectations emerged, of course, "by an " 'invisible hand' process" (Landa 1994: 160).

I cite Landa not to enter into a discussion of alternative ways of interpreting the *kula* or this "total social fact" – as Mauss phrased it – but to show how a new institutionalist model that is built on the foundation of rational choice may be deployed to "explain" the emergence and function of reciprocity, verbal spells uttered over trees and canoes, mortuary food distributions, and more. Landa mystifies local practices that are done for their own sake as being done for the

---

[19] The literature on the *kula* is enormous. See Weiner (1976) for a revision of Malinowski's ethnography and interpretation, and the collected essays in Leach and Leach (1983).

sake of sustaining trade. By cascading her market model, Landa dialectically converts mutuality into its opposite and turns local beliefs into fabrications: the *kula* becomes an illusion of the Trobrianders, reciprocity becomes a fantasy of escape from *Homo economicus*, and both are contingencies. Unlike Becker, Landa does not place mutual ties within the subjective preferences of rational actors but derives them as a consequence of self-interest. Whereas Becker elides local practices, Landa colonizes them. Both explanatory models veil local forms so that competitive trade is freed of commitments and obligations.

And so we return to Polanyi's division. Although worried about the economic transformation Europe had experienced, Polanyi held that market models do work for market economies because the economy there is disembedded. In contrast, I argue that the division is a continuing dialectic in all economies, where it assumes different historical forms and degrees of tension. Disembedded economies cannot exist without mutuality; however, market practices and models erase their contingency and dialectically undermine their existence by continuously expanding the arena of trade, by cascading, by appropriating materials, labor, and discourse, and by mystifying and veiling the mutuality on which they are built. If the standard models of economy offer little hope for understanding and contesting the enlarging wealth differences within and between economies, or confronting the environmental devastation that is fueled by higher and higher consumption levels, an alternative model of economy, partly inspired by Polanyi, may offer a way of confronting these global crises by nourishing that other realm of economy on which we also rely.

3   The great transformation of embeddedness: Karl Polanyi and the new economic sociology[1]

Jens Beckert

Introduction

Over the last 25 years, economic sociology has developed into one of the fastest growing fields of sociology and became an important subfield of sociological scholarship (Smelser and Swedberg 2005; Beckert and Zafirovski 2006). This does not mean that sociologists during the postwar era did not study economic phenomena, but they did so either selectively by focusing primarily on issues of the organization of the industrial work process, labor markets, and industrial relations, or by focusing on the societal and cultural *effects* of capitalist economies. An example of this is the concentration of critical social theory on issues of alienation and the "colonization of the life world" (Habermas 1981). Class theory was primarily interested in the distributional effects of capitalism and various phenomena of exploitation of the industrial worker. What was lost in these sociological approaches to the economy in the postwar period was the comprehensive study of the social preconditions of capitalist economies and their core institutions, especially markets. This broad approach had been developed by the classical sociological authors in their studies of the economy. For Max Weber, Émile Durkheim, and Georg Simmel, the exploration of the institutions of modern capitalism was an important part of their respective social theories, and the neglect of this issue left a void in sociological scholarship during the postwar period.

It is not easy to understand this decline of economic sociology and its reemergence in the late 1970s, but there is widespread agreement on several contributing factors. On the one hand, the decline of sociological interest in the economy is probably related to the "solution" of many of the economic problems that were paramount during the classical era of sociology. Once patterns of stable growth developed in the Western world during the 1950s and 1960s, economic problems became less important for the understanding of social integration. Keynesianism seemed to offer effective political instruments to steer economic growth, which made the fulfillment of "adaptive functions"

[1] I am grateful to the editors and to Akos Rona-Tas for their helpful comments.

(Parsons 1951) a problem that appeared to have found an enduring solution in a regimen of "embedded liberalism" (Harvey 2005; Ruggie 1982). Moreover, the dominant Parsonsian paradigm of structural functionalism advocated a division of labor in the social sciences which left most aspects of the investigation of economic phenomena to the discipline of economics.[2] Even the later critiques of structural functionalism did not touch this division of labor – at least at first – since the Marxist critiques, conflict theory, and interpretative sociology led either to the study of phenomena of distribution and exploitation or, as in the case of Harold Garfinkel, to an orientation which showed little interest in the investigation of economic phenomena.

These developments provide clues as to why economic sociology declined in the postwar era. But why did the field reemerge during the 1980s? First, problems of inflation, increasing rates of unemployment, and low growth rates since the 1970s brought economic problems into the focus of societal attention once again. These macroeconomic changes were accompanied by profound transformations on the organizational level, commonly referred to as the end of the Fordist production regime. Second, during the 1970s and 1980s sociologists, anthropologists, and political scientists "discovered" economic configurations whose success had to be attributed to factors not accounted for in orthodox economic theory: the enormous success of Japan (Dore 1986; Hamilton and Biggart 1992; Yamamura and Streeck 2003), the rise of industrial districts (Trigilia 2006), and the discovery of the informal economy (Hart 1973). Third, the global economic picture started to change significantly in the 1980s because of the pronounced shift to market-oriented economic policies not only in the Western capitalist countries but also in the developing world, especially in Asia and Latin America, and, later, in the transitional countries of the former Soviet bloc. Markets gained in importance relative to political regulation, which dominated the capitalist postwar economies. Though this shift toward markets brought the dominant political orientations closer to the assumptions of orthodox economics, sociologists were sensitized for the social anchoring of economic action and turned to the investigation of markets as the paramount institution of exchange advocated by neoliberalism. After the failure of shock therapy in transition economies, the insight that markets have social and political preconditions also reached policymakers in international organizations like the World Bank, where "social capital," for instance, became a core policy concept.

In addition to the "real" changes in the economy, changes in the relationship between economics and sociology must be mentioned, too. First and foremost, the 1970s saw an expansion of the rational choice approach into substantial

---

[2] The resulting paradigm has been called the "economy and society perspective" (Swedberg 1987; Granovetter 1990). Geoffrey Hodgson (2008: 137) refers to the "Robbins-Parsons Consensus."

fields that were hitherto domains of sociology. The new economic sociology is in part a reaction to this "economic imperialism" and its understanding of action, making the counterclaim that even on economics' home playing field, i.e. "the economy," many phenomena can be better understood by approaching them from sociological perspectives. At about the same time, however, new developments took hold within economics which made the discipline itself more sensitive to the institutional preconditions of market exchange. This holds true for information economics and the new institutional economics. Sociologists started to address the systematic problems raised by economists from these schools.

Given these transformations, the renewed interest of sociology in investigating core institutions of modern capitalist economies, especially markets, might not be surprising. What is surprising, however, is that the essential concept applied in the new economic sociology is not derived from the classical sociologists Max Weber, Émile Durkheim, Georg Simmel, or Karl Marx. Instead, the "founding manifesto" of the new economic sociology, Mark Granovetter's (1985) seminal article "Economic Action and Social Structure – The Problem of Embeddedness" centers on Karl Polanyi's concept of embeddedness. This concept had been introduced by Karl Polanyi in his *The Great Transformation* (Polanyi 2001).[3] Ever since the concept was brought to the attention of sociologists by Mark Granovetter, it has been a focal point of the new economic sociology. Hardly any article associated with the new economic sociology fails to mention "embeddedness" as the core concept indicating a sociological approach to the economy. Few economic sociologists would disagree with the statement "We are all Polanyians now."

I will argue in this chapter that, in its adaptation by the new economic sociology, Karl Polanyi's concept of embeddedness has itself undergone a great transformation. As it has been continually reinterpreted, significant meanings of the concept have vanished, while others have been added. In particular, the social-reformist connotations of the concept have been neglected. I begin by exploring below the different meanings attached to the concept of embeddedness in the new economic sociology. Against the established approaches, I argue that it is not the embeddedness of economic action as such that should constitute the vantage point of economic sociology, but rather three coordination problems that actors face in economic exchange. It is only by starting from these coordination problems that the *necessity* of embedding economic action becomes theoretically comprehensible. I will argue that by proceeding from these coordination problems, sociological, anthropological, and

---

[3] Though Karl Polanyi is usually cited as the originator of the concept of embeddedness, it was used earlier by Richard Thurnwald in his study "Die menschliche Gesellschaft" (Thurnwald 1932). Polanyi was familiar with the works of Thurnwald when writing *The Great Transformation* (see Firth 1972).

historical approaches to the economy can find common research questions which allow them to enter into more fruitful conversations with each other. Later, I draw attention to the social-reformist inclinations of Polanyi's use of the notion of embeddedness and thereby highlight the challenge posed in *The Great Transformation* that was largely not taken up by economic sociologists. Finally, I note limitations with regard to the development of a macro theory of the economy that result from making embeddedness the core concept of economic sociology.

Embeddedness: the ironies of the career of a concept

The career of the concept of embeddedness in the new economic sociology would certainly have come as a surprise to the man who is quoted as its originator. It has been pointed out repeatedly that Polanyi hardly ever used the term (Barber 1995: 401; Krippner 2001: 779), and by no means could one claim that it is a well-defined, central concept in his work. In *The Great Transformation* the term is used only in the chapter on the "Evolution of the Market Pattern." In the relevant paragraphs Polanyi contrasts the market economy with economic configurations based on reciprocity and redistribution: "Instead of economy being embedded in social relations, social relations are embedded in the economic system" (Polanyi 2001: 60). The second use of the term a few pages later also alludes to this contrast:

In the vast ancient systems of redistribution, acts of barter as well as local markets were a usual but not more than a subordinate trait. The same is true where reciprocity rules: Acts of barter are here usually embedded in long-range relations implying trust and confidence, a situation which tends to obliterate the bilateral character of the transaction. (Polanyi 2001: 64)

Evidently the centrality of the concept of embeddedness is an artifact of the *reception* of *The Great Transformation*. Nevertheless, it is possible to identify two core meanings the concept had for Polanyi; first, he sees markets as necessarily limited by institutional regulations which connect them to the moral fabric of society. Unregulated markets cannot be more than a pathological form of organizing the fulfillment of adaptive functions in society and will lead to social anomie. This institutional anchoring of the economy is characteristic of all three types of economic exchange distinguished by Polanyi: reciprocity, redistribution, and market. Second, the term "embeddedness" is not only an analytical term but also alludes to the political or social reformist task of stabilizing a (democratic) organization of society through the institutional regulation of markets, especially in the realms that Polanyi termed fictitious commodities: land, labor, and money. Hence the reference point of embeddedness is not the economy as such, but "the larger social systems in which all economies are located" (Barber 1995: 406). In both connotations of the term "embeddedness," Polanyi's assessment of the modern capitalist economy corresponds fully with the approaches of classical sociological theory.

That "embeddedness" should become the central concept of the new economic sociology with reference to the works of Karl Polanyi is surprising given the limited significance the term has in the works of the author himself. This irony, however, is complemented by a second incongruity: the understanding of embeddedness advocated by Mark Granovetter (1985), which led to the widespread use of the term in the new economic sociology, differs fundamentally from the meaning of the term in the work of Karl Polanyi.

Granovetter introduced the notion in direct reference to two debates. These concerned the dispute between substantivists and formalists in economic anthropology (Schneider 1974), and the controversy between two competing concepts of action in sociology: on the one hand, the "undersocialized concept of action," incorporated from economics, which sees actors as isolated from each other and, on the other, the "oversocialized concept of action," which represents actors' behavior as being entirely controlled by the social norms in which they have been socialized.

For Granovetter, both concepts of action are flawed. As an alternative, he suggested making the patterns of relationships among actors the core variable for the explanation of economic outcomes. According to Granovetter (1985: 487), economic action is "embedded in concrete, ongoing systems of social relations;" in other words, in actors' social networks. This use of Polanyi's notion of embeddedness promotes a structuralist economic sociology in which economic outcomes are explained by the structural properties of social networks (Granovetter 1973, 2005). Networks pattern market exchange and facilitate collective action. The significance of network structures has been validated in a variety of different research areas, such as the diffusion of information on labor markets (Montgomery 1991; Granovetter 1995), immigrant networks (Portes and Sensenbrenner 1993), and the organization of financial markets (Baker 1984; Uzzi 1999; Mizruchi and Stearns 2001). Proceeding from Granovetter's programmatic essay, the network approach has become the most influential advance within the new economic sociology.

Yet Granovetter's linking of embeddedness to the structuralist network approach in economic sociology implies a fundamental transformation of the concept. As Krippner (Krippner 2001; Krippner and Alvarez 2007) has argued, Polanyi's understanding of the embeddedness of the economy is rooted in institutional analysis. For Polanyi, markets are not networks of structurally equivalent producers but "rather fully social institutions, reflecting a complex alchemy of politics, culture, and ideology" (Krippner 2001: 782). The network approach, by contrast, isolates a single aspect of markets – networks of ongoing social relations – "as constituting the proper domain of economic sociology"

(Krippner 2001: 799). This is a limited perspective because an exclusive focus on the structure of social relations leads to a neglect of the social content underlying the observed structure. By not taking attributes of actors and institutional rules into account, network analysis fails to explain how the social structure of markets emerges and why networks are structured the way they are (Beckert 2005). Moreover, the network perspective does away with Polanyi's concern with the stability of social order, by focusing exclusively on the process of market exchange itself and not on the larger social system.

This, however, is not the last irony in the career of the concept of embeddedness. On closer inspection it becomes evident that Granovetter's focus on network structures gives rise to a further inconsistency, this time with regard to his own intention to provide an alternative to the oversocialized and the undersocialized view of action. Far from providing an alternative within action theory, he does away with a grounding of economic sociology in action theory altogether (Beckert 2003, 2006a). Network structures, rather than social action, become the explanatory variable (Granovetter 2005). Small wonder that institutional economists and rational choice sociologists eagerly took up this notion of embeddedness, since they could readily incorporate it into a rational choice framework (Burt 1992; Lin, Cook and Burt 2001).[4]

In short, the central position of embeddedness – and, hence Karl Polanyi's work – in the new economic sociology appear to be the result of cumulative interpretative misunderstandings on several levels.

Coordination problems in market exchange as the starting point of economic sociology

Despite this confusion the notion of embeddedness has become the core concept of the new economic sociology. This was also possible because the meaning given to the term by Mark Granovetter has not remained the only reading. Zukin and DiMaggio (1990 elaborated a taxonomy that distinguished between four types of embeddedness. In addition to Granovetter's "structural embeddedness," they distinguished between cultural embeddedness, cognitive embeddedness, and political embeddedness. This broadening of the concept of embeddedness unquestionably brought it closer to the meaning that may be deduced from *The Great Transformation*. This breadth allowed different

---

[4] The comedy of errors behind the concept of embeddedness took a final turn a few years ago when Mark Granovetter stated that he did not even have Karl Polanyi's work in mind when introducing the notion of embeddedness in his programmatic essay: "I use the term 'embeddedness' [in the 1985 article] in a narrower and somewhat different way than Polanyi meant it. The reason is that I was not trying to borrow the term from Polanyi, or to re-appropriate or to reintroduce it. Something more complicated was going on. I have looked back at my old notebooks and found that I used the term embeddedness in some of my early notes, before I ever read Polanyi" (Krippner *et al.* 2004: 113).

sociological approaches to the economy to be brought together under a single heading, which has contributed to the development of the field over the last two decades. To what extent, however, can any notion of embeddedness provide a satisfying starting point for economic sociology?

Following Polanyi, I take it as axiomatic that the embeddedness of economic exchange makes economic and social integration possible: the attempt to establish a system of self-regulating markets based on the commodification of the "fictitious commodities," land, labor, and money, produced the dehumanizing social conditions that Polanyi held responsible for the social and political instabilities he witnessed in his lifetime. The analytical – and, as I shall argue later, also the political – challenge is to identify the social preconditions for the organization of the economy that allow the fulfillment of economic functions to be combined with the realization of a humane social and political order.

No critique of the notion of embeddedness as the initial concept of the new economic sociology can deny the indissoluble connection of the actor with his or her social surroundings. However, we may question whether sociology should *start* from this notion as its entry point into the field of the economy. My position is that "embeddedness" characterizes a general answer to specific problems without identifying the underlying problems themselves.[5] By starting from the embeddedness of economic action we are putting the cart before the horse. The first proper step would be to identify the problems that can actually be solved by an approach focusing on the embeddedness of economic action. I suggest that we identify these problems and make *them* the analytical starting point of economic sociology. The problems to be resolved in market exchange are found not only in contemporary, highly developed capitalist economies but also in preindustrial market exchange. Since sociologists have largely ignored such societies, the approach I am advocating invites collaboration with anthropologists and historians; in this respect it is fully consistent with the multidisciplinary interests of Karl Polanyi.

If the strict assumptions underlying neoclassical economic theory are relaxed, the embedding of economic action needs be viewed in the light of three problems of social coordination that actors face in market exchange. General Equilibrium Theory posits that markets can stabilize without being "embedded" because exchange allows for individual utility maximization based on fixed and exogenously given preferences and no actor has an interest in changing the equilibrium result. Once the assumption of perfect markets is given up, however, the problem of the social order of exchange reemerges (Latsis 1972), and it is only by the formation of robust expectations with regard to the actions of relevant "alter egos," i.e. the reduction of the social uncertainties entailed

---

[5] Cf. Dobbin (2004). Rather than proceeding from a set of problems, Dobbin's approach proceeds from a set of social mechanisms that resolve underlying problems.

in market exchange, that stable markets become possible. The reduction of uncertainty is an indispensable precondition for the emergence and operation of market economies (Beckert 1996). Market actors need "stable worlds" (Fligstein 2001) or "calculability" (Weber 1978) in order for role sets to be reproduced. Embeddedness is the mysterious substance which provides this stability in market exchange.

Three coordination problems

The three coordination problems actors face in market exchange are the problem of value, the problem of competition, and the problem of cooperation.[6]

Value

The problem of value may be defined as the "difficulties that market participants have in forming clear subjective values for goods in the market" (Koçak 2003: 8). Only if buyers are able to "discriminate between the worth of goods or services that confront them in the market" and sellers are able to reliably demonstrate "the value of goods they bring to the market" (Koçak 2003: 5f.) can market exchange take place. The basis for this is the cognitive process of commensuration, in which actors rank products according to their contribution to the fulfillment of a need and thus provide the basis for attaching value to a product in relation to others.[7] This is to some extent a technical process if standards are defined to distinguish different qualities of commodities and the contribution of a commodity to resolve a technically defined task. However, in large parts this process of valuation is social in character. The emergence of a "market for whale-watching" on Canada's west coast, for instance, depended on cultural transformations that changed the way whales are valued in Western culture. Although whales were perceived for centuries as feared behemoths – a perception most dramatically described by Melville – this perception began to change from the 1950s onward to the point where whales are seen today as a threatened species that symbolize the value of freedom. Only on the basis of

---

[6] An additional social precondition for the emergence of stable markets is the social legitimation of the market exchange of a certain good. Historically, markets have been subjected to numerous limitations in terms of their location, their duration and the goods they are legally allowed to trade (Braudel 1979; Polanyi 1944; 1976a; Walzer 1983; Weber 1922). The prohibition of trade in human beings (e.g. slavery or adoption), organs, or certain substances (e.g. illegal drugs) are but a few examples of such limitations. Clearly, there is no unilinear historical process by which markets become ultimately legitimate mechanisms for the exchange of all goods. Illegal markets face the same coordination problems as other markets. Actors in illegal markets must find different solutions to these coordination problems, however, which makes illegal markets even more precarious.

[7] I do not attempt to develop a theory of market prices here. Understanding why actors think of a product as being valuable and as having more or less value compared to another good is only one element of price formation; see Guyer, Chapter 11 in this volume.

this change in perception did it become possible for the watching – and not the hunting! – of whales to become a valued commodity for which people are willing to pay money (Lawrence and Phillips 2004). In the case of the market for wine, similar social processes lie behind the possibility of differentiating a product that is perceived by outsiders – or "non-experts" – as largely homogenous. Assigning vastly different values to wine based on the grapes used, the producer, the location of the winery, the year of production, the type of bottle used, and the evaluations of third parties is a complex process without which this market would not exist at all. The "quality markers" constituting the reputation of a wine must be established in communicative processes involving producers, consumers, traders, and intermediaries, especially wine critics. Through these processes the social uncertainty inherent in the product is reduced and consumers can develop confidence in the "value" of a wine despite the fact they cannot classify its quality based on its sensual characteristics.

Valuation processes are social in character in a second sense. Value may be based on the recognized contribution of the good or service to the positioning of its owner on the social ladder and thereby contribute to the definition of the owner's social identity. Products constitute and express membership of specific life-worlds. The classic treatment of this phenomenon is Veblen's (1899) discussion of "conspicuous consumption." But it holds true, of course, in a much more general sense: products are located in a social landscape which allows the owners of goods to be positioned and, conversely, to form social identities based on market choices. Only through such socially based processes of the subjective valuation of goods can stable markets emerge. Hence markets must be socially and culturally embedded to be feasible. In the case of valuation, the embeddedness of economic action is a necessary condition for classifying the material world in terms of the relative value of the products offered, i.e. for creating motives for product demand. A sociological theory of markets will aim to understand how the mechanisms of classification emerge and work (Bowker and Star 2000).

It is obvious that the study of processes of valuation is a field in which sociological, historical, and anthropological perspectives meet. The historical perspective highlights the processes of change in the valuation of goods. For example: Zelizer (1979), in her study of the emergence of the life insurance industry in the United States during the nineteenth century, reveals the long process before potential buyers of life insurance overcame their resistance to the product. At the outset of the industry, life insurance was seen by potential customers as morally corrupting since it involved a gamble with God and provided a premium for the death of another person. It was only by taking this cultural resistance into account that a change in marketing strategies could be achieved; the meaning of the product was reframed, and potential customers started to value life insurance. Economic anthropology has investigated such phenomena as the social base of measurement systems (Gudeman 2001: 12), the dependence of the value of goods on their meaning as symbolic representations of social status (Geertz 1973), and the cultural bases of the demand for products (Douglas and Isherwood 1979; Appadurai 1986; Graeber 2001; Hann and Hart forthcoming).

Competition

The second coordination problem actors face derives from competition. From the economist's standpoint, markets are based on competition. But sellers can only make a profit if markets are not perfect in the economic sense. If markets were perfect, marginal utility would equal marginal costs and the incentive to produce for the market would vanish. Profits emerge when markets are imperfect (Chamberlin 1933; Knight 1921; Robinson 1933). Therefore, market actors attempt to create market structures that provide protection from pure price competition. A power-driven "market struggle" (Weber 1922) ensues in which actors try to restrain competition or use existing regulations to their advantage. At the same time, market actors experiencing disadvantages from existing market regulations attempt to challenge incumbents by trying to change the rules of competition (Fligstein 2001). The state plays a major role in these market struggles by laying down ground rules, for instance in competition law or intellectual property law, and by granting subsidies or collecting tariffs. Political embeddedness as well as market differentiation based on the "singularization of the good" (Callon, Méadel and Rabeharisoa 2002: 201) and processes of network closure are mechanisms aimed at resolving this coordination problem. This is a second indication that markets can only emerge through their embeddedness in noneconomic social and political contexts.

Again, the investigation of these market struggles would profit from a close collaboration between sociologists, historians, and anthropologists. In the Middle Ages, guilds had the function of protecting established producers from unwanted competition. The rise of John D. Rockefeller in the oil industry in the late nineteenth century may be described as the result of a strategy of eliminating competition. Rockefeller created a monopoly by taking over the refineries owned by competitors. The government reacted by introducing antitrust legislation leading to the dissolution of the Standard Oil Company (Hohensee 2003: 78). Closing certain labor market segments to persons on the basis of their race, gender, caste, ethnicity, union membership, and so on also serves to protect defined labor market groups from competition. Geertz (1963: 32ff.) showed how competition in a Javenese bazaar takes place between buyer and seller rather than between sellers because no fixed prices exist. Here it is the lack of an institutional provision which inhibits the type of competition usually associated with market exchange. Stephen Gudeman (this volume) cites examples from anthropological research showing how market exchange is regulated by communal bonds as well as social networks and how these bonds restrict the trade of certain goods or trade between certain actors.

Competition and its moderation through regulation, entry barriers, or product differentiation reflects a fundamental coordination problem for market exchange. It allows market exchange to be understood as a political and social struggle over institutional regulation and "blocking action" (White 1992), pointing to the embeddedness of economic action as a *resolution* to a specific problem market actors face.

Cooperation

The third problem of coordination that actors confront in market exchange is the problem of cooperation.[8] It arises from the asymmetric distribution of information about price, product quality, and the possible opportunism of exchange partners in the light of incomplete contracts. Exchange relations are inherently risky undertakings. The resolution of the social risks of exchange, notably that of "defection," is a crucial precondition for the emergence of stable markets. In addition to social networks, clientelistic relationships, reputation systems, formal warranties, and branding, mechanisms such as trust, social norms, power, network closure, and emotions all help to resolve this coordination problem (Beckert 2006b). While trust, reputation, and institutional safeguards have been extensively discussed as forms of embeddedness in the new economic sociology, it is the systematic problem itself which provides the vantage point from which the cultural and institutional embeddedness of markets may be explained.

Again, proceeding from the coordination problem illustrates the commensurability of sociological, historical, and anthropological approaches. For example, from a historical perspective Berghoff (2005) has explored the origins of the credit reporting and rating agencies in the nineteenth century in the USA and Europe. Modern credit markets could only emerge when institutional solutions had been found to the problem of assessing the risks of credit. The historical investigation shows how the establishment of standards of creditworthiness emerged and altered as social and economic conditions changed and new technological and mathematical possibilities arose. Starting from interpersonal relationships in tightly knit religious networks, the instruments became increasingly formal up to the point where creditworthiness today is established through scoring systems. The very same problem has been investigated in a contemporary empirical case study by Guseva and Rona-Tas (2001), who examined the establishment of credit card markets in Eastern European countries. The research shows the specific solutions credit card companies find

---

[8] The distinction between competition and cooperation as two distinct coordination problems does not imply that competition does not involve cooperation between competitors. The solution to collective action problems is a form of cooperation. The distinction refers to the structuring of competition, on the one hand, and the social risks entailed in the exchange process, on the other.

when operating in an environment in which potential credit card holders have no documented credit history. In economic anthropology, Hart (1988: 179), among others, investigated practices of lending in the informal economy of a migrant community in Ghana, identifying the mechanisms by which traders assess the trustworthiness of their clients (cf. Gudeman, Chapter 2 in this volume). All of this research shows how the potentially devastating problems stemming from the asymmetric distribution of information and the freedom of choice of ego and alter ego are resolved through the connection of market exchange with the institutional, cultural, and social contexts in which this exchange takes place.[9]

Combining sociological, historical, and anthropological perspectives

Identifying the three coordination problems makes the cultural, political, structural, and cognitive embeddedness of market relations comprehensible in terms of the actual problems market actors confront. The embeddedness of market exchange is not the vantage point of economic sociology. Instead, it reflects social conditions that help actors in addressing underlying problems of coordination. This approach comes closer to Polanyi's conceptualization of embeddedness. It allows for a much broader perspective that does not have to limit itself to just one type of embeddedness but can investigate the actual solutions market actors find for the identified coordination problems as a combination of all four types of embeddedness and their mutual interdependencies. This corresponds to Polanyi's view that we should see markets as social institutions enmeshed in politics, culture, and ideology (Krippner 2001: 782).

The closer interaction between sociological, historical, and anthropological scholarship on economic exchange also corresponds to the Polanyian perspective. This plea for increased cooperation is not meant to reinforce disciplinary lines, but, rather, to improve the empirical understanding of economic exchange by enlarging the theoretical and empirical scope of scholarship in all three disciplines. How? First, by systematically studying the historical variance of solutions to the identified coordination problems and the historical genesis of current solutions. Second, by identifying and studying the large pool of alternative solutions to the coordination problems, which not only sharpens the understanding of solutions found in a specific situation but also heightens people's awareness of the cultural specificity and contingency of particular solutions. A comparative and historical perspective makes it possible to identify

---

[9] Many other examples of the study of this coordination problem in market exchange and of the investigation of the specific mechanisms by which it is resolved could be cited from the three fields (Kollock 1994; Braudel 1979). Of course the social and institutional context sometimes works to hinder the solution of cooperation problems. The argument is only that the solution to the problems cannot be analyzed in purely individualistic terms.

specificities of modernity and its variances in the organization of the economy in a non-functionalist way. Third, by applying theoretical concepts developed in one of the disciplines to empirical fields that get less attention in the discipline in which the concept originates. An example would be the concepts of gift-giving, reciprocity, and classification as important analytical concepts in anthropology. Despite their origins in sociology (Durkheim, Mauss), they were long neglected in economic sociology. Recently, however, they have been successfully applied to the analysis of economic exchange by economic sociologists (Godbout and Caillé 1998; Steiner 2004; Healy 2006; Adloff and Mau 2006).

Proceeding from the three coordination problems also enables us to connect economic sociology systematically with economics. Value, competition, and cooperation have been subject to extensive research in economics, especially during the last thirty years. What distinguishes a sociological – or anthropological, or historical – approach to the economy from an economic approach is not the questions asked but, rather, the answers given. The most profound difference – though this crosses disciplinary lines – is either seeing economic action from a normative perspective as contained in the universe of rational actors and efficient economic institutions, or understanding the economy empirically as a cultural and political phenomenon from its dialectic interrelation with other societal spheres (see also Gudeman, in Chapter 2). Which of these perspectives we take, however, is not simply a matter of taste. The coordination problems point to fundamental uncertainty for intentionally rational economic actors that impedes the maximization decisions presumed in orthodox economic models (Beckert 1996).

Embeddedness and social reform

I argued in the previous sections that there are two shortcomings in the use of embeddedness in the new economic sociology. The first difficulty is specific to Granovetter's (1985) influential conceptualization, which restricts embeddedness to the investigation of social network structures. The second, more general, limitation is that embeddedness is used as a starting point and not seen in its connection to the particular coordination problems market actors face. However, even if embeddedness is redefined to include the cultural, cognitive, and political contexts in which economic action takes place and is understood as a response to the three underlying coordination problems, another crucial challenge posed by Karl Polanyi would still not be taken up. In *The Great Transformation* Polanyi did not aim to understand the functioning of market exchange in order to explain the social preconditions for market efficiency; he was concerned with what happens to social order and political freedom when economic exchange is organized chiefly through self-regulating markets. This unease is evident throughout *The Great Transformation*, but is most directly stated in the last chapter of the book.

It follows that a sociological theory of the economy that claims Karl Polanyi as its inspirational source cannot be limited to the investigation of the social and political preconditions for the efficient fulfillment of economic functions, but must also pay attention to the effects of the organization of the economic system on society at large. Firms, for example, have increased leverage to exit existing national regulatory regimes. How does this affect the ability of nation-states to organize social solidarity? What impact does the increasing insecurity of employees caused by new employment regimes have on family structures? How does the expansion of markets effect social inequality, working conditions, and local communities? How are actors responding to the increasing uncertainties they face owing to the marketization of "fictitious commodities?" Whatever answers we give to these questions, they must be part of an economic sociology – and economic anthropology – which analyzes adaptive functions as part of the much larger question of the social integration of society. For Polanyi social order is precarious (Streeck 2007). The embeddedness of market exchange does not result from markets themselves or some other resource floating in society. It is the unstable result of social and political struggles, an outcome that has to be shielded by means of deliberate political engagement from the danger of an "institutional separation of society into an economic and political sphere" (Polanyi 2001: 74). The "double movement" is not an automatic response to the devastating effects of self-regulating markets but, rather, is the result of political intervention in markets in the light of their social consequences.[10] The "re-embedding" advocated by Polanyi implied a substantial political authority over the economy as a result of political and social engagement. In this sense Polanyi followed in the footsteps of the works of economic sociologists from the classical period (1890 to 1920), especially Émile Durkheim and Max Weber, whose scholarly work was also written to provide a scientific basis for social reform.

This reading of *The Great Transformation* as a social theory concerned with the question of social integration under conditions of political freedom is not widely accepted in the new economic sociology. Instead, the embeddedness of economic relations is seen as a constitutive element of *all* economies that can be taken as fact and is *only to be discerned* through sociological analysis. To the extent that the embeddedness of market exchange is seen as something to be established deliberately, it is the efficiency perspective that dominates. Embeddedness is then reduced to the optimal design of network structures for economic gain or of efficient economic institutions (Williamson 1985; Burt 1992).

---

[10] For a critique of Polanyi's notion of self-regulating markets see Gemici (2008).

Embeddedness and modernity

I argued earlier that economic sociology, economic anthropology, and economic history can find a common ground for the analysis of markets by proceeding from three coordination problems that have to be addressed wherever markets are found. This perspective does have certain limitations, however, which brings me back to the debate between substantivists and formalists in economic anthropology. For Karl Polanyi the embeddedness of economic exchange applied to modern societies as well and this perspective is shared by today's economic sociology. To quote Granovetter (1985: 483):

> I assert that the level of embeddedness of economic behavior is lower in non-market societies than it is claimed by substantivists and development theorists, and it has changed less with "modernization" than they believe; but I argue also that this level has always been and continues to be more substantial than is allowed for by formalists and economists.

The trouble with this perspective is that it does not help us to discriminate between traditional and modern economies, or between different types of market economies. In stark contrast to theories of functional differentiation, the new economic sociology highlights phenomena that demonstrate structural similarities between traditional and modern capitalist economies. It shows, for example, that particularistic networks remain paramount in the highly sophisticated market exchanges of today's capitalism (Portes and Sensenbrenner 1993; DiMaggio and Louch 1998). "Blocking action" aimed at restricting competitors (White 1992) is as much a feature of today's economies as it was during the time of the medieval guilds. Economic rationality has been deconstructed and shown to be determined by cognitive scripts that are culturally anchored (Dobbin 2001; Beckert 2002b). The rhetorical *mana* of concepts like "outsourcing," "diversification," or "shareholder value" is seen as structurally similar to the power of totems. Such management concepts serve as orientations for action based on the *belief* in their rational outcomes. On closer inspection, however, they are hardly more rational than magical beliefs.

The dominant narrative of economic sociologists is thus one of continuity. Such a perspective on the economy is appealing against the backdrop of modernization theories that see social networks, particularistic exchange, and magical beliefs exclusively as elements of premodern economies that have vanished in the course of rationalization. It is definitely enlightening to examine the cultural underpinnings of the notion of rationality and to call into question the ontologization that characterizes this concept in much of economic theory. This is also a valuable corrective to the agenda of classical sociology, including mid-twentieth century economic sociology, that sought to identify the distinctive characteristics of modernity in opposition to those of earlier economic formations (Parsons and Smelser 1956).

The appeal of Karl Polanyi for the new economic sociology might stem from the fact that his social theory does not imply a linear concept of development of the sort found in Marx, Weber, Durkheim, and Parsons. Embeddedness is *not* a characteristic that separates premodern economies from modern ones.[11] Based on the notion of a "double movement," social change is conceptualized as a dynamic process of oscillation between embedding, disembedding, and reembedding. Thus "all economies are embedded" (Barber 1995).[12] However, "embeddedness" does not provide a theoretical perspective informing us about the *specific* characteristics of the embeddedness of modern capitalist economies. The strong emphasis on similarities of economic systems across time and space, based on the notion of embeddedness, impedes the development of conceptual tools to address differences between economic configurations and, in particular, the specificity of the organization of modern capitalist economies.

This leaves us with an economic sociology that is unspecific with regard to the structural changes taking place in the organization of the economy with the development of modern capitalism. At the end of the day, all economies are embedded. Given the fact that the new economic sociology started from a strong anti-Parsonsian sentiment in American sociology in general, the allure of the notion of embeddedness is understandable. It has allowed for a concentration on meso- and micro level processes of economic organization and relieved sociologists from the task of addressing socioeconomic development at the macro level. This limitation is regrettable, however, because it excludes the possibility of analyzing changing forms of embeddedness from the premises of a sociological macro theory. I am not arguing for a return to the teleological errors of the past (Joas 1992: 218ff.). But we need an historical perspective if we are to understand the *specific* ways in which economic action is embedded in institutions and social structures of modern societies. We also need to identify the (normative) implications of such changes. Bourdieu's work on the transformation of peasant society in Algeria provides a fine example (Bourdieu 1963[6]). He showed how the logic of calculation wins over the logic of the household in the process of modernization, leading to social dislocation. It is not that modernization leads to disembedding in the sense of making networks and social institutions irrelevant, but structural changes devalue specific forms of embeddedness and force actors into new modes of social organization. The traditional *habitus* of the peasant clashes with the rational *habitus* demanded by capitalist society.

---

[11] This line of argument is also followed by Stephen Gudeman (in Chapter 2) when he emphasizes the dialectical relationship between necessity and contingency.

[12] It is true that Polanyi draws attention to the increasing role of the state in the organization of economic exchange (Block 2003: 281). Nonetheless, the dominant reading of Polanyi's work in the new economic sociology singles out the concepts of embeddedness and double movement, and shows little interest in a macrosociological theory of modernity.

A second example concerning the systematic changes of embeddedness in modern societies refers to cooperation, one of the coordination problems discussed earlier. Trust is a crucial facilitator of cooperation since market actors must take risks when engaging in exchange (Gambetta 1988a; Möllering 2006). Trust itself depends on social and institutional contexts that encourage the willingness to trust by improving the possibility of assessing the trustworthiness of the trusted party (Beckert 2005). Trust plays a role in economic exchange in both traditional and modern economies, but this observation should not prevent us from identifying structural differences in the ways in which trust is established.

Anthony Giddens (1990: 100ff.) distinguishes different ways of organizing the integration of exchange in premodern societies. The development of modern capitalist societies, however, tends to destroy the contexts of trust that support cooperation in exchange in traditional societies. Following Giddens, modern societies are characterized by an increasing time–space distantiation of economic exchange and the loss of traditional contexts of action. These changed macrosocial conditions necessitate the development of new forms of embeddedness that are able to support trust between exchange partners. Zucker (1986) has described this development for nineteenth-century America and shown the structural changes that characterize this development. She identifies a process where the sources of pre-industrial trust were increasingly disrupted by high rates of immigration, internal migration, and an increase in transactions across group boundaries and great geographic distance (Zucker 1986: 54). These changed macrosocial conditions led to a push to develop formal mechanisms for the production of trust, mainly through the establishment of formal institutions. The spread of new forms of standardization that were regulated by formal organizations, the increase in surveillance on the company level, the rise of the professions and of intermediaries like rating agencies may all be read as institutional responses to these changed conditions.

This observed increase in formalization of the bases of trust in modern economies does not *exclude* the continued existence of tight networks of interpersonal relations or cooperation based on religious beliefs. However, a structural change in the form of embeddedness of exchange relations occurred in nineteenth-century America as a response to a changing macrosocial situation. A comparative perspective shows, however, that the dissolution of traditional social relations does not automatically lead to efficient institutional forms of this kind. Hart's (Hart 1988) ethnographic description of economic relations among migrants living in the slums of Accra (Ghana) demonstrates unresolved trust issues in their exchange relations that ultimately lead to extremely high transaction costs and unsteady economic exchange. Trust emerges in particularistic friendship relations, but its generalization fails (Hart 1988: 190ff.).

These few examples suffice to show that historical analysis of the phenomenon of trust and trustworthiness makes it possible to identify and theorize systematic elements of modernization processes. Historical analysis of the economy is a key component of general theories of social change. The comparative approach is directed at the historically specific uncertainties actors face in economic exchange and at their particular reactions. This way a comparative perspective can direct our attention to the plurality of possible responses to macrosocial changes and also to possible failures to establish efficient solutions, thus avoiding the traps of teleological claims.

Conclusion

Based on the works of Karl Polanyi the notion of embeddedness has become the core concept of the new economic sociology. I have argued here that reading of embeddedness in the new economic sociology show a "great transformation" of the concept that does not do full justice to the meanings it had for Polanyi. This holds especially true for the reduction of embeddedness to networks of social relations. But the more encompassing understanding developed by Zukin and DiMaggio (1990) also leaves out the normative and social reformist concerns that formed the intellectual background of *The Great Transformation*. The way the new economic sociology has made use of the concept of embeddedness has, however, two further limitations. First, it does not address the coordination problems actors in economic contexts must resolve, which I have identified to be the problems of value, competition, and cooperation. To start from these problems provides a systematic vantage point for economic sociology and a basis for closer collaboration between sociological, anthropological, and historical approaches to the economy. Second, taking embeddedness as a foundational concept directs research in economic sociology to the meso- and micro levels and neglects processes of macrosocial change which were paramount in the investigation of economic phenomena by classical sociologists. For an understanding of the relationship between markets and society, an understanding of modernization processes and their effects on the organization of the economy remains indispensable.

4 The critique of the economic point of view: Karl Polanyi and the Durkheimians

Philippe Steiner

The purpose of this chapter is to examine what Polanyi and the Durkheimians[1] have in common when they study the economic point of view, what Polanyi labeled the "economistic fallacy" (Polanyi 1977) or the "obsolete market mentality" (Polanyi 1947). This may appear to be a paradox, since there is no trace of any direct influence that the French sociological school could have had on Karl Polanyi's thought. There exist a few cursory references to Émile Durkheim's works in some of his writings, but not a single one to François Simiand and Maurice Halbwachs, who were the leading Durkheimians in the field of economic sociology. More surprisingly, there is no reference to Marcel Mauss's path-breaking analysis of gift-giving processes among primitive societies,[2] although Polanyi did read French. However, as we shall see, there is a point in considering Polanyi and the Durkheimians together since it enables us to advance our understanding of the functioning of the market system in a given setting.

I first consider how similar their comparative analyses of modern society are, with a particular emphasis on their move from history to anthropology. Then I focus on the role played by economic knowledge in the shaping of the contemporary economy, since both Polanyi and the Durkeimians' inquiries stressed the importance of this cognitive dimension of modern society, that is to say, the cognitive embeddedness thanks to which the market system works. Finally,

---

[1] By "Durkheimians" I mean the major contributors from the group that Durkheim built around his ideas and, particularly, around his journal, *L'Année sociologique*. The development of the Durkheimian approach in economic sociology is mainly attributed to Durkheim himself, up to the end of the nineteenth century, and also to François Simiand and Maurice Halbwachs, who became the leaders of the school in this respect. In the early 1900s a second strand of research emerged with Mauss's studies concerning the connection between religion and economy. This work relied upon Durkheim's thesis that religion was the crucial institution for understanding society. Finally, this second approach merged with the first (Durkheimian economic sociology proper) in the post-First World War works of Mauss and Simiand (Steiner 2005: Chapter 6). We may add that, after his retirement, Polanyi's works was part of a collective composed of the group of scholars he had influenced in the Interdisciplinary Columbia Project.

[2] There is a brief reference to René Maunier's works in the chapter dealing with North African trade in the book jointly published by Polanyi, Arensberg and Pearson (1957). Maunier was in touch with Mauss and had published an important study of wedding gift-giving in Kabylie (*Twassa*).

I propose a comparative assessment of Polanyi and the French sociological tradition in terms of their sociology of economic knowledge, and suggest how the Durkheimian approach might enhance Polanyi's insights by providing a more accurate understanding of the role of economic knowledge in our societies.

Economy and the comparative approach

Polanyi's work will be considered here in terms of its relationship to history and anthropology, two disciplines that were important for him when he endeavored to understand the role and the place of the economy. This will permit us to draw a parallel with the Durkheimian approach, since it is my claim that both the Durkheimians and Polanyi used similar intellectual tools: an historical comparative approach and then an anthropological one. This claim entails a second: in both cases, the issue at stake is the economy–society nexus[3] since, according to Polanyi and the Durkheimians, modern society is characterized by the place given to economic institutions, in particular market institutions, and by the problem that such prominence raises for understanding the present situation.

Historical comparative approach

In *The Great Transformation*, Polanyi worked mainly with historical material.[4] This historical material described European development from the end of the Napoleonic wars to the interwar period. In the stylized history that opens his book, Polanyi explains that nineteenth-century European societies rested on four institutions: equilibrium between nations; the gold standard; the market system; and the liberal state, but the market system appeared to be of the utmost importance compared to the three other institutions. The emphasis on the market system gave birth to the distinction between "embedded" and "disembedded" economies, a distinction that it is still fashionable to use in contemporary

---

[3] I mean by this the following: from the middle of the eighteenth century to the present, the role and the place of economic activity within the entire set of social relations was considered a major political issue and an intellectual puzzle. This is a major political issue since, from the start, the rising prominence of the economy became either a threat to traditional views of the functioning of society or a major innovation opening the door to a better world. To use Max Weber's words, the economy–society nexus raises the issue of *Menschentum*, the type of humanity that is emerging from the diffusion and legitimization of economic behavior. It is also an intellectual puzzle because there is no agreement on the strategy for understanding the nature of the relations between the economic sphere and other spheres of social life.

[4] There are some anthropological references in chapters 4 and 5; however, at this stage of his work, Polanyi's inquiry did not emphasize this type of data.

social sciences.[5] Nevertheless, it is necessary to emphasize that Polanyi's major point in this respect is the "double movement" thesis according to which, during the nineteenth century, a *tension* existed between the creation of the market system with its price-setting mechanism, free of any encroachment from normative agencies, and the defense of society against the consequences of the creation of "fictitious commodities," in particular the creation of a free labor market (Polanyi 2001: 79–80; Stanfield 1986: 106–24; Baum 1996; Block 2001: xxviii–ix). Thus, on the one hand, there existed social forces pushing toward more disembeddedness (and political economy should be counted as one of these forces),[6] while on the other, different forces opposed this lethal transformation, protecting society from the disruptive effects of the functioning of the market system. In other words, historical inquiry was implemented first to describe and then to understand the nature of the tension at the core of the economy–society nexus.

This approach has many structural similarities with that developed by Durkheim and the Durkheimians in their economic sociology. This is clear when we consider Durkheim's *La division du travail social* (1893) and *Le suicide* (1897). These two books address contemporary issues: the nature of the modern form of social solidarity, so-called organic or contractual solidarity, and its limits, then Durkheim's study of this drawing on European suicide rates throughout the nineteenth century. Durkheim's approach was built on a dichotomy (mechanical/organic solidarity) which is at the root of the more complex typology of the forms of suicide; for altruistic and fatalist suicide are related to the former, whereas egoistic and anomic suicides are related to the latter. It is worth pointing out that Durkheim's theory is now interpreted in terms of the tension between two different social trends defining something like a social "equilibrium," which provide the level of socialization needed for the functioning of modern society.[7] These successive layers of Durkheim's typology were elaborated in order to understand the rise and functioning of modern societies within which the economic dimension of life was recognized as crucial; and it was not by chance that Durkheim found this dimension to be at the root of the ineffective socialization that he diagnosed (1976: 413–51).

---

[5] Nevertheless, this distinction has given rise to a debate among social scientists. Some of them consider it to be too crude (Grendi 1978: 31), whereas others consider Polanyi's distinction still useful in contemporary social sciences, once it is analytically qualified. This last position is the one advocated by Mark Granovetter in his famous article (Granovetter 1985) where embeddedness is no longer considered through its historical and normative dimensions, but is grounded on microsocial mechanisms (flows of information provided by noneconomic bonds, such as friendship and family life) studied in terms of network analysis (Steiner 2002; see also Beckert, Chapter 3 in this volume).

[6] These forces are mentioned in Chapter 12 of *The Great Transformation*, where Polanyi rightly points out that economic liberalism and laissez-faire policies differed since economic liberalism is not foreign to state intervention.

[7] On this point, I follow Philippe Besnard's analysis (Besnard 1987: 58–61, 81–88).

The historical dimension, together with statistics, is a foundation stone of Durkheimian economic sociology. Simiand's book on wage and price cycles is based on historical data and the historical critique of such data because, following Durkheim's rules of evidence, he wished to construct his economic sociology (or positive economics) on the actual behavior of social groups (workers, bosses, finance capitalists, and so on) instead of relying on the normative propositions defining what should be the behavior of a rational economic agent (Simiand 1907, 1932). The strategy was implemented by Halbwachs (1912; 1933) in his work on working-class consumption patterns, even if the historical dimension is mainly limited to the twentieth century, for want of data from the nineteenth century.

Consequently, it may be said that Polanyi and the Durkheimians were trying to achieve the same goal: to demonstrate how a pattern of economic behavior diffused in modern society, how it affected the functioning of the society in a fundamental way. It is also possible to say that Durkheim[8] and Polanyi both considered the economy–society nexus in terms of the *tension* between different social forces. Nevertheless, this similar endeavor makes two noticeable differences clear. First, if we put aside the concluding part of Durkheim's *Suicide* where he offered a possible solution to the defective socialization process in European societies at the end of the nineteenth century, Durkheim and his school distinguished between their political commitments and their work as social scientists; Polanyi, on the other hand, wove them together. This was done to such an extent that we can read Polanyi's work (notably *The Great Transformation* (1944) and *The Livelihood of Man* (1977)) as an uncommon mixture of academic achievement and political commitment, it being impossible to disentangle these two elements. This difference is important and gives a special character to research done under Polanyi's aegis.[9] However, we do believe that this difference should not prevent us from comparing their respective work, once we are aware that Polanyi would have been considered as an *essayiste* according to the Durkheimian methodological canon, whereas Polanyi could have disavowed their decided separation between research and an immediate political agenda. Second, if Polanyi's works offer suggestive studies of Babylonian and Greek markets, or the various markets at work in eighteenth-century Dahomey (Polanyi 1966: Chapter 6), nothing similar exists for, shall we say, the American market system in the twentieth century. In other words, Polanyi rested with the ideal functioning of the market given by formal political economy, whereas the Durkheimians made longstanding efforts to understand the actual functioning of the market economy: wage formation

---

[8] Durkheim's thought needs to be isolated in this way here. Simiand and Halbwachs did not present their research in terms of this fundamental tension.

[9] In the domain of economic sociology Richard Titmuss's book on health policy (Titmuss 1970) is a perfect example of this intellectual position.

(Simiand 1907), money (Simiand 1934, and consumption patterns and practices (Halbwachs 1912, 1933). Consequently, we may say that Polanyi's achievements in economic anthropology and the comparative analysis of economic systems paid a high price: a neglect of the actual functioning of the present market system, and hence an implicit endorsement of the economistic view of this system, even in the case of the three fictitious commodities (labor, money, and land).

Polanyi's turn toward anthropology brings us to a second dimension of this comparative reading, since some leading members of the Durkheimian group made a similar move.

Anthropology and modern economic society

After the publication of *The Great Transformation* Polanyi found a new impetus for his research in primitive and archaic societies (Grendi 1978). This could perhaps be explained by the fact that his political views were in some respects opposed to those prevailing during the Cold War (Block 2003: 298). This new orientation shed fresh light on the economy–society nexus and produced a notable change in his view of the subject. First, there were three possible institutional arrangements that could provide social integration with respect to the economic dimension of life: reciprocity, redistribution, and the market (Polanyi 1957b). Œconomia, which had played a part in *The Great Transformation*, was now left out of the analysis (see Gregory, Chapter 8 in this volume). Second, the anthropological turn provided a decisive change in Polanyi's interpretation of economic knowledge. Fundamental was the fact that Polanyi made an in-depth study of the formal – substantive conceptions of economic behavior. This distinction prompted extensive discussion concerning its relevance for the discipline of economic anthropology and subsequently in sociology (see Hart and Hann, Chapter 1 in this volume; Beckert, Chapter 3 in this volume). But this is not central to the present inquiry. More important is the fact that this distinction led Polanyi to make an original critique of the abstract and normative nature of formal economics, a critique that was usually focused on *Homo economicus* (Gislain and Steiner 1995; Steiner 2005).

This change was important since it offered Polanyi the opportunity to consider in greater depth some scattered remarks made in *The Great Transformation* (Chapter 4) concerning economic psychology and the profit motive, referring to Max Weber (surprisingly since anthropological references are scarce in Weber's works), Richard Thurnwald, and Bronislaw Malinowski. Thus Polanyi rediscovered some of the Durkheimians' leading work, notably that presented by Mauss in his essay on the gift. Let us consider this point in some detail.

Durkheim and the Durkheimians played a major part in the trend that moved sociological study from historical to anthropological data. This is well known as far as Durkheim himself is concerned, with his strong interest in the archaic religion of the Australian natives (Durkheim 1912). An interest in Antiquity and archaic societies was central to Mauss's work and, in this case, the connection between religious and economic sociology was certainly clearer than with Durkheim, who buried his most insightful ideas in the concluding part of his last book. As Mauss himself pointed out at the close of his essay on gift-giving, his own conclusions came directly from Durkheim's insights.[10] But Mauss's own genius added greatly to Durkheim's view of the issue. Two different elements may be noted here in our comparison between Polanyi and the Durkheimians.

First, Mauss's study of the anthropological data on gift-giving was the occasion to generalize his thoughts about the phenomenon of exchange, beyond that which he had so far produced. The conclusion of his essay stressed the permanence of gift-giving and its continuing presence within modern society. Among the illustrations he gave, Mauss endorsed social insurance and decommodification,[11] preceding his praise for the exchange of gifts that lubricate day-to-day activities. Thus, according to Mauss, the labor market did not function as an ordinary market since gift-giving processes (reciprocity) and the socialization of wages (redistribution) were at work; on the other hand, since Mauss did not make a distinction between the two forms of exchange, we may consider that, like Polanyi (1957b: 247), he contrasted these two forms of exchange to market exchange but, contrary to him, he did not straightforwardly oppose them. If we add to this Mauss's statement on the impossibility of eradicating market exchange, a lesson that Mauss learned while studying the Soviet economy (Mauss 1924), then it is possible to say that Mauss's position is an important link in the sociological tradition that runs from Auguste Comte's views on exchange[12] through to Polanyi. All of them stressed that different modes of exchange are simultaneously at work within a given society, and claimed that any unilateral consideration given to market exchange is nothing but historical illusion. Furthermore, we may notice that, in this area of his research, Mauss came close to Polanyi's way of combining academic achievement and political commitment, which explains why they are considered together in Caillé's work (Caillé 1986, 2000, 2005).

---

[10] This point has been studied in our previous study on the Durkheimian approach of the economy (Steiner 2005); on the other hand, Camille Tarot's book on sociology, religion, and symbolism has emphasized how strong the connection between Durkheim and Mauss was when they came to work on this topic (Tarot 1999).

[11] Devised for understanding the modern Welfare State, Gøsta Esping-Andersen's concept is also fitted to this strand of thinking (Esping-Andersen 1990).

[12] In his *Système de politique positive*, Comte (1890: II, 155–73) claimed that there were four modes for conveying resources: war, market exchange, bequest, and gift. He also claimed that it was nothing but our present egoistic view of humanity that made us to believe that market exchange should prevail; on the contrary, Comte argued that the most important social issue of his time was to enhance the role of altruism (gift-giving) within industrial societies.

Second, it should also be clear that, when Durkheim and Mauss turned their interest toward anthropological data, they were not losing sight of the present. Quite the contrary! As Durkheim himself put it in the first page of his *Formes élémentaires* (1912), his study of primitive Australian religion left his topic unchanged: the functioning of modern society. The fundamental reason for this bold statement was an ontological hypothesis according to which man was still the same, be it in southern Australian tribes or in modern European nations. The same is true with Mauss's view, notwithstanding an important difference related to the emergence of rational economic behavior, which appeared to Mauss as a real novelty. Out of his inquiry into archaic forms of exchange, Mauss built something like an oxymoron: in the opening pages of his essay, writing that gift exchange ("*échange don*") is a mixture of interested and disinterested behavior, selfishness, and altruism. Both aspects are so profoundly intertwined that it is impossible to disentangle them. In this respect, Mauss was reflecting the tension that we have found at the core of Durkheim's and Polanyi's view of modern economic society.

Did Mauss's position differ from the one advocated in *The Great Transformation*, where Polanyi argued that the profit motive – considered here as a proxy for rational economic action – has overcome other economic motivations, such as reciprocity or redistribution? I do not think so. In the concluding pages of his essay, Mauss made it clear that, according to his view of the subject, the rational economic actor was not an ancient character but a truly modern one, and he added that *Homo economicus* was not in the past, but the future (Mauss 4: 272).[13] Accordingly, if rational economic behavior has to be considered as a social construction, then an important task for the social sciences was to study how such a construction was made possible, how it happened. As Mauss put it in his Huxley Memorial Lecture devoted to the concept of identity ("*la notion de personne et du moi*"), the French school of sociology aimed at the social history of the categories of the human.[14] Furthermore, Mauss had a very clear position when motivations in the gift-giving process were at stake. Interest and disinterest, freedom and obligation are present in this process and, we suggest, consistently with our previous interpretation of Durkheim and Polanyi in terms of a tension embedded in the economy–society nexus. Furthermore, Mauss's view does not conflict with Polanyi's sharp opposition between the profit and

---

[13] If we read, side by side, Polanyi's Chapter 4 of *The Great Transformation* and Mauss's chapter on economic events in his *Manuel d'ethnographie* (Mauss 1947: 104), we notice how similar are their interpretations of Adam Smith's view of exchange. Both claimed that it was nothing but a mistaken interpretation of Cook's description of natives offering gifts, and not bargaining for a better rate of exchange.

[14] In the course of this lecture Mauss characterized the Durkheimian school in a very specific manner: "In doing this, you will see a specimen – perhaps less significant than that which you anticipate – of the work of the French school of sociology. We adhere in particular to *the social history of the categories of the human mind*." (Mauss 1938: 333; my italics).

the subsistence motive, if we take into account the "double movement" thesis at the core of *The Great Transformation*, and the coexistence of various modes of exchange studied in *Trade and Market* (Polanyi, Arensberg and Pearson 1957).

I conclude this brief comparison between Polanyi and the Durkheimians with a more general remark about the study of the economy–society nexus and, in particular, about the rational behavior that is attached to modern forms of economic activity. Did their move from history to anthropology come by chance? I do not think so. As a matter of fact, such a move was widespread, and some leading thinkers in the twentieth century, having considered in detail the economy–society nexus, took a similar path. This was true of Weber when he launched his lengthy study of world religions, following his work on the religious (ascetic) origins of rational economic action, a move that involved lengthy studies of the origins of various religious ethics (Buddhism, Confucianism, and Ancient Judaism); it was the case, too, with Michel Foucault when, after his two series of lectures on economic liberalism in 1978 and 1979, he came to deal with Antiquity in order to understand what he called the care of oneself ("*le souci de soi*"). This suggests that Polanyi and the Durkheimians, like Weber and then Foucault, felt the need *to study anthropological data in order to understand the present*. They felt the necessity to study data related to an earlier stage of history and then to compare these data with the present: in short, they felt the need to gain a longer view than the one provided by the history of modern Europe. Nevertheless, this also means that history and anthropology appeared to fall into the same category: the economy–society nexus is not only an historical issue, but it is also an issue pertaining to the domain of universal history – to use Weber's words –, a domain that asks for a longer view than the purely historical one because, as Mauss aptly put it, the issue is "the social history of the categories of the human mind." Nevertheless, be it historical or anthropological, the understanding of the economy–society nexus involves a strong dimension of the sociology of knowledge when it is acknowledged that economic behavior may entail the conscious attempt to mould our actions according to the model of formal rationality, and when this issue is explicitly taken up by scholars and experts of various types. It is to this issue that we must now turn our attention.

The market system and the role of economic knowledge

Polanyi's *The Great Transformation* contains two chapters devoted to economic knowledge: chapters 12 and 13 on the liberal credo, a credo directly connected to British classical political economy. What role does this credo play in Polanyi's narrative? This is the first issue to be considered here. The second issue is related to the critique of the present "market mentality" and the substantive or formal meanings of economy that became so central in Polanyi's subsequent writings: how is the formal approach to economic behavior connected to market mentality? Here I will consider the limits of Polanyi's approach, and also how the Durkheimian sociology of economic knowledge, as developed today, offers some key elements for understanding its role in the economy–society nexus.

The role of economic knowledge in The Great Transformation

There are relatively few comments related to political economy and economic knowledge in *The Great Transformation*. Two different approaches are present in Polanyi's book. The first one, which might be named the Tocquevillian approach,[15] considers changes in economic motives as a form of religious revolution. Accordingly, the diffusion of the profit motive among European societies amounted to nothing less than a change similar to "the most violent outburst of religious fervor" (Polanyi 2001: 31). This Tocquevillian approach is pushed further when Polanyi claims that political economy was instrumental in changes affecting modern societies since it produced an explanation of the laws under which modern society was ruled, and contributed to the replacement of benevolence by the profit motive. Polanyi's assessment is straightforward: political economy becomes a form of secular religion (Polanyi 2001: 107). The Tocquevillian approach is also present in Chapter 12, the first chapter devoted to the "liberal credo" where Polanyi explained his perspective using a religious vocabulary (faith, salvation, evangelical fervor, dogma, crusading passion, and the like). With this rhetorical strategy, Polanyi raised an important issue:[16] Social and moral thinking in the eighteenth century was very different from that of the seventeenth, when religion was at center stage. In this respect, Polanyi highlights the fact that political economy became as central for the late-eighteenth century and the beginning of the nineteenth century as religion had been for the seventeenth century. Nevertheless, what is missing here is an explanation of such a transformation. To put it in a nutshell, Polanyi's approach does not provide an explanation of political economy's centrality in social and moral thinking in market society.

The second approach emphasizes the role of the British classical economists in the "double movement" thesis at the core of Polanyi's book. This approach

---

[15] Tocquevillian because in his study on the French Revolution, Alexis de Tocqueville stressed the religious form of what appears to be a purely political event (see Tocqueville 1951: book I, chapter 3).

[16] On this issue, see the final pages of Max Weber's *Protestant Ethic and the Spirit of Capitalism 1904–1905*, and Foucault's lectures in the Collège de France in the year 1977–8 (Foucault 1978). I have dealt with this issue in several papers focusing on the discursive transformation at work and on the spread of economic behaviour considered as an ethos (Faccarello and Steiner 2008; Steiner 2008b, 2009).

considers that political economy was instrumental in the creation of the modern market system. Chapters 10, 12, and 13 of *The Great Transformation* are crucial since they dealt with "Political economy and the discovery of society" and the "liberal credo;" that is to say, with the core of the message conveyed by political economy. However, Polanyi's offering here might be somewhat disappointing for anyone in search of a clear position on the precise role played by political economy in the social changes affecting Europe during the nineteenth century. In Chapter 10, Polanyi rightly argues that the discovery of the economy was of tremendous importance because it opened the way to the creation of the market system (Polanyi 2001: 124–5). How did this happen? Once again, we are left with no clear answer, and Polanyi puts forward instead a questionable distinction between Smith and Ricardo, involving the latter's alleged misunderstanding of the economic system and his responsibility for a theory of the capitalist system lacking a correct view of the distribution of wealth.

However this chapter contains a real gem when Polanyi deals with Jeremy Bentham. Polanyi claimed that the social sciences were more effective in changing society than the natural sciences. The rationale behind such a claim is linked to the fact that political economy and legislation were instrumental in building the market system before engineers were able to transform the communication system (Polanyi 2001: 124–5). This was a bold statement from a scholar who relentlessly stressed the role of machines in the rise of the market system. Was this gem considered more fully in chapters 12 and 13? Unfortunately not, since Chapter 12 deals with a remote dimension of the double movement thesis. In a highly polemical move, Polanyi is busy convincing his readers that society's reaction to the utopia of a pure market was the spontaneous part of the story, whereas the utopia needed state support to gain momentum. The following chapter explains that class interests grounded in economic or material interests were, considered alone, insufficient to explain nineteenth-century history; they must be oriented by social interests reacting to the dangers brought about by a highly disruptive utopia, the market system praised by economists.

Hence Polanyi's position appears to be a dual one. At a macrosocial level, Polanyi makes a functionalist connection between political economy and the rise of the market system. Is classical political economy a cause of this rise? What is the microsociological link between these two macrovariables? The problem is that the possibility of producing such a tremendous change simply through ideas is doubtful, even when the ideas are those of brilliant economists such as Ricardo and Malthus. Polanyi never claimed that political economy had such power. Instead, his hypothesis was to transform political economy into a sign of the ongoing change. This is similar to Durkheim's interpretation of socialism, when he stated that socialism was not the science of market society, as it was often claimed by socialist thinkers and devotees, but socialism was a social fact – a social fact appearing as a way of thinking ("*une manière de penser"*) – in need of sociological explanation (Durkheim 1895–6). My contention here is that Polanyi's approach to political economy may be read in the same way: political economy is a social fact that signals the change going on within the economy–society nexus. This means that studying political economy is not studying the change itself, but a specific way of thinking that comes with the change. This interpretation of the role of political economy is weak since it makes political economy peripheral, something that may be left out of historical explanation of the change, a position that is certainly too mild for a full understanding of Polanyi's thought.

A more robust interpretation may be achieved through Durkheim and the Durkheimians, since they provide us with some microsocial dimensions that can improve our understanding of Polanyi's macrosocial hypothesis. This interpretation considers political economy as a social representation that, on the one hand, is instrumental, building the new goals society provides for itself, and, on the other, it shapes how people living in such a society understand social life, interact, and behave accordingly.

Formal economics and the "obsolete market mentality"

Political economy with its abstract basis (*Homo economicus* and rational economic action) was left almost untouched in *The Great Transformation*. But this topic became central in an important paper published in *Primitive, Archaic and Modern Economies* (Polanyi 1947), in the book edited ten years later (Polanyi, Arensberg and Pearson 1957), and, finally, in chapters 1 and 2 of the manuscript published after Polanyi's death (Polanyi 1977). Polanyi dealt with modern economics in these parts of his work; that is to say, with the type of economic knowledge that appeared as a consequence of the so-called marginalist revolution. Two dimensions of Polanyi's assessment of economics are relevant to our inquiry.

First, he launched a critique of the rational man placed at the core of pure economics. This critique was quite specific since Polanyi was not interested in methodology, as sociologists often tend to be. Rather, Polanyi's comments highlighted what was at the root of rational man: "economic motives," or, more precisely, the fear of starvation and the lure of gain. Obviously, we may find pages where Polanyi stressed the empirical inaccuracy of the supposed behavior of the (theoretical) rational man, and the strict difference between such a model and empirical behavior. But this was not the important point in Polanyi's critique, which was centered on the anthropological specificity of such a character. In various passages he emphasized that the real issue was the confusion existing in the minds of members of market society between the "economic man" driven by "economistic" motives separated from other motives (religion, friendship, prestige, and so on), and the general conception of man, the one that we encounter in any society other than market society. This misunderstanding seemed crucial to Polanyi, who urged his readers to change the way they thought about this point. A first step in this direction was to abandon the "obsolete market mentality" and to acknowledge a more appropriate perspective rooted in the longer view provided by an anthropological approach. The same strategy was at work in the second dimension of Polanyi's critique: the distinction between substantive and formal views of economic behavior. Again, he was interested in emphasizing the great difference between the substantive meaning of economy (nature–man interaction mediated by institutions) and the formal meaning (means–end rationality and scarcity), so that he might explain the historical specificity of the latter.

In either case, Polanyi's rhetorical strategy was based on the anthropological shift that he embarked on after the publication of *The Great Transformation*. In both cases the concern was to emphasize the clear specificity of market society and market behavior compared to what we knew about universal history. This strategy was similar to the one adopted by the Durkheimians, notwithstanding a difference that we will come to shortly.

According to the Durkheimians (see Simiand 1912; 1932, volume II), political economy is an intellectual dead-end on account of its methodological shortcomings, and because economic activity does not occur in the way that economists say it does. Consequently, economic sociology has to create its own set of concepts to facilitate correct understanding of what occurs in this sphere of social life. This intellectual strategy is now most common in the field of economic sociology. Polanyi's approach differs on a decisive point. On several occasions, he noted that *within a market society* the difference to which he had drawn attention, between market behavior and subsistence economic behavior, became elided (Polanyi 1968a: 61; 1977: 12, 24; Polanyi 1957b: 240; see also Caillé 2005). Where that happens, political economy or the formal approach to economy is deemed correct:

The last two centuries produced in Western Europe and North America an organization of man's livelihood to which the rules of choice happened to be singularly applicable. This form of the economy consisted in a system of price-making markets [...] As long as the economy was controlled by such a system, the formal and the substantive meanings would in practice coincide [...] under that market system economics terms were bound to be fairly realistic. (Polanyi 1957b: 240)

This very important statement should have led Polanyi to study carefully the functioning of a society in which the theoretical cleavage he had in mind disappeared, because of the way that we must use the market system to make a living. It is likely that Polanyi considered his previous statement on the utopian and unsustainable character of a pure market society sufficient to rule out such an inquiry. However, from our present position, we can no longer be satisfied by repeating the Polanyian credo, since we know that "market mentality" is far from fading away, to say the least. So we must consider carefully how "market mentality" functions before claiming that it is an "obsolete fallacy," if such a statement may be said to be at all meaningful.

Polanyi did not succeed here in linking his anthropological turn to the present; he limited himself to claiming – rightly – that the market system and market mentality were highly specific, and not common institutions. He thereby left out his own brilliant insight concerning the power of the social sciences to modify the architecture of modern societies, a fact that he – rightly again – pinpointed when he dealt with Bentham and the utilitarians.

Polanyi and cognitive embeddedness[17]

Once we admit that economic knowledge is important in Polanyi's view of the economy–society nexus, we are led to examine this dimension further, so that we might understand how the present market society works. As it turns out, Polanyi was not really interested in the role of economic knowledge, be it folk representations of the economy held by lay people, or rationally constructed representations elaborated by scholars and people whose education encompassed political economy.[18] Here, we are left with no clear analysis of the microsocial, or even of the institutional mechanisms that might explain the formation and consequences of this so-called "obsolete market mentality." Polanyi did not consider the precise role that political economy might have played in the social construction of the present economy–society nexus. This role is merely postulated by him and, despite his claim that we have been overwhelmed by a faulty vision of the functioning of the social world (the so-called "economistic fallacy"), Polanyi never studied in detail how this fallacy entered our minds, or what the practical results are for the everyday activities of people living in modern societies.

In striking contrast, following the lead given by Auguste Comte, the Durkheimians paid attention to social representations and socially constructed representations when they studied the functioning of the economy (Steiner 2005). Two distinct directions are worth considering here.

First, following the importance given by Durkheim to the teaching system (Durkheim 1905), the sociology of economic knowledge has to consider

[17] Sharon Zukin and Paul DiMaggio approach this form of embeddedness in terms of bounded rationality (Zukin and DiMaggio 1990: 15–17). In the present inquiry, cognitive embeddedness refers to social representations related to the teaching of economic theory (constructed representations) or the day-to-day economic activity (folk representations) of actors, on one hand, to the embodiment of economic knowledge in machines (computers with specific softwares) or social mechanisms (from economic indexes to specific forms of market such as financial markets), on the other.

[18] This view of economic knowledge is drawn from a previous study in which these categories were studied in detail, with a Weberian emphasis on the tensions that exist between different types of economic knowledge (Steiner 1998, 2001).

carefully the growing importance of the teaching of economics, particularly after the Second World War. The reason is plain: the functioning of the market system is likely to be modified once there are people with economics training in the various departments of economic life and when the economic point of view is considered as a legitimate, or even *the* legitimate, perspective when social policy is at stake. Contemporary research in the so-called "new economic sociology," especially in France (Heilbron 2000), studies how a training in economics (rather than in law) became a valuable resource in public arenas, and how it came about that a new elite emerged – a *Noblesse d'Etat* since, in the French case, they came from the exclusive system of *grandes écoles* whence they often started their careers within the French high administration.[19] This new elite was characterized by its ability to base its outlook on formally acquired economic knowledge (Lebaron 2000). This may be of great importance when a country has to comply with the demands of foreign lenders, as was the case with France in the 1950s (Fourquet 1980) or South American or Asian countries today (Babb 2001; Dezalay and Garth 2002). At the same time, there have been some important studies of the spread of economic knowledge more extensively with the creation of educational programs in precollege teaching and the creation of a growing number of newspapers, together with weekly or monthly journals devoted to the economy (Duval 2004). This strand of research now actively considers how the economic point of view is instrumental to the neoliberal transformation that has occurred in the last decades of the twentieth century (Blyth 2002) and how the economic point of view migrates from core countries (North America and, to a lesser extent, Western Europe) to peripheral countries in South America, Asia, and Eastern Europe (Babb 2001; Dezalay and Garth 2002 2006; Fourcade-Gourinchas and Babb 2002; Fourcade 2006). In all these cases, economics appeared as a powerful element in the extension of the market system around the world. This process is strengthened by some powerful financial institutions responsible for the economic international order, notably the International Monetary Fund (IMF). Research into such processes helps us better understand how belief in the economic point of view has macro effects, through the operation of financial constraints and adjustment policies, and how such belief is diffused increasingly widely until it becomes "common sense."

Second, the sociology of economic knowledge pays attention to the embodiment of economic knowledge in specific tools and social *dispositifs* (in the Foucaldian meaning of this term: a network of actors, texts, laws, rules,

---

[19] This situation opens the way to studying the formation of a professional ethos through emulation or the competitive aspect of the process of teaching and learning, emulation which is likely to endure in professional activity. In this respect, Marion Fourcade's study of the globalization of the economic profession (Fourcade 2006) is in line with Durkheim (1905) and Bourdieu (1989).

buildings, machines, and so on). This dimension of the market system was less developed by the Durkheimians themselves since it was barely perceptible before mid-century; but it may be linked to their views once we consider how carefully they considered the material dimension of social representations, such as magic, sacrifice, gift-giving (Mauss), or totems (Durkheim). Michel Callon's views on the economic embeddedness of economic activity (Callon 1996)[20] is grounded in the fact that there exist many social *dispositifs* where economic knowledge, formal economics included, is entailed in such a way that economic actions implement what is supposed by economic theory even in sheer ignorance of that theory (Steiner 2001). Contemporary financial markets are the classical locus for this, since ongoing transformation of the markets is strongly related to the presence of software that implements economic theory (the formulas of Merton, Black, and Scholes) in pricing derivatives and in traders' decisions (MacKenzie and Millo 2003; MacKenzie 2006), or in matching supply and demand according to a Walrasian view of what constitutes a perfect market. This approach has been extended (Callon and Muniésa 2003) to encompass a wide range of situations (from consumer to financial markets) in which marketplaces are considered as distributed collective devices for making calculations, broadly defined:[21] this extension is particularly relevant to the present argument since it means that the "market mentality" is much more effective now than was the case when Polanyi claimed that our market mentality was obsolete.

In both cases, the role of economic knowledge appears to be much more than a desideratum in the functioning of the market system, either because the actors in an economy where livelihood depends on market exchange are aware of the rules at work in a market and expect certain behavior from the people they encounter in them, or because material and social devices exist that implement economic theory as a matter of routine. There are thus many "*effets de théorie*" (Bourdieu 2000) or performativity (Callon 1996; Mackenzie 2006) in the present market system, which throws doubt on Polanyi's claim that the "market mentality" is obsolete. In that case, Polanyi's political commitment did not engender accurate judgment since, in retrospect, the last few decades have witnessed the marketization of *mentalité* to an increasing degree. A Durkheimian approach, concerned with the study of economic representations, is highly relevant: instead of making normative claims and rejecting the market, the task before us is to study the numerous ways through which this

---

[20] It is useful to bear in mind the fact that, according to Polanyi, embeddedness is due to economic and noneconomic institutions: "The human economy, then, is *embedded and enmeshed in institutions, economic and non-economic*" (Polanyi 1957b: 244; my italics).

[21] In their view, calculation does not imply the use of arithmetic or algebra. Calculation is close to Beckert's evaluation procedure (Beckert, Chapter 2 in this volume) with classification, physical movement, and then production of a given result (a sum, a schedule, an evaluation, a binary alternative) (Callon and Muniésa 2003: 4–5).

cognitive embeddedness of economic models is gaining momentum. As Mauss correctly stated, *Homo economicus* is not fading away into a past, he is part of our present and probably our future, too.

Conclusion

From this brief comparison between Polanyi's achievements and the Durkheimian school in the domain of the sociology of knowledge, together with its contemporary manifestation in concern with the idea of cognitive embeddedness, I would like to draw out the following conclusions.

First, there is a strong similarity between Polanyi and the Durkheimians owing to their progressive discovery of the importance of anthropological data where the economy–society nexus is at stake. In both cases, anthropological data became a cornerstone of the inquiry into modern society as part of the drive to understand the same political and social issue: what meaning should we attach to the rise of the economic sphere? If historical data provided an initial basis for their respective inquiries into the rise of the modern view of economy ("the market system" in Polanyi's words), they both considered that such data were not sufficient for answering the question they had in mind. I consider that the reason for this move was their common interest in what Mauss called the "social history of the categories of the human mind" (Mauss 1938: 333).

Second, there are strong similarities between the strategies pursued by Polanyi and the Durkheimians, and, more generally, by the "French socio-logical tradition" from Comte to Bourdieu (Steiner 2008a). Thus, we should consider Polanyi not as an exception within the company of scholars interested in the economy–society nexus, but as a member of a larger group of mavericks. But Polanyi's views on the role of economic knowledge in the functioning of the modern economy–society nexus is not sufficiently elaborated to sustain his claim that classical political economy played an important role in the making of the modern market system. A more accurate study of the interplay between economic thought, institutions, and the economy is needed. To this end, the institutional approach of the Durkheimians, and more generally of the "French sociological tradition" is useful, suggesting that due consideration should be paid to the different strategies developed in this tradition.

This last conclusion does not mean that Polanyi's highly specific blend of political commitment and social science should be ignored in favor of a nar-rowly conceived academic approach. Rather, my claim is that, if we take seriously Polanyi's political commitment to a truly humane society, we should try to improve the "scientific" grounds of such a commitment as one way of making it more powerful politically, a task that Polanyi certainly embraced in his own time.

5   Toward an alternative economy: Reconsidering the market, money, and value

Jean-Michel Servet

Karl Polanyi is widely invoked by critics of the extension and intensification of market exchange.[1] Neoliberal globalization is now seen as another attempt to revive the self-regulating market system at all levels, from the local to the global, comparable to the national and international experience of European societies from 1830 to 1930 analyzed in *The Great Transformation* (Polanyi 1944). This work presents a number of possible outcomes, and various lessons may be drawn from it for social struggles and policies today. More than half a century after its publication, can we go further with its theoretical and political arguments? In his preface to the first edition of *The Great Transformation*, when speaking of the establishment of the United Nations, Robert Morrison MacIver[2] notes pertinently:

> Such liberal formulas as "world peace through world trade" will not suffice. If we are content with such formulas we are the victims of a dangerous and deceptive simplification. Neither a national nor an international system can depend on automatic regulation. Balanced budgets and free enterprise and world commerce and international clearing houses and currencies maintained at par will not guarantee an international order. Society alone can guarantee it; international society must also be discovered. (MacIver 1944: xi)

The same observation might be made with regard to structural adjustment, the "Washington consensus" and the World Trade Organization. It might be supposed that Polanyi's critique of market relations and his political proposals with regard to developments in production, exchange, and finance are irrelevant today, since there has been a complete break in recent decades between his

---

[1] The French adjective *marchand* is translated here usually as market, sometimes as commercial. The first draft of this chapter was translated by Niall Bond of the Institute for the Study of European Transformations, London. It draws on Servet (2004, 2005, 2007). The workshops that gave rise to these publications testify to the multidisciplinary topicality of Polanyi's oeuvre in contemporary France.

[2] R. M. MacIver (1882–1970), a US sociologist who was professor in Aberdeen from 1907 to 1915, and then in Toronto before moving to Columbia University in New York in 1927. The new edition of *The Great Transformation* (2001) is prefaced by the former chief economist of the World Bank, Joseph E. Stiglitz, widely known as the author of *Globalization and its Discontents* (2002).

age and our own. Yet his arguments – not just against those who invoke the supposedly "natural" forces of the market, but also against those who merely lash out at the market without specifying concrete alternatives – have remained surprisingly topical. We can not only embrace Polanyi's critical perspective on the effects of the market system, but also his very conception of the market. His interpretation of the functioning and success of this system may be used to produce new propositions for the analysis of relations of production, exchange, and finance in contemporary societies. His definition of reciprocity is generally ignored today, although it can be particularly fruitful when contemplating an economy based on solidarity.[3] From Polanyi's analysis of the evolution of European societies I shall focus on the historically informed concepts underpinning his proposals that are worth reviving for an analysis of present-day transformations all over the world. Projects to develop community currencies[4] as one possible form of response to globalization will serve as a test of the continuing pertinence of his concepts. My aim, in short, is to extend the Polanyian critique of the market, money, and value to the analysis of contemporary societies.

This rereading of Karl Polanyi in the context of applying his concepts to the example of community currencies requires us to draw up an inventory of his thinking on market, money, and value. Some of these thoughts are clearly alive. Even if others in my view are dead, this does not mean that his overall analyses are defunct. In today's ideological context, they must be examined critically so as to produce new concepts that are better-suited for understanding how our societies function and possible alternatives. Every era has to critique earlier texts and ours is one in which globalization and neoliberalism predominate, in which it is claimed that market norms are crucial to the functioning of societies. Seen in this way, the great topicality of Polanyi's work today appears almost paradoxical. In the 1970s the idea that "the market system will no longer be self-regulating, even in principle, since it will not comprise labor, land, and money" (Polanyi 2001: 259) was widely shared.[5] The age of neoliberalism often seems to have discarded such ideas as so much ancient

---

[3] There is no good English translation for *économie solidaire*, since *solidarité* embraces so much more in French than its English equivalent. See entries for *économie solidaire* in Laville and Cattani (2006).

[4] These are known in France as *monnaies sociales* (Blanc 2006, Hart 2006), of which *Systèmes d'Echange Local* (SEL, Servet and Bayon 1999) or LETS (North 2006) are the best-known. But the term includes local, parallel, complementary, and alternative currencies of all kinds.

[5] In his preface to the French translation of *The Great Transformation*, Louis Dumont was able to write, even at the beginning of the neoliberal era: "The central institution of the market – considered to be self-regulating and able to command society's submission irrespective of what happens – has been swept away and no longer exists to all intents and purposes. In thousands of ways, facets of dirigisme or socialism have been introduced, and it was impossible for President Reagan to speak like Herbert Hoover, whose reign Franklin Roosevelt's New Deal definitively ended" (Dumont 1983: vi–vii).

baggage. Today, faced with neoliberalism's ideological pressures, advocates of intervention appear very much on the defensive. They demonize the market, but make few new political proposals because they have come to terms with the "market system", accepting that it is the most efficient means for producing and distributing goods and services, and for finance. Critics limit their ambitions to combating its negative effects, believing somehow that they can make it both more efficient and fairer. But was Karl Polanyi wrong, like Joseph Schumpeter (1948) in *Capitalism, Socialism and Democracy*), to refute Ludwig von Mises and Friedrich von Hayek? His critique of the basic logic of the global market system is still surprisingly topical with respect to both the environment and lifestyles:

To allow the market mechanism to be sole director of the fate of human beings and their natural environment indeed, even of the amount of use of purchasing power, would result in the demolition of society. [...] In disposing of a man's labor power the system would, incidentally, dispose of the physical, psychological, and moral entity "man" attached to that tag. [...] Nature would be reduced to its elements, neighborhoods and landscapes defiled, rivers polluted, military safety jeopardized, the power to produce food and raw materials destroyed. (Polanyi 2001: 76)

If making the market system universal could have consequences as extreme as Polanyi suggests, to grasp the limitations of present-day neoliberal policies is not enough. It is time to reread this author and to reaffirm his analysis of the market system and its theoretical corollaries, money, and value.

Beyond a critique of the market

If we restrict ourselves to its recent history – as Karl Polanyi does, just like Karl Marx, Max Weber, and Joseph Schumpeter – capitalist production,[6] generally conflated with growing subordination of social relations to the "market system," might be understood as a monumental attempt to break with traditional relations of production, exchange, and finance, by ruthlessly privileging economic motives aimed at the commodification of societies and their production. The nineteenth century may be interpreted as an explosion of the economy, trade, money, and finance as autonomous spheres, while the Great Depression and the Second World War constitute an era of countertrends and about-turns, when collectives and the state (in such diverse forms as social democracy, populist, Peronist, or Marxist–Leninist movements) were vindicated and liberalism

---

[6] In *The Great Transformation*, the term "capitalism" has differing meanings. It is applied to the capitalism of the great merchants (p. 29) and to industrialists with employees (pp. 84, 165, 168, 175). The capitalism of 1830 is qualified as *early capitalism* (pp. 84, 166, 231), while that of 1930 is *modern capitalism* or *liberal capitalism* (pp. 245, 251). On p. 188, Polanyi distinguishes *purely commercial forms of capitalism* from the *agricultural capitalism* that preceded the *industrial capitalism* of the early eighteenth century; to the former involved home-based labor in rural areas.

reached its apotheosis in fascist states.[7] The effects of those reversals continued right through to the stagflation, increased unemployment, and workers' loss of purchasing power in the 1970s. This interventionist cycle was decisively broken during the 1980s in a new wave of globalization driven by policies of economic deregulation, privatization, and structural adjustment.

The work of Karl Polanyi is often reduced to a mere critique of commodification. But, rather than restrict ourselves to a factual presentation of events when asking *how* European societies in the nineteenth century escaped from the rules of human economic history – the absorption of the economic by the social, tight control over market relations, and the erection of barriers to the use of money – we should ask *why* Europe's development was unique, especially since the reversibility of the historical trend suggests that it is not a natural or unilinear development. From where do the will, and, above all, the capacity to achieve a transformation which, in the absence of countervailing trends would, according to Polanyi, lead to the self-destruction of human societies, come? Is this an effect of the particular interests of social groups who impose it politically on society as a whole, while claiming to defend the general interest?[8] Polanyi implies as much in passages of *The Great Transformation*:

> [The double movement] can be personified as the action of two organizing principles in society, each of them setting itself specific institutional aims, having the support of definite social forces and using its own distinctive methods. The one was the principle of economic liberalism, aiming at the establishment of a self-regulating market, relying on the support of the trading classes, and using largely laissez-faire and free trade as its methods; the other was the principle of social protection aiming at the conservation of man and nature as well as productive organization, relying on the varying support of those most immediately affected by the deleterious action of the market – primarily, but not exclusively, the working and the landed classes. (Polanyi 2001: 138)

Is it a perverse effect of the rise of individual rights, whose positive aspect is freedom of conscience, with priority accorded to private property to the detriment of all other rights? We shall not answer such questions directly, since this would be to admit their premise, namely that from the eighteenth and nineteenth centuries onwards so-called Western societies offered real autonomy in those fields of social relations commonly referred to as "economic" and "the market." If we were to admit this common interpretation uncritically, Polanyi's extraordinary achievement in penetrating the development of European societies would be reduced to a doctrinaire belief in a purely "catallactic"[9] motivation behind economic activity, the antithesis of the perspective he offers.

---

[7] From Karl Polanyi's perspective, National Socialism and Fascism should be distinguished from protectionism in its various forms, since they represented the logical culmination (and degeneration) of the liberal economy, not its opposite (Polanyi 2001: 244, 250).

[8] For Polanyi's very broad understanding of social group see Polanyi (2001: 160).

[9] This expression for activities related to exchange was often used by Polanyi.

When Karl Polanyi undertook an analysis of the evolution of the systems of production and exchange in Europe from the sixteenth century onward, first as a journalist in Vienna, then as a teacher in England, and subsequently as a researcher in the United States, his purpose was to reveal to his contemporaries a possible path other than that of the doctrine of individual interest, capitalist appropriation, and accumulation, to prove that the categories of economics were the product of an exceptional historical situation rather than universal, and to show that normal societies were founded on something other than the catallactic prejudice, lucrative destruction, and formal rationality of *Homo economicus*. This was the matrix for *The Great Transformation*. Then, benefiting from the expertise and collaboration of his colleagues, for the most part anthropologists, archaeologists, and historians, he undertook the vast project of constructing an economic anthropology of human societies, rejecting the dominant prejudices of economists. As a result, Polanyi realized a new interpretation of the historical and anthropological foundations of what is substantively "economic." When applied to societies and epochs other than European societies based on the institution of private property and capitalist accumulation in *Trade and Market in the Early Empires* (Polanyi, Arensberg and Pearson 1957), the result appeared to represent a compromise with the economists participating in the interdisciplinary project, something of a departure from his position in *The Great Transformation*, leaving the hard core of economic knowledge untouched when it comes to interpreting the workings of contemporary exchange.

Polanyi debunked the Robinson Crusoe myth of classical theory as an antiquated relic. From time to time economists claim to revive it, proposing pedagogical models from game theory, neoinstitutionalism, or the simplifications of ultra neoliberalism. At best, the concepts of economic science, in as much as their potential application is reduced to the societies and cultures where they arose, remain more or less efficient tools for understanding the rationality of contemporary institutions and economic behavior. Economic anthropology has drawn inspiration from more humane social forms based on a different logic and concluded that not all human societies have functioned exclusively on the basis of the mercantile motive, that the capitalist mode of production, exchange, and finance jeopardizes the future of humanity, and that it is possible to reverse the process, since the world did not always work that way.[10]

Even so, an interpretation of Polanyi that stresses his importance for anthropology seems one-sided, since it blinds us to his fundamental critique of classical economic doctrine. Denunciations of the damage caused by the development

---

[10] "In effect, the disintegration of a uniform market economy is already giving rise to a variety of new societies" (Polanyi 2001: 260). According to Louis Dumont, in his preface to the French translation (Dumont 1983: i–ii), the German term *"Umwandlung"* [turn-around] is a more precise rendition of the idea Karl Polanyi sought to convey with the English word, *transformation*.

of the "market economy" are as essential to belief in it as praise of its potential for progress. Critical analysis of the market system is not advanced by mere denunciation of its supposed negative effects; and Polanyi's work would be of scant importance if it were nothing more than that. How then could he claim that the market and socialism are compatible? His account of the social consequences of the market system undoubtedly provides the emotional impetus needed to break with the doctrines of classical economics; but an antieconomic romanticism based on exotic historical, archaeological, philological, or ethnological examples cannot constitute a scientific program. Its politics would be limited to yearning for a return to a protector state or to romanticizing place-based *communitas*; but to show blind faith in either the all-encompassing state or local solutions to all problems is to neglect the complexity of society and the need to resolve problems at the level they occur.

Karl Polanyi's scientific project, his spiritual posture, his engagement with a democratic, decentralizing, and humanist socialism, and with the study of societies that were then considered to lie outside the modern world reveal his vision to be not limited in this way.[11] His work opens up productive channels for the critique of economic doctrine. A number of so-called "alternative" political programs are petering out today largely because of their inability to go beyond denouncing the market and its effects. Polanyi's essential break with orthodoxy lies in his deconstruction of the concept of the market. We will see that he splits this category into antithetical logics: "the market" is a *belief* and not a scientific concept. With this distinction in mind, we can then sort the wheat from the chaff when redefining a hierarchy of individual and collective rights of access to goods and services. On this basis, we can conceive of a principle of subsidiarity, taking in all levels from the top to the bottom of society, which delegates powers to the level appropriate for resolving the problems human communities face. In this way rereading Polanyi can help us to deconstruct the very concept of the market and thereby to consider the future of our exchange practices in a new light.

The fictitious commodities

In *The Great Transformation*, Karl Polanyi makes a distinction between markets and the market system[12] and frequently describes land, labor, and money as "fictitious commodities." The vast movement that took place first in Europe and North America, then throughout the planet, to commodify land, labor, and the means of payment – the basic elements of production, exchange,

---

[11] Polanyi Levitt (2005: 2).

[12] The index (p. 305 *sq.*) contains entries such as: *Market economy, Market system, Markets* alongside *Commercial revolution, Commercial society, Commodity fiction, Commodity money, Commodity prices, Exchange, Exchanges,* and *Trade.*

and finance – must be understood as the imaginary product of belief in a world market; and the "law of competition" is a multifarious expression of this Utopia. For Polanyi, the expression "fiction" applies to land, money, and work when these essential sources of wealth are bought and sold just like any other commodity in the interest of maximizing profit and reducing costs, being subject to the same kind of calculation. He emphasizes that the meaning he gives to the adjective "fictitious" is different from the commodity fetishism analyzed by Karl Marx (1867) in *Capital,* since Marx was here concerned with value in the economic sense (Polanyi 2001: 76). If *fictitious* and *fiction* are to have a meaning, it is that Polanyi's main purpose was not to describe or critique the real effects of the market system, but rather the ideal construction of this principle.[13] It is that Polanyi's main purpose was not to describe or critique the real effects of the market system, but rather the ideal construction of this principle. To deconstruct that principle is to undermine our belief in it and its practical efficacity for the institution of social relations.

For Polanyi, then, the economy should not be understood as a dimension or aspect of the social that we could claim, like Karl Marx, to analyze scientifically, but as a way that society represents itself, making a particular type of logic its autonomous core. Words replace things in a world that has entered into a sort of madness, through the inversion of signifier and signified. Belief in a special kind of rationality lends unity to practices that appear together as "the market." The market system as a unifying abstract category, that is, the totality of exchange transactions, is only real to the extent that we believe in its existence; and economists who claim that their knowledge is based on describing the real world merely promote mystification. This fiction of the market economy, moreover, supports the attribution of an "economic" value to property rights and the products of labor, when this value is really a product of the imagination. The imaginary character of each kind of market (the labor market, the property market, the money market, and so on) makes the state's role indispensable to the functioning of what are in reality pseudo-markets.[14] It is as a work of the imagination that they are brought together in a single category. Accordingly, in what follows, we will break up "the market" by distinguishing two kinds of logic essential to its functioning: the logic of the marketplace and the logic of customer ties.[15]

---

[13] *The New Oxford Thesaurus of English* (2000) associates *fiction* negatively with *works of the imagination* and *untruth* or *invention*; and *fictitious* with *false, fake, untrue* (p. 358).

[14] Polanyi (2001: 155) emphasizes that they are instituted by the state. It is noteworthy that those who claim to defend the laws of the market as a quasi-natural form of organization, take recourse to law, both at the World Trade Organization and the European Union, for instance, so as to ensure that for international trade the technical and social norms of the manufacturing country rather than those of the consumers apply.

[15] The relations established between buyers and sellers through "custom" are perhaps expressed better by the term "ties," with its sense of mutual dependency, than by "customer relations," which today implies a sort of Public Relations (PR) through which firms manipulate their clients.

If, as Karl Polanyi claims, the production of land, labor, and money as commodities is a fiction, we should not forget that this vast scheme is extraordinarily efficient. But, given the essential role of these fictitious commodities in the system of production, the revelation of their fictitious nature should cast doubt on the whole system, especially since no other commodity can be produced without them. If the market system does not reduce complex reality to an abstraction (as we are prone to believe), our task then becomes to seek out the social constants that determine the modern forms of what we imagine to be "economic," such as the social forms of exchange, the institutional means for transferring goods and services, and even the limits imposed on money's circulation; these limitations did not exist only in ancient societies. This reading of Karl Polanyi thus opens up new paths for archaeological, anthropological, and historical studies. Many scholars who criticize him on the basis of what they call facts have simply not understood his radical critique. This vision allows us to bring a new analysis to bear on institutions and behavior in modern societies believed to be economic, particularly when they pertain to markets and money. Such an analysis would emphasize the variety of forms of exchange and transfer of goods. The problems of the market can only be understood if we call into question belief in the autonomy of the economy; in other words, if the economy is conceived not as a reality, but as a certain way of looking at beings and things – as an ideology, as a logic of ideas and representation, in short as a belief system. We can only escape the market's dominance by adopting a different perspective. If we wish to generate practical alternatives to the market, rather than just opposing its effects as a living disaster, we must embrace ideological deconstruction along these lines.

A nonevolutionary vision of the principles of economic integration

According to Polanyi, there exists in all societies a multiplicity of forms for transferring material and immaterial goods. He recognized three concomitant forms of access to goods and services: reciprocity, administered redistribution, and the market. (In *The Great Transformation* he included "householding," only to withdraw it in later work; see Gregory, Chapter 8 in this volume.) In contemporary societies, many forms of transferring material and immaterial goods are conceived as belonging exclusively to the market. As a horizontal mechanism for coordinating the supply and demand of goods, services, and money, and for distributing income, the market is opposed – on the one hand – to whatever is offered "free of charge" and to the state's role of vertical coordination when levying taxes and redistributing income – on the other. This classification is hardly sufficient if we wish to develop "the market" as a relevant category.

Karl Polanyi's main contribution was to expose this widespread modern confusion of all forms of reciprocity, exchange, or circulation with the market. This conflation endows the market with universality in space and time, the first manifestations of which are supposedly "primitive barter." He shows that, although often limited in scale, the circulation of goods and services between groups and people is as ancient as human society and in no way depends on whether the transfer is commercial and competitive or not. Different institutional frameworks organize the circulation of goods according to the specific logics of market, redistribution, and reciprocity, often in combination.

The modern custom is to extend the opposition of gift and market to all human societies. The fact that gifts are generally followed by an immediate or deferred return or by imaginary substitutes (such as deference under conditions of dependency) substantially circumscribes the freedom of actors, unlike a marketed good or service which thereby acquires a universal definition. This claim is all the more remarkable given that what we mean by this one word is rarely found in ancient and non-Western societies, where there are generally multiple terms to describe the social relations involved in transfers. We cannot reduce the difference between reciprocity and market exchange to the sole criterion of whether money payment is involved or not. That would be to reduce reciprocity to a simple economic category for certain forms of transfer. The new institutional economics treats gift, market, and redistribution as complementary forms of the transfer of goods determined by variable transaction costs; but this reductionism is an impediment to analysis.

In *The Great Transformation*, the market is not treated as a single unitary category. Rather, Polanyi distinguishes (2001: 61–7) between *long-distance trade* and *local* or *internal markets*. Each of these institutions could exist separately, serving different types of function and need, while remaining subordinate for a long time to logics other than competition and only exceptionally embracing it. Boundaries were constructed to demarcate different types of exchange within limits compatible with the reproduction of other institutions in society. According to Polanyi, such practices prevailed in Europe until the eighteenth century, with "mercantilist" states regulating domestic trade through a proliferation of laws. The expansion of one form of transfer at the expense of another could in no way be described as a natural evolution.

This attack on the common belief in the market as a transhistorical institution is important because the market idea is often associated with those of private property and individual freedom. In fact, private ownership and other forms of property rights each correspond to specific categories of market. Politicians often invoke "the market economy" to defend private property rights, a conservative justification for inherited inequalities in fortune that ignores destruction of the environment and of established ways of life. How goods and services are circulated and how they are held as property are two different issues. Circulation of products through the market is compatible with extremely heterogeneous forms of appropriation and with a variety of degrees of personal freedom or constraint. Polanyi insisted that the state necessarily intervened in establishing a market economy from the 1830s to the 1930s. He also showed how the fascist states presented themselves as a solution to the contradictions of the market system, by defending private property and organizing the commercial circulation of goods and services. The fact that economic liberalism led to fascism while socialism made a clean break with it shows the error in confusing modes of circulation with modes of appropriation.

Finance has provided a model for understanding and instituting competitive markets. In modern societies, financial markets appear to be the most efficient response to market organization, offering a theoretical archetype of the competitive economy in general – hence their strategic importance in the first two chapters of *The Great Transformation* (see Hart, Chapter 6 in this volume). Yet they are the most regulated of all markets, subject to massive intervention by state-related institutions to limit their potential for excess. The market's limits are revealed by the impossibility of producing and reproducing land, labor, and money as commodities, and by the need for state intervention to create *any* supposedly self-regulating markets. Indeed the state seems to be a precondition for markets to exist as allegedly autonomous institutions at all.

For reciprocity to exist, in contrast to commercial or profit-seeking relationships, the exchange partners should be voluntarily complementary and interdependent (Polanyi 2001: 50–1). In Polanyi's words, "Reciprocity is aided by a symmetrical pattern of organization" (Polanyi 2001: 59). The elements of symmetric figures are reciprocally equal, but their complementarity within a whole makes their superimposition impossible. They are not interchangeable or commutable, like buyers and sellers in the market, whose functions are supposed to be unrelated to status or hierarchy. Seen from this perspective, the market and reciprocity are antinomies. An economy based on solidarity may privilege reciprocity, but this does not preclude other logics of production, circulation, and finance. The difference between the model of the market and principles such as *autarky*, *reciprocity*, and *redistribution* is that the latter have not acquired autonomy through an institutional form designed for that purpose (Polanyi 2001: 59). Their institutions have religious, political, military, and other functions, with no direct link to production, exchange, and finance. They do not seek to absorb social, cultural, and spiritual forms by reducing their functioning to mere economic constraints.

The logic of the marketplace versus the logic of customer ties

Polanyi refused to contrast a unitary category of the market with other forms since, when he studied historical societies, especially ancient Greece and the

African kingdom of Abomey in the eighteenth and nineteenth centuries, he opposed the *market* to *trade*, extending the distinctions he made in *The Great Transformation* between *long-distance trade*, *local markets*, and *internal markets*. If the marketplace can, at first sight, be included within the modern category of the market, which it appears to exemplify, trade is distinct from the market because its rational exchanges are framed by sophisticated administration under the control of political authorities. Although Polanyi may be read as having concluded that the trade–market dichotomy has gradually disappeared, I prefer to reactivate it for modern societies by distinguishing between two opposed logics of exchange, one that I call "marketplace" and the other "customer ties." I contrast these logics, even though they can coexist within the same institutions, one forcing on the other a compromise that is necessary for its functioning. This subordinate relationship may be reversed, if we follow Polanyi's nonevolutionary approach to the modes of access to goods. It is a question of different principles, each with its own logic and system of legitimation,[16] not of the market as a scientific abstraction.

The anonymity that prevails in the marketplace at one point in time is supposed to neutralize social identities and differences between actors. This appears to be a social prerequisite of the exchange, whose character is horizontal rather than hierarchical. Ordinary hierarchies and relations of domination are suspended during the exchange. Provisionally, each party to the transaction becomes the other's equal (i.e. a possible substitute). The conceptual space of this exchange is not a private space belonging only to the participants in the exchange. It is also public, a fictitious world of "individuals," who are likewise supposed to be equivalent.[17] Equality is a norm and a rule of behavior in this marketplace. Differences in status and fortune are temporarily replaced by a citizenship of exchange relations, in the name of an ideal of substitutable equivalents. These citizens are utilitarian consumers and producers, undifferentiated by gender, hierarchical relations or interdependence, or solidarity.

Economics, originally known as "political economy," was built on this egalitarian utopia of the marketplace, eliminating other forms of transfer and remuneration. The market contract, a prerequisite to establishing the convention of equivalence between two partners to an exchange, is made as though there were no debt before or afterward, and certainly no obligations beyond the economic. Payment is a reciprocal operation of debit and credit that is instantly

---

[16] See Boltanski and Thévenot (1991).

[17] We should distinguish here between the individual and the person, and note that most economists confuse the two and misuse the term "individual." The person, which means "mask" in Latin, presents different facets and is only defined through relations with other members of the groups to which the person belongs. The individual is supposed to have unique characteristics making it possible to define him or her without reference to others. A person has desires, while an individual has needs.

concluded: the transfer of money releases the parties from all other obligations of hierarchy or solidarity.

In the microsociety of the founding texts of economics it is assumed that market exchange is, or must become, the main activity, thereby reducing people to vectors of mutually autonomous, individual economic motives. This myth grants legitimacy and value to the eager pursuit of material goods and services (under the pressure of need) and to all activities leading to their accumulation by individuals acting in their own utilitarian self-interest. Everyone must defend his particular interests; there is no *social whole* expressing shared interests that have been set in a hierarchy as recognized relations of solidarity and interdependence; at the most, there is a sum of interests. Solidarity is generated mechanically and objectively out of the interdependence of actions, not from conscious motives. The pursuit of interests described as "economic" (which boil down to cupidity, avarice, and greed) is judged positively, in contrast to the actions of those who defend the interests of the "collective" and work within the political order; the latter are negatively represented as pursuing only their own self-interest.[18] This channeling of individual and egocentric interests by "the market" is presented as a more effective restraint on "passions" than appeals to reason, duty, morality, or religion. Thus, the virtues of the good tradesman are opposed to the mad passions of powerful elites and the populace at large, with the aim of endowing commercial activities that had been despised for so long with legitimacy and prestige. The market is presented as a civilizing agent and the merchant as the prototype of a self-interested individual.

In fact, when we observe buyers and sellers and how prices are set, it is plain that trade at the local and international level diverges radically from this presumed logic of the "marketplace."[19] Neoinstitutional economics and game theory try to account for other dimensions of exchange, without breaking with the illusion of the market's unity as a category. We will designate this dimension, an approach to exchange altogether different from the logic of the marketplace, as "customer ties." In this view, sellers discriminate between buyers in an attempt to generate loyalty and sustain the relationship. The contract does not render parties to the exchange uniform and equivalent, limiting their relationship to a single transaction. In contrast to the juridical interpretation of a sales contract, a major part of contemporary sales strategy consists precisely of seeking to ensure that the customer relationship is not severed, but is, rather, renewed and perpetuated. However, this acknowledgement does not imply that the relationship is part of a social whole. Customers are differentiated, but

---

[18] See Adam Smith's praise of the pursuit of self-interest by butcher, brewer, and baker as opposed to the questionable generosity of public policy in *Wealth of Nations* (Smith 1776).

[19] The present analysis aims at identifying the beliefs underlying market relations. All markets of course require social bonds and networks to function. Thus, the market of the neoliberals is a utopia.

relations are not necessarily seen as being interdependent, so that this type of exchange remains quite unlike reciprocity.

Before the nineteenth century the logic of customer ties prevailed over that of the marketplace, even in Western Europe, where hierarchy in Louis Dumont's sense predominated, and relations formed in the marketplace were relegated to a secondary mode of managed exchange. The context for modern economic practice is the gradual disappearance of hierarchical norms, as Dumont explained in his preface to the French translation of *The Great Transformation* (Dumont 1983). The norms of the marketplace generally correspond to those of *Homo aequalis* (Dumont 1977), just as customer ties may be derived partly from *Homo hierarchicus* (Dumont 1967).

Community currencies (*monnaies sociales*), as they were developed in the 1990s, illustrate well the tension between these two logics. On the one hand, the relationship between two members of a local system of exchange (LETS or SEL) is supposed to be an equal one. The group apparently accepts a market logic and each participant treats everyone as equals, thereby obscuring the hierarchy and inequality that they bring from outside the group. On the other, their relationship does not end with payment for exchange and, indeed, sustains an explicit dynamic of interdependence between members which is characteristic of customer ties. It is precisely this dynamic of renewed exchange that allows community currencies to have a multiplier effect at the local level by stimulating exchange within a group that declares itself to be sovereign.

Limits to the fungibility of money

Karl Polanyi's studies of the boundaries of exchange in ancient societies were continued by anthropologists, in particular by Paul Bohannan. Boundaries of this kind have not disappeared with modernity, but merely taken on other forms.[20] There are still moral limits to the extension of commercial relations. It was once common to sell human beings wholesale (under various forms of slavery) and to obtain honorary titles or military and religious offices against legal tender. Most members of modern societies disapprove of these practices and they have been prohibited by law; so legal frameworks restrict markets. On the other hand, the commercialization of land, labor, and money, which appears natural to most of our contemporaries, was subject to substantial limitations even in Western societies until the nineteenth century because their *free* transaction would have appeared contrary to nature (or, rather, contrary to society). It is remarkable that while Karl Marx and Friedrich Engels were denouncing commodification in *The Communist Manifesto*, a growing number of European countries were prohibiting trade in and the use of slaves in their

---

[20] For a topical discussion of spheres of exchange, see the interesting work of Guyer (2004).

colonies, greatly reducing the sphere of commercial practice, not for economic but for moral reasons.[21] Like Marx and Engels a century earlier, Polanyi, in *The Great Transformation*, seems not to recognize what an extraordinary limit these laws placed on the commodification of labor on Europe's periphery.[22] In ancient societies, many denounced what they considered to be excesses of commodification. Such assertions, which may be encountered in various epochs, are not reliable indicators of a real extension of the "profit-seeking sphere." Rather, they manifest shifts in the moral limits of exchange: the establishment of certain rights, goods, and activities as belonging to the field of circulation goes with the exclusion of other rights, goods, and activities from that sphere.

Polanyi understood perfectly well, drawing on ethnological publications from before the Second World War, that money cannot be reduced to what is needed for the functioning of what we call today "the market" or "trade," nor could it be limited in the imagination to being the only accepted intermediary for these transactions. Money defines norms and social relations at a more general and deeper level, and market transactions are only a part of that. These norms gained lasting and universal recognition through dowry payments, ritual offerings, instruments of political alliance – indeed, any social act that required codification and abstraction. We find here rituals of transfer and sophisticated codes, forms for conserving debts, credit, and the like – all of them requiring means of payment that correspond to established norms and units of account. Money did not emerge as a functional necessity in response to the difficulties inherent in barter at all; it did not originate directly through relations of production and exchange either. Polanyi could therefore maintain that the use of money is universal, just as the spoken word is universal among human beings. There is a plethora of dialects and languages, but all human beings can potentially use speech and its substitutes. Likewise, all human societies have monetary instruments for accounting or payment; they may vary greatly in form, but all function to establish norms for assessing value and for coordinating mutual relations at the level of society as a whole.

The general categories Polanyi applies to ancient or exotic forms of money have been validated by numerous anthropologists and archaeologists. He opposes "modern money" (*all-purpose money*) to the uses of money in antiquity or exotic money, where *special-purpose monies* were typically reserved for specific groups of people or classes of activity. Here again, we can apply Polanyi's concepts to contemporary reality to highlight the contradiction

---

[21] Two independent countries did not abandon slavery until the end of the Civil War in the United States (1865) and in 1888 in Brazil. Slavery has still not been stamped out, if we take account of *bonded labor* as practiced in southern Asia.

[22] His focus is on the transformation of European societies. Non-European societies are basically treated as lying on the periphery of Europe. Hence our surprise when we read about the "hundred years peace" of 1815–1914 (a chapter title in *The Great Transformation*).

between the supposed fungibility of money and actual practices, even in so-called "developed" societies.[23] The ancient limits were generally achieved by using differing physical instruments, while modern barriers are usually determined by sources of income and assets that can be valued by a unitary currency. As a result it is more difficult to demonstrate the barriers and limits to fungibility, which are determined morally and through use of a variety of instruments to distinguish types of expenditure, for instance, by systematically resorting to different credit cards or deposit accounts.

Community currencies offer a perfect contemporary example of how exchange may be closed off. Each local group defines a more or less extensive range of products and services that may be offered for exchange within its circuit. The purchasing power of each of these currencies is restricted to voluntary transactions between members of each local group. Only exceptionally are agreements reached between groups in order to allow for an extension of the range of trade; the national currency is completely banned.[24] In this way each group achieves a sort of monetary sovereignty.

A permanent tension exists between the apparent fungibility of monetary instruments and the moral demarcation of boundaries related to their use. Social hierarchies and moral orders, in distinguishing uses and articulating taboos, promote diversification and fragmentation of the uses of money. This does not entail, however, a complete sealing off of the instruments and uses of money, even if all societies generate such compartments. How do we explain this? Why did Polanyi think it appropriate to distinguish between *primitive money* and the *all-purpose money* of so-called "modern" societies? Where does this central feature of how modern money is commonly represented, its supposed fungibility, come from?

One hypothesis is that this representation of the universal usage of modern money, its fungibility, is a result of sovereignty (Aglietta and Orléan 1998). The theoretical equality of subjects with respect to the sovereign, the power of the issuer of a currency and belief in God make it possible to circulate a unique monetary instrument on a lasting basis. How else can we explain how non-Christians (such as Jews) in a Christian commonwealth or non-Muslims (such as Jews or Christians) in a Muslim state were able to pay taxes and to preserve their differences? By the same token, how is it possible in a caste society, where people practice intricate rituals of avoidance to the point of never eating the same dish together or where *dalits* (untouchables) are obliged in some public places to

---

[23] This has been a central hypothesis in work on monetary socioeconomics carried out by the Centre Walras at the University of Lyon since the mid-1990s. See Blanc's (2004), which builds on Guérin (2003); Pahl (2000); Servet and Bayon (1999); Singh (1997); Vallat (1999); Weber (2004); Zelizer (1994): see also Blanc (2006).

[24] This was the finding of Servet and Bayon (1999) for SEL in France, but in Anglophone countries it is quite commonplace for LETS groups to combine use of local and national currencies in their exchanges (Hart 2006).

drink tea from throw-away cups, while members of the so-called higher castes drink their tea in metal (and thus reusable) cups, that they still share a single form of money? Coins are nowadays exchanged readily and no one wonders who has touched them before. Similarly, in the France of the Old Regime, the universal use of money and a strong hierarchy of social groups existed side by side: there were few restrictions of access to particular types of coins according to social appurtenance (although certain social groups had no access to gold coins, for example), yet privileged groups (the nobility and the clergy) did not pay taxes that were limited to the Third Estate, because they indicated servitude and were considered to be defamatory. We also find differences in the tax obligations of the military elite, the farmers, and other social orders in the Ottoman Empire. Issues of taxation are never simply a matter of income, expressed in terms of money; they also always involve questions of status between the various classes in society. In modern democracies, the potential equality of the republic or commonwealth is expressed by treating the national currency as a medium linking "economic" subjects conceived of as equal, indeed equivalent within "the market." Notwithstanding this leveling of value in an economic order to which universal access is guaranteed through legal tender, hierarchies, and moral orders persist in the social fabric; and this is where the permanent tension between the fungibility of money and the barriers erected around money originates.

The enigma of economic value

We may now reconsider the theories of value that emerged in the foundational discourse of economics and find new meanings there, taking into account: 1. Polanyi's critique of the economists' approach to the market system; 2. the opposition we have suggested between the logic of the marketplace and that of customer ties; and 3. the moral boundaries that structure access to and the use of money. Polanyi rejected the labor theory of value, but he did not bother to elaborate any alternative, despite the fact that theories of value occupied a privileged place in debates between economists, particularly between Marxist and neoclassical ideologies, up until the 1970s .[25] The reason is clear. For him, to acknowledge a specifically economic value of commodities underlying their price would entail ignoring all the noneconomic aspects that shape production, exchange, and finance (Polanyi 2001: 42, 161–2, 205). This would hardly be compatible with his critique of materialism or with his claim that land, labor, and money are "fictitious commodities."

But power and economic value are a paradigm of social reality. [...] Economic value ensures the usefulness of the goods produced; it must exist prior to the decision to

---

[25] Polanyi 2001: 76 note 3, 129, 132. It should be pointed out that the index does not have an entry for *value*, although we do find *prices*.

produce them [...]. Its source is human wants and scarcity [...]. Any opinion or desire will make us participants in the creation for power and in the constitution of economic value. (Polanyi 2001: 267)

In the eighteenth century, economists took their place in the emergent social division of knowledge production as a scholarly order entrusted with revealing the masked relations between value (essence) and prices (appearance). After all, most of them, certainly those who adhered to classical economic doctrines, claimed that goods have a value. Beyond the *value* of the "things" lie relations between the social groups engaged in exchange and their members. Thus, in most ancient societies, barter is not primarily aimed at establishing a balance between supply and demand, but at asserting the relative social status of the partners to an exchange relationship, just as the Greeks' *nomismata,* according to Aristotle in the *Nicomachean Ethics*, allowed people who were as socially distinct as an architect and a cobbler to "settle accounts."

Let us recall the myth of barter, which in substance overlapped with the first modern debates on value (Servet 2001: 15–32). This fiction of a natural price for value came relatively late and had a direct relationship with the need to identify social relations and a set of mechanisms and institutions characteristic of what was understood as a *market*. Economists of the eighteenth century, in building up their knowledge as an autonomous discipline, invented an "economic" world whose essential characteristic was that relations based on self-interest regulated the social order and all other motives for action were subordinated to them in a classification of whatever activities constituted production, exchange, and finance. The market, with the features that we have listed as typifying the marketplace, appears to be the ideal forum for exercising this particular form of rationalism, giving autonomous expression to economic motives without their being embedded in the social.[26] Thus, in early economics, value theories were opposed to the traditional hierarchy of customer ties, giving priority to new exchange relations and structuring contracts accordingly. Barter scenarios generally involve an encounter between two "individuals" supposed neither to know one another prior to the exchange nor to create bonds lasting beyond the exchange. No one lays any claim to or confirms their status before, during, or after the transaction, nor to any quality or identity, apart from their readiness to engage in the transaction and hence to be substituted by another person engaging in a similar transaction. This dual fiction of relationships without a history and based on complete equality is considered typical of "market-place" situations in modernity.[27]

---

[26] The metaphor, "embedded," it may be mentioned in passing, is only used by Polanyi six times in *The Great Transformation*; he expresses the same idea in a number of other ways (see Beckert, Chapter 2 and Hann, Chapter 14, this volume).

[27] "this was the result of a market-view of society which equated economics with contractual relationships, and contractual relations with freedom" (Polanyi 2001: 266).

With economic theories of value, the proportion of goods exchanged seems to be fixed not through the money imposed by the authorities (which is their measure and the means of their exchange), but on the basis of their usefulness, scarcity and the quantity of production factors necessary to produce them. In contrast to money as a unit of account, value is seen as a natural measure independent of a higher political power: people create for themselves the order they want, independent of any state or hierarchy. But these definitions of value assume that the economic actor is an individual outside society, faced with his own work or the hierarchy of his needs. Even while engaging in an exchange, he may be ignorant of the conditions in which his partner to the transaction works and of his needs, relying solely on what is offered in the course of bargaining. This ego is somehow projected on to the scarce things exchanged, whether they be desired and consumed (as utilities) or acquired and transformed (by labor). The relationship posited between value and labor creates an image of equality, freedom, and potential equivalence between human beings.[28] To acknowledge the hierarchy underlying the process of remuneration would render this equality chimerical. Utilitarian value theories ignore, for example, the effect of imitation, which makes a good infinitely more valuable when it is desired by others. Value, however defined through labor, scarcity, or utility, allows the "individual" engaged in the exchange – which the rationale of the marketplace presents as self-interested and isolated – to give full vent to his ability to calculating costs and benefits rationally and above all to choose freely. Economic theories of value (labor, utility, scarcity) developed within the framework of this myth were objective in the sense that they rationalized the relationship between a person (conceived of as by nature an egotistical individual) and a world of things where others exist only through competition for access to those things.

Beyond this rationalized construction of a supposedly objective expression of value in price, the prices of things (as opposed to relations of hierarchical subordination) created an ideology of equality among "individuals." The democratic ideal of egalitarianism, a moral value to which Karl Polanyi subscribed, conceives of people not as independent atoms with complete possession of their belongings, but as beings invested with the potential for solidarity, consciously interdependent with others (in that they are members of society with commitments) and endowed with both rights and duties, including duties toward future generations. Thus, at the heart of debates over value lay a problem that classical economics found impossible to resolve, one that was made explicit by Polanyi: namely, the problem of production and the articulation of

---

[28] "In a mistaken theorem of tremendous scope he [David Ricardo] invested labor with the sole capacity of constituting value, thereby reducing all conceivable transactions in economic society to the principle of equal exchange in a society of free men." (Polanyi 2001: 132).

collective and individual needs, or how to give adequate recognition to both persons and the social whole.

This issue has been made conspicuous, even acute, as a result of the unprecedented scale of globalization today. Community currencies are only one, perhaps minor response to these conditions. They give full rein to a price differentiation made possible by the fact of the circuit's autonomy and by the prevalence of intertemporal relations between members. In his or her negotiations, each participant is able to practice positive discrimination in the form of compassion or affection; the group itself may choose to impose rules equalizing the rate at which work is remunerated. All of this is based on a principle of local sovereignty that recalls some of Polanyi's (1922, 1924) arguments when he was critical of Bolshevik socialism in the 1920s. It also evokes his definition of reciprocity, based as it was on acknowledged inter-dependence and recognition of necessary submission to a social whole. These social experiments, echoing Polanyi's work of half a century ago, point to the possible development of an economy based on solidarity, *une économie solidaire* (Laville and Cattani 2006).

6 Money in the making of world society[1]

Keith Hart

A "Magellan moment"

According to writers as varied as John Locke and Karl Marx, ours is an age of money, a transitional phase in the history of humanity. Seen in this light, capitalism's historical mission is to bring cheap commodities to the masses and break down the insularity of traditional communities before being replaced by a more just society. It matters where we are in this process, but the answers given differ widely. When a third of humanity works in the fields with their hands and a similar number has never made a telephone call in their lives, I would say that capitalism still has quite a way to go. This chapter takes off from Karl Polanyi's perspective on his moment in history, in *The Great Transformation*, for analysis and inspiration when addressing our own moment. I will also draw on the work of Marcel Mauss (Hart 2007a), whose name is increasingly joined with Polanyi's by those who advocate more socially responsible versions of economy. My focus will be on the evolution of money at a time when world society is being formed rapidly at considerable risk to us all. I prefer to call this "the new human universal" rather than the normal term, "globalization."

Magellan's crew completed the first circumnavigation of the planet some thirty years after Columbus crossed the Atlantic. At much the same time, Bartolomé de las Casas opposed the racial inequality of Spain's American empire in the name of human unity. We are living through another "Magellan moment." In the second half of the twentieth century, humanity formed a world society – a single interactive social network – for the first time. This was symbolized by several moments, such as when the 1960s space race allowed us to see the earth from the outside or when the Internet went public in the 1990s, announcing the convergence of telephones, television, and computers in a digital revolution of communications. Our world, too, is massively unequal

[1] I am grateful to Eric Worby and the School of Social Studies, University of the Witwatersrand, Johannesburg for the visit there in April–May 2007 when I wrote and presented the first versions of this chapter; also to Alain Caillé for posting a version online on *La revue du MAUSS permanente* at that time; and to my colleagues and students at Goldsmiths College who suffered a semi-improvised inaugural lecture in October 2007.

and the voices for human unity are often drowned. Emergent world society *is* the new human universal – not an idea, but the fact of our shared occupation of the planet crying out for new principles of association. The task of building a global civil society for the twenty-first century, perhaps even a federal world government, is an urgent one. Money, instead of being denigrated for its exploitive power, should be recognized for its redemptive qualities, in particularly as a mediator between persons and society. Money – and the markets it sustains – is itself a human universal, with the potential to be emancipated from the social engines of inequality that it currently serves (Hart 2000).

A lot hinges on where in the long process of human evolution we imagine the world is today. The Victorians believed that they stood at the pinnacle of civilization. I think of us as being like the first digging-stick operators, primitives stumbling into the invention of agriculture. In the late 1990s, I asked what it is about us that future generations will be interested in and settled on the rapid advances then being made in forming a single interactive network linking all humanity. This has two striking features: first, the network is a highly unequal market of buyers and sellers fueled by a money circuit that has become progressively detached from production and politics; and, second, it is driven by a digital revolution whose symbol is the Internet, the network of networks. So my research over the last decade has been concerned with how the forms of money and exchange are changing in the context of this communications revolution.

My case for a recent speed-up of global integration rests on three developments of the last two decades: 1. the collapse of the Soviet Union, opening up the world to transnational capitalism and neoliberal economic policies; 2. the entry of China's and India's two billion people, a third of humanity, into the world market as powers in their own right; and 3. the abbreviation of time and distance brought about by the communications revolution and the population's restless mobility. The corollary of this revolution is a counter-revolution – the reassertion of state power since September 11 and the imperialist war for oil in the Middle East. Certainly we have regressed significantly from the hopes for equality released by the Second World War and the anticolonial revolution that followed it. On the other hand, growing awareness of the risks for the future of life on this planet entailed in current levels and forms of economic activity might encourage more people to take globalization seriously. The ecological ("green") paradigm – manifested as concern for global warming and for total food, water, and energy supplies – is powerful enough to replace market fundamentalism as the natural religion of this emergent world society.

Marcel Mauss's position on markets and money is a persuasive basis for an "institutionalist political economy," complementary to Polanyi's ideas. *The Gift* (Mauss 1924) is an extended commentary on Durkheim's (1893) argument that an advanced division of labor is sustained by "the non-contractual element in the contract," a largely invisible body of state-made law, custom, and belief that could not be reduced to abstract market principles. Mauss held that the attempt to create a free market for private contracts is utopian and just as unrealizable as its antithesis, a collective based solely on altruism. Human institutions everywhere are founded on the unity of individual and society, freedom and obligation, self-interest and concern for others. The pure types of selfish and generous economic action obscure the complex interplay between our individuality and belonging in subtle ways to others.

Mauss (1997) was highly critical of the Bolsheviks' destruction of confidence in the expanded sense of sociability that sustained the market economy. In his view, markets and money were human universals whose principal function was the extension of society beyond the local sphere, even if they did not always take the impersonal form we are familiar with. This was why he disputed Malinowski's (1921) assertion that *kula* valuables could not be considered to be money (Mauss 1924: 102n). Mauss advocated an "economic movement from below," in the form of syndicalism, cooperation, and mutual insurance (Fournier 2006). His greatest hopes were for a consumer democracy driven by the cooperative movement. The true significance for him of finding elements of the archaic gift in contemporary capitalism was to refute the revolutionary eschatology of both right and left. Most of the possibilities for a human economy already coexist in our world; so the task is to build new combinations with a different emphasis, not to repudiate a caricature of the market in the name of a radical alternative. Here Mauss follows Hegel (1821) – rather than Aristotle (Polanyi 1957a) and Marx (1867) – in seeking the integration of institutional possibilities that have been variously dominant in history rather than representing them as mutually exclusive historical stages.

Mauss (1924) was interested in how we make society where it didn't exist before. Hence we offer gifts on first dates or on diplomatic missions to foreign powers. How do we push the limits of society outward? For him money and markets were intrinsic to this process. Thus giving personalized valuables could be considered to be an exchange of money-objects if we operate with a broader definition than one based on impersonal currencies and focus rather on the function of their transfer, the extension of society beyond the local level. This helps to explain his claim that "the great economic revolutions are monetary in nature" (Fournier 2006: 212), meaning that they push us into unknown reaches of society and require new money forms and practices to bridge the gap. The combination of neoliberal globalization and the digital revolution has led to a rapid expansion of money, markets, and telecommunications, all reinforcing each other in a process that has extended society beyond its national form, making it much more unequal and unstable in the process.

Social and cultural theorists talk of little else these days than "financialization" (Epstein 2005), the idea that financial services have become the dominant arm of capitalism; and the media are obsessed, as I write, with "the credit crunch," the first sign that this period of dominance is coming to an end. Money has acquired its apparent preeminence because the economy was being extended rapidly from a national to a global level without any of the social regulation that existed before or will likely follow eventually. Naturally, the specialists in money used their newfound freedom from the Keynesian consensus of the 1940s to 1970s to loot the world in scandalous and damaging ways that we will have to repair, if we can. But, in addition to drawing people en masse into unsustainable credit schemes, they also began to put in place some of the institutional mechanisms that will be necessary if we wish to make the market work for all of us and not just for them. A lot of the wealth piled up in recent decades came from exploiting discrepancies ("arbitrage") in a world market that was rationalized and made more unitary in the process. Capitalism clearly is instrumental in making world society. It is unlikely to be the basis for its stable functioning, but it does get us some of the way there. That is what future generations will say of us; but they will be most interested in the new social and cultural forms we are making, probably not in the money as such.

In what follows, I seek to throw light on our moment in history, first by examining Polanyi's analysis of the part played by money in "the great transformation" of the nineteenth century and in the disaster that followed from it (1914–1945). Then I will sketch my own version – which takes off from Polanyi's emphasis, even as it differs from his – of "the long twentieth century" going back to the revolutions of the 1860s.[2] From this I will develop some general arguments concerning money's role in "the human economy," a concept that Polanyi sometimes referred to. I end with some remarks about the political lessons to be gained from revisiting *The Great Transformation* today.

Money in *The Great Transformation*

Karl Polanyi's (1944) masterpiece opens with a highly selective account of the making of world society in the nineteenth century, a society that Polanyi not unreasonably considered to be lying in ruins as he wrote. Money was a central feature of all four pillars of this civilization (see Hart and Hann, Chapter 1 in

---

[2] Shortly after the collapse of the Soviet Union, Eric Hobsbawm (1994) published *The Age of Extremes: The Short Twentieth Century, 1914–91.* Giovanni Arrighi (1994) came out simultaneously with *The Long Twentieth Century* in which he sought to place recent capital accumulation within a historical framework of 700 years. My own approach to the twentieth century focuses on the rise and fall of "national capitalism" (see Hart and Hann, Chapter 1 in this volume), a process whose origins lie in the 1860s and whose end is not yet complete, despite three decades of subversion by neoliberal globalization (Hart 2000: 123–30).

this volume). Polanyi identified the interest that had sustained a century of peace with what he insisted on calling *haute finance*,

an institution *sui generis*, peculiar to the last third of the nineteenth and the first third of the twentieth century, [which] functioned as the main link between the political and economic organization of the world in this period. (Polanyi 2001: 10)

The international gold standard "was merely an attempt to extend the domestic market system to the international field," the balance-of-power system was a superstructure built on its foundation, and the gold standard's fall "was the proximate cause of the catastrophe" (Polanyi 2001: 3). The self-regulating market was "the fount and matrix of the system," it had "produced unheard-of material welfare," but it was utopian in its pursuit of an autonomous circuit of commodities and money. The liberal state, in the name of market freedom, forced all other interests in society to submit to the freedom of capital, another word for money.

Later in the book, Polanyi listed money as one of the three "fictitious commodities." Labor, land, and money are essential to the industrial system; they must therefore be bought and sold, but they were definitely not produced for sale. Labor is human activity that is part of life itself, land is another word for nature, and "actual money ... is merely a token of purchasing power which, as a rule, is not produced at all, but comes into being through the mechanism of banking or state finance" (Polanyi 2001: 75–6). Here, Polanyi comes close to suggesting that a free market in money entails buying and selling society itself. Consistent with this approach, Polanyi inverts the liberal myth of money's origin in barter:

The logic of the case is, indeed, almost the opposite of that underlying the classical doctrine. The orthodox teaching started from the individual's propensity to barter; deduced from it the necessity of local markets, as well as of division of labor; and inferred, finally, the necessity of trade, eventually of foreign trade, including even long-distance trade. In the light of our present knowledge [Thurnwald, Malinowski, Mauss, and so on], we should almost reverse the sequence of the argument: the true starting point is long-distance trade, a result of the geographical location of goods and of the "division of labor" given by location. Long-distance trade often engenders markets, an institution which involves acts of barter, and, if money is used, of buying and selling, thus, eventually, but by no means necessarily, offering to some individuals an occasion to indulge in their propensity for bargaining and haggling. (Polanyi 2001: 61–2)

Money and markets thus have their origin in the effort to extend society beyond its local core. Polanyi believed that money, like the sovereign states to which it was closely related, was often introduced from outside, and this was what made the institutional attempt to separate economy from politics and naturalize the market as something *internal* to society so subversive.

Polanyi distinguished between "token" and "commodity" forms of money.[3] "Token money" was designed to facilitate domestic trade, "commodity money"

---

[3] I borrowed these labels for my own analysis of the two sides of the coin as symbolic of the state/ market pair (Hart 1986).

foreign trade, but the two systems often came into conflict. Thus the gold standard sometimes exerted downward pressure on domestic prices, causing deflation that could only be alleviated by central banks expanding the money supply in various ways. The tension between the internal and external dimensions of economy often led to serious disorganization of business (Polanyi 2001: 202–3). Another way of putting this contradiction is to oppose the liberal definition of money as just a "medium of exchange" to one as a "means of payment." Money was thus:

… not a commodity, it was purchasing power; far from having utility itself, it was merely a counter embodying a quantified claim to things that would be purchased. Clearly, a society in which distribution depended upon the possession of such tokens of purchasing power was a construction entirely different from market economy. (Polanyi 2001: 205)

Here, Polanyi echoes Keynes's (1930) contrast between "money proper" (medium of exchange) and "money of account" (unit of account and means of payment), with the emphasis on the latter, similarly drawing attention to the political possibilities for state manipulation of "purchasing power."

The final collapse of the international gold standard was thus one consequence of the ruinous attempt to delink commodity and token forms of money. In a trenchant discussion of the economic crisis of the 1930s that has echoes of the world economy today, Polanyi highlighted the separation of the money system from trade. As restrictions on trade grew, money became more free:

Short-term money moved at an hour's notice from any point of the globe to another; the modalities of international payments between governments and between private corporations or individuals were uniformly regulated. … In contrast to men and goods, money was free from all hampering measures and continued to develop its capacity of transacting business at any distance at any time. The more difficult it became to shift actual objects, the easier it became to transmit claims to them. …the rapidly growing elasticity and catholicity of the international monetary mechanism was compensating, in a way, for the ever-contracting channels of world trade. …Social dislocation was avoided with the help of credit movements; economic imbalance was righted by financial means. (Polanyi 2001: 214–5)

But, of course, in the end, political means of settling the imbalance outweighed market solutions and war was the result. Polanyi concluded in his notes to *The Great Transformation* that:

… money is not a decisive invention; its presence or absence need not make an essential difference to the type of economy. … Money, like markets, is in the main an external phenomenon, the significance of which to the community is determined primarily by trade relations. (Polanyi 2001: 282–3)

When he returned to the subject, as an American academic after the war, much of his polemical intensity had been replaced by a more dispassionate concern to launch the comparative study of preindustrial economies by anthropologists and historians (see Hart and Hann, Chapter 1 in this volume). In "Money objects and money uses" (Polanyi 1977: 97–121), Polanyi approaches money as a semantic system, like language and writing (cf. Polanyi 1968; Hart 2009). His main point is that only modern money combines the functions of payment, standard, store, and exchange, and this gives it the capacity to sustain the set of functions through a limited number of "all-purpose" symbols. Primitive and archaic forms attach the separate functions to different symbolic objects which should therefore be considered to be "special-purpose" monies. Here, too, Polanyi is arguing against the primacy of money as a medium of exchange and for a multistranded model of its evolution. There is no sense now, as there was in his passionate wartime book, that the future of civilization depends on getting this question right.

The 1940s did indeed see a world revolution. Its immediate outcome was not foreseen by Polanyi. Yet interest in his work has never been greater than now and this may be related to his prophetic value in the present crisis of world economy. Since the last three decades have seen a replay of the "self-regulating market" scenario and the beginning of its demise, Polanyi's vision offers one perspective on the political and economic origins of our own times. But other visions are possible and for my own we need first to retrace our steps to the great transformation of the mid-nineteenth century.

The origins of our times revisited

The 1860s saw a transport and communications revolution (steamships, continental railways, and the telegraph) that decisively opened up the world economy (Hart 2000: 123ff). At the same time a series of political revolutions gave the leading powers of the coming century the institutional means of organizing industrial capitalism. These were the American civil war, the culmination of Italy's *Risorgimento*, the abolition of serfdom in Russia, the formation of the Anglo-Indian superstate, Britain's second reform act, and Japan's Meiji Restoration. German unification at the end of the decade spilled over into the 1870s through the Franco-Prussian war, the Paris commune, and the formation of the French Third Republic. Karl Marx published *Capital* in the same decade (1867) and the First International was formed in 1864. The concentration of so many epochal events in such a short time would indicate a degree of integration of world society even then. But in the 1870s, international trade accounted for no more than one percent of Gross National Product in most countries (Lewis 1978), and the most reliable indicator of Britain's annual economic performance was still the weather at harvest-time.

Capitalism has always rested on an unequal contract between owners of large amounts of money and those who make and buy their products. This contract depends on an effective threat of punishment if workers withhold their labor or buyers fail to pay up. The owners cannot make that threat alone: they need the support of governments, laws, prisons, police, even armies. By the mid-nineteenth century, it became clear that the machine revolution was pulling unprecedented numbers of people into the cities, where they added a wholly new dimension to traditional problems of crowd control. The political revolutions of the 1860s were based on a new and explicit alliance between capitalists and the military landlord class to form states capable of managing industrial workforces and of taming the criminal gangs that had taken over large swathes of the main cities.[4] Germany and Japan provided the clearest examples of such an alliance which took a specific form in each country.

Before long, governments provided new legal conditions for the operations of large corporations, ushering in mass production and consumption through a bureaucratic revolution. The implicit author of this new synthesis ("national capitalism") was Hegel who argued in *The Philosophy of Right* (1821) that states, run by university-trained bureaucrats, should regulate capitalist markets with a view to containing their extreme consequences, while allowing their material benefits to accrue to the people as a whole. The national system became general after the First World War and was the dominant social form of twentieth-century civilization. Its apogee or "golden age" (Hobsbawm 1994) was the period 1948–1973. This was a time of strong states and economic expansion when the idea of "development" (poor nations growing richer with the help of the already rich) replaced colonial empire for most "Third World" countries. When, shortly before his downfall, Richard Nixon announced that "We are all Keynesians now," he was reflecting a universal belief that governments had a responsibility to manage national capitalism in the interests of all citizens.

The 1970s were a watershed. United States' expenditure on its losing war in Vietnam generated huge imbalances in the world's money flows, leading to a breakdown of the fixed parity exchange-rate system devised at Bretton Woods during the war. America's departure from the gold standard in 1971 (Gregory 1997) triggered a free-for-all in world currency markets, leading in 1975 to the invention of money market futures in Chicago to stabilize export prices for Midwestern farmers. At the same time, the world economy was plunged into depression in 1973 by the formation of the Organization of

---

[4] Martin Scorsese's 2002 film *Gangs of New York* (based in part on Herbert Asbury's (1927) book of the same name, whose subtitle is *An Informal History of the Underworld*) shows how the Irish gangs of Southern Manhattan were subdued in the context of the civil war by shelling from battleships in the East River. Mass protest over conscription was put down by the army shooting into crowds on Fifth Avenue, and this spilled over into America's first urban riots involving poor whites and black refugees from the South. The movie's final scene fades in Manhattan's contemporary skyline over its 1860s predecessor, suggesting that capitalism today was made possible by state violence then. The American civil war wasn't just about conquering the slave owners; there was unfinished business in the industrial North, too.

Petroleum-Exporting Countries and a hefty rise in the price of oil. "Stagflation" (high unemployment and inflation) increased, opening the way for conservatives such as Reagan and Thatcher to revive the strategy of giving economic priority to "the market" rather than "the state." The economic conditions of three decades ago and the policies devised then find their denouement today.

In 1975, all but a minute proportion of the money exchanged internationally paid for goods and services purchased abroad. Thirty years later, this function in turn accounted for only a small fraction of global money transfers, the vast bulk being devoted to exchanging money for money in another form. This rising tide of money, sometimes known as "the markets," represents the apotheosis of financial capitalism, with the actual production and sale of commodities and political management of currencies and trade virtually abandoned in favor of an autonomous global circuit of capital. The conditions Polanyi described above for the decades leading up to the First World War have been closely replicated in the last quarter-century. As the smoke rises from the rubble of neoliberalism's demise, we should revisit the story of national capitalism's rise and fall, and Polanyi's account of that earlier cycle has lost none of its fascination for us.

Money in the human economy

To call the economy "human" is to insist on putting people first, making their thoughts, actions, and lives our main concern (see Hart and Hann, Chapter 1 in this volume). Such a focus should also be pragmatic: making economy personally meaningful to students or readers, relating it to ordinary people's practical purposes. "Humanity" is a moral quality, implying that, if we want to be good, we should treat other persons, people like ourselves, kindly. Since theoretical abstraction is impersonal and leaves no room for morality, a human economy would have to pay attention to the personal realm of experience; but it would be a mistake to leave it there. Humanity is also a collective noun, meaning all the people who have existed or ever will. So the human economy is inclusive, in the sense reinforced by our contemporary witness to the formation of the new human universal that is world society.

Anthropologists and sociologists have long rejected the impersonal model of money and markets offered by mainstream economics. Zelizer (1994), for example, shows that people refuse to treat the cash in their possession as an undifferentiated thing, choosing rather to "earmark" it – reserving some for food bills, some as holiday savings, and so on. Her examples generally come from areas that remain invisible to the economists' gaze, especially domestic life. People everywhere personalize money, bending it to their own purposes through a variety of social instruments. This was the message, too, of *Money and the Morality of Exchange* (Parry and Bloch 1989). When money and markets are understood exclusively through impersonal models, awareness of this neglected dimension is surely significant. But the economy exists at more inclusive levels than the person, the family, or local groups. This is made possible by the impersonality of money and markets, where economists remain largely unchallenged. Money, much as Durkheim (1912) argued for religion, is the principal means for us all to bridge the gap between everyday personal experience and a society whose wider reaches are impersonal.

Money is often portrayed as a lifeless object separated from persons, whereas it is a creation of human beings, imbued with the collective spirit of the living and the dead. Money, as a token of society, must be impersonal in order to connect individuals to the universe of relations to which they belong. But people make everything personal, including their relations with society. This two-sided relationship is universal, but its incidence is highly variable (Hart 2007b). Money in capitalist societies stands for alienation, detachment, impersonal society, the outside; its origins lie beyond our control (*the market*). Relations marked by the absence of money are the model of personal integration and free association, of what we take to be familiar, the inside (*home*). This institutional dualism, forcing individuals to divide themselves every day, asks too much of us. People want to integrate division, to make some meaningful connection between their own subjectivity and society as an object. It helps that money, as well as being the means of separating public and domestic life, was always the main bridge between the two. That is why money must be central to any attempt to humanize society. It is both the principal source of our vulnerability in society and the main practical symbol allowing each of us to make an impersonal world meaningful.

Money thus expands the capacity of individuals to stabilize their personal identity by holding something durable that embodies the desires and wealth of all the other members of society. Money is a "memory bank" (Hart 2000), a store allowing individuals to keep track of those exchanges they wish to calculate and, beyond that, a source of economic memory for the community. The modern system of money provides people with a wide repertoire of instruments to keep track of their exchanges with the world and to calculate the current balance of their worth in the community. In this sense, one of money's chief functions is *remembering*. If the proliferation of personal credit today could be seen as a step toward greater humanism in economy, this also entails increased dependence on impersonal governments and corporations, on impersonal abstraction of the sort associated with computing operations and on impersonal standards and social guarantees for contractual exchange. If persons are to make a comeback in the postmodern economy, it will be less on a face-to-face basis than as bits on a screen who sometimes materialize as living people in the present. We may become less weighed down by money as an objective force, more open to the idea that it is a way of keeping track of complex social networks that we each generate. Then money could take a variety of forms compatible with both personal agency and human interdependence at every level from the local to the global.

The reality of markets is not just universal abstraction, but this mutual determination of the abstract and the concrete (Hart 2007b). If you have some money, there is almost no limit to what you can do with it, but, as soon as you buy something, the act of payment lends concrete finality to your choice. Money's significance thus lies in the synthesis it promotes of impersonal abstraction and personal meaning, objectification and subjectivity, analytical reason and synthetic narrative (Wardle 2005). Its social power comes from the fluency of its mediation between infinite potential and finite determination. To turn our backs on markets and money in the name of collective as opposed to individual interests reproduces by negation the bourgeois separation of self and society. It is not enough to emphasize the controls that people already impose on money and exchange as part of their personal practice. That is the everyday world as most of us know it. We also need ways of reaching the parts of the macroeconomy that we don't know, if we wish to avert the ruin they could bring down on us all. Perhaps this was what Simmel (1900) had in mind when he said that money is the concrete symbol of our human potential to make universal society.

The two great means of communication are language and money (Hart 2009). Anthropologists have paid much attention to the first, which divides us more than it brings us together, but not to money whose potential for universal communication is more reliable, in addition to its well-advertised ability to symbolize differences between us.[5] We cannot afford to neglect money's potential for universal connection, choosing rather to demonize it as the source of our vulnerability to people with a lot more of it. It is high time for anthropologists to return to an earlier philosophical tradition, building on Kant's (1798) example, but also on the early twentieth-century neo-Kantianism of Durkheim (1912), Mauss (1924) and Simmel (1900). I have been driven to this conclusion by studying money as the most tangible manifestation of the new human universal that is our shared occupation of the planet.

Mauss (Hart 2000: 191–6; 2007a) held that there are two prerequisites for being human: to be self-reliant to a high degree and to belong to others, merging our identities in a bewildering variety of social relationships. Much of modern ideology emphasizes how problematic it is to be both self-interested and mutual, to be economic as well as social. When culture is set

---

[5] The word *money* comes from *Moneta*, a name by which the Roman queen of the gods, Juno, was known (Silver 1992). *Moneta* was a translation of the Greek Mnemosyne, the goddess of memory and mother of the Muses, each of whom presided over one of the nine arts and sciences. For the Romans at least, money was an instrument of collective memory that needed divine protection, like the arts. As such, it was both a memento of the past and a sign of the future.

up to expect a conflict between the two, it is hard to be both. Yet the two sides are often inseparable in practice and some societies, by encouraging private and public interests to coincide, have managed to integrate them more effectively than ours.

Confronting the money crisis then and now

Jean-Louis Laville has recently reminded us of the two lessons to be drawn from the history of the twentieth century.

First, market society sustained by a concern for individual freedom generated huge inequalities; then submission of the economy to political will on the pretext of equality led to the suppression of freedom. These two solutions called democracy itself into question, whether in the form of totalitarian systems or, with a similar result, through the subordination of political power to that of money. If we reject both of these options, it is then a question of developing institutions capable of guaranteeing a plural economy within a democratic framework, exactly what is compromised when the rationale of material gain without limit has a monopoly.[6]

Laville, following Mauss and Polanyi, pillories those who would reject a caricature of the economy in the name of some future alternative, since all economic possibilities coexist now, including those that have been variously dominant in history. Our task is to build economic solidarity (*économie solidaire*)[7] through new institutional combinations and with a new emphasis (cf. Servet, Chapter 5 in this volume). This means combining the equal reciprocity of freely self-organized groups with the redistributive powers of the state.

It is, however, no longer obvious, as it was for Mauss, Polanyi, and Keynes, where the levers of democratic power are to be located, since the global explosion of money, markets, and telecommunications over the last quarter-century has severely exposed the limitations of national frameworks of economic management. We are clearly witnessing the start of another long swing in the balance between state and market. Central banks are pumping liquidity into failing asset markets, especially housing. The rapid switch by the "masters of the universe" from market triumphalism to the public begging bowl would be surprising if it were not so familiar. The banks want to privatize their profits and nationalize their losses; but such a political recipe may be running out of popular support. Before long, a genuine revival of Keynesian redistributive politics seems to be inevitable. But the imbalances of the money system are now global, as the financial rescue operation recently performed on failing

---

[6] Jean-Louis Laville and I worked together on the text from which this quote is taken. It is available online at: www.rethinkingeconomies.org.uk/web/w/www_26_en.aspx.

[7] This notion, originating in the World Social Forum at Porto Alegre, Brazil in 2000, has entered English, via Portuguese and French (Laville and Cattani 2006), rather awkwardly as "solidarity economy"(Allard, Davidson and Matthaei 2008).

American banks by the "sovereign funds" of some Asian and Middle Eastern governments shows. Society is already taking the form of large regional trading blocs like the European Union, the North American Free Trade Agreement, the Association of South East Asian Nations, and the Mercado Común del Sur, and the Bretton Woods institutions (the World Bank, International Monetary Fund, and World Trade Organization) promote no interest beyond that of Western capital. The strength of any push to reform global institutions will depend on the severity of the current economic crisis. A return to the national solutions of the 1930s is bound to fail.

So what are the lessons to be drawn from comparing our situation with the one Polanyi depicted before; and how might the analysis of money offered here help us to find an orientation to the present crisis? Polanyi explained the world crisis then as the outcome of a previous round of what many today would call "globalization." There are substantial parallels between the last three decades and a similar period before 1914. In both cases, market forces were unleashed within national societies, leading to rapid capital accumulation and an intensification of economic inequality. Finance capital led the internationalization of economic relations, and people migrated in large numbers all over the world. Money seemed to be the dominant social force in human affairs; and this could be attributed to its greater freedom of movement as the boundaries of society were extended outward, then by colonial empire; now by the digital revolution and transnational corporations. The main difference is that the late-nineteenth century saw the centralization of politics and production in a bureaucratic revolution, while a century later these same bureaucracies were being dismantled by neoliberal globalization. Moreover, the immediate winner of "the second thirty years' war" (1914–1945) was a strengthened national capitalism whose synthesis of state and market was hardly anticipated by Polanyi.

It is odd that Polanyi appears sometimes to reduce the structures of national capitalism to an apolitical "self-regulating market." For his analysis of money, markets, and the liberal state was intensely political, as was his preference for social planning over the market. His wartime polemic, reproducing something of his opponents' abstractions, was more a critique of liberal economics than a realistic account of actually existing capitalism. This would explain the lingering confusion over whether he thought a "disembedded" market was possible or just a figment of liberal ideology, "market fundamentalism" (see Hart and Hann, Chapter 1 in this volume). Similarly, we might argue either that neoliberalism did effectively disembed the market economy or that its claim to have done so was a mystification of the fact that markets were still embedded in largely invisible political processes. In either case, the postwar turn to "embedded liberalism" (Harvey 2005a) or social democracy – what I have called the apogee of national capitalism – is only weakly illuminated by *The Great Transformation*.

I have made much here of Mauss's idea, cousin of Durkheim's (1893) concerning the organic division of labor (see Robotham, Chapter 15 this volume), that the principal function of money and markets is to extend society beyond its existing limits. Thus Malinowski's (1922) ethnography of the *kula* ring could be taken as a metaphor for the world economy of his day, with island economies that were not self-sufficient being drawn into trade with each other by means of personalized exchange of valuables between local leaders. These canoe expeditions were dangerous and magical because their crews were temporarily outside the realm of normal society. This always happens when society's frontiers are pushed rapidly outward, as they have time and time again in the last two centuries and long before that. The period of "neoliberal financialization" might be compared with previous episodes in the history of global capitalism, such as the dash to build continental railroads, the gold strikes in California, Alaska, and South Africa, or the wild rubber boom of the mid- to late-nineteenth century. There are many analogous episodes to be found in the mercantilist economies that emerged during the period 1500–1800, notoriously the "South Sea bubble" and the "Tulips craze." Similarly, the last three decades have seen a rapid extension of society's frontiers after the postwar convergence of state and market in national capitalism reached its limit in the 1970s. The quick wealth and cowboy entrepreneurship we have just witnessed was made possible by the absence of regulation in a period of global economic expansion. The end of the bubble marks an opportunity to consider how world markets might now be organized in the general interest.

It is easy enough to harp on the irrational excess and sheer inequality of the neoliberal era – the heedless speculation, corporate skullduggery, outrageous looting of public assets, and not-so-creative destruction of nature and society. But there are lasting institutional effects, just as there were to previous booms which generated new transport and communication systems; a mildly inflationary gold standard; new industrial uses for rubber; stock markets, and colonial empires. I have suggested here that the extension of society to a more inclusive level has positive features, and, before we demonize money and markets, we should try to turn them to institutional ends that benefit us all. The world economy is more integrated than it was even two decades ago; we need new principles of political association with which to put in place more effective regulatory frameworks. Fragmentation would be a disaster. I for one would not wish to return to currency controls and state-managed money, even if it were feasible. Clearly, the political questions facing humanity today concern distributive justice. The long period of Western dominance of the world economy is coming to an end. New actors on the world stage will have their say about who gets what. An escalation of war and general fractiousness is quite likely. Under these circumstances, a focus on the socially redemptive qualities of money and markets might be quite salutary. In this constructive sense, I depart from Polanyi's conclusions; but I fear that his time as a prophet is yet to come.

The new combinations of money, machines, and people emerging today must be addressed squarely. The world society that has developed in the last half-century has some features never seen before and many that are perennial. Any way forward will be worked out by China, Europe, the United States, and regional leaders such as India, Brazil, Russia, and South Africa. They will build on an existing diversity that is hardly illuminated by catchall phrases like "neoliberalism." People everywhere are already asking loudly "What happened to our money, our jobs, and our houses? Why did we let them get away with it? How can we make sure it doesn't happen again?" Debates about political economy today could use the historical substance and prophetic vision that Karl Polanyi brought to the last time our incipient world society was threatened with disintegration. I have suggested here that, whatever the deficiencies of his analysis, *The Great Transformation* is still a crucial resource for the making of the new human universal.

7 Debt, violence, and impersonal markets: Polanyian meditations

David Graeber

If *The Great Transformation* will be remembered for anything a century from now, it will be as the definitive refutation of the great liberal myth of the market. By this I refer to the assumption that "self-regulating markets", as Polanyi calls them, are in some sense natural: that markets will always arise of their own accord as long as governments don't prevent it, just as they inevitably did in Europe once civil society was freed from the stifling effects of feudalism. Polanyi examined the very time and place when this myth first emerged – Britain in the eighteenth and nineteenth centuries – and demonstrated that no such "self-regulating market" could ever have emerged without elaborate government intervention to begin with, and none could survive without continual government support.

Polanyi's insight is clearly as relevant as ever. The free-market ideology that Polanyi felt was gone forever in the 1940s has returned with a vengeance – returned to reap a terrible vengeance, in fact, on the most vulnerable people of the earth. Yet at the same time our intellectual landscape has shifted. Grand sweeping theory in the Polanyian tradition has fallen largely out of favor, at least among what passes as the intellectual opposition to neoliberalism. Yet economists – at least, the most sophisticated of them – often appear more than happy to incorporate many of Polanyi's insights. Most of them, if challenged on the issue, will admit that "the market" isn't really an empirical object. When they refer to "markets" they are really talking about abstract models: models constructed by selecting only certain features of reality and intentionally ignoring all others. It requires constant political work to maintain conditions where those models will take on any semblance of empirical reality. Of course, when giving policy advice, these same economists will almost invariably turn around and say the exact opposite, warning that "the market" – now transformed from an abstract model to an all-powerful deity – will surely punish anyone who disregards its dictates.

When arguments don't even have to make logical sense, critique might seem to lose its point. Why bother pointing out the inconsistencies in such positions? I do think there is a reason though to continue in Polanyi's critical tradition: and that is because how we conceptualize the moment has everything to do with how we imagine alternatives. Polanyi himself wrote at an historical moment when it seemed the West European governments that had originally created self-regulating markets were in the process of moving beyond them. Today we have had to watch some of those very same social democratic regimes leading the way in stripping away social protections, while anticapitalist movements have increasingly departed from any notion that the state – which is, after all, basically a means of organizing violence – can help solve anything.

In this chapter I would like to make a few suggestions about how we might begin to reconceptualize Polanyi's approach to economic history from this current, very different historical vantage point. This means coming up with new terms to supplement, and to some degree supplant, Polanyi's distinctions between reciprocity, redistribution, and market, or between special- and general-purpose monies. For instance, I will contrast "human economies" with different sorts of market, some dominated by credit institutions, others by anonymous exchange of metal bullion. In both cases, I will consider the importance of war and violence as critical elements in allowing the transformation of one form into the other.[1] The easiest way to begin to do this is by looking at the history of money.

Value versus debt

The approach to economic history I will propose here has larger theoretical implications. We have moved past the hoary opposition between individual and society, and might better begin instead from an opposition between value and debt; that is, between webs of dyadic relations based on various forms of (usually mutual) obligation, and the creation of virtual arenas for the realization of human creativity. This point may seem obscure. Perhaps it would be best to explain how I came to it.

In 2001, I wrote a book that aimed among other things to rethink some of the intricacies of Marxian value theory. My key point was that our distinction between "value" (in the economic sense) and "values" (in the social sense) really turns on the commoditization of labor. Wherever human energies are primarily directed at getting money, we assume we are in the domain of what we call "the economy" or "the market", which is thought to operate according to the law of value. Whenever we enter into other pursuits, such as domestic life, religion, politics, and so on, we start talking instead about "values:" "family values" (housework being probably the most important form of unremunerated labor in industrial societies), faith, political ideals, the pursuit of beauty, patriotism, and so on. All these are seen as commitments that ought to

---

[1] This might be considered an extension of an argument about the similarities between impersonal market relations and violence itself as forms of radical simplification (Graeber 2006).

be uncorrupted by the market. At the same time, they are also seen as utterly unique, effectively incommensurable. It would be absurd to search for a mathematic formula that allowed us to calculate just how much personal integrity it is right to sacrifice in the pursuit of art, or how to balance responsibilities to God and to your family.

The entire argument here turns on money as impersonal abstraction. "Value" is assumed to be whatever it is that money measures. Money is treated as a generic substance (aside from its denomination, one banknote is precisely the same as any other), whose only real quality is that it may be precisely counted. Therefore no particular banknote can ordinarily develop a history. The memory of each transaction vanishes with the next. Bills are thus rendered pure potentiality. Without such a generic medium, however, we are left with a series of historical crystallizations: love, faith, integrity, and so forth.

Marx, as we know, saw the value of money as being ultimately rooted in human capacities for creative action, or "labor power." He also argued that it was only through the institution of wage labor that such creative potential itself becomes a commodity. One interesting concomitant is that, as a result, wage laborers – who are working in order to get money – are effectively working to obtain symbolic tokens that represent the importance of their work. Money, then, is a symbol that effectively brings into being the very thing it represents. As such it seems to be the source of the value of the labor, rather than its product. The premise of the book was that any system of value tends to operate this way. Value is simply how we represent the meaning or importance of our own actions to ourselves. These become meaningful and important by being part of some larger social totality, real or imagined; this must also necessarily happen through some material medium: if not money, then treasures, tokens, performances, privileges, and so on. The medium can be almost anything, but its nature has very definite implications as to how this realization of value takes place. With a quantifiable abstraction like money, we can develop systems of abstract value; when the most important tokens of value are unique but permanent heirlooms, betokening "fame," we might end up with something more like a *kula* system (Munn 1986); when they are elaborate, but ephemeral, ritual performances that express "beauty,", we obtain something more like the Kayapo rituals described by Turner (1984; 1985; 1987). Nonetheless, there are always certain constants. One is that, since value may only be realized in the eyes of others, what we think of as "society" largely emerges as the audience for different projects for the realization of value. From the perspective of the actor, at least, "society" is simply all those whose opinions he actually cares about. It is always to a certain degree an imaginary totality. Another constant is that the tokens through which this is realized tend to be fetishized: from the point of view of the actors, they are the source of that which they motivate. The desire to acquire tokens of honor inspires honorable behavior; the desire to attain tokens of faith, or certificates of educational attainment, comes to inspire piety or learning, even to organize the form such actions take. The result, as in the case of money, is that it often seems as if these tokens, rather than the human actions aimed at acquiring them, bring piety or learning into the world – since, from the actors' point of view, this often might as well be true.

Value theory, then, is about how desire becomes social. It is about how our actions become meaningful by being reflected back at us in the form of representations – ultimately, of those very actions – that seem to be their aim and origin. And this is about how different conceptions of "society" are constantly being thrown up, like shadows on a wall, as a necessary part of that process. The main weakness in this approach was its treatment of money. Like Marx, I emphasized the anonymous, impersonal qualities of money. These do exist. There is absolutely no way to know where a dollar bill in one's pocket has been; the result is that the history of objects bought and sold by dollar bills tend to be effaced as well. This is the key to Marx's conception of fetishism, where objects come to embody the intentions of their designers and producers, since we has no way of knowing who those people actually were.

The problem is that, while this may be true of cash, most transactions in contemporary societies do not employ cash. And the largest, most significant transactions almost never do – unless they are criminal in nature. There is a reason why bank robbers and drug kingpins are the only people who prefer to operate with suitcases full of hundred-dollar bills. Ordinary monetary transactions do indeed leave a history, since they usually operate through credit and, as law enforcement agents are well aware, it is quite possible to keep exact and detailed tabs on the movements of any citizen simply by monitoring their bank and credit card transactions. While this does not change Marx's main point about commodity fetishism – I still don't have the slightest idea who was involved in designing and assembling my cell phone or my toaster – it means that money is a far more complex object than we might otherwise assume. Where some see money as wiping away the possibility of memory, Keith Hart (2000: 234), for example, insists instead that money "is mainly ... an act of remembering, a way of keeping track of the exchanges which we enter into with the rest of humanity."[2]

Hart's work is a good place to start for a reconsideration of this problem because he is one of the few authors who looks at money neither as a means of recording history nor as a means of effacing history, but, rather, sees its peculiar quality as lying in the fact that it is an unstable suspension of both:

Look at a coin from your pocket. On one side is "heads" – the symbol of the political authority which minted the coin; on the other side is "tails" – the precise specification

---

[2] In fact, the very word is derived from memory: the English "money" ultimately derives from the temple of Juno Moneta in ancient Rome, where coins were struck during the Punic Wars – Moneta being the goddess of Memory and mother of the muses (Hart 2000: 15, 256).

of the amount the coin is worth as payment in exchange. One side reminds us that states underwrite currencies and the money is originally a relation between persons in society, a token perhaps. The other reveals the coin as a thing, capable of entering into definite relations with other things, as a quantitative ratio independent of the persons engaged in any particular transaction. In this latter respect money is like a commodity and its logic is that of anonymous markets. (Hart 1986: 638)

Marx, of course, argued that in fetishism, relations between persons are displaced and made to appear as if they were relations between things. Mauss's distinction between gifts and commodities works by an analogous logic: a transaction is a gift if it is largely concerned with the relations between persons; a commodity exchange if what is being established is instead equivalence between things. Hart is pointing out that this distinction is inscribed into the very nature of money itself, so much so that economists have produced completely contradictory theories as to what money even is. On the one hand we find the familiar "metallist" or "commodity" theory of money (what Hart would call the "tails" approach) that sees money as having first emerged from the inconveniences of barter. We have all heard this story.[3] At first human beings bartered useful objects directly one for another; after a while, they came to realize that it would be much easier to denominate a single commodity as a means to pay for every other one. For various reasons, precious metals seemed the most convenient choice. According to this view (for example, Samuelson 1948), modern economies are still really just elaborate systems of barter, a way for economic actors to trade useful commodities, with money merely serving as a convenient technology of exchange. This view has become economic orthodoxy: the overwhelming majority of professional economists accept it, despite there being virtually no evidence that anything like this ever occurred.

Ranged against this is a variety of heretical, "chartalist" approaches that rely on the other side of Hart's coin. These assume that money did not arise from individual actors trying to maximize their material advantage, but rather from public institutions aiming to calculate and manage social obligations: that money arises, in effect, from debt. The paradigm is Knapp's *State Theory of Money* (1928). Knapp argued that money arose not as a medium of exchange but as a unit of account (and secondarily, means of payment), specifically, as a way of assessing and levying tax payments. Money here is a way of managing debt, starting with the debt that subjects or citizens were assumed to have to their sovereign. In order to do so, the state must establish the nominal units of account, and fix the conversion rates between commodities.

Moreover, as colonial governments rediscovered in the eighteenth and nineteenth centuries, demanding cash payments from one's subjects is the most

---

[3] This theory of the origin of money already appears in Adam Smith (1776), though in its canonical version it was most famously laid out by Jevons (1875) and Menger (1892).

effective way to encourage a market in goods and services, and this might often have been at least half the point. It is, in fact, much easier, from the point of view of a government, to create a market for goods and services and then buy what it needs, than to requisition everything directly, either in labor or in kind. The key point, as Michael Innes (1913, 1914) originally put it, is that "money is debt:" the state issues tokens of its own obligations that become validated and go into general use by citizens seeking to cancel their debts with one another, because the state is willing to accept them to cancel debts which (it has declared) citizens owe to it.[4]

The chartalist view has always been in a minority among professional economists – even though almost all the existing historical evidence supports it. Still, it has its exponents, especially among the followers of John Maynard Keynes. However, the two camps, as Hart notes, have tended to state their positions in absolute terms, arguing that money is purely one thing or the other. Hence "Keynesians" end up arguing for state-managed manipulation of the money supply as a tool of policy, while "monetarists" insist that the government's role is simply to back up a stable currency but otherwise let the market do its work, and policy swings back and forth wildly between them.

As Hart also observes, for the most part anthropologists have simply ignored these debates. They have had especially little to say about the phenomenon of debt. This is rather surprising, since over the years anthropologists have had a great deal to say about social obligation. Structural functionalist anthropology was, more than anything else, an elaborate system of mapping out "rights and duties" (two concepts which are, like credit and debt, themselves two sides of the same coin). In fact, such an opposition between value and debt opens up a much more interesting set of theoretical problems than more familiar (and increasingly sterile) divisions between "individual" and "society." The metallist view, for example, doesn't begin with one individual who confronts society: it begins with a series of dyadic relations (mainly buyer–seller) and then tries to show how an endless network of such relations can gradually produce an imaginary totality it calls "the market." The chartalist view starts from the state – an entity that I have argued always begins as a utopian project (Graeber 2004) – and works its way down to the regulation of networks of obligation. The state in this view creates money in much the same way as it regulates justice: as a means of balancing moral accounts.

This, in turn, raises two sticky conceptual questions. The first is about the origin of the idea of debt. How do social obligations, rights, and duties that people have with one another end up becoming attached to objects of material

---

[4] Innes also noted that banks, which specializing in canceling credits against debts, developed as intermediaries with the state: in every case we know, it was governments (even, in the case of Medieval Europe, no longer existing governments: see Einaudi 1953) that were seen as establishing the abstract units of exchange, just as they established systems of weights and measures.

wealth, so that the mere transfer of such objects can often render one person entirely at another's command? The second is even larger: how *does* one relate a theory of value to a theory of debt? It is possible to conceive what we call "societies" either as an endless web of interpersonal relations or as imaginary totalities that serve as arenas for the realization of value. It is very difficult to imagine them as both at the same time.

I cannot solve all these problems here. But I will attempt to outline what a theory of debt might look like, because this is critical to conceptualizing the current historical moment in a way that allows for alternatives. Certainly the problem is profoundly undertheorized. The modern state, after all, is often said to have emerged through deficit financing; the economies of wealthy countries are now driven largely by consumer debt; international relations are increasingly dominated by the debt bondage of the poor to the International Monetary Fund (IMF) and the World Bank and by the debt of the United States to East Asia. Yet there is remarkably little written about the nature of debt itself. It is a question of particular political interest, since debt has long been a way for relations based on exploitation and even violence to be seen as moral in the eyes of those living inside them. Throughout history there have been classes of people who essentially live off the labor of others; in a large number of cases, they appear to have convinced them that they are somehow in the former's debt. They do not do this, normally, as a class. They do it through an endless multiplication of individual – or, more accurately, dyadic – ties.

On infinite debt and transactional logics

The obvious place to begin a theoretical inquiry into the nature of debt would seem to be Marcel Mauss's (1924) essay on *The Gift*. Ostensibly, Mauss wrote that essay to explain why those who receive a gift feel obliged to make a return present: in this sense of debt, he argued, one could find the origins of the current notion of contractual obligation. Still, Mauss never develops this connection explicitly; even worse, on those few occasions that he does, he writes as if commercial principles like credit and interest can already be found within gift economies in almost exactly the same form. Michael Hudson (Hudson 2004:100; Hudson and Van de Mieroop 2002: 9), complains that, as a result, Mauss's work has actually stood in the way of any attempt to understand the actual history of credit institutions – and in particular, the development of the custom of lending money at interest. The latter, he argues, is hardly universal. It appears to have been invented in third-millennium BCE Mesopotamia and to have spread out from there, surprisingly slowly. There is no evidence for interest-bearing loans in Pharaonic Egypt, for example and, even in the first century CE, Tacitus claimed that most Germans were completely unaware of the institution. Hudson suggests that in some cases Mauss was reporting practices inspired by European influence and assumed that they were a traditional part of gift economies.

There is every reason to believe that he is right. Mauss only mentions debt and credit explicitly when discussing the potlatch;[5] for example, in claiming that that unlike Melanesians Northwest Coast societies appear to have developed a system of credit (Mauss 1990: 35–6), or that potlatches:

> must be reciprocated with interest, as must indeed every gift. The rate of interest generally ranges from 30 to 100 per cent a year ... The obligation to reciprocate worthily is imperative. One loses face for ever if one does not reciprocate, or if one does not carry out destruction of objects of equivalent value. (Mauss 1990: 42)

The problem with these statements is that, except for the last, they turn out not to be true. Boas's claim that items given at potlatches had to be repaid at 100 percent interest was simply a mistake (Graeber 2001: 209–10): in reality, gifts given at potlatches do not have to be reciprocated at all. When two aristocrats were dueling over a title, they would sometimes try to out do each other in generosity, which could lead to tit-for-tit battles of one-upmanship. But the only gifts that had to be paid back double were those presented as a means of assembling resources from allies or followers before a potlatch. These were really just ways of soliciting contributions and the specification of an exact interest rate even here was so unusual that later ethnographers (Drucker and Heizer 1967: 78) suggested that the idea was probably originally inspired by the example of an early Canadian loanshark.

Actually, there is only one reference to "debt" anywhere in *The Gift*, and it follows immediately on from the above-cited line about interest rates:

> The punishment for failure to reciprocate is slavery for debt. At least, this functions among the Kwakiutl, the Haïda, and the Tsimshian. It is an institution really comparable in nature and function to the Roman nexum. The individual unable to repay the loan or reciprocate the potlatch loses his rank and even his status as a free man. Among the Kwakiutl, when an individual whose credit is poor borrows, he is said to "sell a slave." There is no need to point out the identical nature of this and the Roman expression. (Mauss 1990: 42)

This is not true either. While the people in question did have an institution of chattel slavery (they were among the few Native American societies that kept slaves in any numbers), these appear to have been war captives. Debt bondage of the Roman variety appears to be limited to commercial economies, although, significantly, it appears around the same time as lending at interest

---

[5] He appears to draw his material here mainly from the researches of Robert Davy, whom he mentions as his co-researcher on a more general project to investigate the origins of contractual obligation. Only one other work appears to have come out of this project, Georges Davy's *Foi jurée* (1922) on the potlatch complex of the Northwest Coast, and Mauss cites it frequently in the text.

itself. We appear to be dealing rather with the notorious Kwakiutl flair for the dramatic (Testart 2001).

Still, it is such a constant metaphor – repeated, for instance, in the famous Inuit proverb that "gifts make slaves like whips make dogs" – that we might do well to begin by asking why it should occur to anyone that receiving gifts one cannot repay should be considered comparable to being in the condition of a war captive? We must first of all reexamine what is meant by "the gift." The term is commonly used to lump together a wide range of different forms of economic interaction that, in fact, proceed by very different logics. For present purposes allow me a highly abbreviated list – which among other things may give the reader a sense of just how varied what I have been calling "dyadic relationships" actually can be. Here I identify just four different types.

Communistic relations

I use "communistic" in the sense of relations that operate on Louis Blanc's famous principle "from each according to his abilities, to each according to his needs." While there has almost certainly never been a society in which everyone interacts on this basis all the time, in any social system there is always a form of communism, at least for certain basic needs or for help in dire emergencies (i.e., you offer directions to strangers because you assume any stranger would do it for you; just as in some societies, no one would normally refuse a request for food). Sometimes communistic relations are institutionalized: two clans might each have responsibility for burying the other's dead. Here the responsibilities are rigorously specified, but no accounts kept: obviously no one would keep count of who has buried more. In relations between very close kin, close friends, "blood brothers," and the like, the range of responsibilities may become so wide as to encompass almost anything. It was for this reason that Mauss (1947: 106) suggested most societies may be seen as threaded with relations of what he called "individualistic communism." Communistic relations are reciprocal only in the sense that both sides are equally disposed to help one another; there is no feeling that accounts ought to balance out at any given moment – in part, because there's no assumption that such relations will ever end.

Reciprocal exchange

Under this rubric falls the exchange of compliments, or favors, or rounds of drinks. Such relationships may be broken off after every round because the return is considered to be a more or less exact equivalent to the initial gift. With the exchange of material goods, relations are often kept up by delaying the response in time: I buy dinner for a friend, he will likely feel in my debt until he is able to reciprocate. Or people make a point of ensuring the response is not quite an equivalent (if he buys me a much more expensive dinner, or a much cheaper one, the feelings of debt do not quite cancel out). There are numerous variations here, ways of testing the limits. The critical thing is that, unlike communistic relations, these are by no means assumed to be permanent and, in fact, can usually be broken off at any point. Reciprocity of this sort is about maintaining one's personal autonomy in a relatively equal relationship. (It also implies some implicit standard of value by which wealth could be compared; otherwise, it would be impossible to say a return was of equal value, unless it was of exactly the same thing.)

Hierarchical relations

Relations between masters and slaves, patrons and clients, parents and children, and so on, do not tend to operate in terms of reciprocity but rather by a logic of precedent. If one gives money to a beggar (or to a charity), the recipient will almost certainly not feel obliged to return something of equal value; rather, they will be likely to ask for more. Similarly, if parents allow a child an indulgence, that child is likely to expect the same in the future. The converse is equally the case: if a medieval serf or vassal presented an unusual gift to a feudal superior, it was likely to be treated as a precedent, added to the web of custom, and thus expected to be treated as an obligation in the future (Bloch 1961: 114). There are endless variations here too – from institutionalized plunder or ritualized theft to redistribution, inheritance, or other gifts that pass the superior status to former inferiors – but, except for the last, they all presume a permanent, or at least ongoing, relation that has nothing to do with reciprocal exchange because it is not assumed to have anything to do with equality.

The agonistic or heroic gift

Tit-for-tat exchange may also mount into contests of one-upmanship, where each party tries to present a gift or countergift so lavish their rival cannot reciprocate; in these the equal standing of the two parties is up for grabs at any moment, with the danger that they might degenerate at any moment – at least symbolically – into subordination and hierarchy.

None of these is in any way peculiar to what those following Mauss have called "gift economies." We are all communists with our closest friends, and feudal lords when interacting with small children. What varies is how they knit together, and, when they are present, with more impersonal commercial relations. Such transactions are by no means uniformly governed by principles of reciprocity, and communistic and hierarchical relations are not even really forms of exchange.

Mauss's text deals first and foremost with the agonistic or heroic gift. As a public institution, this seems to reach its fullest flowering in heroic societies – that is, stateless aristocratic societies like Vedic India, Homeric Greece, or Celtic or Germanic Europe; or for that matter the Maori of New Zealand or the First Nations of the Northwest Coast. Such contests could occasionally descend into destruction of property, or even outright violence. The stakes here can be very high. Mauss (1925) cites a Greek text about Celtic festivals where noblemen engaged in public duels that could occasionally turn deadly; and at the same time they vied to outdo each other with gifts of gold and silver treasures. If anyone were presented with a gift so magnificent that he could not possibly repay it, the only honorable response was to kill himself (and distribute the wealth to his entourage).

We might, again, wonder if this every really happened, or how often. But, if nothing else, it makes the "slave" metaphor easier to understand. According to Roman law, for example, a slave is first and foremost a person captured in war who, spared by his captor, therefore effectively owes his life to him. He stands in a relation of unlimited debt or obligation. This is what is referred to in the literature on slavery as "social death;" all previous rights and obligations held by the slave (citizenship, kinship ties, and so on) are voided; the only relationship remaining is that with his new master, and the demands that new master can place on him are in principle limitless. Clearly, the stakes in the most dramatic gift transactions between aristocratic rivals can be equally high: this is why, in Posidonius's Celtic festivals, duels and contests of generosity are treated as variations on a theme, and their consequences, potentially at least, are equally fatal. To best an opponent completely in a contest of liberality, then, becomes equivalent to defeat in war: it, too, establishes an infinite debt and, if it does not lead to actual death (which presumably is rather exceptional), it leads to something very much like "social death," at the very least to the destruction of one's honor and social standing, rendering one the hierarchical inferior of the giver.

In *Primitive Mentality* (1923), Lucien Lévy-Bruhl devotes a whole chapter to the apparently inexplicable response of Africans and Melanesians to having their lives saved by modern medicine: rather than seeking to repay their benefactors in any way, many appear to have reacted by demanding to be fed, given clothing, knives, or other valuables:

You save a person's life, and you must expect to receive a visit from him before long; you are now under an obligation to him, and you will not get rid of him except by giving him presents. (Bulléon, in Lévy-Bruhl 1923: 425)

Accounts like this became something of a cliché: how many of us have not heard the rumor that, among some exotic people (in my childhood I heard it variously ascribed to Eskimo, Buddhists, and Chinese), if you save someone's life, you have to take care of them forever. Such stories are striking because they seem to completely defy the norms of reciprocity, as the missionaries in Lévy-Bruhl's accounts were invariably quick to point out. But not all transactions are governed by norms of reciprocity. These accounts make a great deal of sense if we assume that those whose lives were saved therefore concluded that they were, in fact, now within a relation of complete hierarchical dependency. Hierarchies operate in terms of precedent, rather than reciprocity, so that the terms of this new relationship had now to be negotiated. In dealing with foreign missionaries, they were negotiating the terms of their newfound dependence with alien creatures of apparently infinite wealth. And, anyway, to abandon the assumption of equality with a stranger is no little thing; it is hardly surprising many were shocked when they discovered they were dealing with such apparently niggardly patrons.

On "Primordial Debt" and the State

So the analogy between debt and slavery seems to occur to people because slavery itself is conceived of as a permanent, absolute, and unpayable debt, a life-debt. This is presumably why, in commercial economies, defaulting on a cash loan can reduce one to the same status as a war captive. In either case, a situation of formal equality (combat, market exchange) is converted to one of absolute subordination. It is only in retrospect, when one is trying to justify such unequal relations, that one tries to demonstrate that they are really reciprocal after all. All of this is critical to understanding debates about money itself and particularly the chartalist approach.

Anyone looking for the origin of money in tax debts immediately runs into at least two conceptual problems. One is the question why, if the state creates money, it would need to levy taxes in the first place. What is the point of minting coins, distributing them, and then demanding that subjects deliver them back? The answer, as I have already pointed out, is that by doing so the authorities create a market in goods and services – based on the exchange of these same debt-tokens – that makes it much easier for them to acquire the things they need than by systems of direct requisition. The other question concerns the basis on which the state collects taxes. We could see taxes simply as a system of institutionalized plunder, but chartalists, being for the most part social democrats, would generally wish to avoid such a conclusion.

In so far as theorists of money address themselves to this question, the usual solution is to see the state as having simply adopted a much more fundamental or "primordial" debt that everyone could be said to owe to society.

At the origin of money we have a "relation of representation" of death as an invisible world, before and beyond life – a representation that is the product of the symbolic function proper to the human species and which envisages birth as an original debt incurred by all men, a debt owing to the cosmic powers from which humanity emerged ... Payment of this debt, which can however never be settled on earth – because its full reimbursement is out of reach – takes the form of sacrifices which, by replenishing the credit of the living, make it possible to prolong life and even in certain cases to achieve eternity by joining the Gods. But this initial belief-claim is also associated with the emergence of sovereign powers whose legitimacy resides in their ability to represent the entire original cosmos. And it is these powers that invented money as a means of settling debts – a means whose abstraction makes it possible to resolve the sacrificial paradox by which putting to death becomes the permanent means of protecting life. Through this institution, belief is in turn transferred to a currency stamped with the effigy of the sovereign – a money put in circulation but whose retour [sic] is organised by this other institution which is the tax/settlement of the life debt. So money also takes on the function of a means of payment which makes it possible to "settle" a debt, in other words to "finance" it. (Théret 1999: 60–1)

This argument has developed largely within France, spearheaded by the work of economist Michel Aglietta (Aglietta and Orléan 1992, 1998). It is largely inspired by certain texts in the Vedas that, as Charles Malamoud (1983, 1988, 1998) has shown, do propose a theory of existential debt. As one typical text puts it, "in being born every being is born as a debt owed to the gods, the saints, the Fathers and to men" (Malamoud 1983:27). The word used is not the same as that for a duty or obligation, but is what one would use for a borrowed object or a commercial loan. Ultimately, the gods will reclaim this loan by taking back your life; in the meantime, one can offer the lives of cows and sheep in sacrificial rituals, as a kind of interest payment.

There are a number of problems, however, with making such statements the basis of any broader theory of the origins of money. First of all, while the notion of an existential debt might appear in Vedic theories of sacrifice, there's no hint of it in Near Eastern or Classical texts. Second, and even more serious, the very idea of a universal sovereign inventing money by transforming cosmic debt into tokens of value appears to be contradicted by the historical evidence.

It is telling that primordial debt theorists almost never consider the example of Mesopotamia, even though Mesopotamia saw both the world's first states and first money. This is all the more striking since the evidence from there in many ways confirms chartalist assumptions. For example, money did indeed begin as a unit of account, and existed as such for thousands of years before the creation of a uniform medium of exchange. It also developed within large public institutions: specifically, in Sumerian and Babylonian palaces and temples. These institutions did indeed establish standards of conversion, starting with a conversion rate between silver and barley. One *shekel* of silver was made equivalent to one *gur* or "bushel" of barley, considered an adequate month's ration. Hence one silver *mina*, one-sixtieth of a shekel, was equivalent to one of two allotted daily meals – since the year, for ease of calculation, was divided into months of exactly 30 days. The state also set price schedules, interest rates, and so forth (Hudson 2002, 2003, 2004; cf. Henry 2004 on Egypt). All this is precisely as chartalist theory would predict. The problem is that there does not appear to have been a single unified state; and there was no generalized system of taxation.

Palaces and temples operated autonomously, were major landholders, maintained craft workshops, and collected revenues from renting their land, selling merchandise, and (in their own capacity, or via officials working in a private capacity) lending out money at interest. Neither palaces nor temples, however, levied taxes. The ruler of a given city-state might impose tribute on the citizens of conquered rivals, but their own citizens were not subjected to uniform state levies, for the very reason that it would imply servile status. Even more strikingly, in so far as rulers did intervene in their cosmological capacity as universal sovereigns, it was not to impose debts, but rather, to eliminate them. While the precise origins of making interest-bearing loans are not entirely clear,[6] by c. 2400 BCE it seems to have been common practice on the part of palace or temple local officials, or other wealthy individuals, to provide such loans to needy farmers – particularly during times of famine or other disasters – and then to appropriate lands, family members, and, ultimately, the farmers themselves. Often, in fact, debt peons ended up as dependents in temple workshops. The social dislocation so caused was such that it became customary for each new sovereign, on taking the throne, to wipe the slate clean, voiding all outstanding consumer loans, returning all land to its original owners and sending all debt peons back to their families. Hudson suggests it was because Sumerian and Babylonian rulers saw themselves as sacred kings that they could make such gestures of cosmic renewal. Societies lacking sovereigns of such universal pretension, he notes, were much less able to contain the dangers inherent in the creation of widespread structures of monetized debt when these diffused from the ancient Near East. In ancient Israel, prophets substituted the notion of a periodic "jubilee," but in the Classical Mediterranean sacred kings had long since vanished.[7] As a result, periodic debt crises led to endless social dislocation and movements for reform or revolution. When the latter were stymied, the results were often catastrophic.

What I hope comes through from all this is that the very notion that there must always be something that one can label "society" – a single totality to which everyone is born with a set of obligations – is not itself primordial. True, imaginary totalities must be created in the process of creating value. But

---

[6] Hudson (2002) hypothesizes that the custom of lending money at interest originated in officials loaning handicrafts produced in temple or palace workshops to merchants engaged in long-distance trade, so as to collect a share of the proceeds (though others – e.g. Steinkeller 1981; van de Mieroop 2002: 64 – suspect it might have originated in rental fees).

[7] Classical Greeks, incidentally, also "looked upon direct taxes as tyrannical and avoided them whenever possible" (Finley 1981: 90).

these can often take an endless variety of overlapping forms. The logic of debt, however, is not totalizing in this way. It is inherently dyadic. Even Malamoud (1983: 32) notes that, in the actual Vedic texts, there is a strong tendency to emphasize not the universal debt to the gods but the more particular debt of a man to his father, one that can only be repaid by oneself bearing a son. As with so many theories of "primitive society," one wonders if what lurks here is the shadow of the nation-state.

It is quite likely that, when one does find the notion of primordial debt, it arises in reaction to the logic of the market. Egoism and altruism, as Maussian theory has repeatedly taught us, are terms that only make sense in relation to each other; they are themselves "two sides of the same coin" that appear to have only become conceptually possible with the advent of a commercial logic. It is quite possible that the early Vedic texts are attempts to work out the morality of this new situation. The same may probably be said, in a different way, of the ideology of the modern nation-state. It is significant, in this context, to recall that the word "altruism" was coined by the nineteenth century social thinker, Auguste Comte, one of the first European authors to articulate a notion of primordial debt. In his *Catéchisme positiviste*, Comte completely rejected the notion of basing rights on this premise:

Positivism will never admit anything other than duties of all to all. For its social point of view cannot tolerate the notion of rights, for such notion rests on individualism. We are born under a load of obligations of every kind, to our predecessors, to our successors, to our contemporaries. After our birth these obligations increase or accumulate before the point where we are capable of rendering anyone any service. On what human foundation could one thus seat the idea of "rights"... ? (Comte 2002: 295)

The "final state" would consist only of duties, which in turn, could be boiled down to the famous imperative "to live for others" (Comte 2002: 47): altruistically.[8]

Comte's proposal that we are all born in debt to society appears to have been picked up, at the end of the century, by French political thinkers like Alfred Fouillé and Léon Bourgeois, who called it the "social debt." They, in turn, provided much of the political inspiration for Durkheim. In each case the assumption was that "society" is the nation, and that governments, being representative of society, have the right to dictate how that social debt can be dispatched: not only through taxes, but, for instance, through service in war. It is in other words essentially a nationalist doctrine. And, like nationalist doctrines almost everywhere, it is ultimately based on appropriating the emotional intensity of very local and particular forms of commitment – for instance, of

---

[8] The fact that Comte developed this notion in the course of proposing a new religion, broadly modeled on Catholicism, strongly suggests that the real origin of such notions goes back less to Vedic ideas than to Christian doctrines of original sin.

debt to fathers – and attaching to them to an abstraction. In this way, one might even suggest that what theorists of primordial debt have in fact produced is something of a nationalist myth, the chartalist counterpoint, one might say, to the notorious "barter myth." A less idealized theory of the state could express the matter of absolute debt – when indeed it was invoked – in terms of a much simpler logic. Sovereignty, after all, is the power of life and death. Ultimately, then, governments claim the same power over their subjects as victorious warriors do over their prisoners; and their (usually, in principle, unlimited) right to extract resources from them follows for exactly the same reason.[9]

Less totalizing alternatives: marriage and vengeance

All this seems very far from anthropological writings on the origins of money, which, such as they are, tend to focus on what Polanyi called "special-purpose monies" and what early ethnographers referred to as "primitive currencies" (e.g., Quiggin 1949; Einzig 1949). These tended to be employed in societies without strong states, neither primarily for taxes nor for buying and selling commodities, but first and foremost in matrimonial transactions.

There has been surprisingly little theoretical reflection on such currencies in recent anthropological literature. One of the great exceptions is a book by French economist Philippe Rospabé called *La Dette de Vie* (1995). Based on a survey of the literature from North and East Africa and Melanesia, Rospabé makes a compelling argument that tokens transferred in marriage also typically represent recognition of an infinite (or at least, unpayable) debt. Rospabé's central point is that such goods always seem to be given "as a substitute for life, as a pledge by which givers promise to render a life for one which they have taken from another group" (Rospabé 1993: 35). "Savage money," as he prefers to call it, is a means of payment, not of purchase; and what it "pays" for is ultimately life itself.

This is because such currencies are first and foremost ways of making marriage payments. The only equivalent to a woman given in marriage is another one. Bridewealth is only paid when direct exchange does not happen: and, though it consists of objects of wealth, these are never treated as the equivalent of a woman (or more precisely, her fertility). In many cases people are quite explicit that we are dealing here with a mere acknowledgement. In other words, in paying bridewealth you are recognizing the existence of a debt – a debt of life, since what bridewealth really secures is the paying clan's right to claim any of the woman's children as their descendants – that can only be expunged in later generations when one gives one of one's own daughters as a bride in her turn.

---

[9] This appears to be the reason why centralizing states almost always try to limit or even eliminate forms of private slavery – see Testart (2002).

As Rospabé emphasizes, the power to generate life is an incommensurable, ultimate value. It cannot be purchased because there is no possible material equivalent. Shells used as money are often explicitly compared to wombs, but no one suggests that any amount of shell money is actually worth the same as the procreative potential of a woman's uterus. They are tokens representing the very thing for which they are an obviously inadequate substitute: the immutable abstraction of generative power. The logic of bloodwealth, he argues, may be seen as a variation of this: again, the price of a life (in this case, a life taken) can never really be repaid, unless, perhaps, by the gift of a woman as compensation.[10]

In so far as one can speak of primordial or absolute debts, life-debts in Rospabé's sense, they take the form not of cosmic but of dyadic relationships – or, to be more accurate, they are cosmic relationships that can only take a dyadic form. The question of course is how tokens meant to express recognition of a debt that cannot be paid eventually become the means of settling debts; how such inherently unique dyadic ties can eventually knit together to create a uniform system for the measurement of value. Rospabé does not attempt to answer this question. Even so, he implies that commodity money simply could not have arisen from such a system: it had to develop from outside.[11] But there are examples of such currencies (in parts of Melanesia, for example, or aboriginal California) where the use of tokens that in certain places are restricted to matrimonial transactions and the like are, in other places, extended to buying fish, houses, pots, and so forth.

The closest I know to a proposed solution is the theory of the origins of money developed by a numismatist, Philip Grierson (1977, 1978). His is often referred to as the "*wergeld* theory," as he focused not on bridewealth but on bloodwealth. It is largely based on his reading of what are often referred to as the Barbarian Law Codes, or "the laws of the Germanic peoples who settled

---

[10] Occasionally, compensation can be paid in the form of a woman whose children will then be considered replacement for a murder victim (sometimes they will even be given the same name). In other cases, as most famously with the Nuer, the rate of compensation is exactly that required to obtain a wife who can then be "married" to the victim's ghost, in parts of North Africa to the "owner of the blood;" again, in order to secure progeny. This is as close to true compensation as one might come. According to Rospabé, the logic of ceremonial exchange, such as the *tee* or *moka* rituals of Highland Papua New Guinea, would seem to be the result of a gradual process of abstraction where the tokens, in circulating, gradually achieve a kind of autonomy from the powers of life to which they ultimately refer.

[11] This certainly was the conclusion reached by any number of theorists, who concluded that what Polanyi called "general purpose money" did indeed emerge from barter, but that barter occurred between societies, and not within them. Marx (1858, 1867) was already suggesting in the mid-nineteenth century that commerce, and therefore commercial money, had first emerged "in the pores" of the ancient world, only later to be adopted within. Karl Bücher (1904) adopted this position, as did Max Weber (1961). One could argue that Polanyi (1968b) agreed. My own position is that, since money does not have a single origin, both the internal and the external theories of the origin of money are likely to be in some part correct.

within or along the old frontiers of the Roman empire in the fifth and sixth centuries A.D." (Grierson 1977: 19). These legal systems were generally meant to provide scaled compensation payments for death or serious injury that were intended to head off blood feuds. Generally they were calculated according to a single unit of account: cattle in Wales, gold in Germany, furs in Russia. These payments were never imagined to be material equivalents to the loss of life or limb – such injuries were seen as incalculable – but emerged from "the need to assuage the anger of the injured party and make good his loss in public reputation" (Grierson 1977). He adds:

> The conditions under which these laws were put together would appear to satisfy, much better than any market mechanism, the prerequisites for the establishment of a monetary system. The tariffs for damages were established in public assemblies, and the common standards were based on objects of some value which a householder might be expected to possess of which he could obtain from his kinsfolk. Since what is laid down consists of evaluations of injuries, not evaluations of commodities, the conceptual difficulty of devising a common measure for appraising unrelated objects is avoided. (Grierson 1977: 20–1)[12]

Grierson and those who have taken up his argument provide a good deal of compelling linguistic evidence that, just as the English word "to pay" is ultimately derived from the Latin *pacere*, "to pacify," many terms for "debt" or even "money" in European languages appear to be derived from terms for "sin," or "fault," or "guilt" (see also Hudson 2002: 102–3; Ingham 2004:90).

  This does allow one to imagine how the system could expand to a more general system of currency: two gold plates for a broken knee, five for a severed arm, and so on. Still, it doesn't resolve the fundamental conceptual problem. If *wergeld* is originally a recognition of the incommensurable value of a human life, how then does it ultimately become the measure of a man's "worth" or "price" – which is, in fact, what the word appears to mean etymologically? Even more, how we may move from such profoundly dyadic relations (tokens, in effect, of the recognition of and desire to assuage another's justifiable anger) to a systematic measure of the value of pots and chickens? Grierson thinks it was unlikely to have occurred through attempts to systematize the value of the objects used in payment. Instead, he is forced to fall back on the longstanding earlier involvement of most of these barbarian populations in the Roman slave trade (Grierson 1977: 23). Roman slave traders, he notes, were familiar figures beyond the Rhine and Danube in the centuries immediately before these laws were recorded, and etymological evidence again suggests that most of the

---

[12] Note here that Grierson carefully avoids any suggestion that these schedules of tariffs were created by rulers, even though most were, in fact, attributed to individuals who considered themselves kings. Presumably he is more interested in using medieval records as a way of reconstructing an earlier, presumably more egalitarian period, more like that described by Tacitus, in which standards of value were not imposed, but worked out in "communal assemblies."

terms for buying and selling in Germanic languages originally referred to trade in people: many of the victims were precisely sold because they were unable to pay some fine or compensation. This became a very common pattern all over Africa and South East Asia as well as in zones where powerful commercial economies came into contact with those organized on a very different basis: legal systems, even bridewealth systems, are converted from ways of regulating relations between people into ways of turning human beings themselves into commodities. A slave, as I have noted, is considered to owe an absolute life-debt to his owner. But at the same time a slave can be traded for a specific amount of money. The conversion of an unpayable debt into the "price" of a man or woman, then, appears to have been brought about principally through an alchemy of violence.

On the relation of human economies to market economies

Scholars studying the rise of impersonal market relations – even those who see them as arising first between societies, only later extending to relations within them – rarely pay adequate attention to the role of violence, and in particular, to the formative role of the slave trade. I have space here only to propose the barest outlines of a theory; but let me begin by suggesting that there are two possible ways to make the jump between absolute debt and the logic of the market. One is the power of social creativity. As I often point out (Graeber 2001), the central concern of any social system is creation, and that means, first and foremost, the creation of human beings and social relations. Here, we might suggest that, just as for Marx the value of money in a capitalist society is ultimately the value of the human creative powers invested in creating marketable commodities, so in the societies that Grierson or Rospabé describe – I would call them "human economies" – the predominant forms of currency are invariably representations of the powers of *social* creativity. Women's reproductive powers are merely the concrete symbol for the more general power to nurture, shape, and foster human beings. That is why, as I have suggested elsewhere (Graeber 1996), money tends to be symbolically identified with the owner's inner capacities, the "promise of power" they embody.

"Human economies:" the phrase appeals in part because it is so obviously paradoxical. Are not all economies, ultimately, human economies? Clearly they are. But they are so, above all, because they are always, ultimately, concerned with the creation of (certain valued sorts of) human beings. What is unusual about market economies is that, they can pretend to be about anything else, at least in some contexts. Commodity money is what really makes this possible. Substituting the phrase "human economies" for "gift economies" therefore seems a nice way to capture the paradox. It also helps to underline Mauss's most important point about gift economies: that outside of commercial markets, even in what might seem to us to be economic transactions, it is always the status of human beings and relations between them that is ultimately at stake. There is also a relatively easy way to identify a human economy: we need merely check to see whether the main form of currency is used primarily to rework relations between people or to purchase things like noodles, furniture, or shoes.

This does suggest a common conceptual basis to all forms of currency. Creative capacities are, like credit, a potential for future productivity. Debt is a claim on future creativity. It is only the monetization of debt that allows anyone to specify the depth of this future; in fact, to charge for each unit of time by which this creation is delayed. In terms of human production, any such calculation seems quite absurd. In general, the gulf between human economies and market systems is such that any attempt to move directly from one to the other would have profoundly jarring effects on the entire system of social production. This is indeed what happens the moment impersonal markets begin to develop – usually, I suspect, in relation to the spread of new forms of predatory violence. The moment the same forms of wealth that were once used exclusively for arranging marriages and paying fines can be used for buying and selling goats and leather pouches, one invariably witnesses intense social struggles over the dangers of the potential commoditization of human beings – specifically, over prostitution and slavery. All this is quite apparent in the ancient Near East and Mediterranean, where elites strove to define themselves specifically as people whose daughters' reputations were in no sense to be sullied by the market (Lerner 1983, 1986; Kurke 2001). But we see the same thing on the fringes of the system, wherever commercial and human economies meet. The history of the expansion of the slave trade into Africa and South East Asia, as I have mentioned, is a story of the abusive manipulation of forms of debt and of the abusive transformation of obligations into commodities.

Notes on the history of monetary instruments: commodity, credit, trust, and violence

Predatory violence has been the main instrument enabling the conceptual leap from a human to a commodity economy, of transforming tokens that served to acknowledge one's inability to repay acts of cosmic creativity into instruments for the marketing of people. Ideologies of debt, in turn, have been and continue to be the single most effective way of making human relationships created and maintained by violence seem to be rooted in morality. Most of the arguments marshaled here, from the discussion of hierarchical versus egalitarian modes of gift exchange to the various ideologies of absolute or primordial debt, ultimately aim at trying to understand how this comes about.

Turning from the peripheries to the centers of great civilizations, let me offer in outline a new historical architecture, constructed around the shifting relations between credit and commodity monies. The historical evidence confirms, as Geoffrey Gardiner (2004: 139) succinctly put it, that "bullion is the accessory of war, and not of peaceful trade." Commodity money, in particular in the form of gold and silver, is distinguished from credit money most of all by one spectacular feature: it can be stolen. An ingot of gold or silver is indeed an object without a pedigree; throughout much of history bullion has served the same role as the drug dealer's suitcase full of dollar bills, an object without a history that will be accepted in exchange for other valuables just about anywhere, with no questions asked. As a result, credit systems seem to arise in periods of relative social peace, across networks of trust, whether created by states or, in most periods, international institutions; precious metals replace them in periods characterized by widespread plunder. Predatory lending systems certainly exist at every period; but they seem to have the most damaging effects in periods when money is most easily convertible into cash. The story is too long to tell in any great detail, but a very tentative breakdown of Eurasian history might go as follows.

Age of the first agrarian empires (3500 BCE to 800 BCE): dominant form, virtual credit-money

Our best information on the origins of money goes back to ancient Mesopotamia, but there is no particular reason to believe that matters were radically different in Pharaonic Egypt, Bronze Age China, or the Indus Valley. The Mesopotamian economy was dominated by large public institutions (temples and palaces) whose administrators effectively created money of account by establishing a fixed equivalent between silver and the staple crop, barley; debts were calculated in silver, but silver was rarely used in transactions: payments were made in barley or in anything else that happened to be handy and acceptable. Major debts were recorded on cuneiform tablets kept as sureties by both parties to the transaction.

Markets certainly did exist. Prices of certain commodities that were not produced within temple or palace holdings, and thus not subject to administered price schedules, would tend to fluctuate according to the vagaries of supply and demand. Even here though such evidence as we have (e.g., Hudson 2002: 25, 2004: 114) suggests that most everyday purchases, such as beer advanced by "ale women" or local innkeepers, were made on credit, with tabs accumulating to be paid, typically, at harvest time.

Interest rates, fixed at 20 percent, remained stable for two thousand years. This was not a sign of government control of the market; at that stage, institutions like this were what made markets possible. In so far as governments did intervene, it was to deal with the effects of debt. In bad years the poor tended to become hopelessly indebted to the rich and would often have to surrender their lands and, ultimately, family members into debt peonage; hence, it became customary for each new ruler to wipe the slate clean, cancel debts, and return bonded laborers to their families.

Axial Age (800 BCE to 600 CE): dominant form, coinage, and metal bullion

This is the age that saw the emergence of coinage as well as the birth in China, India, and the Middle East of all major world religions.[13] From the Warring States period in China and fragmentation in India to the carnage and mass enslavement that accompanied the expansion (and later dissolution) of the Roman Empire, it was a period of spectacular creativity and in much of the world, of almost equally spectacular violence.

Coinage, which allowed the use of gold and silver as a medium of exchange, also made possible the creation of markets in the now more familiar, impersonal sense of the term. Precious metals were also far more appropriate for an age of generalized warfare, for the obvious reason that they can be stolen. Coinage certainly was not invented to facilitate trade (the Phoenicians, the consummate traders of the ancient world, were among the last to adopt it). It appears to have been first invented to pay soldiers.

Throughout antiquity one can speak of what Ingham (2004: 99) has dubbed the "military-coinage complex." He might better have called it a "military–coinage–slavery complex," since the diffusion of new military technologies (Greek hoplites, Roman legions) was always closely tied to the capture and marketing of slaves; and the other major source of slaves was debt: now that states no longer periodically wiped the slate clean, those not lucky enough to be citizens of the major military city-states were fair game. The credit systems of the Near East did not crumble under commercial competition; they were destroyed by Alexander's armies – armies that required half a ton of silver bullion a day in wages. The tax systems of the Hellenistic and Roman empires, which demanded payment in coins the state itself had mined and minted, were designed to force their subjects to abandon other modes of circulation and enter into market relations, so that soldiers (and government officials) would be able to buy things with that money. The effects of the constant wars conducted by the legions in turn guaranteed that much of the consequent trade was, in fact, in human beings, or in the products of slave-labor.

---

[13] The phrase "Axial Age" was originally coined by Karl Jaspers to describe the relatively brief period between 800 BCE and 200 BCE in which, he believed, just about all the main philosophical traditions we are familiar with today arose simultaneously in China, India, and the Eastern Mediterranean. Here, I am using it in Lewis Mumford's more expansive sense as the period that saw the birth of all existing world religions, stretching roughly from the time of Zoroaster to that of Mohammed (see, for example, Mumford 1966: 268).

The creation of new media of exchange, however tawdry their origins, appears to have had profound intellectual effects. Some (Shell 1978, 1982; Seaford 2004) have even gone so far as to argue that early Greek philosophy only became possible because of conceptual innovations introduced by the technology of coinage. Certainly, it is significant that this was precisely the age that saw, in India, China, and the Eastern Mediterranean, the emergence of all major philosophical trends and world religions. What is more, they appear in the times and places that also saw the emergence of coined money. While the precise links are yet to be fully explored, one thing is clear. Ideals of charity, altruism, and selfless giving typically promoted by these new world religions seem to have arisen in direct reaction to the logic of the market. As Mauss liked to point out, outside of a commercial economy, either pure selfishness, or pure selflessness, would be almost inconceivable. To put the matter crudely, if we relegate a certain social space to the selfish acquisition of material things, inevitably someone else will soon set aside another domain in which to preach that, from the perspective of ultimate values, material things are unimportant, and selfishness – or even the self – illusory. The fact that these markets were based on coinage, which allowed for far more impersonal and hence potentially violent forms of market behavior than earlier credit relations presumably made the distinction all the more compelling.

The Middle Ages (600 to 1500):[14] the return of virtual credit-money

If the Axial Age saw the emergence of commodity markets and universal world religions, with their complementary ideals of egoism and altruism, the Middle Ages was the period in which those two institutions began to merge, so that monetary transactions were increasingly carried out through social networks defined and regulated by those same world religions. This enabled the return, throughout Eurasia, of various forms of virtual credit-money.

In Europe, where all this took place under the aegis of Christendom, coinage was only sporadically and unevenly available. Prices after 800 AD were calculated largely in terms of an old Carolingian currency that no longer existed (it was actually referred to at the time as "imaginary money" – Einaudi 1953), but ordinary day-to-day buying and selling was carried out mainly with tally-sticks, notched pieces of wood that were broken in two as records of debt, with half being kept by the creditor, half by the debtor. Such tally-sticks were still in common use in much of England well into the sixteenth century (Innes

---

[14] I relegate most of what is generally referred to as the "Dark Ages" in Europe to the earlier period. The Viking raids, and the famous extraction of *danegeld* from England, might be seen as one the last manifestations of an age in which predatory militarism went hand and hand with hoarding gold and silver bullion.

1913, 1914; MacIntosh 1988). Larger transactions were handled through bills of exchange, with the great commercial fairs serving as their clearing-houses. The Church, meanwhile, provided a legal framework, enforcing strict controls on the lending of money at interest and prohibitions on debt bondage.

The real nerve center of the medieval world economy, though, was the Indian Ocean, along with the Central Asian caravan routes, connecting the great civilizations of India, China, and the Middle East. Here, trade was conducted through the framework of Islam, which not only provided a legal structure highly conducive to mercantile activities (while absolutely forbidding the lending of money at interest), but allowed for peaceful relations between merchants over a remarkably large part of the globe, allowing the creation of a variety of sophisticated credit instruments. China in this same period saw the rapid spread of Buddhism, the invention of paper money, and the development of even more complex forms of credit and finance.

This period did see its share of carnage and plunder, of course (particularly during the great nomadic invasions), and coinage was, in many times and places, an important medium of exchange. Still, what really characterizes the period appears to be a movement in the opposite direction. Money, during most of the medieval period, was largely delinked from coercive institutions. Money-changers, we might say, were invited back into the temple, where they could be monitored; the result was a flowering of institutions premised on a much higher degree of social trust.

The age of European empires (1500–1971): the return of precious metals

With the advent of the great European empires – Iberian, then North Atlantic – the world saw both a reversion to the use of chattel slavery, plunder, and wars of destruction, and the consequent rapid return of gold and silver bullion as the main form of currency. Historical investigation will probably demonstrate that the origins of these transformations were more complicated than we ordinarily assume. One of the main factors in the movement back to bullion in China, for example, was the emergence of popular movements during the early Ming dynasty in the fifteenth and sixteenth centuries that ultimately forced the government to abandon not only paper money but any attempt to impose its own currency. This led to the reversion of the vast Chinese market to an uncoined silver standard. Since taxes were also gradually commuted into silver, it soon effectively became official Chinese policy to try to bring as much silver into the country as possible, so as to keep taxes low and prevent new outbreaks of social unrest. The sudden enormous demand for silver had effects across the world. Most of the precious metals looted by the conquistadors and later extracted by the Spanish from the mines of Mexico and Peru (at almost unimaginable cost in human lives) ended up in China. The global connections that eventually developed across the Atlantic, Pacific, and Indian oceans have been documented in great detail. The crucial point is that the delinking of money from religious institutions and its relinking with coercive ones (especially the state) was here accompanied by an ideological reversion to metallism.[15] Credit became, on the whole, an affair of states who sustained themselves largely by deficit financing, a form of credit which was, in turn, invented to finance increasingly expensive wars. Internationally, the British Empire was steadfast in maintaining the gold standard even through the nineteenth and early twentieth centuries.

Current era (1971 onward): the empire of debt

The current era might be said to have been initiated on August 15, 1971, when US President Richard Nixon officially suspended the convertibility of the dollar into gold and effectively created the current floating currency regimens (Gregory 1997). We have returned, then, to an age of virtual money in which consumer purchases in wealthy countries rarely involve even paper money and national economies are driven largely by consumer debt. All of this has been accompanied by what is often called a "financialization" of capital (see Hart, Chapter 6 in this volume), with speculation in currencies and financial instruments becoming a domain unto itself detached from any immediate relation to production or even commerce (e.g., Arrighi 1994; Harvey 2005b).

Historically, as we have seen, ages of virtual credit-money have also involved creating controls of some sort over the destructive social consequences that ensue when debt spirals entirely out of control. So far the movement this time has been if anything in the other direction: we have begun to see the creation of the first effective planetary administrative system, operating through the IMF, the World Bank, corporations, and other financial institutions, largely in order to protect the interests of creditors against debtors. However, this apparatus was very quickly thrown into crisis. The new age of virtual money has only just begun and the long-term consequences are as yet unclear.

Conclusion

Let me turn briefly in conclusion to the question of debt versus value: or, to be more specific, society seen as a network of dyadic relations of obligation rather than as an imaginary forum for the realization of some conception of the Good.

I noted above that hierarchical relations, for example within feudal or patronage systems, operate in practice on a principle of precedent that is in many

---

[15] The myth of barter origins and the commodity theory of money was, of course, developed in this period.

ways the opposite of reciprocity. An unexpected gift is likely to be taken as a precedent and similar gestures will be expected in the future. But the moment native theorists of feudalism felt the need to represent society in the abstract, they invariably argued that relations between the different ranks and statuses of society were ultimately based on reciprocity after all: nobles provide protection, peasants provide food, and so forth. The reason would seem simple enough. While reciprocity may or may not be the basis of any given transactional logic, of how people actually interact with each other immediately on the ground, it everywhere underpins conceptions of justice.

The list of transactional logics above was meant to illustrate the proposition that what we call social or economic systems are, in reality, an endless interweaving of dyadic relations that often operate according to completely different principles. Some are based on forms of pragmatic communism, some on a hierarchical logic of precedent, some on principles of balanced exchange – which may, in turn, be relatively personal or impersonal, ephemeral or sustained. Others are based on outright theft or extortion. In no case – even assuming we could draw a bounded circle and call it a "society" – do accounts all balance out. And, of course, any such drawing of circles is itself an ideological gesture: there are no natural boundaries; real social relations always overflow any such limits.

It is, however, an extremely important ideological gesture. For much of its history social anthropology has wrestled with the problem of how to square these abstract representations with what one actually finds on the ground. Take as an example the famous problem of "circulating connubium." In certain societies, just about everyone insists that society is organized into a series of clans that each marry in a circle: clan A giving women to clan B, B to C, C to D, and D back to A again. When we examine actual practice, we find instead an infinite complexity of principles and arrangements. Edmund Leach (1954) was probably the first to recognize that all such claims are merely ideological statements, ways of moving beyond the untidiness of social existence by conjuring up an image of totality, a single "society." How is this done? In just about every case, by plucking certain dyadic relations – dyads based, as they are, on a certain notion of mutual indebtedness – from that infinitely complicated reality and creating an image of justice, an imaginary sphere in which all accounts balance out.

The market is, of course, the same. "Markets," as I pointed out at the beginning, don't really exist. Economists are perfectly happy to admit this. The market is a model. The question is what kind of model? At this point I think we can answer the question: it is a model created by isolating certain principles within a complex system (in this case by fixing on a certain form of immediate, balanced, impersonal, self-interested transactions that we call "commercial exchange," which is almost never found in isolation but always surrounded by and drawing on other logics – hierarchical, communistic ...), and then creating a totalizing model within which the books all balance and all debts and credits ultimately cancel one another out. No such bounded entity could ever exist, either in time or space. Nonetheless, such bounded entities are endlessly invoked: in part, so as to create theaters for the realization of certain forms of value and partly in order to make ideological statements about the legitimacy of existing social relations. We need *a* market to exist in some immediate concrete form whenever we have to determine the value of our house or art collection, especially if we wish to realize that value by selling it. We need *the* market to exist, at least at the level of rhetoric, when we wish to represent capitalism as ultimately just. What vanish, in any such operation, are the innumerable acts and threats of violence that are required to create any such system – as Polanyi observed when he pointed out how much state power was required to create the "self-regulating market" – and that ultimately lie hidden behind our very conceptualizations of the nature of money itself.

8   Whatever happened to householding?

Chris Gregory

Introduction

Polanyi's contribution to the history of economic thought is not so much as a theorist of value but as a conceptual tool-maker and tool-user. "The study of the shifting place occupied by the economy in society," he noted (Polanyi 1957b: 250), is "no other than the study of the manner in which the economic process is instituted at different times and places. This requires a special tool box." Polanyi the "tool-user" is the historian, the author of *The Great Transformation* (1944), his classic study of the "shifting place" occupied by the economy in nineteenth-century England. Polanyi the "tool-maker" is the concept-builder who fills his toolbox with general concepts gathered from single-case studies, refines them with logical distinctions of the sharpest kind, and orders them neatly in the rows and columns of his conceptual tool-box.

We first meet Polanyi the tool-maker in Chapter 4 of *The Great Transformation* where his four general principles of behavior – reciprocity, redistribution, householding, and money-making – are distinguished by social relationships and institutional pattern. His concept of "reciprocity," a process embedded in family and kinship, and instituted by symmetrically arranged groupings, was inspired by Thurnwald's (1916) ethnographic study of dual organization among the Banaro of Papua New Guinea; his concept of redistribution was inspired by Malinowski's (1922) study of the Trobriand Islands; and his concept of householding – "the etymon of the word 'economy'" (Polanyi 2001: 55) – comes from Aristotle.

We meet Polanyi the tool-maker again thirteen years later as the author of the influential essay, "The Economy as an Instituted Process," in the collection, *Trade and Markets in the Early Empires,* he edited with Arensberg and Pearson (1957b). In this essay he is concerned to sharpen his tools and to re-order them. Here "money-making" is reclassified as a species of "exchange," a general concept that takes its place alongside reciprocity and redistribution. What comes as a surprise is that his other generic concept, "householding," is not only no longer in the toolkit, it does not even rate a mention in the index of the book of which this essay is part; but in his final, posthumously published work, *Dahomey and the Slave Trade* (Polanyi 1966), householding re-enters the picture once again with the familiar quartet of terms – redistribution, reciprocity, householding, and exchange – used to structure Part II of the book.

The final twist in this now-you-see-it-now-you-don't history of householding comes in 1987 with the founding of the Karl Polanyi Institute of Political Economy. The second statement of purpose of the Institute reads: "The extension of economics beyond the narrowly defined study of the laws of market exchange to embrace *redistribution* (the role of the state) and *reciprocity* (the role of the community) as organizing mechanisms of economic activity."

Why did Polanyi remove householding from his toolbox and put it back in again? Why did the Polanyi Institute remove it again? Archival research could no doubt provide an empirical answer to these questions, but this is not what I want to explore here. My concern is more conceptual, with the adequacy of Polanyi's toolbox for an anthropological investigation of the economy today. We can all agree with the Polanyi Institute that the study of the economy should embrace the role of both state and community, but what about the role of the household? Doesn't this have a role to play today? If so, how *should* the concept be formulated? A critical examination of Polanyi's methods of conceptual tool-making and using may help us answer these questions.

Polanyi the conceptual tool-maker

Polanyi's writings fall into two discrete categories. On the one hand, we have the tool-maker who is primarily concerned with conceptual issues; on the other, we have the tool-user who is primarily concerned with historical questions. *Trade and Market in the Early Empires* falls squarely into the first camp. The introduction to the book makes this clear: "the main task of this book is conceptual; it argues that only a small number of alternative patterns for organizing man's livelihood exist and it provides us the tools for the examination of non-market economies" (Polanyi, Arensberg and Pearson 1957: xvii–xviii). His other two books, by contrast, are primarily historical: *The Great Transformation* (1944) has nineteenth-century England as its focus; *Dahomey and the Slave Trade* (1966) is concerned with the economic history of West Africa before the nineteenth century. Chapter 4 of *The Great Transformation*, however, stands apart because the aim here is conceptual. Indeed, the various authors in *Trade and Market in the Early Empires* are concerned to refine and develop the conceptual framework Polanyi first sketched in Chapter 4 of *The Great Transformation*.

Polanyi's method, like Marx's and many other great thinkers in the European tradition, is paradoxical in that complex, highly sophisticated historical analyses are performed using extremely simple conceptual frameworks. This method of "simple complexity" produces clear thought, nowhere more so than in *The Great Transformation*, where the simple conceptual framework of Chapter 4 stands opposed to the empirical complexity of the rest of the book. We do not have to agree with the substance of Polanyi's arguments to appreciate clarity as an academic value. Given that much anthropological thought today is the obscure product of complex simplicity (the use of a jargon-ridden conceptual framework so complex that it cannot even handle the simplest of historical questions), we can learn much by paying close attention to Polanyi's conceptual tool-making methods, whether or not we like what he produced.

The fundamental problem Polanyi addresses in Chapter 4 is how to develop a positive conception of the negation "non-market economy." The negation he sought to negate, in Hegelian terms, was the ethnographic evidence for an absence of wage-labor, the profit motive, and the other features of capitalist economy. He posed the question of how production and distribution could be ensured given these absences and found the answer in "two principles of behavior not primarily associated with economics: *reciprocity* and *redistribution*" (2001: 49–50). These principles of behavior, he added (2001: 50–1), "cannot become effective unless existing institutional patterns lend themselves to their application." Reciprocity requires *symmetry* and redistribution *centricity*. While he was inspired by Melanesian ethnography, Polanyi stressed that these notions were of great generality and were to be formed to some extent in all human groups. Redistribution, for example, has a "long and variegated history which leads up almost to modern times" (Polanyi 2001: 53). Other examples include the kingdom of Hammurabi in Babylonia and the New Kingdom of Egypt.

Householding as a "mode of behavior" is not advanced as a concept in answer to the question of "absences." This principle is "a feature of economic life only on a more advanced level of agriculture" (Polanyi 1944: 53). Its institutional pattern is that of the "closed group," *autarky*. Examples include the despotic Roman *familia*, the democratic Southern Slav *zadruga*, the great domains of the Carolingian magnates, and the small peasant holding of Western Europe.

Polanyi's concept of householding, then, is distinguished from reciprocity and redistribution in important ways. Whereas the latter were inspired by a reading of the ethnographic literature of "tribal" economies in Melanesia, the former derives from Aristotle and Polanyi's own reading of the historical literature on the "peasant" economies of Europe. Householding, moreover, is a historically specific concept that does not have the generality of reciprocity and redistribution. Here lies a contradiction in Polanyi's analysis. Having just told us that householding is "a feature of economic life only on a more advanced level of agriculture," he adds just a few lines later that the "principle is as broad in its application as either reciprocity or redistribution" (Polanyi 2001: 56).

This equivocation about the status of householding runs throughout Polanyi's thought, only to be "resolved" by the Polanyi Institute. An institutional resolution to a problem of this type, however, is the last thing we need. For me this ambiguity in Polanyi's thought is the most exciting part of it, for it suggests a new way forward, a point I will return to when we have finished looking at his toolbox.

His final principle of behavior is that of "production for gain," the money-making principle underwritten by the institution of the "self-regulating market." This principle stands opposed to the other three, which are embedded in social relations. The "great transformation" in the early nineteenth century ushered this disembedded form into a position of dominance after 1834. "Money-making" is, therefore, the most historically specific of all four forms of behavior.

Polanyi's first conceptual toolbox is represented in the table below. He never presents his argument in terms of tables or visual forms of any kind, but the logic of his prose suggests that he conceived of the interrelationships between his concepts in this way.

The following "Porphyrian tree" (Figure 8.1) captures the key distinctions differentiating his concepts.

This diagram reveals that an ethnographically informed modification of Aristotle's distinction between production for use and production for gain – "probably the most prophetic pointer ever made in the realm of the social sciences"(Polanyi 2001: 56) – is the logic-chopper that divides the concepts into two mutually exclusive parts. This logic may be represented by means of a Venn diagram (Figure 8.2).

I express Polanyi's argument in this way to highlight another contradiction in his analysis. If these concepts are to have the logical status that Polanyi wants to give them, then they must be *general*. If they are general then they

Table 8.1 *A tabular presentation of Polanyi's first conceptual toolbox*

Principle of behavior	Reciprocity	Redistribution	Householding	Money-making
Social relations	Embedded in family and kinship	Embedded in territorial chiefdoms, tribes, city-states, despotism, or feudalism	Indifferent: may be patriarchal family, village settlement, seigniorial manor	Social relations embedded in economy
Institutional pattern	Symmetry	Centricity "Long and variegated history which leads up almost to modern times"	Autarky "a feature of economic life only on a more advanced level of agriculture"	Self-regulating market 1834–1931

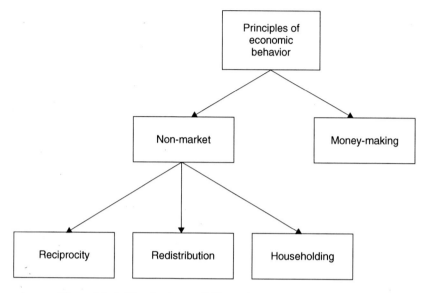

Figure 8.1 A "Porphyrian tree" illustrating the key distinctions in Polanyi's (1944) concepts.

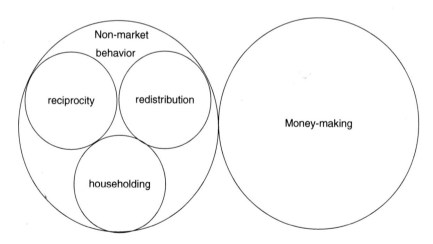

Figure 8.2 A Venn diagram to illustrate Polanyi's (1944) interpretation of Aristotle's distinction between production for use and production for gain.

are not, by definition, historically *specific*. Polanyi hints at this problem when he notes that reciprocity and redistribution are "present to some extent in all groups." Householding and money-making, however, are historically specific, he tells us. These problems are overcome in the redefined 1957 toolbox where householding drops out and a new generic concept, *exchange,* takes the place of the historically specific concept "money-making."

In this new toolbox *reciprocity, redistribution*, and *exchange* are now called "forms of integration." "Exchange" is a general concept that consists of three subtypes: "gift trade," "administered trade," and "market trade." "Gift trade" links partners or friends in relations of reciprocity that are often ceremonial, such as the relations between kings or chiefs. "Administered trade" is based on treaties with set prices. "Market trade" is the familiar money-making activity where prices are set by a self-regulating market. "Reciprocity" as a form of integration requires symmetrical groupings as institutional support, but these need not be dual. Polanyi generalizes this notion by allowing for multiple symmetry where three, four, or more groups may be reciprocal with regard to two or more axes. Redistribution is redefined so that it:

… may apply to a group smaller than society, such as a household or manor irrespective of the way in which the economy as a whole is integrated. The best known instances are the Central African *kraal*, the Hebrew patriarchal household, the Greek estate of Aristotle's time, the Roman *familia*, the medieval manor, or the typical large peasant household before the general marketing of grain. However, only under a comparatively advanced form of agricultural society is householding practicable, and then, fairly general. (Polanyi 1957b: 254)

Here then is the first answer to the question of "Whatever happened to householding?" It disappears with a wave of the tool-maker's wand. The 1957 essay, quietly and without fanfare, redefines it as a species of redistribution and tucks it away out of sight. No explanation is given. Key sentences from the 1944 discussion have simply been cut and pasted into the 1957 essay as part of a larger paragraph dealing with redistribution.

The effect of these operations is to elevate the trinity to a conceptual level that is now completely general. Furthermore, the three concepts are sufficiently elastic to allow for different historical forms of coexistence. The three concepts may coexist in such a way that one form of integration dominates the others. For example:

Reciprocity as a form of integration gains greatly in power through its capacity of employing both redistribution and exchange as subordinate methods. Reciprocity may be attained through a sharing of the burden of labor according to definite rules of redistribution as when taking things "in turn." Similarly, reciprocity is sometimes attained through exchange at set equivalencies for the benefit of the partner who happens to be short of some kind of necessities – a fundamental institution in ancient Oriental societies. In non-market economies these two forces of integration – reciprocity and redistribution – occur in effect together. (Polanyi 1957b: 253)

Thus the three "forms of integration" create a logical triad for possible encompassment and subordination of the other two. When this happens the subordinated forms become mere patterns of behavior. The toolkit thus attains its generality and logical perfection. Now it is only a matter of putting it to use.

I have no desire to become a Polanyian mechanic, since I believe that empirical analysis must always involve some creative conceptual work. On the other hand, there is no sense in being unnecessarily creative when it comes to concepts. If the toolboxes of our intellectual ancestors contain some useful concepts, why not use them? The utility of a concept cannot be decided a priori; it always depends on the historical problem being addressed.

Polanyi's problem, it must be remembered, was not primary data collection. He was not an ethnographer. His concepts were developed primarily for secondary-level analysis of a comparative and historical kind. General concepts like this are of limited use to the ethnographer who, by definition, is concerned with specifics; the ethnographer's aim is not so much to apply concepts and theories but, where necessary, to critique conventional orthodoxy in the light of new data. Understanding indigenous concepts is one of ethnography's prime aims. This necessarily involves a theoretically informed approach that confronts the dialectical relationship between the specific data and the general theory. Such work is primary and provides the raw material for a more general comparative and historical understanding. Without the primary reports of Thurnwald, Malinowski, and other ethnographers, Polanyi would have had nothing new to say.

Polanyi's tools and his mode of constructing them, however, are of critical importance for the ethnographer and for any anthropologist concerned with more general comparative questions. This is because his tools are *general* concepts rather than *universal* ones. In this sense his tools are similar to Marx's but radically different from those of the "formalist" economist.

Universal and general theories of value

Polanyi's distinction between "formalist" and "substantivist" conceptions of the economy is really a distinction between universal concepts and general ones. A general concept is one whose applicability is decided historically on empirical grounds. A universal concept, by contrast, is transcultural and transhistorical. It belongs to the realm of human nature rather than historically specific forms of human society. Thus, while a general proposition admits of exceptions, a universal proposition admits of none. The proposition "All men have two legs" is a general one, the fact that it is possible to find men with one or none (or even three) does not falsify it. Considered as a universal proposition "All men have two legs" only requires one exception to be falsified.

Marx's concepts and theories of the economy are also general in this sense. While his historical and theoretical approach differs quite sharply from

Polanyi's, his conceptual toolbox is almost the same. Marx's conception of the economy, as Polanyi (1957b: 256) notes, "flows from the conviction that the character of the economy was set by the status of labor." But, adds Polanyi, "the integration of the soil into the economy should be regarded as hardly less vital." Thus, for Polanyi:

> ... dominance of a form of integration is ... identified with the degree to which it comprises land and labor in society. So-called savage society is characterized by the integration of land and labor into the economy by way of ties of kinship. (Polanyi 1957b: 255)

His analysis does not rest on a single theory of value as it does for Marx; and his multivalent approach draws attention to the importance of noneconomic values in structuring economic life, such as religion, for example.

The similarity of Marx's toolbox with Polanyi's may be seen by examining the following diagram (Figure 8.3), which captures the relationship between Marx's central concepts: slave-, serf-, and wage-labor. For Marx (as for Polanyi) the great transformation occurred when labor-power emerged as a commodity, that is, when the market for wage-labor became a dominant form of social organization. This was the final phase of the evolution of class struggle that originated in slavery and progressed via feudalism into capitalism. These evolutionary stages, like Polanyi's (1957b: 256), are historically untenable; but this is not to deny the generality of the concepts he develops.

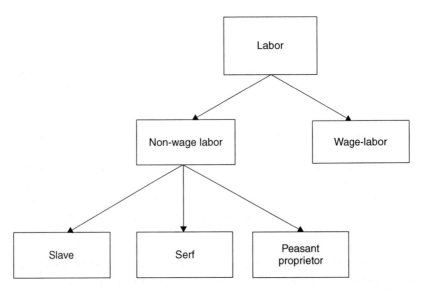

Figure 8.3 The relationship between Marx's central concepts: slave-, serf-, and wage-labor.

Marx's (1970: Volume III, Chapter 47) notion of the "peasant proprietor," who is both capitalist and worker, land-owner and farmer, is of some interest. This figure made an appearance in the early stages of capitalist agriculture in Europe, when land became a marketable commodity. In England, where land was the entailed property of aristocratic families, the proletarianization process created a class of people who were forced to enter the market as sellers of their labor-power, but in Europe they had the option of entering the land market. They were successful bidders for small plots of land because, as Marx notes, "If sold in small lots, the land in this case brings a far higher price than it does by its sale in large estates, because the number of small buyers is large and that of the large buyers small" (Marx 1970 Volume III, Part VI, Chapter 47, para 51). This figure is none other than Polanyi's autarkic householder, "a feature of economic life only on a more advanced level of agriculture" (Polanyi 2001: 55).

The generalizing approach to concept-making that Marx and Polanyi share is opposed to the universalist approach of the "formalists" (more accurately described as "marginal utility theorists" or "neoclassical economists"). The generalist is concerned to understand historically specific forms of human economy and the social relations that constitute them. The universalist, by contrast, strives to understand human nature transculturally. The study of *Homo economicus* as a fact of human nature is a valid enterprise, but the "formalists" have been not been successful in persuading anyone except themselves of the universality of the model they present. This is because the argument, based as it is on market-centric assumptions about the nature of economic activity, is unconvincing. Second, even if a persuasive universalist theory of value could be developed, what is the point of a theory that can explain everything but nothing in particular? At best, a persuasive universalistic explanation for a specific event still leaves room for a historically specific general explanation of that event. Thus good universal theory and good general theory are complementary rather than contradictory.

The question of what constitutes a "good" universal theory is, of course, highly problematic. A minimum requirement would be that it is based on some fundamental psychological trait in human nature and does not reflect some unexamined Eurocentric assumption about economic behavior. The founding fathers of neoclassical economics, for example Jevons (1871), based their universal theories on the psychology of pleasure and pain. In this respect their theories deal with an aspect of human psychology that does seem universal; however, as Malinowski, Mauss, Polanyi, and a host of anthropologists have pointed out, formalist theories are based on problematic Eurocentric assumptions about commerce and trade. The formalists, for their part, are uninterested in this dialogue because, as their spokesman, Milton Friedman (Friedman 1953: 3–43) argued, whether its assumptions are realistic is irrelevant to a scientific theory: what matter are valid and meaningful predictions. In this respect, then, the generalizing comparative and historical method of Polanyi, Marx, and others constitutes an incommensurable paradigm. Academic debate presupposes some common ground, some shared assumptions, from which disputation can proceed; but the universalist, psychologizing, ahistorical, abstract, assumptions-do-not-matter approach of neoclassical economics seems to have nothing in common with the generalist, comparative, historical, and concrete approaches of Polanyi and Marx.

This difference is best illustrated by comparing Polanyi's approach to the family and economy with that of Gary Becker – who won a "Nobel Prize" "for having extended the domain of micro-economic analysis to a wide range of human behavior and interaction, including non-market behavior." The extraordinary breadth of Becker's "extension" may be found in his *A Treatise on the Family* (Becker 1981), which covers not only the analysis of marriage, births, divorce, division of labor in households, prestige, and other non-material behavior of "persons from all walks of life" (Becker 1981: ix), but also nonhuman forms of biological life as well. This is because Becker believes that "nonhumans as well as humans allocate scarce resources while competing in various situations"(Becker 1981: x). In other words, his analysis extends beyond *Homo sapiens* to include Neanderthal man, *Homo erectus, Homo habilus*, the great apes, and beyond primates to birds, fishes, and so on.

Becker has taken the "universalism" of formalist economics to its outer logical limits. His theory is not only transcultural and transhistorical, it is trans-species; it can explain everything. The downside, of course, is that it can explain nothing in particular about *Homo sapiens* located in specific times and places, and nothing about the historically specific instituted processes we have consciously and unconsciously developed to organize our economic livelihoods. This is Polanyi's problem: if the formalist's agenda is "extension," then the substantivist's agenda is just the opposite, a concern with the historically specific and with its generality.

Polanyi's concepts can be arrayed along a general/specific continuum. Reciprocity and redistribution are the most general. For example, the latter, we have seen, has a "long and variegated history which leads up to almost modern times." Money-making of the kind based on the self-regulating market comes next. It is a more historically specific category, being limited in its generality to the period 1834–1931. Householding of the autarkic peasant proprietorship kind is the most specific (or least general) of all, being "a feature of economic life only on a more advanced level of agriculture."

Toward a critique of Polanyi's concept of householding

To critique is to dignify, to acknowledge common ground from which to criticize, modify, and transcend. My concern here is to lay the grounds for a critique of Polanyi's notion of householding, to attempt to move it forward while sharing the methodological assumptions on which it is based.

Householding as an autarkic form of peasant proprietorship is a concept whose sell-by date has passed. Whatever its merits as a concept for understanding a particular historical period in the development of capitalist agriculture, it is no longer useful for today's economy. Money-making is a principle of economic behavior that has conquered the globe, but in ways that vary from place to place and to a relative degree. Autarky as an institutional pattern is of relatively minor importance today. The peasant proprietor, a key figure in debates between Lenin and Kautsky, Chayanov, and so forth in the early twentieth century, has all but disappeared from the scene. The dying stages of this debate took place in the *Journal of Peasant Studies* from its inception in 1971 to its demise in 2001 when it became the *Journal of Agrarian Change*, a transformation that has been comprehensively charted by the editors in an essay that explains the name change (Bernstein and Byres 2001).

Just as money-making is not limited in its historical significance as a principle of economic behavior to the era when the self-regulating market was the dominant institutional pattern, so too "householding" as a general category is not defined solely by its realization as an autarkic form of peasant proprietorship. My own research on markets, merchants, and kinship in middle India (Gregory 1997) reveals that, contrary to orthodoxy, householding is not always autarkic and is sometimes embedded in market relations. In other words, "householding" may be either autarkic or non-autarkic, or both. This situation suggests a modification of Polanyi's basic framework, which may be represented in the following Venn diagram (Figure 8.4).

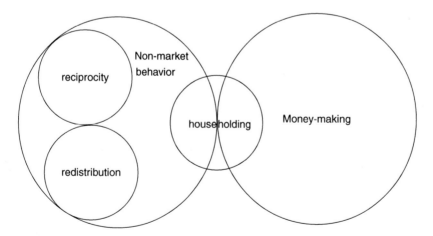

Figure 8.4 "Householding" may be either autarkic or non-autarkic, or both – a modification of Polanyi's (1944) basic framework.

Thus "householding" as a principle of economic behavior may straddle both the market and nonmarket domains. What is the substantive content of that part of householding which is embedded in the money-making domain? This entails questioning Polanyi's fundamental assumption that the economy is an *instituted* process. While *some* economic behavior is instituted, can we say that *all* economic behavior is an instituted process? Although economic behavior is often clearly enmeshed in institutions of a socioeconomic or religious kind, with distinct values and motives, is all economic behavior enmeshed in institutions? If not, what is the significance of the part of the economy that is not an instituted process?

Economy as a non-instituted process

The "institution" is to Polanyi's theory of the economy what the "incest taboo" is to Lévi-Strauss's theory of kinship (Lévi-Strauss 1949). Just as the incest taboo is the bridge that enabled *Homo sapiens* to cross from nature to culture in Lévi-Strauss's theory, the invention of the institution enabled the mechanical and biological elements of economic process to acquire a social reality in Polanyi's thinking. "The instituting of the economic process", notes Polanyi (1957b: 249–50):

vests that process with unity and stability; it produces a structure with a definite function in society; it shifts the place of the process in society, thus adding significance to its history; it centers interest on value, motives, and policy. Unity and stability, structure and function, history and policy spell out operationally the content of our assertion that the human economy is an instituted process.

An "instituted process" therefore is one that has evolved as an organizing mechanism to enhance social order among people in given places and times. An institution is the creation of two or more individuals and, if it continues to serve a useful purpose, it acquires a life of its own transcending human lives and intentions; its servants make rules and enforce them on others to ensure cooperative human behavior. An institution, like a human being, has an origin, a useful life, and an end; this lifetime can be anything from a few days to hundreds of years.

Polanyi was primarily concerned with the economic significance of three institutions: dual organization of the moiety kind; centralized territorial organizations in the form of chiefdoms, kingdoms, or states; and the self-regulating market. These institutions regulated economic behavior of a reciprocal, redistributive, and money-making type.

It is obvious that these three institutions transcend individual human lives and intentions in the sense that they are socio-centric. Take a moiety for example. An individual member may say that the eaglehawk moiety is "my moiety" or "our moiety" and that the crow moiety is "his moiety" or "their moiety," but the definition of a moiety is always socio-centric and absolute, never ego-centric and relative. This is because the boundary between two moieties is objective and not relative to the perspective of one ego. This form of dual organization is widespread throughout Amazonia and Oceania, but in middle India, where I have conducted fieldwork, there is another kind of "dual organization" that does not have an objective socio-centric institutional form. As there is almost no ethnographic data on the Indian form of dual organization and what little there is often confuses it with the moiety form, it is necessary to provide a brief ethnographic account, since I take it to be of fundamental importance for understanding economic processes of a non-instituted kind.

Unlike the Oceanic and Amazonian forms of dual organization that developed in locations where markets were virtually nonexistent and money-making was a relatively unimportant principle of economic behavior, the middle Indian form of dual organization developed in a society where money-making was important and so ancient that it is listed as the occupational specialization of one of the four original castes (*varna*) in the classic Sanskrit myths of creation. The Laws of Manu, for example, tell us that Vaisya were created "to tend cattle, to bestow gifts, ... to trade, to lend money, and to cultivate land" (Mueller 1979: 24).

The caste system is a classic example of the economy as an instituted process in Polanyi's sense. But at the household-level, "dualism" refers to a non-institutional, "us-centric," kindred-type group whose boundaries vary according to the perspective of ego's group, the "us." This non-institutional form is embedded in the caste system and the wider market economy, but has distinct values and motives of its own. The particular linguistic form of this opposition among the Halbi speakers of Bastar District is *dadabhai/saga*. The term *dadabhai* is a compound consisting of *dada*, "elder brother," and *bhai*, "brother." Thus *dadabhai* may be glossed as "brotherhood." *Saga* has the general meaning of "marriageable" and may be glossed as "the others." The terms are like kinship terms in that they are relative to an "ego," but unlike ordinary kinship terms the ego is a group rather than an individual. The ego-group in this particular case minimally comprises actual brothers, their wives, and their unmarried sisters.

The effect of this linguistic device is to divide the world into two groups, "us" and "them," but, unlike dual organization of the moiety kind, the boundary between the brotherhood and "the others" will vary according to the point of view of a particular brotherhood. Suppose, for example, that we have three groups of siblings A, B, and C. From the perspective of A, the others consist of B + C; from the perspective of B, the other consists of A + C; and from the perspective of C the others consist of A + B. If the three groups of siblings were part of a moiety system, the boundary between the two would be fixed from a socio-centric point of view. Suppose, for example, that A and B belonged to moiety X and C belongs to moiety Y, then the boundary between the two moieties is always A + B = X and C = Y, no matter whose perspective.

This oversimplified example assumes that sibling groups are discrete entities. In reality they are overlapping kindreds with elastic boundaries. These create ambiguities that are either resolved or made more ambiguous according to the contingent history of local-level politics. The brotherhood, by definition, has no objective socio-centric form and, when viewed from a socio-centric perspective, it may appear as an amorphous ethnic group without any internal structure because one person's brotherhood becomes someone else's "the others" at the level of society as a whole.

The middle Indian brotherhood is therefore not an institution in Polanyi's sense. It does not produce unity and stability nor a structure with a definite function, but it is a social form in that it has distinct values and motives. These values are us-centric rather than socio-centric; they are local rather than global and produce disunity, instability, and ambiguity. This is because they are not oriented toward a structural whole in the sense that a "global" institution like caste could be said to be. The household-level values of the "brotherhood," then, may be said to be "embedded" as Polanyi would say (or "encompassed" as Dumont would say) in the institution of caste as a social whole.

The values of the brotherhood are many and complex, but those that relate to money-making and exchange are very simple, and are clearly articulated by the people themselves: among the brotherhood money is shared, while for transactions involving the others money is either unilaterally given or reciprocated. For exchanges involving the "rest of the world" – that is, those who are neither *dadabhai* nor *saga* – it is profit-making of the familiar type. The values of the brotherhood are sometimes harmonious with the institutions in which they are embedded, sometimes dissonant. Thus, what is illegal activity from the socio-centric perspective of the state, may from the brotherhood's perspective be classified as legitimate.

Polanyi's conceptual toolbox, then, requires us to add a new concept: householding of the non-autarkic kind that is embedded in the market sphere where money is shared, given or taken depending on the relationship of the us-centric brotherhood to the rest of the world. The following diagram (Figure 8.5) captures these divisions. It should be noted that the concepts "sharing," "giving," and "taking" are generic categories that have many subdivisions. For example, "giving" may be one-way or two-way. "Taking" refers not only to profit-taking in the legal sense, but also to misappropriation, pilfering, embezzlement, plunder, and so forth, which, from the perspective of the brotherhood, may be legitimate under some circumstances. Similarly, "giving" includes "legitimate" gifts and bribes but, from the perspective of the brotherhood, what is important is the ambiguity, which it is a conscious and deliberate strategy to create.

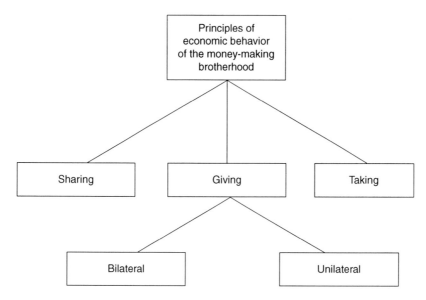

Figure 8.5 A new concept: householding of the non-autarkic kind.

The values of the brotherhoood

These different forms of exchange that I have distinguished under the heading of the non-autarkic household have their analogies in the classic types of exchange distinguished by Polanyi and by Sahlins (1972). Indeed, given the generality of the concepts, it would have been surprising if they didn't; but the market context in which the brotherhood is embedded and its non-institutional character mean that the "values and motives" informing and governing economic behavior are quite distinct. In what follows I provide some ethnographic evidence to illustrate something of the substantive content and generality of these concepts.

Sharing

One of the defining characteristics of the us-centric brotherhood is sharing. This idea is not just restricted to the people of middle India, but it seems to be general throughout India. Indeed, in many places, it is reflected in the language used to define the us-group. In the Tamil language of South India, for example, the brotherhood is called *pangali*, literally those who share (Dumont 1950–1951: 6). Among Hindi speakers in the North, the us-group is called *sapinda*. The word *pinda* refers to death-ritual gifts that serve to define the scope and limits of the *sapinda* (Trautmann 1981: 246ff). The Bengali word for this kindred grouping is *jnati*. This is not etymologically linked to sharing but, according to (Inden and Nicholas 1977: 17), the ideology of sharing is a defining characteristic of the *jnati* group. The actual constitution of the us-centric kindred varies across the country, but respect and trust are the key values that govern relationships within the brotherhood; the obligation to share is but one manifestation of the complex working out of these values.

The obligation to share in day-to-day economic behavior varies in reality too, of course. Of particular interest is the operation of the principle in money-making merchant families. My studies of such families in Bastar (Gregory 1997) reveal that sharing capital keeps rich families rich and poor families poor. This is because the "secret" to the success of a family business is access to credit and hence trading capital. Rich families share credit within the brotherhood and deny it to others. In poor families, on the other hand, demands from relatives for loans are a hindrance rather than a help.

In the markets of Bastar District merchants are economically differentiated by commodity and caste. For example, marketing of high-valued gold and silver jewelery is controlled by rich Marwari-speaking merchants from Rajasthan, while the marketing of low-valued glass bangles is in the hands of poor local families who are either landless or own a few hectares of land. The trading stock the rich merchant displays to attract customers has a market value of around (rupees) Rs 50,000 or more, while that of the poor merchant's glass bangles is around Rs 500 or less. Trading capital not only includes stock for sale but also the ability to extend retail credit. This is crucial for securing sales in rural areas where income streams are irregular. The poor merchant – aptly called the "penny capitalist" by Tax (1953) – is unable to extend this retail credit.

The trading capital required to become a rich merchant is a barrier to entry that few poor merchants manage to overcome. The rich, for their part, only share their capital within a generation group of real or parallel brothers, or across generations with sons and patrilateral nephews; the brotherhood may also include fictive kin. The trading capital of the poor merchant, on the other hand, is forever at risk of being depleted. At the end of a day the poor merchant may have sold goods to the value of Rs 100, of which Rs 20 represents profit while the other Rs 80 must go to replenish stocks. But some of the Rs 80 capital is often spent to meet the demands of relatives.

Sharing of money capital within the brotherhood, then, is a value that divides and differentiates a community rather than uniting it. It is embedded within market institutions that provide unity and stability, but in a different sense. The periodic market system in north Bastar is an "instituted process" and provides a classic example of "unity and stability" in Polanyi's terms. The center of this system is Kondagaon, the biggest town in the region. Tens of thousands of people gather here every Sunday for the big weekly market. During the weekdays the rich merchants of Kondagoan travel in different directions to many smaller markets in the towns and villages of the region each occurring on a fixed day. On any one weekday, as many as ten or twenty small markets are going on in different parts of the region; these attract from a few hundred to a few thousand people, depending on the size of the town or village. On Saturdays three intermediate-sized markets are held in the second-level centers of the district. The spatio-temporal structure of the system is such that villagers living anywhere in the district have a market they can attend on any day of the week no more than a few hours walk away. From the perspective of the community as a whole the system of periodic markets is a highly structured institution serving the important function of exchanging locally produced surplus grain with the manufactured imports the people need for their socio-cultural and biological reproduction.

The importance of the sharing of money-capital for the success of the merchant brotherhood has a generality that extends beyond Bastar and possibly beyond India as well. "The genius of a trading community," argues Timberg in his study of the Marwari merchant families of India, "*lies in its manipulation of credit*" (Timberg 1978: 29, emphasis added). Timberg shows how this enabled them to acquire the capital to become the leading trading and business community in India. The Marwari merchant family is to India what the Chinese are to South East Asia and the Jews were to Europe. Marwar was the name of the princely state now known as Jodhpur District; the term "Marwari" is used today as a generic label for people who come from this area and its surroundings. It includes a heterogenous collection of people from different castes and tribes, but the Marwari dialect they speak sets them apart at this very general level of classification. Within the Marwaris, the Jains are the undisputed mercantile elite. Jainism is an ancient Indian religion originating in anti-Brahman protest (Carrithers and Humphrey 1991). Jains deny the sanctity of the Vedas. They question the ideological claim that Brahmans were the indispensable intermediaries with the gods. They protest the hereditary power of the Brahmans and their costly animal sacrifices. In its place, they have developed a doctrine of non-violence and vegetarianism of an extraordinarily uncompromising kind. "Jains," as Carrithers and Humphrey (1991: 1) note, "are to avoid harm to even the smallest living thing, to purify themselves strenuously through self-mortification, and to conduct lives of strict moral rectitude." Jains are also known for their mobility: every major city and market town of any importance in India has a resident Jain community. These communities, and the broader Marwari grouping of which they are part, often control most of the mercantile activity in any given town. One estimate has it that Marwaris control over 60 percent of the assets of Indian industry (Timberg 1978: 11). This is mere guesswork, but few people familiar with the workings of the Indian economy would question it.

The Marwari Jains, then, offer an example of the brotherhood in the socio-centric form of an endogamous ethnic group. To understand the concrete workings of the economy as a non-instituted process, it is necessary to take the us-centric perspective of a particular group of brothers; but as my concern here is to make the general point about the role of sharing of capital in the brotherhood as a means of accumulation for the brotherhood, I refer the reader to the concrete illustrations in my book *Savage Money* (Gregory 1997: Chapter V).

The benefits of manipulating credit have also been discovered by brotherhoods who specialize in illegal commodities and violence elsewhere. The Mafia is the classic example. The etymology of the word "mafia" is "scoundrel" or "thief," clearly an outsider's perspective. From the us-centric perspective of the brotherhood it is *L'Onorata Societa* and *N'Dranghita* in the Calabrian dialect, "The Honoured Society" (Woodward 1979: 18). This self-definition highlights the values of honor and respect that inform internal dealings of brotherhoods everywhere. Indeed, as Ianni and Reuss-Ianni (1972) point out in their ethnography, *A Family Business: Kinship and Social Control in Organized Crime,* the *mafioso* is a "man of respect" who has "friends" (1972: 24–5). The origin of the mafia is found in the private armies maintained by landowners to protect lands and families from bandits (Ianni and Reuss-Ianni 1972: 25). Following the industrial revolution in Europe, the migration of Italians overseas, and the development of a self-regulating global market, the brotherhoods extended their kinship webs globally and some moved into illegal commerce. These extended family networks were the foundation on which their wealth and power grew (Ianni and Reuss-Ianni 1972: 156); and, because the wealth required policing, private armies were developed to protect it. The brotherhood, then, is not only an informal bank that distributes credit to its members, but it may also be an informal state to the extent that it deals in violence.

If the sharing of property within the brotherhood is a means of capital accumulation for the rich, then it can work in precisely the opposite way for the poor and the urban *lumpenproletariat* more generally. Such a process is often romanticized as a "sharing and caring" ethos that celebrates the egalitarian nature of kinship relations. While this no doubt happens in many cases, especially between very close kin, a closer examination of the concrete workings of the values of the us-centric brotherhood reveals that it often shades into "taking and self-interest." This is because, as mentioned above, the boundary between the brotherhood and the others is an ambiguous gray zone that is redefined with every transaction. Those in need are naturally inclined to cast the brotherhood net as wide as possible to ensnare their better off relatives; those who are relatively better off are naturally inclined to limit the kindred net as much as possible and to *dodge* requests for money. "Dodge" is the key word here, for to refuse is to cut off relations and spark a dispute which may cause problems in the longer term. The limits of the brotherhood are decided by a never-ending struggle between the ethos of caring and sharing, on the one hand, and taking and self-interest, on the other.

A case study from my fieldnotes illustrates this point. The glass bangle trade in Bastar is dominated by a local community who have turned it into their caste speciality. By any measure these merchants are poor, with a trading capital of Rs 500 or less (equivalent to about 200 kg of rice). This takes the form of stock which is neatly laid out in rows on a mat on the ground in front of them. At the big Sunday market in Kondagaon some twenty or thirty sellers gather in one alley with close relatives sitting beside one another. Two of these were married sisters, Sita and Anita. Married women in Bastar are severed from their natal brotherhood at marriage and become members of their husband's brotherhood. However, it is a particular quirk of the Bastar system that the husbands of two sisters are regarded as brothers and hence members of the same brotherhood (*dadabhai*). This linkage, though, is the weakest of all brotherhood links because the "us" linkage is affinal rather than agnatic. Sita's husband, for example, will be much closer to his own brothers than he will be to Sita's sister's husband.

Sita was obviously much better off than her sister Anita: her display of glass bangles was twice the size of Anita's, a disparity that was mirrored in the quality of Sita's sari and her adornments. Sita's husband, too, was a hard worker and had various sources of informal income. Anita's husband, by contrast, was not so industrious and was fond of the local liquor. Needless to say, Anita was constantly pressuring Sita for trading capital in the form of glass bangles. Sita, in her dual capacity as sister and member of the same *dadabhai*, had a double motive for sharing and caring for her sister, which she did. However, tensions developed between their husbands, for Sita's husband regarded Anita's as a good-for-nothing who should be ignored. Anita's husband, by contrast, was constantly pressuring his wife to dun Sita and her husband for money. The tension between the husbands spilled over to the sisters whose loyalties were divided. Finally Sita, fed up with her sister's demands, began to ignore her repeated requests, making a token gesture of help now and then. On my last visit in 2005 the sisters were estranged and no longer talked to each other.

I have many case studies of successful sharing among poor merchants, but I have stressed estrangement here because, while kin relations of this kind are extremely important, they are often ignored in the literature. Estrangement is a particular fate of kin relations because only previously related kin can become estranged. Estrangement requires studied avoidance of eye contact and feigned deafness to the words of the estranged relative; indifference is not an option because only complete strangers have this luxury. The effect, of course, is eventually to alienate kin and turn them into others.

This form of market-embedded sharing differs from the classic form of generalized exchange defined by Sahlins (1972) in that there kinship relations define sharing, whereas here sharing defines kinship. This is a distinction between economy as an instituted process and as a non-instituted process. In the classic case, the socio-centric institutions of kinship, such as moieties, exogamous descent groups, and the like, structure the form of the transaction; but in the case of us-centric brotherhoods the boundaries of the brotherhood are a matter of day-by-day negotiation as kin become others and others become kin.

Anthropologists have only recently turned their theoretical attention to this form of sharing among the *lumpenproletariat* embedded in a market economy. Peterson (1993), in an important article dealing with Australian Aborigines, has coined the term "demand sharing" to describe it. Having observed that Aboriginal people are constantly confronting each other (and outsiders) with forthright demands of the kind, "I want to owe you five dollars," he was led to the paradoxical question of why recipients often have to demand generosity (Peterson 1993: 861). He observed that, *pace* Sahlins, demand sharing often extended well beyond closely related people, that the demands made accumulation difficult, and that they were blocked by hiding, secretive behavior, and lying, but never by outright rejection. His conclusion was that demand sharing reflects an underlying tension between autonomy and relatedness that runs throughout Aboriginal life (Peterson 1993: 871). "Relatedness" here does not refer to the institutionalized relatedness defined by their moiety organization, but is a kindred-like notion of the brotherhood kind.

The idea seems to be one of great generality among the poor of the world, but it takes on culturally specific variations that reflect the historical, geographical, and ethnographic contexts of its operation. For example, Hart's classic study of the "informal economy" of the slums of Accra reports variations on the themes I have developed above. We find commodity specialization by ethnic group:

Ethnic group concentrations act as informal rings inhibiting entry into certain commodity trades. The whole of meat distribution, from cattle trading to butchering, is dominated by the Islamic Hausa community, and non-Muslims have great difficulty breaking in, even at the lowest level. (Hart 1973: 73)

We also find an ethos of sharing that inhibits accumulation:

The egalitarian philosophy of peoples, inured by generations of peasant insecurity to the disbursement of surpluses as a form of social insurance, makes private accumulation a difficult, though not impossible, task, and allows those who do not benefit from the informal economy to consume the earnings of those who do. (Hart 1973: 87)

In his most mature reflection on his Accra fieldwork (Hart 1988) we learn more about the values and motivations of this "barely differentiated Dickensian mob, of water carriers, bread sellers, shit-shovellers, taxi drivers, pickpockets, and prostitutes" whose economy seemed as if it was "being made, unmade, and remade from day to day." The reason for this was that it was "not easy for migrants to transfer their customary rural *institutions* to the city" (Hart

1988: 179, emphasis added). Institutions provide form, structure, and ethical standards to follow; an informal economy, by definition, is without institutions of this kind. When the migrants moved to the city they were confronted with new institutions – the state and the market in particular – but, to the extent they were denied access to the rewards of this new formal economy, they had no option but to involve themselves in the non-instituted processes of the informal economy. Hart does not use this Polanyi-inspired language but his ethnography may be interpreted in this way:

> At home kinship is structured by lineage organization, lending the full authority of ancestors to fathers, husbands, and senior brothers. Away from home the migrants abjured any simulation of this religion of descent. Genealogical differences of generation were collapsed into a single conceptual brotherhood; ancestor worship could not be practised since the structure of home groups necessary to make up a sacrificial congregation could never be replicated. The sheer unequal power of parenthood writ large was mainly absent in the slums, where ethnic solidarity found expression in beer talk and kinship was a domestic relationship of uncertain moral provenance. (Hart 1988: 179)

The brotherhood he speaks of here is similar to the one I have described for India, with generational difference elided. Hart also speaks of a "zone of *association,* [whose] strongest form of expression is *friendship,* the negotiated order of free individuals joined by affection and shared experience rather than by legal sanction or the ties of blood." It is in this area of social life, he adds, "that trust plays so prominent a role, relatively unmediated by the formal obligations of kinship and contract" (Hart 1988: 179; cf. Gudeman, Chapter 2, and Beckert, Chapter 3, in this volume). I noticed in the small market town were I did my fieldwork that friendship and trust were more important among the poor migrants than the rich. Poor migrants tend to marry "incorrectly," have short genealogical memory, and often cannot afford to maintain links with home. The kin-based brotherhoods of the rich, by contrast, are recorded in books kept by a special genealogist caste, go back many generations, and, because of migration, cast their web over the whole of India. Whatever the case, friendship in India is more concerned with giving than sharing, and I now turn to this topic.

Giving

If sharing as a non-instituted process among us-centric brotherhoods embedded in a market economy must be distinguished from the sharing that occurs in a non-market economy embedded in social institutions of kinship (e.g. the moiety), so too giving from the brotherhood to the others as a non-instituted process must likewise be distinguished from its classic instituted form.

Giving in its more general form is either bilateral or unilateral. As an instituted process in Polanyi's work, this distinction is between "reciprocity" and "redistribution." In Lévi-Strauss (1949) it becomes one between "restricted" exchange and "generalized" exchange. Whatever label we choose, the socio-centric institution is invariant as a rule: exogamous moiety or unilineal descent group; bilateral cross-cousin marriage or matrilateral cross-cousin marriage. Giving from an us-centric brotherhood to the others ("them") does not obey any rule because giving, by definition, is always to the others.

The situation in India is extremely complex because both exogamous clans and brotherhoods exist, and there is much confusion in the literature as a result. In middle India, for example, where the brotherhood exists in it classic form with a distinct appellation, *dadabhai*, it is often mistaken for an exogamous moiety of the type found in Amazonia or Australia. Another distinguishing feature is that the brotherhood has always been embedded in a money economy in India, but the extraordinary economic development of recent years has transformed this situation.

In spite of its complexity and the unresolved nature of many of the theoretical debates, the broad outlines are relatively unproblematic. Unilateral giving is informed by Brahmanic values and obliges inferior wife-givers to make continual gifts of money and property to superior wife-receivers; bilateral giving, on the other hand, is more of a low-caste form of giving among equals. These forms of giving are associated with dowry and bridewealth, respectively, and recent developments have seen their increasing monetization, indeed their hyperinflation. This has been associated with another change in the wedding ritual: the introduction of the "reception" (the English word is used in Bastar District).

This is a classic example of conspicuous consumption. Prestige is the obvious motivation for the bride's father, but the obligation to spend derives as much from the expectations of others as from the desire of the father for social recognition. The cost of a wedding in India is a direct function of one's wealth. "As much money as you have, a wedding will cost that much," an informant once told me. The result is that the wedding industry has become one of the biggest in India and weddings are one of the greatest single causes of indebtedness there.

For the elite this potlatch behavior seems to have no limits, as the following newspaper report shows.

PARIS 5/12/05 – An Indian steel tycoon reportedly paid US$60 million for his daughter's wedding – a six-day bash for 1,500 guests in France's most sumptuous settings, including Versailles. Lakshmi Mittal rented the Tuileries garden in Paris one night and a gallery at Versailles another night to celebrate the marriage of his 23-year-old daughter, Vanisha, to 25-year-old Amit Bhatia, according to Thursday's edition of Paris Match magazine. Louis XIV's lavish chateau apparently was not enough – Mittal also had a makeshift castle built at a park in Saint-Cloud, outside the capital, Paris Match said. The actual wedding took place Tuesday at another chateau, Vaux-le-Vicomte. The $60 million price tag was about the cost of an Airbus A320 passenger jet. The wedding put on by Mittal, named by Forbes magazine as one of the richest people in the world, cost more than the recent royal wedding in Spain. Paris Match said the wedding of Spain's Crown Prince Felipe to TV anchorwoman Letizia Ortiz cost $35 million. (AP 2004)

In the same year I witnessed in a remote town of middle India an equivalent situation when a local *nouveau riche* "tribal" (to use the official Indian word) spent Rs 100,000 (US $2,500) on a wedding the likes of which had never been seen before in the community. For the first seven days the ritual followed the tradition, but on the last night a "reception" was held in the classic form seen in Bollywood movies (and in Hollywood movies such as *Monsoon Wedding*).

These cases suggest some theoretical pointers and paradoxes in the sharing and giving behavior of the commercial brotherhood: whereas the sharing of credit among the brotherhood is a source of capital accumulation for them, the giving of gifts and hospitality to the others is a major drain on resources and, for some, a source of financial ruin. The dilemma arises because the brotherhood needs the others for its own social reproduction. Giving to the others creates alliances, but its meaning will vary according to the concrete situations in which it occurs.

When the motive is commercial reproduction, giving to the others enters that gray zone between what the state defines as black or white, legal or illegal, legitimate or illegitimate. When does a gift become a bribe? When does acquiring become stealing? Institutions resolve these questions by appeal to an abstract law, ethical code, or practice. For a non-institution such as the brotherhood it is a question of morality, and this is contingent on the concrete facts in question. The morality of the brotherhood is often at odds with the ethics and law of the state, but if the brotherhood is powerful, well-connected, and a generous giver (e.g. unilateral gifts to charity), then the contradiction is non-antagonistic.

This double standard helps us understand the paradox of the respectable Mafia family. In the Australian town of Griffith, Italians now make up more than 50 percent of the population. Roughly half of these migrated from one village in southern Italy, called Plati, the others having come from various places in northern Italy. The Sergi clan from Plati are well known for their mafia activities, such as the production and sale of drugs, murder, and so on. In 1977 a leading Christian businessman and antidrugs crusader was shot dead in the main street. A royal commission inquiring into his death publicly named twenty-one members of the Sergi family to be charged with drug trafficking and possibly with murder. The local newspaper identified them by means of a kinship chart on the front page. None of these men has been charged. Instead, one made the 1997 Australia Day honors list; on the same day his father was made Griffith citizen of the year award for his generous gifts to charity. The family pursues respectability and honor with the same ruthlessness and efficiency that it pursues wealth; unilateral giving is a means to this end, but when it is successful it brings rewards of both a material and immaterial kind (Woodward 1979 Bottom 1988; Moor 1989).

Taking

Taking as a non-instituted economic process, like sharing and giving, is defined always with respect to the values of the us-centric brotherhood. In Bastar sharing is among brothers (*dadabhai*), giving to others who are friends or remote kin (*saga*), and taking from others who are strangers (*pardesia*). This tripartite division of transactors divides "them" into two subcategories, *saga* and *pardesia*. Another way to split the trichotomy is to lump the *dadabhai* and *saga* together as "tribal brothers," as opposed to the alien others. We find this dichotomy in the Christian tradition; it is the basis of what Nelson (1969), a Weberian sociologist, has called the "Deuteronomic Double Standard," after the famous commandment in the Bible:

- XXIII: 19. Thou shalt not lend upon usury (*neshek*) to thy brother (*l'ahika*); usury of money, usury of victuals, usury of anything that is lent upon usury.
- XXIII: 20. Unto a stranger (*nokri*) that mayest lend upon usury; but unto thy brother thou shall not lend upon usury, that the Lord they God may bless thee in all that thou settest thine land to in the land whither thou goes to possess it. (Deuteronomy 23.19)

This Deuteronomic Double Standard is a particular variation on a theme of great generality that defines taking as "usury of money, usury of victuals, usury of anything that is lent upon usury." The general idea here is that you profit from the other, not your tribal brother. Profiteering, from the perspective of the brotherhood, is any activity that it deems legitimate, be it interest from moneylending, profit from commercial trade, exploitation, stealing, or plunder. These values have informed the economic behavior of Christians and non-Christians, believers and non-believers, Europeans and non-Europeans from all corners of the planet.

Consider once again Hart's account of the slum dwellers of Accra, where thieving – one activity among many – covers the whole gamut from pickpocketing to armed robbery. "Thieves," he notes (Hart 1973: 76), "practise openly, but usually outside their home neighbourhood. This explains the paradox … that while respected and even admired by his immediate social milieu as long as his victims are outsiders, the thief is hounded by crowds, beaten up and vilified wherever he is caught."

These subaltern values are also graphically illustrated in Gary Kildea's *Celso and Cora*, a film about a street vendor in Manila. Here is an extract. It is nighttime; Celso is talking to the camera while selling cigarettes to two customers,

Celso: Ah … about these police. As they say, they're so irritating sometimes but there's nothing we can do. It's just the way it is. They're the rules of the game here in the Philippines. For example, they take it on themselves to prohibit sidewalk vendors but it's actually an honorable profession. They can't catch any of these hold-up men. But sidewalk vendors ... they're more in their league. Just like what happened to me one day, right here. A man came asking for "blue ...." See "blue-seal" import brands are banned. They're illegal. Or, as they say, they're illegal if you get caught. But if you don't, they're not. So he asked if I had any. I didn't know he was police. So I handed him some. That's when he produced his badge. 'Look here I'm police. What's the price for me?' Naturally I was startled. I was taken off guard. I said "10 Sir," which was, anyway, my usual price. I stood my ground. He said to me, "I'm from the police. Is it still the same?" "That's the correct price, Sir," I said. So then he grabbed a whole handful of candy like this. "These are included, huh?" he said. It was around 3 pesos worth that handful of candy. My "capital" for "blue" is 7.50, so I ended up short by 50 cents. Which was OK. It's just how it goes. (Kildea 1983: shot 44 at 27.53 min)

Here, Celso is talking to a man behind a trade store counter where he went to buy some timber to fix the ceiling of the slum dwelling he is renting:

Celso: That's it. Just pad the receipt a bit. It'll be deducted from the rent. Because ... you know ... that'll come off my rent. But what about my labour? Naturally I deserve something for the work. (Kildea 1983: shot 71 at 41.50 min)

Understanding the economy as a non-instituted process, then, depends on the point of view; but the shift from the socio-centric perspective of the institution to the us-centric perspective of people like Celso and his family introduces ambiguity. From the perspective of the state, they are petty criminals who engage in illegal trade and steal from their landlord; but from Celso's perspective, the law is unjust and the police are the real thieves. Furthermore, the absence of wage-labor as an institutionalized process means that wages have to be taken because they will not be given. As Celso explained to the filmmaker,

> That's really how it is, pare,
> With the life of the poor,
> It's not equal.
> (Kildea 1983: shot 120 at 102.12 min)

Conclusion

The fate of householding as an instituted process should by now be clear. Of all the tools in Polanyi's conceptual toolbox, this one had the least generality, or, to put it the other way round, the greatest historical specificity. Its rise was tied to the development of capitalist agriculture, and so was its demise, because production for use in an economy geared to production for exchange was an anomaly. Whatever merit the concept has for understanding the past, it is clearly of little or no use in today's world, where even agriculture has gone beyond the Green Revolution. This, perhaps, is why the Polanyi Institute removed it from the conceptual toolbox. The state, the community, and the market are the key economic institutions today; the household has no – or at least very little – institutional function.

My experience of fieldwork in India, however, suggests that Polanyi's concept of the economy needs to be extended. The economy is an *instituted* process, but it also needs to include "non-instituted" processes like the "brotherhood." I have distinguished between householding when embedded in non-market social relations and a version that is embedded in the market, and have proposed the notion of "brotherhood" as a positive form of the negation "non-instituted process."

Brotherhood is a generic concept of which the householding brotherhood – the concern of this chapter – is but one species among many. The householding brotherhood is a minimal category. Other more inclusive conceptions include the tribal brotherhood, the ethnic brotherhood, the religious brotherhood, and so on, each with its own distinct values and motives. The word commonly used to describe these larger groupings is "identity," a concept more usually associated with the politics of violence and the taking of lives than with the taking of profits. Consideration of the economic significance of the brotherhood in this larger sense is a subject for further research.

The economy is not only a non-instituted process at the level of the household, but also more generally for brotherhoods, especially the religious brethren, who have a global spread. Furthermore, the world economy today has become a non-instituted process. This is because, as Polanyi noted in *The Great Transformation*, the gold standard was the centerpiece of the self-regulating market as a nineteenth-century institution. The UK pound sterling gold standard of which he wrote ended with the Great War, but was replaced by a US dollar gold standard in the 1930s. This lasted until the breakdown of the Bretton Woods fixed-parity exchange rate system in 1971. Since then the world economy has had no institution to unify and stabilize international trade. The "informal economy," to use Hart's term, has now become the dominant mode. Violence, corruption, plunder, and theft are fast becoming the norm rather than the exception, as Hart's important contributions to the analysis of this global problem suggest:

Rapidly expanding religious movements, especially Pentecostal Christianity and Sufist Islam, establish connection with world society for their members, bypassing local and national structures that serve only to impede their progress. The issue of criminal organization inside and outside the formal bureaucracy cannot be wished away. These forms fuse in new hybrid organizations, as the following story illustrates. An illegal trade has grown up in the southern French cities of Marseilles and Montpellier. It supplies cars and car parts to Africa and is staffed mainly by North Africans. Some of them dream of reclaiming the Mediterranean for Islam and they all ignore official paperwork, relying on word-of-mouth agreements between religious brothers. This traffic has grown so big that the French car industry has shifted its operations significantly southward to meet a demand that the official records miss entirely. Now Russian and Latin American mafias are becoming involved and the gangs are diversifying to Brussels and Hamburg as part of a global strategy. Nor is mainstream French politics without its criminal side. We are now learning about President Mitterrand's slush fund supplied by petrol companies and wholesale distributors in Africa. And his successor remains tainted by corruption in the Paris mayor's office. (Hart 2004)

Understanding the economy today both at the household and global levels poses new conceptual and ethnographic challenges because the economy has moved away from its previous location in society. We can usefully draw on our intellectual ancestors, such as Polanyi, because their concepts, limited as they are by history and geography, have substance that allows them to be modified for new times and places. The more important conclusion to be taken from Marx and Polanyi, however, is that theoretical advances must be grounded in historical and ethnographic research.

9 Contesting *The Great Transformation*: Work in comparative perspective

Gerd Spittler

Karl Polanyi deserves great credit for including the results of anthropological research in his studies on the development of capitalism in Europe in *The Great Transformation* (1944). This distinguishes him from most other historians not only in his own time but still today. However, the effectiveness of his enterprise was limited by his method of comparison, which relied heavily on dichotomous categories, and by his failure to give enough attention to the subject of work. In this chapter I will first discuss Polanyi's ethnographic sources and show how these are embedded in a longstanding German debate on work. I will then give two examples of how work can be systematically analyzed, "work as interaction" and "working abroad: expeditions and migrants," in order to suggest what a comparative anthropology of work might look like.

The Great Transformation: ethnographic sources and the subject of work

The fourth chapter "Societies and Economic Systems" is only one of the twenty-one chapters of Polanyi's great work, but it is crucial for his argument. In this chapter he formulates alternative concepts of economy that contrast with the capitalist market economy of the nineteenth century. He shows that there were and are cultures in which society is not subject to the market economy, but where the economy is integrated into society. In the latter the economy is not an isolated institution, but is embedded in social relations. Man is not addicted to exchange and profit by nature, but seeks social acceptance. The embedded economy does not function according to the principle of *exchange*, but according to the social principles of *reciprocity, redistribution*, and *house-holding*. Polanyi finds examples of such economies in the Middle Ages and in the ancient world, but, above all, in the literature of social anthropology, which he began to read at this point for the first time.

Polanyi quotes a number of English, German, and American anthropologists, but his most important sources are Bronislaw Malinowski's *Argonauts of the Western Pacific* (1922) and Richard Thurnwald's *Economics in Primitive Communities* (1932). The latter is frequently quoted from the German version

(*Werden, Wandel und Gestaltung der Wirtschaft im Lichte der Völkerforschung*), which was not identical with the English version although published simultaneously.[1] Polanyi takes his ethnographic examples mainly from Malinowski and his theoretical concepts from Thurnwald. For the concepts of *embeddedness* and *reciprocity*, Polanyi refers to both Malinowski and Thurnwald, while the concept of *redistribution* is attributed to Thurnwald alone: "Thurnwald discovered that apart from, and sometimes combined with, such reciprocating behaviour, the practice of storage and redistribution was of the most general application from the primitive hunting tribe to the largest empires" (Polanyi 2001: 279). Throughout his life Thurnwald was interested not only in primitive societies but also in the archaic cultures of the Middle East for his comparative "ethno-sociology."

Thurnwald is also an important source for Polanyi's subsequent chapter, "Evolution of the Market Pattern," where he shows that trade, market, and money also exist in non-capitalist societies, although they function according to different rules, since they are embedded in the society. "Thurnwald established the fact that the earliest forms of trade simply consisted in procuring and carrying objects from a distance. Essentially it is a hunting expedition" (2001: 281). Thurnwald also noted the presence of money in many societies which had not developed into a market economy. He is also mentioned in later chapters, where Polanyi compares the destructive tendencies of colonialism with those of early capitalism with reference to Thurnwald (1935). The anthropologist is credited with a better vision of the parallels than historians had been able to develop: "Thurnwald's penetrating mind recognized that the cultural catastrophe of black society today is closely analogous to that of a large part of white society in the early days of capitalism. The social historian alone still misses the point of analogy" (2001: 166).

Polanyi's interpretations are sometimes personal and even idiosyncratic. Although he gives long quotations in the appendix, these do not always represent the nuanced argumentation of the authors. In particular, he largely ignores a basic element in the economic analyses of the authors he cites: work. For Polanyi work is not an independent analytical category. Work is mainly defined in terms of what it is not: "the absence of the principle of laboring for remuneration; the absence of the principle of least effort" (2001: 49). The positive side appears only in a heading in the appendix: "The usual incentives to labor are not gain but reciprocity, competition, joy of work, and social approbation" (2001: 277). Here we find elements of an analysis of work as human action, but they are not elaborated in the subsequent argument.

---

[1] Polanyi explicitly acknowledges the central importance of Malinowski and Thurnwald for this chapter (see the note on page 50). Other anthropologists are also quoted, but less systematically: Lowie, Radcliffe-Brown, Goldenweiser, Benedict, Herskovits.

In Chapter 6 "The Self-regulating Market and the Fictitious Commodities: Labor, Land, and Money," Polanyi returns once more to the subject of work. The transformation of labor, land, and money into commodities forms the heart of *The Great Transformation*. "Of the three, one stands out: labor is the technical term used for human beings, in so far as they are not employers but employed ... But as the organization of labor is only another word for the forms of life of the common people, this means that the development of the market system would be accompanied by a change in the organization of society itself. All along the line, human society had become an accessory of the economic system" (1944: 75). Here we can see clearly that Polanyi is not interested so much in work as in the life of the working class in general. A discussion of the conditions of the working class which omits the experience of work is bound to focus on the poor as victims, and this is what we find in Polanyi. However, more goes on in the workplace than just exploitation. We need to pay attention to discipline, time organization, cooperation, relations with machines, self-assurance, and many other factors to understand the history of the labor movement.[2]

This lack of interest in work distinguishes Polanyi from Malinowski and Thurnwald, who both represent a long German-speaking tradition that places work in the center of the analysis. Polanyi quotes some of the earlier authors (Karl Marx, Karl Bücher, and Max Weber), but not with respect to work. From them he could have learned to define work in ways going beyond his dichotomy "differentiated versus embedded." They stressed the importance of the human capacity for work (*Arbeitsvermögen*), which includes physical strength and manual skills, but also energy, knowledge, and perseverance. The act of work is not exhausted in performance, but includes other aspects. It may bring satisfaction or frustration. The worker may do his work more or less efficiently. He may be eager or unwilling. Work may be regarded as meaningful or meaningless. The worker may realize his identity in it, or be alienated. He can, but does not have to, see it as a purely instrumental activity. He may also turn it into play, a struggle, or a creative art form.

Few careful ethnographic studies of work were undertaken in the nineteenth century. A serious ethnography of work was launched only in the twentieth century by three professional anthropologists who built on earlier German social scientists. Karl Weule (1908), Richard Thurnwald (1932a and b), and Bronislaw Malinowski (1922, 1925, 1935) all maintained their interest in the subject of work throughout their anthropological careers. No one has described the different aspects of performance more precisely than Thurnwald: knowledge and skill, performance and compulsion, care and accuracy, perseverance

---

[2] This is what Thompson realized when he wrote his famous article (1967). On the later evolution of the relation between work and the labor movement today, see Price 1982, 1983.

and patience, discipline and force, diligence and laziness, effort and fatigue, devotion and indifference, ability to withstand strain, concentration and the intensification of work, the intertwining of mental and physical elements, feelings of pleasure, but also of a tedious and dreary burden.

Not only performance but also the rationality of work is an important subject for these three scholars. Weule does not doubt that the work processes of primitive people are rational, taking into account their limited technical equipment. Thurnwald's analysis is much more thorough: for him, any use of tools, even among primitive peoples, is necessarily based on a specific "technical theory." The rationalization of work has a history which for Thurnwald does not simply begin with the separation of empirical experience and science (Weule) or with the influence of higher religions (Weber). Malinowski's great contribution to the rationality debate is his discussion of the relationship between magic and religion, on the one hand, and work and technology, on the other. His ideas in this respect changed over the years. In his early works (e.g. 1912), religion and magic are the only forces capable of making people perform regular, coordinated, and strenuous work. Primitive people do not distinguish between magic and technology. However, in his studies of the Trobrianders, Malinowski assumes that they make a strict distinction between technology and magic. The fact that work is based on empirical experience does not mean that it is organized only on the basis of technical efficiency. The *economic principle of the maximum of effect for the minimum of effort* holds only with reservations. Rather, it is the joy derived from work and artistic motives that dominate.

I do not wish to discuss these authors in detail here, since I have written a whole book about them (Spittler 2008a). I owe much to them, but "on the shoulders of giants" we can now look to the future and compare work in different societies in a fresh way. In what follows I will give two examples of such comparisons.

Work as interaction

Whatever else work may be, it serves – by definition – to attain a goal. Work that does not achieve its goal is ineffective. Effectiveness is thus an important feature of work. Effectiveness has to be distinguished from efficiency. Efficiency is measured not only by the results, but by the relation between the means and the result. However, the efficiency, or in more general terms, the rationality of work is not at all self-evident.

Work may basically be conceived of in two different ways: as transformation of an object or as interaction with a subject (Spittler 2003). The first paradigm, which I call the "technical paradigm," implies the transformation of a passive object. The process is controllable and may be planned. When one has the appropriate knowledge, skill, and power, one can form an object according to one's ideas. The means for this are tools or machines. The second paradigm, which I call the "interactive paradigm," assumes an object that is not fully controllable. An element of unpredictability is involved. One devotes great attention to the object, tries to become acquainted with it, interprets the messages that this object emits, and reacts to them.

The first paradigm seems to be constitutive of the modern position. We "work over" a piece of wood in order to make a spoon. We work on a piece of raw stone and produce a club or a blade. We transform the soil in order to make it agriculturally useful. Production means for us making a product through the transformation of material, of things. Habermas assumes the universal existence of this technical paradigm. In his essays "Arbeit und Interaktion" (Work and Interaction) (1968) and "Technik und Wissenschaft als Ideologie" (Technique and Knowledge as Ideology) (published together as Habermas 1968) he makes a distinction – based on an interpretation of Hegel and Marx – between two types of action, "work" and "interaction." Work is "instrumental action" and follows technical rules. Interaction is "communicative" action and follows its own norms. The two types of action have to be kept strictly separated. Work is absolutely essential, but as Habermas observes – criticizing Marx – interaction should not be derived from work. Conversely, and here Habermas directs his remarks against Herbert Marcuse, work cannot be organized as an interaction (Habermas 1968: 56). If we want to be technically successful, we cannot communicate with nature; we have to work on it. Work belongs to the area of technique and economy. The task of the cultural sciences is to examine interaction. Habermas has adhered to this approach consistently and refined it in his *The Theory of Communicative Action* (1984).

But can work and interaction really be so clearly divided? Is interaction free of instrumentality? I shall argue that work is not only a matter of working on objects but can also be a matter of interaction between subjects. The idea that not only humans possess their own sense of self-will or self-determination (*Eigensinn, Eigenwillen*), but also animals, plants, even things that we regard as dead material, is widespread in non-industrial, non-capitalist societies. Many objects, or rather subjects, have their own peculiarities (*Eigenarten*), which one must know and take into account, and also a self-will, which is not fully controllable. This self-will may be so strong that these subjects are as powerful as humans or even may dominate them. Work becomes a *game*, a *fight*, a *service*, a *caring*, an *exchange*.

Let me give just one example. According to the Kel Ewey Tuareg, humans and animals, and even things, have a well-developed self-will (Spittler 1998). This self-will may turn into resistance as soon as others try to influence it. *Tugey*, to refuse, is a frequently used word that emphasizes the sense of self and self-will in humans, animals, and things. When the goats refuse to come at the call of their women herders, this is a type of refusal that is familiar to us. It becomes more difficult for us to understand when we hear that the goats refuse to give milk or even that the dates refuse to be sold. Such a refusal may not be insuperable but it constrains the work principle in several respects. The limits to what is feasible and what may be induced are more narrowly drawn. This is not only because opposition is experienced at work; this can be overcome in many cases. The important thing is that the refusal is often respected, even when it could be technically overcome. This respect is shown in the handling of camels or goats. Goats are especially self-willed. (Europeans also held this view in the past, for our word "capricious" comes from *capra*, goat.) The goats make the work of the herdswomen difficult. For example, some goats (referred to as "gazelles") do not allow themselves to be milked at all, or only when several women herders have captured them. Milking them, which normally should take a few minutes, lasts half an hour and requires the cooperation of several women. But we may also imagine that this makes the work more fun. If the women were to see the goats as pure instruments for achieving their aims, then the lonely work in the wilderness would be intolerable. But to watch a quarrelsome goat is fun, and to capture a shy goat is a game that relieves the monotonous work of milking.

Respect for the distinctive personality and self-will of animals can be developed into a specific service ethic. A conception of work as a service is common among nomads. Much more so than farmers or sedentary cattle keepers, nomads adapt their entire way of life to the needs of the animals. Kurt Beck has described this in detail with reference to nomads in Kordofan (Beck 1994, 1996). The herders put their life at the service of the herd.

Up to this point I have spoken about animals. But what about the craftsman who works with "raw materials," with wood, with stone, and metals? The most interesting test for the question of interaction is not the handling of tools by a craftsman, but working with machines. This is the prototype of instrumental activity; it is the model for Marx's, Weber's, and Habermas's conceptions of work. Research is dominated by the technical or economic paradigms, and nearly all studies assume this framework. There, are, however, some noteworthy exceptions: sociologists and social anthropologists, using the method of participant observation, have arrived at other views, closer to the perspective of interactive work that I describing here.

Manufacturing Consent. Changes in the Labor Process under Monopoly Capitalism is the title of a book by Michael Burawoy (1979). Its subject is an old topic: how do humans perform incessant and strenuous work? Burawoy's study is based on his own experiences as a worker in a machine manufacturing factory. He found that supervision, monetary incentives, and punishments were insufficient to explain the motivations of the workers. It was neither force nor wages which guaranteed successful production, but, rather, the fact that the work process was treated as a kind of game. The playful-antagonistic character with which this work was done and conflicts settled with management and other workers gave a meaning to the work, which otherwise under Tayloristic conditions it could never acquire. The game drove away boredom and fatigue. It made the basic deprivations of work tolerable and even satisfying. Contrary to the assumptions of Marx, Polanyi, and many others, the playful character of work is not lost even under the extreme conditions of capitalist factory work.

Burawoy writes of playing with machines, but they are more an instrument in the game between coworkers than a partner or opponent. This becomes clear when we look at ethnographic studies which focus on the relationship between the worker and things. Lucy Suchman's investigation of *human–machine communication* (1987) begins with a quotation: "Thomas Gladwin has written a brilliant article contrasting the method by which the Trukese navigate the open sea, with that by which Europeans navigate. He points out that the European navigator begins with a plan – a course – which he has charted according to universal principles, and he carries out his voyage by relating his every move to this plan ... If unexpected events occur, he must first alter his plan, then respond accordingly. The Trukese navigator begins with an objective rather than a plan ... He utilizes information provided by the wind, the waves, the tide and current, the fauna, the stars, the clouds, the sound of the water on the side of the boat, and he steers accordingly." (Suchman 1987: VII)

At first this distinction seems understandable, and it would also explain why "primitive" peoples, in this case the Trukese, have a close relationship with nature and things, while Europeans do not. However, Suchman argues that this interpretation is wrong. Her book is devoted to demonstrating that we too do not, or at least do not only, just execute plans; we too get involved with the objects and feel their effect. Work is always related to a context.

In her empirical study, which is in the tradition of ethnomethodology, Suchman investigates the way people behave when using a copy machine. The "intelligent" copy machine is designed in such a way that plans of action are "built in" both for the processes in the machine and for potential users. But the actual behavior of the users is also shaped by a variety of elements, not only the instructions given by the copier, but also faulty results. Most importantly, users talk to each other about their problems. They try out different possibilities, and the instructions given by the copier are only one out of many elements guiding their actions. Their actions, according to Suchman, depend on the specific context and not on a given plan. Users credit the machine, like a person, with pragmatic intentions. Problems then arise from the fact that these do not correspond to the internal communication of the copier. The users and the copier can interact, but they cannot communicate.

Suchman's book triggered a sustained debate and is today considered a classic in the literature on human–machine relations. Twenty years later, in 2007, a new, expanded edition was published (under the title *Human–Machine*

Configurations. Plans and Situated Actions), in which Suchman responds to critics and extends her argument beyond the human–machine relationship. She underlines that actions must always be seen in relationship to a concrete situation. Elements of the environment form obstacles that have to be taken into account by an actor, but they also provide opportunities to be grasped. Plans are one element in a situation. They do not completely determine actions, but can help in shaping particular actions; above all, they provide the basis for a rhetorical strategy to lend uniformity to an action before, during, and after its realization.

We could object that the users of Suchman's copier were laymen who had only a very limited knowledge of the inner workings of the machine. It is therefore interesting that an ethnographic study was carried out in the same firm to investigate how technicians treat copiers. In the United States during the second half of the twentieth century, technicians were the fastest growing professional group. Even more than service providers and administrators, they may be seen as the prototype of a post-industrial economy (Barley and Orr 1997). So how do they interact with machines? Julian E. Orr (1996) examines the triangular relation between service technicians, customers, and copying machines. He worked for many years as a service technician before undertaking his anthropological research.

Orr finds that some technical service and repair work corresponds to the technical paradigm, but machines are also subjects, in this case both partner and opponent. "War stories" narrate both heroic successes and also tragic defeats. Even the heroic stories assume that the machines are difficult and incalculable. "These tales of the heroism required to service early machines seem balanced between celebrations of the perversity of the machines and celebrations of the technicians for coping. It is not clear whether the technicians more admire the coping or the perversity" (Orr 1996: 139). Even when many are of the same type, each machine is an individual, and it is named individually by the users. The machines are (like a livestock herd) in principle domesticated, but only in principle. When describing the negative characteristics of machines, moral and value judgments are used. Machines can be "filthy," "perverse," "crotchety," and "odd", but these characteristics are seen not only as negative. "The machines are both perverse and fascinating ... Catastrophes resulting from oversight are described with the same pride as part of the process of becoming a real technician ... Indeed, how could they resent the machines, for such a machine is a worthy opponent, partner, other" (Orr 1996 98f.).

Orr compares the way technicians deal with machines to Lévi-Strauss's account of the *bricoleur*, who works with whatever happens to be available. This corresponds, however, only partially to the self-image of the technician. In practice the technician interacts with the machine as though it were an individual. The stories told by technicians are character descriptions and moral value judgments. On the other hand, they have a technical world view in so far as they try to harness the chaos through orderly and systematic behavior, based on knowledge and skill. We might argue that many technical processes are so complex that not even experts find them easy to master. The habit of anthropomorphizing machines would then be a strategy to reduce this complexity. In a manner reminiscent of the way Tuareg goatherds describe their relationship with the goats, the technicians express their relationship with the machines as a master–servant relationship in which, although they are the masters, the machines behave as wayward servants. However, Orr leaves unclear how this way of speaking relates to actual working practice.

The use of anthropomorphism to express complex technical facts may be observed in many other situations. Today, this idiom is also used for programming languages. We can speak of the beliefs, capabilities, choices, and commitments of certain software components (Rammert and Schulz-Schaeffer 2002: 36). The programs can then communicate with people on that basis. The answer to the question whether agency is only attributed to technical artefacts (anthropomorphism) or whether it is based on observable properties that they have, will depend on how one defines "agency." Rammert and Schulz-Schaeffer propose a graded concept of action. A weak concept of action limits itself to the fact that a change is effected. In this sense, speed-control humps or heavy key tags, which Latour offers as examples, also possess agency and can interact with people. A strong concept of action stresses the intentionality and reflexivity of action. It is from the outset related to a human subject, capable of self-awareness. However, Rammert and Schulz-Schaeffer point out that the human actor is himself a social construct (2002: 52ff.). Historically, the limits of his agency have been variously defined in theology and law. Actions are basically constituted by processes of attribution. From this point of view the distinction between attributed or real agency of artefacts then becomes questionable. If one goes this far, it would also be interesting to take the results of anthropological research seriously. Rather than diagnosing the fetishization of things and the anthropomorphization of nature and technology among the "primitives," we should examine ourselves from the point of view of these societies (2002: 40).

Theoretical stimuli for such research may be found among peoples who, although they recognize differences between humans, animals, plants, and stones, do not raise these to the status of fundamental ontological differences. Philippe Descola (2005) has taken steps in this direction, though non-anthropologists will find it difficult to follow him in taking seriously the worldview of peoples such as the Australian Aborigines or Indians of the Amazon region. But Western philosophers can also be invoked. When Martin Heidegger quotes Master Eckehart, who refers to the soul as a great thing and God as the greatest thing, but then turns to such mundane things as a jug or a pair of shoes, he is without doubt postulating a hierarchy of things, but not necessarily any ontological difference. Heidegger advises us not to approach things as if in a raid or ambush (*überfallartig*), but to let them work on us. His emphasis on the independence of things is consistent with a conception of work as interaction rather than as transformation (Heidegger 1950).

In sociological and anthropological consumer research, the symbolic meaning of things, their social life, and their biography have been a prominent object of research for some decades. However, things are scarcely ever studied in connection with work. This perspective seems to me unbalanced. Consumption takes place mainly within the household and housework, that is, caring for the things in the household and keeping them in order, is closely bound up with their meaning. Jean Claude Kaufmann (1997) shows that women, who are normally the ones who do the housework, often have a different relationship to things from men, who merely consume them.

Working abroad: expeditions and migrants

Viewing work as interaction allows us to compare non-industrial and industrial societies in a non-dichotomous way. A similar approach may be pursued in the field of migration. Contemporary international migration involves workers who are integrated into the economy of the host country in low-paid occupations. This kind of migration might be compared with other historical and present-day forms that are very differently structured, including the form of long-distance trade referred to by Karl Polanyi as a *tribal expedition* (2001: 62). When we think of long-distance trade, we first of all think of professional traders, i.e. people who control the purchase, transport, and sale of goods in order to gain a profit. It is mainly this form of long-distance trade which has been studied in the anthropological and historical literature. However, there is another form of long-distance trade, in which local needs and the procurement of goods are not separate phenomena concerning different groups of people, but are united within one group. In the *trading expedition* the households that consume the final product themselves organize the procurement of goods from far-off places. The starting point is an economy which is chiefly organized as a subsistence economy, but which procures some goods from outside. A classic description of such a system may be found in Malinowski (1922). The *kula* trade is organized in the form of an expedition In his *kula* studies, Malinowski focuses on the ceremonial exchange of bracelets and necklaces, but also mentions a "subsidiary exchange of ordinary goods" (Malinowski 1961: 361). Yams, betel nuts, and coconuts are exchanged for each other or for craft products. Later, Malinowski revised his opinion and came to accept that what he here refers to as subsidiary exchange is actually a main object of the *kula* expedition: "in the *kula* the most important economic fact is that the non-utilitarian exchange of valuables provides the driving force and the ceremonial framework for an extremely important system of utilitarian trade" (Malinowski 1965: 456).

Malinowski repeatedly described the *kula* ring as an example of intertribal trading, but he did not make a general analysis of *expeditions*. This was done by Richard Thurnwald (1932: 145–9). Expeditions are collective enterprises with many participants under a single leadership. They may be conducted according to various principles, including hunting, gift exchange, or "collective trade," of which caravan trading is an example. The expeditions described by Thurnwald cover long distances and last for weeks or months. In *The Great Transformation* (2001: 61f.), Karl Polanyi took up Thurnwald's ideas.

Claude Meillassoux (1971: 68f.) also took up the notion of the expedition in his discussion of long-distance trade. He argued that it constituted one of the first forms of long-distance trade, preceding the development of "trade," in which exchange value is more important than use value, and later still "commerce," in which goods are exchanged for money. Expeditions are carried out not by professional traders but by peasants whose interest is in the immediate use value of the goods. They try to exchange as advantageously as they can, but their aim is not to make a profit. This remains true even if they are obliged to make another exchange before obtaining the goods they desire. Meillassoux briefly discusses the conditions and limitations of these expeditions: since they are carried out by peasants, they are constrained by the conditions of the agricultural cycle, and are seasonally limited.

All these authors assume that the expedition precedes long-distance trade by professional traders in an evolutionary sequence. Such expeditions are nowadays rare. However, the Kel Ewey Tuareg have for centuries organized trading caravans and practiced transhumance which regularly took them into areas belonging to other ethnic groups and, since the beginning of the colonial period, also across borders into other countries (Spittler 2008b). Between the ages of ten and sixty, Kel Ewey men spend about six months of each year in Hausaland. In this respect they may be compared with migrant laborers who spend a large part of their active life away from home, but who do not lose contact with their families. Such migrant laborers are frequently the first to bring home new consumer goods, which then spread among the rest of the population. This is not the case among the Kel Ewey, whose resemblance to migrant laborers turns out to be rather superficial. The Kel Ewey do not arrive empty-handed in their host country, as laborers do, but as independent "entrepreneurs." They put their own camels out to pasture there, they sell their own products, and are completely equipped with everything they need. They are not dependent on local people and can live as they please. The herders who tend the camels live isolated in the bush, far from the towns. This is quite different from the situation of a migrant laborer who is exposed to frequent contacts with the local people, occupies a subordinate position among them, recognizes their superiority, and uses them as a reference group when it comes to adopting new consumer goods. The Kel Ewey do not feel any temptation or pressure to adopt the norms of the local people. The caravaneers know exactly what they are looking for. They do not wander through a market gathering information about the variety of products available; they are looking for a particular item, such as a wooden bowl, a clay pot, or a pair of sandals. Unlike the Hausa, who stroll leisurely around a market, they walk quickly and purposefully, without looking to right or left.

Modern labor migration to Libya and Algeria offers an alternative to these traditional expeditions. Young Kel Ewey men hire themselves out in these countries, especially in the oasis towns of Tamanrasset and Djanet (Algeria) and Ghat (Libya). They can earn more money here than in Nigeria, but are also exposed to police raids. Since they enter the country without documents, they live in constant fear of being expelled. Moreover, in the unsafe areas close to the border, they may encounter robbers who snatch all their savings. In this case, too, complaints about the hardships involved are mixed with pride. These Tuareg migrants call themselves *ishumagh*, derived from the French word *chomeur*, meaning unemployed, but here designating a self-assured way of life which has found expression in a large number of poems and in songs.

The caravaneers and the migrant workers among the Kel Ewey differ not only in their destination countries (Nigeria for the former, Algeria and Libya for the latter) but also structurally. The caravaneers take their workplace with them when they travel to foreign places. They travel south not only with their camels but with all the equipment they need: tools, transport sacks, dishes, even food. They act independently in the sense that they sell their goods (salt and dates) and from the earnings buy millet and clothing for their families at home. Everything they do is related to the needs of those at home. While they are in the south, they mainly have contact with people like themselves, and in the case of the herders exclusively so. When the herders take their camels to new pastures, they perform the same work. The migrant laborers, on the other hand, are employed by strangers and are exposed to foreign influences in a very different way in their work, in their consumption habits, and in their social contacts. They are more easily overwhelmed by the foreign culture than the herders and come to see their own culture more critically, even though both groups remain oriented toward their home area. It is no coincidence that the Tuareg rebellion in the 1990s in Mali and Niger was mainly the initiative of Tuareg migrants in Libya and Algeria.

Toward a comparative anthropology of work

A comparative anthropology of work presupposes a unified category of work, but in this unity there is also diversity, with many variations. We could build on this foundation. It is necessary to avoid the pitfalls of established dichotomies that characterize whole societies and historical periods. Polanyi shares the fondness of many other social scientists for dichotomies: industrial versus non-industrial (Friedmann 1950, Bücher 1896); capitalist versus pre-capitalist (Marx, Polanyi); natural versus artificial (Friedmann 1950; Thompson 1967); world of work versus life world (Habermas 1968); rational versus non-rational (Weber 1958, 1978, 1982); primitive versus civilized; or *Naturvolk* versus *Kulturvolk* (Bücher, Malinowski).

Some of these dichotomies, which at times assume the character of ontological distinctions, represented important insights in their time. Today they are less helpful, among other reasons because they hide the huge differences that exist within categories such as non-capitalist or non-industrial. This problem was emphatically pointed out by Richard Thurnwald, who, when writing of the great differences between primitive peoples, had in mind not contingent cultural variations but, rather, a typology based on natural, technical, and social conditions. Since the cultural turn, anthropologists have become more sensitive to cultural variations and some have explored the semantic content of the term "work" in different cultures, including those of Melanesia. Unlike Malinowski, later anthropologists have tended to consider magical and aesthetic practices as an integral part of work. For the Maenge in Melanesia, working in the gardens is their most important work (Panoff 1977). But the conception that the gardener produces something is foreign to them; rather, the garden owes him something for all the trouble he has gone to. On the other hand, the Baining in New Guinea, as shown by Fajans (1997), have a completely different conception of work. Everything that is natural is considered to be asocial and menacing. Work is the central social concept of the Baining, through which natural products are transformed into social products. Working in the garden converts nature into food, cooking renders raw things edible. This work includes the education of children. After the insignificant and rather embarrassing procedure of biological birth, the child is fashioned into a social being (usually not by its own mother but within an adoptive relationship). Play is viewed negatively, because it is natural and animal-like. If there has ever been a "laboring society" (Arendt 1958), then it is that of the Baining!

In addition to studies of the semantics of the term "work," attention has also been paid to emic theories on the dynamics of the work process. It is not uncommon to find that farmers have a conception of labor power similar to that of Marx. Work requires physical strength. When a peasant in Átány looked back after finishing work in the field, the anthropologist remarked that they had left nothing behind. "Yes we have, our strength," answered the farmer dryly (Fél and Hofer 1972: 163). Many peasants all over the world hold that work alone does not guarantee success. The physiocrats adapted the common perception that work is a form of additional caring (Gudeman 1986). However, cultivation is not only caring but may also be destructive, for instance when clearing the ground or removing weeds. For this reason it is sometimes seen as a struggle (Richards 1939; Spittler 1978).

Dichotomies not only conceal huge structural and cultural differences between non-industrialized societies; they also hinder interesting comparisons that cross the dividing line of the Great Transformation. A true laboring society is not an exclusively modern phenomenon but is to be found among Melanesian horticulturalists. Concepts work as care, or as struggle, or as exchange, are not to be confined to one side of a great divide. As we have seen, the interaction perspective has wide application. Things are not necessarily inert but may possess a spirit. The worker may take them as objects that he can treat as he likes, but sometimes his work is better understood as an interaction between subjects. Anthropologists researching in societies where this kind of interaction is regarded as normal may contribute to sharpening awareness of these phenomena.

One of the most insidious dichotomous clichés is the idea of an absolute contrast between embedded work in non-capitalist societies and work in capitalist societies that is held to be non-embedded because it is performed in distinct places, at distinct times, and by distinct people. Such processes of distinction can also be found among farmers and herders, sometimes to a more marked degree. Although it is commonly said that the separation of working and living was one of the most important consequences of industrialization, this is patently untrue. The typical workplace in agrarian societies is in the fields, where people go to work and not just for amusement. The spatial distinction between work and other spheres of life is even more marked among herders. While the cultivator goes home at the end of the day, the herder spends the night with his flocks. And herders, to a greater extent than cultivators, frequently perform their work alone and not in the company of others. Spatial and chronological differentiation is widespread in non-industrial work situations, perhaps more so than in industrial societies, at any rate if we disregard the craftsman and the cottage industry worker and focus on cultivation and herding, the dominant forms of work in agrarian societies. Of course these distinctions reflect the modern Western point of view with its emphasis on the home. It is also possible to feel at home in the forest or the field.

The theory that work is intensified under capitalist conditions is more justified than any dichotomy. However, it is frequently overlooked that, even in capitalist society, wage-labor is not the only form of work, and today less so than ever. Work in the home was never organized as wage-labor. Everywhere in Europe today freelance work of all kinds is on the increase and new terms are invented to describe it. The competitive conditions of neoliberal markets may or may not be conducive to the greater "rationalization" of work. Even if we accept that capitalist wage-labor is particularly rational in the sense that it promotes the intensification of work, this does not mean that non-capitalist labor was irrational. Result-oriented work exists in all societies. The question of efficiency (the means by which goals are achieved) arises everywhere. A kind of "practical reason," which some anthropologists may turn their noses up at, can always be found. But beyond this, the task of defining rationality in relation to the performance of work has not yet adequately been addressed by anthropologists.

Non-industrial, non-capitalist work has many special features that distinguish it from capitalist, industrial work. However, I have tried to show in this chapter that this does not justify seeing them as a dichotomy, a pair of absolute opposites. A comparative anthropology of work should cross the dividing line of the Great Transformation. The art of anthropology consists in navigating carefully between Scylla (the other as the opposite) and Charybdis (the other as the same).

10 "Sociological Marxism" in central India: Polanyi, Gramsci, and the case of the unions[†]

Jonathan Parry

The framing

In a suggestive recent article, Michael Burawoy (2003) discovers a complementarity and an at first sight unlikely convergence between Karl Polanyi and Antonio Gramsci. Though they came from different backgrounds, and had roots in the different Marxian traditions of Lukacs and Lenin, both broke with, and in comparable ways superseded, "Classical" Marxism. Taken together they lay the ground for the development of a rejuvenated and more "sociological" recension of the tradition. While most variants occlude society in their preoccupation with the state, the market, and their interrelations, they make it central to the analysis. Polanyi's focus is on the relationship between ("active") society and the market; Gramsci's focus is on that between ("civil") society and the state. But, crucially, they converge "on a similar conception of society as both the container of capitalism's contradictions and the terrain of its transcendence" (Burawoy 2003: 21–2). On Burawoy's reading, however, Gramsci has a more compelling analysis of "containment" than of "transcendence." Polanyi provides genuine scope for a theory of counter-hegemony but is Pollyanna-ish about the obstacles to it.

Both reject the linear teleology of Classical Marxism and the mechanical determinism of the German Marxism of their day. History is not pre-ordained. "We can only know what is or has been, not what will be – for this does not exist, and is therefore by definition unknowable," says Gramsci (quoted in Kolakowski 1981 3: 234). "The concept of a future that awaits us somewhere," says Polanyi, "is senseless, because the future does not exist ... (it) is constantly being re-made by those who live in the present" (quoted in Burawoy 2003: 11). And with regard to the role that social classes play in making that future, their ideas are similar.

[†] Funded by the Economic and Social Science Research Council, Nuffield Foundation, and London School of Economics, the fieldwork on which this chapter is based has extended over approximately 26 months between 1993 and 2008. I gratefully acknowledge the invaluable research assistance of Ajay T.G. (who is not, however, in any way responsible for the contents or any of the conclusions in this chapter).

Where – as in the West – civil society is highly developed, argues Gramsci, and "a proper relation" exists between it and the state, revolutionary change will involve the working class in patient "trench warfare" aimed at destabilizing the hegemony of the "political class" and at establishing its own.[2] The state is protected both by coercion *and* by its hegemonic control over the ideology of subaltern classes and the institutions of civil society. The working class must win others over to its view of the world, to its social, cultural, and moral values, and cannot therefore triumph by confining itself to "corporate–economic" struggles – to its own *class* interests. It must forge alliances with others on issues that are not purely economic, and must patiently build up its own counter-hegemony and bloc of support in "a war of position."

In *The Great Transformation*, Polanyi similarly stresses that for a class to act as an effective historical agent it must stand for something more than its own particular interests. It must persuade other classes that it represents the interests of society. Thus, in early nineteenth century England, it was the middle classes who were "the bearers of the nascent market economy," and who – when business flourished – were seen as the guarantors of employment and rents. When it didn't, it was industrial workers and the rural gentry who, respectively, spearheaded the struggle against the commodification of labor and land. So "at one time or another, each social class stood. ... for interests wider than its own" (2001: 139). Ultimately, says Polanyi, "it is the relation of a class to society as a whole which maps out its part in the drama, and its success is determined by the breadth and variety of the interests, other than its own, which it is able to serve" (2001: 163). In the long term, class interests provide only "a limited explanation" of social transformation. It is society that determines the fate of classes, rather than classes that determine the fate of society. They are only the "mechanism" for social and political change, not its "ultimate cause." "The 'challenge' (of laissez-faire) is to society as a whole; the 'response' comes through groups, sections, and classes" (2001: 160). Though it is plausible to suppose that *in a market society*, in which material self-gain has become the "instituted value," classes mobilize around narrow economic interests, in the general case their standing, rank, and security are the concerns that really drive them.

The revolutionary moment that followed the end of the First World War had evaporated, the Turin factory councils movement had foundered, the fascists had come to power in Italy. The key question for Gramsci was why capitalism proved so resilient. His answer lay in the hegemony that the political class

---

[2] His contrast was with Russia, where civil society was only "primordial and gelatinous" and "the state was everything." For that reason it was more susceptible to frontal assault ("a war of movement"), whereas modern democracies are protected by the "sturdy structure of civil society," the "trenches" and "permanent fortifications" of the system of domination (Gramsci 1971: 238, 243). These must be painstakingly captured in a preliminary "war of position."

exercises over civil society, including the trades unions. Though the autonomy of such institutions from the state creates theoretical space for resistance, civil society has been generally co-opted by it to contain class struggle, organize consent, and reinforce hegemony. This outcome is sometimes partly secured by a "passive revolution." Fundamental change is aborted by a revolution initiated from above that does not involve the active participation of the people. In the United States, Fordism and Taylorism permitted high rates of productivity and therefore high wages, which in turn gave capital leverage over the private lives of workers – a reflection of industry's "need to elaborate a new type of man suited to the new type of work and productive process" (Gramsci 1971: 286).

Gramsci's analysis, for Burawoy, has two major shortcomings. First, he makes no attempt to explain how civil society arises, or why it takes deeper root in some countries than others. Second, he does a better job of persuading us of the power of hegemony than of the possibilities for subverting it. "Without an ideology to found a new order, without material concessions to attach its allies, and without a state to organize its domination through a combination of force and consent, how can the working class ever replace capitalist hegemony with its own?" (Burawoy 2003: 35).

Polanyi provides us with a plausible answer to the first problem, and with the beginnings of one to the second. What he calls "active society" – the unions, the Chartist and cooperative movements, and their like – arises in direct response to the dehumanizing effects of the market. But if Gramsci's capitalist hegemony is so stoutly protected by the "trenches" and "permanent fortifications" of civil society that it appears all but invincible, the problem with Polanyi is the opposite. He does not appreciate the formidable obstacles that "active society" must confront in its quest to rein in the market, nor explain how a downtrodden and demoralized working class was able to assert itself.

Building on a key passage in *The Great Transformation* (p. 173f), Burawoy accounts for this contrast by crucial differences between the contexts with which they were dealing. In England, Speenhamland led to "degrading pauperization" and the Industrial Revolution to "cultural catastrophe." To mainland Europe, the latter came fifty years later, and Italian and German unification were accomplished with worker support. Workers consequently exerted greater political leverage, got the vote earlier, and enjoyed higher status and wages. The state protected them from the excesses of the market, the incursions of which were more gradual and less violent. Polanyi's stress on the ravages of the unregulated market and on the compulsions to curb it reflects the English situation; Gramsci's focus on the hegemony of the state and its stranglehold on civil society the continental one.

Whether Polanyi and Gramsci provide the most promising platform for a rejuvenated Marxism does not concern me here. Nor do I want to enter the lists over whether – and in what sense – Polanyi was "really" a Marxist.[3] My limited purpose is rather to explore the light that Burawoy's juxtaposition of the two theorists might shed on a specific ethnographic situation. Though the differences between them might have been an artefact of the different national contexts on which each focused, my suggestion is that the insights of both might be usefully applied to different tendencies within the same setting. Gramsci offers a handle on the way in which the union movement functions among *organized-* (and largely *public-*) sector workers in central India; Polanyi on the impetus behind one brand of unionism that has grown up among the *contract* labor force in the *private* sector. Different "fractions" of the (not so unitary) "working class" experience the state and the market in different ways.

The "double movement" in India

As Polanyi famously argued (2001: 145–7), "laissez-faire was planned; planning was not." There was "nothing natural about laissez-faire … (it) was enforced by the state" – whereas the collectivist reaction against it was largely spontaneous. This "double movement" – the unleashing of the market and the reaction against it – was simultaneous rather than sequential. It was not, as Isaac (2005: 15) supposes, "*first*, the disembedding of the economy under the self-regulating market, *then* the emergence of countermeasures 'designed to check the action of the market relative to labor, land, and money'" (emphasis added). For Polanyi, the Poor Law Reform Act of 1834 was the real beginning of a competitive labor market, and thus the true origin point of industrial capitalism. Speenhamland had been "a preventative act of intervention, obstructing (its) creation …" (2001: 231). Thus the "reaction" of society anticipated the real blow that revolutionized our world by making a commodity of labor.

In India, as Neale (1994) argues, things happened differently. The East India Company did not *plan* to impose a self-regulating market. It resulted from "accepted assumptions about the world." But the left hand did not clearly know what the right was doing, and while the British were instituting measures to create a market in land they were also legislating to protect the peasantry from it (cf. Servet, Chapter 5 in this volume). While in England landed interests resisted the commodification of land, in India large landlords embraced the new system with enthusiasm and "pushed the logic of market gain beyond what the

---

[3] Dalton (1981; cf. Dalton and Köcke (1983)) had it right, I believe, when he said that "the differences between Marx and Polanyi distinctly outweigh their similarities." Halperin's (1984) claims to the contrary I find unconvincing. Many non-Marxist theorists similarly stress the social embeddedness of the economy and a broadly "institutional" approach to comparative economics. Her suggestion that in the prevailing climate of McCarthyism in the United States he masked his Marxism is unfalsifiable and ungenerous.

British themselves had done at home. In the middle decades of the nineteenth century Indian landlords had become thoroughgoing rent-maximizers, while many British administrators had become more 'pro-tenant' than their peers at home" (Neale 1994: 151). Though the imperial order was caught in two minds, it was in the long run those who favored "protection" who dominated policy – as it continued to be for some time after the British had left.

The Indian Independence movement has been described as a "passive revolution" in the Gramscian sense (Chatterjee 1986). Constitutional democracy based on universal suffrage was not demanded by the people, but was "gifted" to them by the nationalist elite. In 1947, the new Congress government's economic policy was still uncertain; and it was not until the death of Patel (the Deputy Prime Minister and a severe critic of planning), that the "socialist" Nehruvian modernizers were able to get their way (Khilnani 1997: Chapter 2). The commanding heights of the economy – including manufacturing industry – would be closely controlled by the state. Nehru himself regarded laissez-faire as "bullock-cart" economics, and planning *was* certainly planned. Where the principle that labor should find its price on the market was applied in organized-sector industry, that was largely as the result of spontaneous guerrilla action on the part of management (including the management of many state enterprises). A "free" labor market developed *sub rosa*, outside the law, in reaction to planning, and in defiance of state regulation.

But the state has sought to limit not only the freedoms of capital, but also of labor. In the organized sector, union membership has long been a right. During the Second World War, however, union activities were restricted under the Defence of India Rules that gave government the power to prohibit strikes and impose compulsory arbitration. The end of the war brought a period of violent industrial unrest, and – as a "temporary" measure – the new Congress government perpetuated these powers through the Industrial Disputes Act of 1947 (Myers and Kannappan [1958] 1970: 142–3). They have never been revoked. So labyrinthine is the law on arbitration, and so protracted the procedures, that most strikes today are technically illegal (Saini 1999; cf Holmström 1984: 167) – though that does not prevent them. In the name of political stability and economic development, the state insists on its right to regulate industrial relations and represent the wider interest of society (Myrdal 1968: 2, 882; Myers and Kannappan 1970: 149). When, in the late 1960s, the Governor of the Reserve Bank of India appeared before the National Commission on Labour, he argued that collective bargaining was a product of laissez-faire (though, in fact, its original champions had been bitterly hostile to industrial "combinations"). It was therefore, he claimed, irrelevant to "socialist" India with its planned economy. Representatives of the Congress Party-affiliated unions who backed him added that you can only bargain over a "commodity," and that no progressive thinker would accept that labor can be treated as such.

The "community" must be a third party in industrial disputes and its interests paramount (Rudolph and Rudolph 1987: 284).

Most of India's industrial legislation applies only to fairly large-scale, bureaucratically organized, capital-intensive factories – to the so-called "organized" sector. Workers in it are (at least theoretically) the beneficiaries of employment laws governing enforceable minimum wages, hours, and conditions of work, job security, safety procedures, union recognition, and the like. They account for less than 10 percent of the total labor force.[4] Fewer than half of them are unionized (Harriss-White and Gooptu 2000); more than half are employed in state enterprises (Saini 1999). Relative to those who work in the unorganized sector, they are privileged – and this has been especially true of those who work in government factories. The state represents itself as an enlightened and benevolent employer – which, comparatively speaking, it is. That provides it with another "just" reason for retaining the power to curb militancy. It equally adds to the difficulty that public-sector workers have in identifying a clear class antagonist.

Though a small proportion of the workforce, organized-sector workers *are* organized and – since many of them work in key industries – have the capacity to seriously disrupt the state. After Independence, the nationalist leadership could sense potential trouble and adopted three strategies to head it off (Breman 1999). First, they allowed such workers to develop into a privileged enclave enjoying high wages, and good benefits and facilities that detached them from the rest of the working class. Second, the government made every effort to defuse industrial conflicts by insisting on compulsory arbitration; and, third, they encouraged the rise of unions affiliated to political parties – especially to Congress and its allies. And when the parties weren't allies, the unions could be relied on to compete with each other and divide the workers.

Thus, through its labor legislation and industrial policies, the state helped to create deep divisions within the working class. In the case I now turn to, trades union politics reflects and entrenches these divisions – between organized and unorganized sector workers; and within the former between those employed in public and private factories, between "company" and contract labor, and between local "sons-of-the-soil" and outsiders. Regional ethnicity overlaps with union affiliation in a potentially explosive way. In the public sector, unions are instruments of state hegemony and management control. In the private sector they are largely the tools of private capital. That is why most workers are militantly apathetic about them and stridently scornful of their leaders. There is, however, a notable exception. This union's appeal derives – as Polanyi would predict – from its resistance to the employers' determination to treat labor as just another "commodity."

---

[4]   Harriss-White and Gooptu (2000) give a figure of 7 percent; Saini (1999) says 8.3 percent.

The local landscape of labor

Until the mid-1950s, Bhilai was another small village in the rural region of Chhattisgarh, then part of Madhya Pradesh but now a separate state. That village has given its name to a large urban agglomeration, the site of one of the largest steel plants in Asia. The Bhilai Steel Plant (BSP for short) was built with Soviet aid and is one of several public-sector steel plants run by the Steel Authority of India Ltd (SAIL). It is the only one that has consistently shown a profit[5] and is commercially much more successful than its "sister" plants constructed in other states by the British and West Germans. This is widely attributed to its record of relatively harmonious industrial relations[6] – relative both to other SAIL units and to the private-sector factories that now surround it and for which it provided a magnet.

Employment provision was as important as profit in the planning priorities of the time when BSP began. By the late 1980s it had around 65,000 workers on its *direct* pay-roll. Of these, perhaps three-quarters worked inside the seventeen square kilometre plant or in its adjacent company township; the rest for its mines. Another 5,000 were employed in or around the plant by associated public-sector corporations specializing in steel plant construction, scrap recovery, and the manufacture of refractory bricks. 8,000–10,000 contract laborers toiled for daily wages in the plant. That is, some 80,000 jobs in all. Since then, however, a new economic wind has blown and BSP has slimmed its *direct* labor force down to around 35,000. It has thus shed some 30,000 permanent posts in twenty years.

This contraction is so significant because such jobs are so privileged. BSP workers are the local labor aristocracy. "Down-sizing" has been accomplished by a moratorium on recruitment, natural attrition, and voluntary retirements; and BSP employees continue to enjoy considerable security, pay, allowances, and fringe benefits that make them the envy of all other workers. Economically, and in lifestyle and values, they frequently have more in common with their line managers than with the contract laborers who work alongside them (and often at their lordly direction). Regardless of caste and religion, the BSP ethos is that workmates eat together, shoveling delicacies brought from home onto each other's plates. When they meet at the start of each shift, all shake hands – Brahmans and Untouchables, Hindu and Muslims, officers and men. But no regular BSP worker deigns to eat or shake hands with the contract laborers who spend the shift at his side. He characteristically has a strong sense of his identity and dignity *as a BSP worker*, and little sense of identity with those outside

---

[5] It has been in profit every year since 1972–1973 and through several recessions in the steel market.

[6] Other reasons include the relative simplicity and reliability of its Soviet technology, the fact that depreciation costs are by now largely discounted, and steady domestic demand for its principal product, railway lines.

the citadel of secure employment (of *naukari*). Nor – most of the time – does he see his interests as being fundamentally opposed to those of his officers. We are used to thinking of miners and steelworkers as the vanguard of the proletariat. Here they are increasingly "embourgeoisified."

Not only are BSP jobs lucrative, but the demands they make on a worker's time are generally light – in "hard shops" rarely more than three or four hours in a shift (Parry 1999a). Many then go home to attend to some moonlighting business. The Indian state runs a "mixed economy," as do many of its workers for whom a public-sector job is the bread and private enterprise the butter. Entrepreneurial profit is a respectable pursuit, and private property is not a moral peril (cf Ramaswamy 1983: 100f).

Many jobs in the plant are potentially dangerous, and workers routinely place their lives in the hands of their colleagues. Between bouts of intense productive activity, there are long fallow periods during which there is little to do but fraternize. Intense loyalties develop within the work group (which in terms of caste, religion, and regional ethnicity is almost invariably heterogeneous); and these relationships extend beyond the plant gates (Parry 1999a 1999b). Especially for those who live in the Township (around three-fifths of the regular workforce), being a BSP crane operator or loco driver is in most daily interactions as salient an identity as being a Brahman or Bengali (Parry 2003).

The children of a BSP worker are likely to be born in the BSP hospital (one of the best in the region); to attend a BSP school (superior in standard to state government schools); to box, bowl googlies, or jump hurdles at a BSP sports club; and be taken to see its Nehru Art Gallery, the musical fountain in its Maitri Bagh ("Friendship Garden"), or the tigers in its zoo. Should one of his teenagers run off the rails, or should the worker himself develop a drink problem or desert his wife, he might be referred to the BSP Family Counselling Cell (Parry 2001). And should he die in post, his obsequies will be subsidized, even perhaps organized, by the plant. It is a cradle to grave provision, the company assuming the raja's mantle as "Mother and Father" (*Man-Bap*) of his people.

It was almost forced to, for this gargantuan new complex required a core workforce of skilled operatives with a long-term commitment to their jobs. But there is more to it than pragmatism. Initiated just after Independence, built with the fraternal aid of the "anti-imperialist" Soviet Union, Bhilai epitomized the Nehruvian dream. A trail-blazer for the rapid development of the country, it was a beacon for modern India. Its purpose was not only to forge steel but a new kind of man in a new society. The aim, as Gramsci said of Fordism, was to create workers in a mould suited to a new productive regime – and here a new nation. The result is a remarkably cosmopolitan place in which caste and communal identities are comparatively muted (Parry 2008a).

At a little remove from the plant is an industrial estate that houses around 200 private-sector factories, and others are strung out along the main highway that runs through Bhilai. In size, this private-sector workforce now probably equals that of BSP. Perhaps one-third of is directly employed. The rest are on contract and liable to summary lay-off. It is a way of circumventing the labor laws. The rights of contract workers are much weaker, and their labor is consequently more flexible, susceptible to discipline, and cheaper.[7] Until recently, most private-sector factories would recruit such workers through a contractor, who becomes the notional employer of those under him. He might have charge of a bank of five lathes and would hire kin, caste fellows, and co-villagers to run them. By contrast with the BSP "melting pot," where work groups are generally very solidary but socially extremely heterogeneous, the private-sector shop floor was characteristically divided into mini ethnic or caste enclaves (Parry 1999a). Since the industrial strife of 1990–1991, however, the employers have abolished the right of contractors to recruit and have dispersed their work-teams. They have not got rid of them. The contractor shields the company against the requirements of the law – which are needless to say never met.[8]

Aside from all these is a vast "multiplier" labor force in the informal sector doing tasks related to industry (like sorting scrap or loading trucks). Very few have ever been unionized, and then only ephemerally. For that reason they do not figure in my discussion; but they exist off-stage, the silent, un-unionized and downtrodden majority.

The Bhilai working class is thus divided between formal and informal sector workers. Formal-sector workers are divided between those employed in public and private industry. Both of these workforces are again split between secure company workers and insecure contract labor. The distinction is between *naukari* ("regular employment") and *kam* ("work"). Company workers, like university professors, have *naukari* – a matter of security, not skill. The skilled/unskilled distinction has little ideological salience. BSP workers are privileged, not because they bring particular capacities to the market, but because the state has decreed that they should be.

The working class is further fragmented by religion, regional ethnicity, and caste. In Bhilai, Hindu–Muslim tensions are low-key (Parry and Struempell 2008) and the more significant cleavage is between the local sons-of-the-Chhattisgarh-soil and long-distance migrants. The locals were initially reluctant recruits to BSP's labor force (Parry 2008b) and in the pioneer days workers

---

[7] Engineering and metal-work dominate locally. In these labor is a major component of total production costs: 25–30 per cent according to Ramaswamy (1990: 161). I judge, however, that in routinely circumventing the law, the industrialists are motivated as much by their concern to *control* labor as to cheapen it.

[8] The local office of the Labour Commissioner is a toothless bureaucracy; and cynics say it is a source of cheap advice on evasion for the industrialists. They do not even have a list of all the factories on the Bhilai industrial estate. Though they have a right to access the company register of workers, they are invariably denied it. The maximum fine for non-compliance is a paltry Rs 200 and lawyers advise management never to make it available.

flooded in from all corners. Many stayed on and brought their families to join them. Times changed. BSP jobs became increasingly attractive and the locals began to insist that the plant had been built on their land and their boys should be preferred for employment. Currently, I estimate, just over half of the *permanent* BSP workforce is Chhattisgarhi. Proportionately "outsiders" remain hugely overrepresented. Twenty years back that was even more true. Among BSP *contract* workers, by contrast, Chhattisgarhis predominate overwhelmingly. On the industrial estate, the same division obtains. Locals are thus likely to do the least remunerative, and most arduous and insecure jobs. While outsiders are divided by their heterogeneous origins, the locals are divided by caste – especially by the division between the so-called "Hindu" castes and the Satnamis, the most populous "untouchable" caste in the area, and now well represented in the regular BSP workforce as the result of the policy of "protective discrimination" (or affirmative action) in public-sector employment (Parry 1999b). Company workers are almost all male. Much contract labor is female, and women were conspicuous in the union militancy that emerged among private-sector contract workers in the early 1990s.

In Bhilai, society as a whole is *not* "more and more splitting up into two great hostile camps" (Marx 1977: 222). In fact, much "class" conflict is between different "fractions" of "the working class" and runs along fracture lines created by the state and by capital. I say "*the* working class" with much hesitation. If there is *one*, I am not sure that BSP workers can *now* be said to belong to it (Parry n.d.). I say "class" conflict because these sometimes antagonistic strata are at bottom economic groups. The crystallization of their consciousness is, however, inhibited by social mobility and linkages between them (Giddens 1973: 107). In its early years, BSP provided secure remunerative employment for many from the most disadvantaged groups. Over time the barriers to such mobility have hardened, largely because recruitment to plant posts has dried to a trickle, and because of inflation in the educational qualifications required to get one. As a result of the superior standards of its school system (Parry 2005), it is today a good deal more likely that the son of a BSP worker will make it into a managerial job than that the son of a contract laborer will get one with BSP. Though many BSP workers have kin and neighbors in the informal sector, they are increasingly prone to distance themselves from them, and now just as many have family members in management. BSP households often hire women from what they call this "labor class" as domestic servants, employ members of it in their moonlighting businesses, or lend them money at interest. Those of peasant origin hire labor to cultivate their holdings – which BSP incomes have often enabled them to expand.

The local union scene

Nearly all local unions are federated with an umbrella organization that is affiliated to a political party. Thus, the BSP Steelworkers' Union is federated to the Indian National Trades Union Congress (INTUC), which is affiliated with the Congress party. Regular workers in the BSP mines are represented by the Sanyukt Khadan Mazdur Sangh (Joint Mineworkers Union) which is federated with the All-India Trade Union Congress (AITUC), which is affiliated to the Communist Party of India (CPI). Other local unions belong to the Centre of Indian Trade Unions (CITU), which is the union wing of India's other major parliamentary communist party, the Communist Party of India (Marxist) (CPI[M] or CPM).[9]

Union agendas are often a product of party maneuvring. Local party power brokers have close links with the union leadership. They are often the same people. Party in-fighting may paralyze a union. Industrial harmony is partly contingent on the relationship between the local union and party leadership, and the state and national government. BSP has enjoyed industrial peace because its INTUC union has been "reasonable." It was "reasonable," an ex-Chairman of SAIL told me, because the local Congress leadership wished to ingratiate itself in Delhi. Things went differently in other SAIL units.

For at least twenty-five years after BSP started, the CPI and the "progressive" wing of Congress shared many objectives. In the industrial field, these included nurturing the public sector and making its workers a model in terms of wages and conditions for the industrial working class as a whole. In the foreign policy field, it meant cementing relations with Moscow. BSP had iconic status for the CPI as *the* exemplar of the benefits of Indo-Soviet collaboration and the Kremlin directive was "hands off Bhilai" (Zinkin 1966: 106). In 1974, when the steel industry was entering a recession, there were tensions between Moscow and Delhi over the expansion of BSP's capacity (Krishna Moorthy 1984: 106), and AITUC was challenging INTUC's hegemony in the plant, a one-day strike was called in it and the mines. S. A. Dange, the Party General Secretary in Delhi, telephoned the local leadership and cautioned them to call it off. Now was not the moment to rock the public-sector boat and Moscow's prestige was at stake. On other occasions in the late 1970s and 1980s, these same local leaders were directly approached by senior SAIL management to rein in their militants and concentrate on counteracting the growing influence of the more radical Chhattisgarh Mukti Morcha that was championing the cause of contract labor in the mines.

The strategy worked in that it produced very tangible gains – for BSP labor. What it did *not* do was provide their private-sector peers with sufficient leverage to ratchet up *their* wages. The result was the creation of an increasingly privileged enclave of public-sector labor aristocrats, and an increasingly wide gulf between them and the rest of "the working class" – especially with contract laborers in the private sector. It was this that made space for the rise of a much more militant union movement.

---

[9] For simplicity, I follow popular usage by referring to particular unions by the acronym of their federations rather than by individual title.

Union membership does not imply allegiance to the party with which it is associated. The legislation requires that any factory with a hundred or more workers should have a "recognized union" chosen by the majority of its workforce. It is with this union, and this union alone, that management must negotiate. It might sound like a strength, a way of preventing management playing one union off against another, but in fact it is a weakness. The employers ensure that the majority of their workers belong to the most compliant union available (generally one that they sponsor themselves). They then refuse to talk to anybody else. Given that no other can speak for them, workers have every incentive to join the one that is "recognized." It is therefore no surprise that a worker may be a member of a communist union but vote for a right-wing Hindu nationalist party, or may join one union out of prudence and another from conviction.

More precisely, the relevant legislation distinguishes between "recognized" unions and those that are also "representative." The rights of the latter are stronger in that the employers are obliged to talk only with them on *all* matters affecting any worker in the enterprise, consult them on changes in work practices, and admit their representatives to the board of management. Though a union that is merely "recognized" has the exclusive right to negotiate with management on matters (like pay and conditions) that affect the whole workforce, other unions have the right to represent their individual members (in disciplinary proceedings, for example). The INTUC union in the plant is a "representative" one, while the AITUC union in the mines is simply "recognized." But while the plant is governed by a state government Industrial Relations Act, which lays down such stringent rules for compulsory arbitration that it is virtually impossible to call a legal strike, the mines are governed by a central government Industrial Disputes Act that is less restrictive. In both cases, however, the procedures for deciding which union has majority support are the same. These notionally require that every two years a senior government Labour Officer verifies a 2 percent sample of the membership lists of all the unions in an enterprise. Only if he is satisfied that a rival union has more genuine members than the "recognized" one will a secret ballot be held. But while the recognized union remains employer-friendly he is very unlikely to draw that conclusion. In practice, even the pretence of a verification exercise might happen only once in a couple of decades. It's a crucial point for what follows. In public-sector enterprises like BSP, no union has any serious chance of being "recognized" without political backing from the state and central governments. In the BSP mines, AITUC had been well organized from the start; but it was not until 1971 that it achieved recognition. That was in the wake of Mrs Gandhi's election landslide following the Bangladesh war when she brought Mohan Kumaramangalam, a well-known communist, into her cabinet as Minister for Steel. His backing was decisive.

The union and party loyalty of even senior union leaders cannot be taken for granted. Factionalism results in frequent defections. Nearly all of this older generation of leaders originally came from outside, many from Bengal and Kerala. They are relatively highly educated (to get a grip on the legislation, they need to be), and most started out with technical or clerical jobs in the plant. Some are now independent unionists, or work in BSP and "moonlight" as leaders of unions on the industrial estate. None speak Chhattisgarhi. And when they speak, they do so *on behalf of* the workers but not *at their behest* (Ramaswamy 1988: 74). Indeed, their attitudes to them are often unselfconsciously patrician, and they are separated from them by a considerable gap in lifestyles. Today they generally have cars and cordless phones, and live in *pakka* mansions in salubrious middle-class housing colonies.

How are such lifestyles funded? Not by membership dues, which are paltry – an *annual* subscription is a small fraction of one *day's* pay for a BSP worker.[10] True, union coffers don't need large floats since they don't provide strike pay.[11] True, union leaders in the plant are BSP workers with a company wage, routinely supplemented an income "on top" from grateful contractors and workers. In the private sector, a serious source of earning is the percentage they take on wage settlements (cf. Heuzé 1999), and the regular retainer and contracts they accept from management. One AITUC leader, the union boss for the notoriously volatile workforce of a distillery owned by a notorious industrialist, held a transport contract with it (in his son's name) and the bottle-washing contract (in his son-in-law's name). His trucks would cross picket lines. The problem, an AITUC leader confided, is especially acute on the left. Parties need funds to fight elections. Those on the right can rely on subventions from businessmen, contractors, and industrialists. The communist parties cannot and treat their affiliated unions as milch cows. Where will such contributions come from? Corrupt deals with contractors and industrialists.

No wonder most workers describe union leaders as "thieves" and "eaters of bribes." It is a vicious circle. What worker would pay higher dues to leaders he believes to be bent? What leader would impose them at the cost of his membership melting away and with it his credibility with employers? Without other means of funding campaigns or sustaining their lifestyles, many sail close to the wind. But it would be a mistake to conclude that unions are irrelevant to workers. Union *netas* (leaders) are needed for all sorts of instrumental purposes that have nothing to do with class struggle.

---

[10] Even so, many resist paying. An aspiring BSP union activist must enlist a certain quota of new members to be eligible for office, and so often pays the (easily affordable) dues of their reluctant coworkers.

[11] Only the Chhattisgarh Mukti Morcha has issued a daily ration of rice and *dal* to those on strike.

INTUC and the BSP workforce

As the child of Nehru's modernizing vision, it was all but preordained that BSP's recognized union would be a Congress one. While Congress retained power at the center a leash was kept on its leadership. Management was grateful for a moderate union and anxious to preserve its influence. At times there were pockets of AITUC and CITU support in the Blast Furnaces and Coke Ovens, and among the contract labor force.

Though BSP boasts of its industrial relations record, press coverage for the period from 1960 up to the beginning of Mrs Gandhi's Emergency in 1974 suggests some amnesia. There was serious unrest among construction workers facing retrenchment, who demanded permanent production jobs, and among the displaced peasantry. The latter angrily protested that BSP was tardy in honoring its pledge to the peasants of ninety-six villages to provide employment to one member of every household from which land had been compulsorily purchased for its complex. INTUC showed little interest in either constituency. Though other unions organized among construction labor, their actions were largely spontaneous and, except in the Coke Ovens, none was supported by production workers.

In the most dramatic incident, strikers invaded the Power Plant and forced its shutdown. Power is a strategic target. BSP is an integrated plant: if production is disrupted at some critical point in the cycle, the whole plant grinds to a halt and major items of capital investment – like blast furnaces – are at serious risk. (It is entirely different with the mines: ore may be stockpiled and what is left in the ground today is still there tomorrow.) The police were called in and fired tear gas and rifle rounds. Violent disturbances continued over the next couple of days; only 6,000 out of 30,000 plant construction workers reported for duty, and there was a heavy police presence throughout the plant and township. The issue continued to smoulder for several years and there were more protests – many orchestrated by the Chhattisgarh Mazdur Kalyan Sabha (Workers' Welfare Association) on behalf of retrenched Chhattisgarhi labor and of the jobs for land demand.

Not only did the INTUC leadership lack influence with these malcontents, it was crippled by factionalism. What management needed was a stable set of union officials who could deliver their members' compliance. What it got was a floating cast-list of rival claimants who could not. Under pressure from the Steel Ministry and SAIL, the INTUC national leadership eventually intervened and ordered fresh union elections. These were held in 1973, and Ravi Arya, a Punjabi, emerged as the union's General Secretary – allegedly with direct backing from the Minister for Steel (Kumaramangalam again). For the next thirty-odd years, Arya remained the most powerful figure in it. He and a small oligarchy developed a cosy relationship with management that ensured unconfrontational labor relations.

Those lower down the union hierarchy were discouraged from dissent by numerous perks, by exemption from normal duties, and by the patronage put their way. Shop-floor representatives acquired a lien on the workforce that rivalled that of any line manager. Though it might cost, the union hierarchy could influence recruitment and postings, the allocation of quarters, places in BSP schools, and beds in its hospital. Until overtime was abolished in 1986, shop-floor representatives decided who would do it. They could get your leave sanctioned, plead your case when you had been drunk for a fortnight and had not reported for duty, and defend you in disciplinary hearings. It is for such reasons that BSP workers need *netas* ("leaders"); and it is why they regard them with disdain.

During the mid-1990s, manning levels on the BSP shop floor were extremely generous, absenteeism was rife, and time discipline was very relaxed (Parry 1999a). The reason that BSP experienced very few strikes, a union leader explained, is that "the gate is always open" (so workers can leave). There was, in short, little cause for labor to develop deep collective resentments over managerial discipline; and the *neta* would ensure that officers did not officiously exceed their rather circumscribed authority.

What even senior plant leadership has had little influence over, however, is pay negotiations. The basic wage and major allowances are bargained in Delhi between SAIL and union representatives from all its units. Only the annual bonus is negotiated locally. During Arya's hegemony, however, SAIL wages improved steadily. Unions representing its more militant plants forced management's hand. BSP has been able to keep its workforce happy and sustain harmonious industrial relations because its workforce could "free-ride" on benefits extracted by less compliant unions in other SAIL plants.

One union demand that SAIL and the Steel Ministry consistently refused to concede was that jobs should be heritable.[12] As a sop, however, they implemented a system of "compassionate appointments" that provided employment to a dependant of any employee who died (from whatever cause) during his period of service. The system was widely abused and helped perpetuate the dominance of "outsiders" in the labor force. That set the local political leadership against it, with the result that in 1987 the scheme was radically curtailed with union acquiescence. "Weren't your members unhappy?" I asked one of their negotiators. "Yes," he agreed, "but there was nothing they could do. We decided it all in Delhi."

Most workers know little of union politics at this level, nor of the occasional campaigns the leadership launches. When, in 1994, the union called a token strike in protest at the government's liberalization policies, hardly any worker

---

[12] Such a provision had long existed at the Tata plant in Jamshedpur. See also Ramaswamy (1983: 18) on the Coimbatore factory she studied.

I knew had heard of it. A BSP worker could be unofficially absent for weeks at a stretch without much risk to his job; but a single day on unofficial strike is sufficient to get him the sack. Management crows that during strikes production invariably *increases*. It's possibly true. The persistent absentee realizes that this is the one day he *must* report for duty.

Most workers are, however, passionately interested in the election of their shop-floor representatives. While considerations of caste and regional ethnicity seem largely irrelevant at the top of the union hierarchy, on the shop floor the Chhattisgarhi–outsider split assumes real significance at election time. Among the group of workers I know best, both elections for which I have detailed information were contests between locals and outsiders. The successful candidate in the second was a local Satnami "Untouchable" who was voted in with the support of his higher caste Chhattisgarhi workmates – for whom regional identity plainly took precedence over caste. But it is not the only consideration. What workers also want is a representative who can stand up to their officers. The ability to do so is greatly enhanced by patrons higher up the union hierarchy. What officers want is a union leader who carries enough clout to persuade workers to work when necessary.

At the time of writing, however, this is scarcely relevant. The union has fallen back into factional disarray. The blurred boundary between union and party is partly responsible – schisms in the state Congress Party and competition between union leaders for the Congress ticket to contest in successive State Assembly elections. So, too, is factionalism among INTUC leadership in Delhi, this reproducing itself within plant leadership and filtering down to the shop floor. And senior management, it is said, has stirred the pot. The spin-offs include rigged elections, protracted court cases, the suspension of the union, repeated attempts to browbeat management and the state bureaucracy into recognizing one contender or another, and violent confrontations between different factions, which multiply like amoeba. As a result there has, for the last few years, been no legitimate leadership whom management can deal with. The strategy, as one personnel officer disarmingly told me in 2004, was to talk with all sides and listen to none. Since 2005, even that has been unnecessary. The courts have again suspended the union.

The consequences are not trivial. The world market for steel has been buoyant, and BSP profits unprecedented, but in the name of liberalization BSP has sold off some of its housing, reduced its welfare provision, cut subsidies and allowances, dragged its feet over implementing High Court rulings regularizing certain groups of workers, and offered annual bonuses that are in *absolute* terms lower than those paid a decade ago in the midst of a market recession. Most serious is the reduction of the permanent workforce and its replacement by contract labor. Though chronic absentees are now vulnerable, most individual workers still feel secure since compulsory redundancies have not been mooted. But since there is hardly any recruitment, they despair for their sons. Though with some hyperbole, they also complain of tighter time discipline, heavier workloads, and increasingly autocratic line managers. With no come-back from the *netas*, the only way to manage management is *chamchagiri* (sycophancy), and the earnings gap between officers and workers has wid-ened significantly. Moan as they do about the uselessness of unions, many now better appreciate what it is to be without one.

Not that workers are without redress. "What happens now," I recently asked some friends, "when you have an altercation with an officer and there is no *neta* to frighten him?" "We accuse him of calling us a *Chamar* (Leather-worker)," came the immediate response, "and threaten to lodge a FIR (First Information Report) with the police." When management recently attempted to require workers to sign out at the end of their shift as well as in at the start – in an effort to force them to stay throughout it – production slumped dramatically. Rollers got jammed, a plague of fuses suddenly blew, and the experiment fizzled out. When, at about the same time, a worker met with a fatal accident, his colleagues suspected that – with the union suspended – no compassionate appointment would be offered his family. They went *en masse* to the hospital morgue and refused to allow his corpse to be removed until management had agreed that one of his sons would be recruited.

In theory, it might seem that the current disarray of the recognized union should provide a golden opportunity for AITUC or CITU to stage an electoral coup to replace it. During the decades of INTUC hegemony, however, their organization and leadership have atrophied and their following among the regular workforce is small. But even if it were not, and as I have already indicated, the formal procedures for replacing a recognized union are so complex, protracted, and subject to manipulation that, without the direct backing of the state and central governments, the prospects of doing so are regarded as negligible. Indeed, without government intervention, it will now be constitutionally impossible to resurrect the INTUC union because its cen-tral committee is elected by those who have been "active members" over the past two years. Since there are no longer any "activists," there is now no electorate.

Plant contract labor and the unions

CITU has, however, had a significant impact on the conditions of contract workers in the plant. Though they all receive a fraction of a BSP operative's wage, the unionized 20 percent of them do much better. Although liable to lay-offs when not required, they are in theory guaranteed re-employment under another contractor when work is available, and they get the legal minimum wage and statutory benefits.

In law (though it is infinitely interpretable), workers who perform tasks for which there is "a permanent and perennial need," and those who have been continuously employed for 240 days must be made permanent and provided with all benefits. BSP is routinely in breach of these provisions and its contractors systematically circumvent the "continuous days" rule by short-term lay-offs, rotating work sites to make workers impossible to track, and by falsifying records. The recognized union primarily represents permanent workers and is apt to shrug. Though it has maintained a cell to "look after" the interests of contract workers, its officials are reputed to look after themselves by accepting tokens of the contractors' gratitude for their willingness to avert their eyes.

With little prospect of a mass following among BSP employees, it is CITU that has championed the cause of contract labor and taken BSP to court. Ironically, however, most unionized contract workers are members of INTUC. Though CITU won legal battles on behalf of some 3,000 contract workers doing demonstrably "permanent and perennial" jobs, management would only talk with INTUC, and it was largely those who defected to INTUC who benefited from the reclassification of tasks.[13] This led to violent confrontations between supporters of the two unions in the early 1980s, and CITU loyalists have been subject to harassment by the contractors, management, and INTUC. Trouble flared up again in 1997 when a female laborer was raped and murdered in the plant. The Contractors' Association wrung its hands in ostentatious anguish. How could its members responsibly continue to employ women in the plant without guarantees for their safety? The women "at risk" and who were therefore laid off, it transpired, were members of CITU; the men who replaced them were sponsored by INTUC.

Most contract workers are un-unionized and liable to summary lay-offs. They have a significantly higher accident rate and their chances of receiving proper compensation or adequate medical attention are slight. For each worker, BSP pays the contractor a sum in excess of the legal minimum. Most contractors pay their workers substantially less. Contract labor is lucrative – for the contractors, for those BSP officers who accept a "commission" on the contracts they control, for everybody except the un-unionized worker.

In recent years, some of the toughest unskilled production jobs have been given on contract – like that of doorman on the Coke Oven batteries. So taxing is this task that no BSP worker was ever required to perform it for more than four hours a shift. The contractors require their workers do it for eight, and those most desperate for cash do two shifts back-to-back everyday. For

---

[13] CITU fought a similar case on behalf of the canteen workers, in which the Supreme Court ruled that BSP must treat them as regular workers. The details of their contract were left to negotiation between management and union. When management dragged its feet, CITU returned to court. BSP pleaded that it could only negotiate with INTUC, with whom they were already in discussion.

sixteen hours on a job that no BSP worker would do for more than four, they earn around half his wage – but without any of the allowances and perks, the monetary value of which would add at least 50 percent more. When I started research in Bhilai in 1993, contract labor in the plant was nevertheless more remunerative than day-labor work outside. That situation is now reversed. One reason that many still work there are the opportunities for petty pilferage. These, in effect, provide another subsidy to the contractors, who can pay their labor at less than the market rate because of the value of the wood, coal, wire, and metal scrap that is smuggled out of the plant. The "weapons of the weak" (Scott 1985) are not always progressive. Pilfering plays a significant part in sustaining contractors' profits.

BSP's associated public-sector corporation, Hindustan Steel Construction Limited (HSCL), has long been a failing enterprise, but under government pressure BSP has recently channelled a large proportion of labor supply contracts through it as a way of keeping it afloat. HSCL then recruits through a pyramid of petty contractors. This has the advantage that HSCL becomes (or so BSP claims) the "principal employer" and therefore ultimately responsible for any breach in the law regarding the use of temporary labor in "permanent and perennial" jobs. It is these workers – probably two-thirds of all contract labor in the plant – who are most likely to receive wages far below the legal minimum. Though BSP does invariably pay its contractors for labor at the regulation rate, it well understands that its contractors generally pay their workers only half of that sum, and that this is how they make money. The visible above-board margins on any contract can therefore be pared to the bone. BSP is thus complicit in deregulating the price of labor. With the liberalization of the Indian economy, it is forced to compete in a global market for steel; and so it edges toward a competitive market for labor in a surreptitious reaction to "planning" that might price it out of the market. It is Polanyi's "double movement" in reverse.

Though regular BSP workers may feel for contract workers, they do not regard them as allies. This is not only a matter of "culture" and lifestyle, but also because at least some sense that their interests are opposed. With liberalization, it is only because many of the most gruelling tasks are performed by cheap flexible labor that regular BSP employment can remain so secure and remunerative, and its pace of work so relaxed.

The unions and the mines

This lack of common cause between company and contract labor applies equally to the private sector; and that division again overlaps with regional ethnicity. Before the industrial turmoil in the early 1990s, the unionized workforce in the private sector mostly belonged to an AITUC or CITU union, consisted of company labor, and was largely made up of outsiders. But many managements refused to recognize unions, and fired or intimidated workers who joined them. The predominantly Chhattisgarhi contract labor force was mostly un-unionized.

The roots of the present situation lie in BSP's iron ore mines at Dalli-Rajhara, some hundred kilometres away. When the plant produced its first steel in 1959, work on its *mechanized* mines lagged behind and BSP faced a problem of supply. There was, however, plenty of ore lying close to the surface, and all that was needed to extract it was dynamite and brawn. So the interim solution was labor-intensive *manual* mining. The workforces involved in these systems had very different characters. The minority *mechanized* miners were skilled migrant workers, exclusively male, BSP employees, and mainly belonged to an AITUC union. The more numerous *manual* miners were peasants from nearby villages. Many were women, some "Tribals," and all worked under contractors for much inferior pay. Though AITUC made some efforts to organize them, they were never regarded as its natural constituency. The union saw manual mining as a temporary measure; and their brand of Soviet Marxism assumed that the torch of history belonged, not in the hands of a "primitive" caste-ridden peasantry, but with a "real" industrial proletariat whom the mechanized miners appeared to resemble.

Discontent over the disparity in pay, over the inhumanly harsh conditions in the manual mines, and the retrenchment that would follow mechanization soon boiled over. To compound the injustice, in the mechanized mines the cost of production per tonne was two to three times higher. The basic wage was five times more, with generous allowances and benefits on top. Contract miners, moreover, were required to present themselves for work on six days a week, but – owing to bottlenecks in production – might be employed for only two. One of their persistent (but long denied) demands was a "fall-back" wage – a proportion of the standard daily rate paid for days on which, through no fault of their own, they were unable to work.

In 1966, 8,000 manual miners came out on strike, and in 1968 trouble arose when 4,000 were declared redundant and further job losses threatened. AITUC lobbied for them to be "departmentalized" (taken on as BSP employees). Management said it was impossible to "absorb" them all, and refused to offer any of them the same conditions as the mechanized miners. In such a gruelling environment, who would put his back into the job if wages were fixed and nobody could be fired? Following a seven-day strike in 1971, BSP created a new category of Departmental Piece-Rated (DPR) workers who were guaranteed wages equivalent to a BSP worker in the lowest grade on fulfillment of a production quota determined by time–work studies. Based on length of service, nearly 4,000 of the 14,000 manual miners became DPR workers over the next two years.

That left 10,000 no better off. Many still worked for contractors, but – as part of the deal struck with AITUC – others joined cooperative societies that took contracts for raising and transporting ore. Characteristically, these were organized around kinship and neighborhood clusters. Some were run by AITUC members with regular BSP jobs and were reputed to be as exploitative as the contractors, and some of the latter had close kin of senior AITUC leaders working for them. By this stage, then, there were four kinds of workers in the mines: regular BSP employees; DPR workers; society workers; and contract labor. Trouble erupted once more in 1976–1977 when contract and society workers agitated for parity with DPR workers and demanded an annual bonus equal to BSP labor. AITUC pressed their case, and the campaign escalated from a series of short stoppages to a 57-day strike. But, in the end, the AITUC leadership agreed a bonus of Rs 308 for the regular and DPR workforce and to a paltry Rs 70 for them. The manual miners went back on strike. It was a bad misjudgment, AITUC leaders now admit, and some whisper that their seniors were bought. The latter claim that they were under instructions from party headquarters. In any event, the union's credibility in the manual mines was destroyed and Shankar Guha Niyogi's moment had come.

Niyogi, a Bengali railway contractor's son, had been sacked from the BSP Coke Ovens in 1968 on the strength of a vetting report from the West Bengal police that claimed he had been associated with the (Maoist-style) Naxalite movement. He had subsequently lived a peripatetic and semi-underground existence as a radical activist, had supped – it was said – with Naxalites, himself worked as a manual miner, married an Adivasi ("Tribal") wife, learned Chhattisgarhi, and developed an astute appreciation of the power of local cultural symbols for political mobilization – of "sacrifice" and "martyrdom" in particular (Parry 2008b). He was subsequently to rediscover a forgotten home-grown Chhattisgarh "revolutionary" hero – Vir Narayan Singh – who had been executed by the British in 1857 and who became an icon for his movement. On Niyogi's release from detention at the end of the Emergency, the manual miners – who had deserted AITUC en masse and set up a new union[14] – invited him to Rajhara as its Organizing Secretary.

His impact was immediate. By June 1977 he had orchestrated another strike and more demonstrations. During one of these, with crowds of miners and a contingent of armed police outside, the district authorities requested a meeting in the union offices – a pretext for arresting him. The strikers retaliated by surrounding a dozen or so policemen and announcing they would hold them until their leader was released. Their colleagues opened fire on the crowd,

---

[14] The Chhattisgarh Mines Shramik Sangh. Along with other unions that looked to Niyogi for leadership, and that were founded in other industries elsewhere, this subsequently became an affiliate of the Chhattisgarh Mukti Morcha, which has (sometimes successfully) contested a small number of State Assembly constituencies.

which scattered into the evening but returned early next morning to renew their protests. The police again fired. Eleven strikers were killed and scores wounded. The movement now had martyrs and subsequent demonstrations produced more – as when, in 1980, an angry crowd protesters gathered outside the Central Industrial Security Force headquarters to demand the arrest of three of their constables for the attempted rape of an Adivasi girl. Again they were fired on.[15] Niyogi's fame spread: his organization began to attract national – even international – attention and spread to nearby industrial centers.

One of these was Rajnandgaon, where the sizeable workforce in the BNC mills – "represented" by a supine INTUC-affiliated recognized union – came out on an unofficial strike that lasted for more than two and a half months and was accompanied by serious violence. At the start of it, police attacked "sitting-in" workers with batons in the blacked-out mill at night. The majority of strikers were Chhattisgarhis, and the company managed to keep minimal production going with help from about 10 percent of the workforce who were from Uttar Pradesh and Bihar – from where they now imported *lathait* (toughs with staves) to provide backbone. The strikers formed a new union. But Niyogi, who had moved into one of the industrial neighborhoods, and other leaders of the new union that the strikers formed, tried to downplay the sons-of-the-soil against "outsiders" aspect of the conflict. A union march was set on by thugs armed with iron bars and axes; next morning they attacked a workers' district, fired shot-guns, beat workers, and molested women, and that evening the police opened fire on a crowd of protesters, killing three. That was in 1984. By 1986 Niyogi's followers were beginning to organize in Bhilai.

The Chhattisgarh Mukti Morcha ("Liberation Front") – the CMM – was no ordinary union movement. Initially structured around work groups in the manual mines, each under its *mukhya* (or headman), a large proportion of its members and activists (if not of its most influential strategists) were Chhattisgarhis who were often as dependent on their small peasant holdings as on their industrial jobs. Many were women. The CMM concerned itself with agrarian as well as industrial problems (as its green and red flag supposedly symbolized), campaigned on environmental issues like river pollution, Adivasi rights in the forest and against the logging contractors, and took up issues important to women in their domestic capacities.[16] Its agenda went far beyond the "economism" of most Indian unions. Though over a decade it achieved a more than sixfold increase in the daily wage of contract miners, it rapidly realized that many families were little better off since a significant proportion of the increment went on liquor. It therefore organized a vigorous anti-alcohol campaign that involved the public humiliation of backsliders and the forcible closure

---

[15] One was killed and about twenty others were treated for bullet wounds.
[16] Not only were many women manual miners, but in Chhattisgarh many agricultural tasks are also done by them.

of the businesses of big liquor contractors. It founded schools for workers' children, set up a technical training institute and a cooperative garage, and built – through voluntary labor – an impressive hospital staffed by idealistic Bengali doctors and dedicated to the memory of the martyrs of the 1977 firing. The movement is charged by its detractors with fostering xenophobia and deepening divisions in the "working class." As an unintended consequence of the predominant ethnic character of its contract labor constituency and its play on local cultural symbols, there is some truth in this – though those hostile to it probably did more to foster antagonism by raising the bogey of local chauvinism to unite outsiders against it. Niyogi's agenda was undoubtedly a politics of class, not regional ethnicity. More than almost any other Indian trades union, the CMM took up the cause of contract labor and attempted to address the concerns of peasants and workers of both sexes.

Though not known for his attention to financial detail, Niyogi needed money to sustain his campaigns, and he had a shrewd appreciation of the need to develop sources of income to fund them. The manual miners union set up cooperative societies that took transport contracts from BSP, and it was out of their profits that the union was able to feed workers' families when they went on strike. It is therefore not surprising that there were bitter wrangles when the Assistant Registrar of Cooperatives decided – at BSP's behest – to de-recognize seven societies affiliated to them, or that BSP dragged its feet over the payment of arrears.

There was also a long-running propaganda battle over Niyogi's relationship with the Naxalites. The local administration, the AITUC and INTUC leaderships, and senior CPI office-bearers (who simultaneously accused him of being an agent of the "bourgeois interests" and the CIA) consistently tried to tar him with that brush. But, at least in his public pronouncements, Niyogi repeatedly distanced himself from the Naxalites – from their violence, their view of the peasantry as the only "revolutionary" class, disdain for unions, and pessimism about the progressive political potential of industrial labor. Where Niyogi had stood on Naxalism has now, years after his death, once more become a matter of political relevance and controversy.

The Dalli-Rajhara mines remained the centre of CMM activism until the end of the 1980s. Much of its energy went into opposition to their mechanization, which Niyogi predicted – despite BSP's strenuous denials – would result in large-scale job losses. Matters came to a head when BeeKay Engineering – one of the big private-sector engineering companies in Bhilai – was given the contract for a new crushing plant. Niyogi vowed it would never be built. The BeeKay union – run by Sambal Chakraborty, an old CPI activist – had other ideas, as did the AITUC leadership in the mechanized mines. AITUC offered a deal whereby a quota of contract workers would be "departmentalized" when the new plant was completed, but Niyogi would have none of it.

AITUC claimed that was because they would then be represented by AITUC. Niyogi claimed it was because a few workers would benefit at the expense of the rest.

Throughout the late 1980s, CMM pickets disrupted work on the new unit. AITUC supporters retaliated. Though there was a history of violent skirmishes between them that went back to 1977 when the breakaway union was formed, there had in the interim been occasions on which they had collaborated on issues like pay. But now there were pitched battles and riots; activists on both sides were murdered; Rajhara was several times placed under prolonged curfew and families were split. Few of the AITUC foot-soldiers in these confrontations were mechanized miners with regular jobs. They were far too comfortably settled. BSP anticipated trouble and BeeKay got the contract for the new plant with generous margins for contingencies. Sambal had a war chest, and he deployed this to buy one of the cooperative societies formed to raise ore. In reality it existed only on paper and had never yet won a contract. Mines' management, however, put work its way (thereby expanding its membership), and AITUC promised that those who turned out for them would be first in line for new posts. The violence, then, was largely between CMM workers and job-seekers from the same villages.

The local AITUC leadership, I was told by one of those most directly involved, was charged by the SAIL Chairman with finding a way to contain the CMM, and Sambal was given the task. But in the end his troopers proved too disruptive for SAIL. They repeatedly blocked the rail link from Rajhara, interrupting supplies of ore to the plant. AITUC was asked rein in Sambal, who was instructed by party leadership to confine his activities to the industrial estate in Bhilai.

Mechanization proved inexorable and Niyogi proved right: large-scale redundancies followed. Perhaps because he saw his Rajhara constituency being progressively whittled away;[17] or perhaps because he wanted a larger stage for his movement or to confront AITUC in one of its power bases, from 1989 Niyogi shifted his focus to Bhilai.

The CMM on the industrial estate

His opening campaign on behalf of a group of contract workers in the ACC cement plant was a resounding success, and others joined his union in droves and staged strikes. The employers retaliated with intimidation and lock-outs; there were murders, assaults, and threats of rape. Around 4,000 CMM workers were summarily dismissed and replaced by blackleg labor recruited largely

---

[17] In 2008, the Dalli-Rajhara mines are fast approaching exhaustion, their workforce is reduced to a total of around 4,000 and there are very few contract miners left.

through the AITUC leadership. With Niyogi temporarily in jail, one of the big private conglomerates that had formerly refused to have any truck with unions decided to recognize an AITUC one, and Sambal imported some of his Rajhara jobseekers to replace locked-out CMM labor. Once again there were outbreaks of violence between the two sets of workers, with the police and district administration extending a fraternal hand to the combination of Communist union and their capitalist sponsors. Under fire, capital proved itself more capable than labor of acting in concert.

Though the class-consciousness of the CMM leadership was clearly "revolutionary," and CMM activists certainly perceived a conflict between their interests and those of capital, many rank-and-file supporters were swept along by the tide. Kamin, a contract laborer in a large distillery, was one of the CMM workers dismissed. It wasn't a bad job and the money was better than she had previously earned on a construction site. They marched and shouted slogans each morning outside the factory gates, but she never knew why they were on strike or what they were demanding. She bore no ill-will toward the black-legs who had taken her job. Kamin was sacked and they got a job; they'll get sacked and it will the next person's turn. On the opposite side, Adhikari was a supervisor for one of the distillery's contractors. He had thirty labourers under him, all of whom belonged to the CMM, and six operators who were with the "red flag" AITUC union, to which he belonged. He had to: his contractor was a friend of the union boss. He, too, recalls the marches and slogans, but what he remembers most vividly is how the AITUC workers were instructed to remain in the factory one night. Next morning the CMM laborers were locked out and they ran production at 80 percent capacity for the next two days while a crowd armed with staves bayed at the gates. Then they too were given staves and ordered to confront the opposition. Adhikari was mightily relieved to find that the gates were heavily locked and barricaded, and he was glad to sneak out of the back of the factory on the third night when the picketing slackened. The CMM workers were then dismissed and replaced by rough rural Biharis recruited straight from the AITUC's leader's home district.

In February 1991 Niyogi was arrested again, apparently at the instigation of the industrialists. On his release three months later, he was "externed" from (prohibited to enter) five Chhattisgarh districts and appealed to the High Court to have the order declared unconstitutional. In September, he was assassinated by a hired gunman. The outcry was enormous and it took four hours for his funeral procession to file past the union office in Rajhara. The industrial estate in Bhilai was closed down for a week and the situation remained tense for months.

It emerged that shortly before his death Niyogi had received anonymous warnings of an attempt on his life that were passed on to the police. He had also left a tape-recording predicting his assassination by a contract killer hired by five leading Bhilai industrialists.[18] The state police were accused of dragging their feet and the case was transferred to the Central Bureau of Investigation.[19] The alleged gunman, three members of a leading industrialist family, and five other co-conspirators were eventually arrested and charged. Six of the nine were convicted, but in 1998 the Appeal Court overturned all these verdicts. The CMM and CBI appealed to the Supreme Court, which, in 2005, finally acquitted all but the now dispensable hitman.

The CMM has since struggled to sustain its momentum and morale. In July 1992, a big rally was held near the Bhilai Power House station demanding that the Labour Court order the immediate reinstatement of the 4,000 sacked union members. Stones were thrown and the police opened fire. One policeman and sixteen workers were killed, and forty more were seriously wounded. Fifteen years later the case of the dismissed workers still grinds through the courts; and the union has increasingly become bogged down in lawsuits. Its leadership is now split by factional rivalries and allegations of corruption, and its rank-and-file following in Bhilai is furtive and cowed. It is also even more heavily dominated by Chhattisgarhis, who have local landholdings to sustain them when they strike or are sacked.

It is now more or less business as usual. The distillery has seen a succession of new unions, and I should have known better than to ask a friend who worked there why the workers kept switching. Of course, "it's the owners that decide who we join." At one of the big engineering firms on the industrial estate, management has co-opted a second-generation AITUC leader to front their new "pocket" union and has cajoled most workers to join it. When its senior organizer comes to the factory, he is generally found in the Personnel Manager's office, where for my benefit they ritually bicker like an old married couple. Once, when I wanted to check the regional origins of some workers, I asked him to take me through the list. "You don't think he knows," the Personnel Manager snorted. "You'll have to ask me." He is indeed knowledgeable. Through the dispensation of small favors, he retains roughly one worker in ten as an informer, who keeps him abreast of what others are saying and doing inside and outside the gates. Of those I am able to identify, all are union "activists," company workers and outsiders – and some are very well-built. It is hardly surprising if workers are cynical about unions, and if the sons-of-the-soil are resentful.

Not everything is quite what it was. In the larger private-sector units I know best, there is now no difference in pay and allowances between "company" labor and "permanent" contract workers. It is just less legally problematic

---

[18] As early as 1981, he had previously alleged plots on his life.
[19] There was at the time a BJP government in Bhopal, the then state capital, and at least one of the industrialists whom Niyogi named was closely linked to it. The central government in Delhi was Congress.

to lay off the latter. A few have become labor contractors, who recruit and discipline a third tier of workers that had previously hardly existed, so-called "supply workers." Today these constitute a majority of the workforce. The contractor is paid a retainer equivalent to the wage of a permanent contract worker, but can expect to make a significant income on top. He may, for example, receive wages for several skilled workers but pay them only at the unskilled rate. He may also exact a levy on the wages of workers under him and charge them a "commission" each time they are "rotated" and waiting hopefully for re-employment. None of these contractors may operate without the goodwill of the union – which is why they pay the leadership off every month and offer a job to the occasional worker they nominate. Routinely laid off and forced to compete with each other to be re-employed, supply workers have little solidarity with each other. None are unionized; most are Chhattisgarhis.

Hegemony and resistance: conclusion

The inescapable conclusion is that union politics in Bhilai reflect – and exacerbate – structural divisions in the working class that have largely been created by the state and its labor legislation, and that are dangerously congruent with regional identities. Conflict not only characterizes the relationship between capital and that segment of "the working class" whose labor is most transparently treated as a commodity, but also between these flexible contract workers and other working class fractions. The unions that represent the company workforce are sponsored by the state and/or management, and defend the citadel walls that surround this enclave of organized-sector labor and protect its privileges against a more radical union movement that has attempted to represent the interests of workers outside it. The state has been their patron through the concessions it has granted them, and their protector through the legal labyrinth that shields them against competitors. As Gramsci saw they might, they contain class struggle, organize consent, and entrench hegemony. Through a "passive revolution," the state has incorporated "the vanguard of the proletariat" into its own bloc of support. Decent schools, medical facilities, and other amenities were granted them from above. The aristocracy of labor has never needed to fight for them in the name of "the working class" as a whole. For much of it as a consequence, many rights of citizenship hardly exist.

But Gramscian hegemony is as much a matter of winning hearts and minds as of controlling civil society institutions. Not only are BSP workers among the most materially privileged segments of the Indian working class, but the world of the company "saturates" their lives. Work-group relationships are a central focus of social life outside the plant; jobs in it a major source of identity. "Mother-and-father" to them, the company sees its "children" from cradle to grave. As Nehru's beacon of India's industrial modernity, BSP had a significant place in the national imagination. Employees are proud to work for it, and it is their commonsense that the political order that created it can claim their consent.

No hegemony is, however, absolute, and workers are also often distrustful of management and deeply cynical about parties and unions. But rather than see in this the seeds of a possible counter-hegemony, I regard it as a major support for the status quo. It is so completely obvious to most workers that party and union leaders will ultimately be revealed as corrupt and self-serving that they conclude that things couldn't be otherwise and that nothing can change – at least not without the miraculous appearance of a truly disinterested messiah, a Mahatma Gandhi or a Niyogi. Whoever had the latter assassinated had insight. Without such a saintly exemplar, his movement was doomed to political entropy.

It did nonetheless briefly represent a real counter-hegemony, the constituency for which was a working class fraction whose compliance was always secured more by economic and physical coercion, and by the leverage that could be exerted through the "primordial" ties that bound workers to their contractors than by the compulsions of the hegemonic culture of the "political class." Their resistance, as Polanyi would suggest, has preeminently been a reaction to the employers' attempts to treat labor as a commodity that must find its price on the market and which may be hired and fired at will.

But, as Polanyi and Gramsci both stress, a counter-hegemony can only gain ground when the class that leads it allies itself on a broad front with other groups, and takes up struggles that are not confined to its own immediate material interests. In its heyday, the CMM began to do that with its alliance with the peasantry, its collaboration with other civil society organizations in campaigns against bonded labor and against alcoholism, and its support of civil liberties. The present significance of these alliances is hard to assess. The one that would matter most is with the Naxalites, the Maoist guerrilla movement that has made large swathes of Chhattisgarh's forested countryside into no-go areas for the state. The prospects for such an alliance are, however, difficult to gauge. It is said, and top-ranking police brief, that some segments of the CMM are sympathetic to Naxalites; and Niyogi's relationship with them has become a topic of renewed controversy. As the Chhattisgarh state government has become increasingly repressive of all forms of political dissent under the cover of its counter-insurgency program, it is hard to dismiss that as unlikely – even if the extent of the sympathy and its practical import are at present unclear.

What is clear is that the union's energies are largely taken up by bushfires on the industrial estate, and that it has made no serious attempt to organize contract labor in the plant. As to winning the hearts and minds of the regular BSP workforce, the task seems utterly hopeless. As Burawoy observed, what Polanyi did not properly weigh are the obstacles to creating a counter-hegemony that seriously challenges the market when the odds are stacked so heavily against it.

11   Composites, fictions, and risk: toward an ethnography of price

Jane I. Guyer

Introduction: fictions and prices

The topic of this chapter – popular understandings and social processes of commodity price formation – has engaged me for a long time, and weaves its way through much of my work, from urban food supply to bride-wealth to second-hand automobile spare parts. It has seemed, however, too vast to take on directly and there will never be enough time to address the economists systematically on an issue that they have owned for a hundred years. Only on an occasion such as presented here, an invitation to review aspects of economic anthropology in light of a re-reading of Polanyi's (1944) *The Great Transformation*, has it seemed worth placing some thoughts into circulation. Those thoughts focus on how price is produced, presented, revealed, and concealed as a *composite* as distinct from a *singular* amount.

In all but catastrophic inflationary conditions, market participants are describing and judging absolute and relative prices all the time. Allusion to the composition of prices, through distinct but converging processes, has recently become one of the regular reference points in popular and even corporate justificatory discourse. This is a departure from concepts that take price "as a whole," such as "worth" in a religious register, and the intersection of supply and demand (scarcity and desire) in the marginalist neoclassical register. Although the use of a composite idiom seems on the rise at present, the component categories in circulation actually refer back to classical theory: to returns to land, labor, capital, and the state. So although the price instabilities of recent years have provoked a more explicit compositional idiom, its terms diffuse the evidence of very innovations whose broader influences have made composition so compelling an idea to invoke. Novelties in financial futures and insurance technologies, and possibly the effects of intellectual property rights and contractual engagements, are all embedded in other terms by the time that price enters public discourse. I concentrate on these popular terms, trying – where I can – to identify places where direct evidence or circumstantial argument can show both the increasingly explicit reference to classical elements and the existence of other elements that are concealed by them.

Anthropological theories of price have always been implicitly composite, in order to encompass and recognize sociocultural components. Marx argued that the commodity and its price is a fetish that conceals the social relationships on which it is based and confuses the analytical components of use and exchange value. For the component costs of land and labor, Polanyi refers to them as "fictions," since there are no market relations at all behind their production. The concealment of composition would then be one of the main functions of price ideologies, since it dampens reasonable doubt about worth and circumvents the moral and political commentary that might ensue from close analysis. Indeed, throughout history, many authorities have aimed to maintain "customary" or "just" prices so as to avert negative commentary, at least in certain domains that are crucial to political purposes. As E. P. Thompson (1971) argued and illustrated so forcefully, the questioning of simple equations between things and their prices is a sure sign of fundamental unrest. In Thompson's case of the price of bread in the eighteenth century, it was the miller's margin that came under violent selective scrutiny when price was questioned. Restoring a meaning to the price–livelihood equation can restore and buttress the legitimacy of government. For example, during my childhood, living on post-war rationing in Britain, people knew that prices were artificially stabilized and subsidized, although no-one knew by how much, and were thereby coaxed into a permanent position of collective gratitude (even when tempered by grumbling). Conversely, under antitax ideologies, public attention is deliberately drawn to sales and value-added taxes, in part to keep their levels clearly in the public eye in time for the next election.

In the twenty-first century, however, an interesting phenomenon has begun to emerge, namely, an increasingly open recognition that prices are composites, across the board. People are actually reminded that all prices are fictions – literally the results of narratives of creation, addition, and subtraction – in ways that go far beyond Polanyi's discussion of "fictitious commodities" in the mid-twentieth century or Marx's theory of commodity fetishism in the mid-nineteenth. Consumers are now trained by discount outlets to notice retail mark-up rates; by the Lou Dobbs Report to know about differential global wage rates; by foreign travel to pay attention to currency exchange; by many prices – from airline tickets to retail commodities – to know about added taxes, fees, and payments, which are often now itemized; by e-Bay and the automobile market to know about depreciation; and by their own experience with financial institutions to read the bills for compulsorily itemized charges and fees. Since the 1980s, we have become aware of a premium for celebrity on an expanding range of goods, for the brand image as glamor rather than guarantor of quality. Each of these additions is a quite familiar concept in itself; consumers themselves have just not focused on isolating and measuring each one so

self-consciously until recently.[1] The experience of doing so probably persuades
all of us that there must be other components we don't yet know about and still
others we don't understand.

The result is a moral economy of transparently composite prices, which
nevertheless retain the mystery of their components. My exploration here is far
from exhaustive, and the ethnographic examples come from domains of which
I already have particular knowledge, rather than from full-scale research. But
I can point to where it is going, in anticipation of the kind of revitalized debate,
apposite to our own moment in history, which the editors have launched. The
question is: now that prices are popularly recognized and vigorously engaged
with as fictional, fetishistic, and composite, what can and should analysis focus
on, and about what is analysis revelatory? I will argue, following the logic if
not the substance of Polanyi's argument, that we pay attention to elements of
price that are hidden in plain sight among the multiple traditional price elements
by the very diffuseness of their presence.

Price composites, historical moments, and the moral economy of prices

Prices have always been understood as fictions and composites at some historical moments, and they have been naturalized and moralized at others. My own
orientation comes partly from living up to the age of about ten in the moral
and political economy of administered market prices. I passed my childhood
taking regular trips to the shops with money in one hand and a ration book in
the other, knowing the official rhetoric of justice behind a wartime rationing
system and participating in the local calibrations of shortage and access. For
the money-price to be stable and unitary, ancillary prestations were made but
not considered a part of the price. To be assured of items during peak periods of
seasonal demand – chocolates for holidays, fruit for jam-making in summer – we
needed friendly relations with the local retailers. As errand-runners for the
family, children bore a pretty serious responsibility to be deferent and cheer-
ful to the shopkeepers at all times. And then some things came free: Ministry
of Food (MoF) orange juice, the compulsory one-third of a pint of milk per day
during mid-morning break at school, and – if my memory serves me right – cod
liver oil. We also received food parcels from Australia, with luxuries like sugared
almonds. The morality and civility of the gift thereby entered the commodity distribution system, alongside government redistribution, with all the implications
for personal status cultivation within an egalitarian ideology. A decade later at

---

[1] For example the British Airways online booking service gives a flight price, and then adds: an
online booking fee; a share of taxes and fees demanded by governments, authorities, or airport
owners; an insurance and security surcharge (since 9/11); and a fuel surcharge.

university, our generation needed the textbook training of Economics 101[2] to get the hang of equilibrium prices in self-regulating markets, in part because it implied a different nexus of citizenship, different local transactions, and a shifted responsibility for managing personal budgets. The one thing we all knew deeply from our own pre-rationing past, "by heart," was that there were severe sanctions backing our ability to adjust to the relative prices that would be produced by the market. They should fit into a budget. The Dickensian saying from *David Copperfield* was often quoted: "Annual income twenty pounds, annual expenditure nineteen and six, result happiness ... annual expenditure twenty pound ought and six, result misery." The latter could easily lead to debtors' prison. Personal debt was culturally imbued with danger and horror; the unique price and selective availability nexus of rationing had offered protection.

My familiarity with one regime of administered prices fostered my interest in how others had been created under other political regimes. It was price formation in the urban food supply system of colonial Cameroon that took me into studies of money in the first place, over twenty years ago. The price of food in the urban markets of colonial Africa (see Guyer 1987) seemed arbitrary: not the currency itself, which was by definition an arbitrary symbol of value and imposed from above, but the amounts, the numerical aspect of commensuration. Labor was not paid for in Southern Cameroon. Neither was land. The French mandate state set price ceilings, still known in administered systems as the *mercurial*. But, clearly, officials worried about food supply. In the early colonial system food was a "fictitious commodity" in Polanyi's specific sense of that concept (1944: 72): not initially produced for the market nor through market relations. Economic commentaries on African urban food prices have referred to prices as "high" or "low," with no obvious theoretical or practical referent except civil service salaries, which were also set by administrative fiat. "Getting the prices right" (as a much later policy called it), that is, getting all relevant prices to work in synergy, proved an elusive process. The continuing colonial and post-colonial impasse about bringing the price–wage–tax nexus into a dynamic and plausible systemic relationship lies at the heart of today's "fiscal disobedience," according to Roitman's (2005) trenchant analysis. So price fictions can also fail. They can be incoherent in themselves and become vulnerable to other and competing narratives and moralities of entailment, consequence, and avoidance under changing historical conditions.

Rapid fluctuations, however, probably always test the systemic tolerance, even in otherwise plausible price configurations. Price movements in Nigeria in the 1990s rose and fell in ways that may only be explained, if at all, in rather distant retrospect (see Guyer, Denzer and Agbaje 2002). In the longer run we

---

[2] Samuelson's (1948) famous textbook was deeply exotic at the time, with its image of equilibrium being like an olive in a martini, always drifting to the same position after disturbance.

are all living through price shifts that have been difficult to comprehend in terms of a simple version of demand and supply. A house we bought in 1977 went on the market twenty-five years later at about fifteen times our purchase price. On the other hand, many consumer goods go on sale for up to "80 percent off." And, yet again, in the summer of 2006, the Baltimore public turned intensely inquisitive about the sale, deregulation, and merger of the domestic energy company, which was projected to result in a 72 percent rate hike, just at the same time as an unprecedented rise in the price of gasoline. For many goods, there is a vast vista for hunting and gathering forays on the Internet, where comparative pricing constitutes a big part of the excitement of the chase on e-Bay and Craig's List. For many things, people's acceptance of customary price explanations has been shaken loose of its moorings. For services and insurance, we are increasingly aware of getting stuck in a maze of mini-monopolies, trick clauses, qualifying conditions, and other channeling devices that are almost as profoundly sanctioned by a revised bankruptcy law as in Dickensian Britain. Warranties, service contracts, membership dues, and so on tie the buyer to the seller to specific dates over time, and when conditions alter, unforeseen clauses swing into view. The aftermath of Hurricane Katrina in the insurance and real estate sectors, and the explosion of Enron in the energy sector, have opened up to public view many profit-making maneuvers and components of prices of which they had been unaware.

There are several ways to study the moral economy of composite prices; the most important at this stage would be through ethnography. This preliminary foray is written from secondary sources. The next section takes a key commodity, oil, and looks at representations of its price-as-composite in several contexts. It ends by showing how the place of finance and financial institutions remains fairly hidden, even after various decompositional exercises.[3] This matters enormously, and especially for comparisons between price regimes in financial institutional settings that are quite different from each other: Euro-America and West Africa, for example. So the next part of this chapter asks whether there is a gain in dropping back in time to Polanyi (and Marx) for the concept of "fictitious commodity" to apply to the risk and risk-mitigation instruments that are now incorporated into price, and then work forward from there. Like land, labor, and capital in their own times, risk now figures pervasively in price composition and capital accumulation, as both an addition and

---

[3] Here I would agree with Bill Maurer that there can be convergences of analytical and vernacular terms. But there is one aspect that has not been discussed enough: there is bound to be a *range* of vernaculars within any "society." For the layperson all may seem mysterious, whereas for the specialist it is hidden in plain sight. ("*Of course* we are looking for loopholes!" as one American accountant said to me as I was working on a paper of that name, mainly about Nigeria). Money, insurance, statistical economics, and so on, as entire domains of expertise, are bound to use different terminologies and forms of argument from the "public." The question is how closely they track each other.

a subtraction. But it is far more diffuse and difficult to identify than the classical factors.

A note first on oil as an example. We might argue that it is not a very good example of principles of price composition because of its uniquely political dimensions. I would argue, however, that this actually helps to throw some general processes into relief and especially the processes of self-representation to the consumer public. Because we know that finance is a hugely important and growing component of the petroleum sector at every level, its diffusion throughout the pricing process makes it possible to trace at least some of the price implications.

Custom and composition in oil prices

The following three small junctures in the massive edifice of oil-pricing illustrate parts of price creation and representation to which we, the public and scholars, can have access, and they open up vistas beyond which are far more opaque.

Representations of custom:the United States, summer 2006

The retail price of gasoline in America rose from around US $2 per gallon to over US $3 per gallon during the first half of 2006. This is still a low price by European standards, but the rapidity of change had a large economic and psychological impact. It instilled fear that all projections were now suspect: from domestic budgets for owning this or that kind of car to ticket prices in an airline industry already in deep financial trouble. In the face of public outrage, the petroleum industry had to explain the forces shaping the market. And since the "majors" cover the entire commodity chain from exploration to the pump, there was no evading the question or passing it on to another party. The price of crude oil is said to be difficult for corporations to influence. Even the major private companies hold direct control of a very small proportion of world reserves because of the prominence of national companies in most of the producer countries. And certainly it seemed plausible that increased demand from China and India would put uncontrollable pressure on world energy prices. The striking thing about the companies' explanations for my purposes here was not the possibility of self-serving reporting or an equally possible avoidance of mentioning all the smaller points at which price advantage may be gained (the judgment of quality, the criteria for setting royalty payments, and so on). It was their reliance on the notion of a *customary level* to proportional shares in the price received by the traditional market participants: producers, the government, the processors (refineries), and the retailers. A bargram that was widely published in newspaper advertisements and explanatory literature showed that, despite a large rise in the *nominal* price, there had been a fairly steady *proportion* of returns over several years among: (1) the crude product (53 percent in 2005); (2) taxes (19.7 percent); (3) refining costs and profits (18.1 percent); and (4) distribution and marketing (9.0 percent) (American Petroleum Institute 2006). Profit on capital is not included, although one newspaper version did give a profit rate of "8.5 cents on every dollar of sales", but externally to the graphic, so implicitly accruing to all parties.[4]

Finance is a component of all capitalist enterprise, but "profit" was not presented in the historical sequence, thereby implying that it does not change much. One result of the status and undeveloped nature of this category is that any new aspects of the extremely complex set of costs of finance are then indiscernible: capital investment, insurance, participation in futures and derivatives markets, and doubtless many other financial instruments, including speculation on the markets. Indeed, Rex Tillerson, CEO of ExxonMobil, expressed doubt that it would be possible for the public to understand the price composition of oil, although he committed himself to trying to explain "the fundamentals" during the maelstrom of confusion on Capitol Hill in May 2006 ("Last year alone the top 10 oil companies spent more than $30 million on their lobbying battalions." Phillips and Bosman, 2006.) The costs of finance are, in fact, diffused across actions and actors at every stage. I know from involvement in the Chad–Cameroon Pipeline project that financial instruments are inserted in several places, sometimes under non-obvious names, possibly in relation to categories in the tax code. For example, what is referred to as the "transport tariff" includes two financial elements, beyond the material and labor costs of maintaining the pipeline itself: an amount ensuring debt service (at an agreed rate, not pegged to the market price of crude) to the lenders, shareholders, and affiliates with respect to the immediate project, and a contribution per barrel to permit recovery and remuneration of company shareholders' investments. Since these rates are fixed in the contracts, for the duration of the agreements they are the "price of doing business" and also a non-proportional obligatory payment, irrespective of the price of the product. So large and so numerous are the total payments in the early years of production in a new field that the varied kinds added together – from royalty rights and customs duties to insurance against oil spills – may add up to the entire price of the crude oil under certain world price scenarios. Below that level, a company would suspend production since finance payments take priority over income. Some payments are mandatory

---

[4] This advertisement does not reproduce well. It consists of a dollar bill cut into three pieces: 55 percent crude oil, 26 percent refining distribution and service stations, 19 percent taxes, with the 8.5 percent profit as a footnote (see the *New York Times* April 28, 2006, page A5 and article May 3, 2006, page C1). Anyone studying the sources would immediately notice that these proportions differ from those in other publications of the American Petroleum Institute, including those reproduced with this paper: possibly the newspaper figures are more recent.

only as long as production continues, so suspension offers temporary relief. Price is presented to the general public, however, in a different way: as proportions of the retail price, based on *actors* ("producers," government, refiners, retailers), and crafted to appear customary.

One sensed that the China–India demand explanation of the oil price in the spring and summer of 2006 could not be sufficient, so rapid was the rise. I had written these paragraphs of the draft chapter before reporters started indicating a whole new element. The concept of "contango" entered the discussion, and then was referred to routinely, although it was never fully assimilated into the public explanations of price movements. National Public Radio reported:

Chief among (the factors) is "contango," a market term for the situation in which a commodity – like oil – has a higher future value than its current price. Oil companies and others like to buy futures contracts to make sure they've got oil coming to them well into the future. But lately, people who have nothing to do with the oil industry are buying oil futures, holding them as can't-lose investments that can return well over 10 percent. Investment banks from Morgan Stanley to Goldman Sachs are making so much money from oil futures that they've become a hot investment for all sorts of big-money players. Some of the biggest players are U.S. pension funds, which have put billions of dollars into oil futures. At least one analyst thinks that pension funds have become part of the machinery driving higher gas prices. "I think if you saw all the pension funds walk away," says Ben Dell, an oil analyst at Sanford Bernstein, "you'd probably see a $20 drop in the crude price." (Davidson 2006)

The final interpretation was that investment in futures was driving up the oil price, which then combined with rising consumer demand which, in turn, intensified an incentive to invest in the oil markets (although not necessarily in oil exploration and production). Twenty dollars per barrel would be about 28 percent of the price at the time. A contango condition indicates riskless profit, and indeed Goldman-Sachs earned the highest profit it had ever registered in 2006. When we return to the artisanal diagram, this profit can only figure as part of the market price of crude. But why then do the proportions of the price break down so similarly in 2006 as they did in the past? The naive consumer becomes a probing skeptic, increasingly demanding breakdowns into new components that seem buried in antique reporting customs in which whole new industries of risk management and consulting disappear.

Consumer petrol prices in Nigeria

Since the early 1980s, the Nigerian consumer public has been in intermittent insurrection over the price of petrol at the pump. There have been strikes, demonstrations, shortages, government pronouncements, and a great deal of consequent suffering. It became clear that people were certainly willing to pay money for petrol but that everyone, in one way or another, thought that citizenship in an oil-producing country entitled the buyer to a price that bore a stronger relationship to the cost of living than to anything else. In other words, the payment – if any – should go in the opposite direction as a right of birth. In another work (Guyer with Denzer forthcoming), we show how Nigerian commentators resisted referring to such an implicit payment as a "subsidy," and tabulated at least six different arguments from the press about how the petrol price *should* be composed. Twenty years before the American Petroleum Institute tried a "shares metric" for public education, the Nigerian government tried a similar tactic. In the face of critique and continuing price fluctuation, they eventually got totally lost in the layers of actual and imputed costs of the commodity chain. Several newspaper articles tried to break it all down and add it up again: production, refining, transport, retail, global markets with changing exchange rates, etc., etc. It never made any sense. But neither did other arguments. The reading public clearly thought that the price ought to be intelligible, which meant being able to trace out a logic of composition as a narrative connecting the oilfield to the petrol pump. In the absence of other logical explanations, one growing theme in the popular accounts became the cumulative margins skimmed off by the military leadership, the civilian leadership, the companies, and, increasingly, the illegal activities of bunkering. In the popular mind, insisting that there should be, in fact, identifiable components of the national petroleum price gave rhetorical traction on the political reality of a price that could not be explained in technical or economic terms.

At the petrol pump

One chapter of *Marginal Gains* (Guyer 2004) was devoted to the negotiation of the "real" price in a single buying event at a rural station in Nigeria in 1997, at the height of a profound petrol drought, and under mandated prices The unemployed youth who made a living from motorcycle taxi services were destitute; the farmers' and transporters' goods were rotting before they could reach the great urban markets; the professionals could not get to work or circulate around their networks; and the officials could not officiate. The arrival of one tanker truck in a somewhat remote area would provoke an enactment of price composition that was charismatic in its skill on the part of the station-owner. There was a mandated money price, from the government. Everyone on that day knew that rationing by a self-regulating price mechanism of allowing a bidding war would have brought social chaos, even if it had been possible, under and around the perspicacity of the police and the army. In the event, the station-owner worked the customary, named, components of a market price, in a manner that was similar in structure, even though different in content, to the company advertising described above. After standard Yoruba marketing practice, there are add-ons and subtractions, measurement adjustments and social recognition factors, indices of relative suffering (exposure to sun, need, and so forth), which translated into longer and shorter waiting times, more or less of the amount one wanted, "dashes" (tips) to the helpers and the soldiers, and so on. No-one expected the station-owner to operate at anything less than a profit. But she herself had to be careful that her practices kept within the limits of the discernible and recognizable, against the sanction of being accused of extortion at best and witchcraft at worst. This was not the same composite as the American Petroleum Institute, but still profoundly framed in familiar customary terms.

Inferences

The relationship between customary price, old and novel compositional logics, and popular political culture is a crucial one, and one to which theory itself contributes. Breaking out the components has been seen as a method of intellectual and political insurgency, event though its reference points may be "traditional" or perhaps visionary. Faced as we are now by price skepticism, economic anthropologists could try to sort through the empirical situations and the dynamics of rhetoric and theory. E. P. Thompson (1971) argued that a moral economy imbued the stability of prices in pre-capitalist England. People were enraged and selectively punitive when they moved out of customary equivalences. The impression is given by scholars in the Polanyi tradition that certain pre-capitalist commitments survived enough to deeply influence how the fictitious commodities were treated. It is unclear, however, what he thought about a moral economy of the "genuine" commodities and markets in general, particularly with respect to inevitable price fluctuations. What these junctures in oil markets suggest is that "custom" emerges at many points as a stabilizing representation, but that its own techniques of identifying actors and defining categories of cost eventually invite further skepticism when realities break out of the framework: from contango effects to disappearing subsidies to the works of witchcraft. We may clearly imagine that the classic functions of money – as equivalent exchange, as hierarchical payment, as fixed standard unit of account – each comes with its own moral compass and its own justifiable version of custom, and therefore that "multipurpose" money and price must always carry the potential for falling apart into conflicting moralities. But each instance of challenge is not necessarily a generic reiteration of this predictable falling apart. A "modernist" effect of the kind that Latour (1993) theorized, where definitions inevitably breed hybrids, must sometimes generate novelties that fail to fall into any obvious consensual or moral categories. So do customary accounts, even those drawing on old and familiar non-market moral terms, come to conceal as well as reveal, to stand in the way rather than point the way (as Polanyi hoped)?

Where is finance? And is risk a new fictitious commodity?

I am not making a "for or against" argument with respect to risk technologies. This would be futile and presumptuous (since I do not know this field other than through the anthropological and popular literature and personal experience). I am simply moving back and forth from "risk" to the classic work on "fictitious commodities" to clarify each in light of the other, and to pose anthropological questions about the public's changing culture of composite prices.

The extraction of risk from its common-sense matrix – designated variously as "danger, the wild, hazard" (Beck 1992), "rigid long-term commercial arrangements" (Lexecon 2006) or most broadly, a human condition that combines too much exposure with too much commitment – is claimed to be as pervasively important a shift as any that has taken place in the past fifty years. Writers from within the financial sector (e.g. Bernstein 1996; Gleason 2000) seem in agreement with Beck (1999) and Latour (2005) that the measurement and mitigation of risk/uncertainty have moved us into a new era of market practice, sociality, and social theorizing. Those who operate within the new financial markets describe ever-expanding frontiers of innovation.[5] So important do they consider these interventions that Bernstein rewrites the history of modernity as the history of "the mastery of risk … rooted in the Hindu-Arabic numbering system that reached the West seven to eight hundred years ago" (Bernstein 1996: 1, 3). "The past twenty-five years have seen more changes in capital markets than were introduced in the entire prior history, which spans centuries" (Gleason 2000: 3). Niall Ferguson (2001: 409) even attributes the final crisis of Russian communism to the "substantial risk premium" Gorbachev had to pay to borrow on international capital markets that had become more and more precise about profile and reputation.

The rise of risk and its mitigation was not predictable when Polanyi wrote *The Great Transformation* (1944), even though it had precursors in the credit and insurance sectors. But according to its practitioners, new financial instruments based on risk calculation have become a fundamental means of global market integration (LiPuma and Lee 2004) by allowing the vicissitudes in a range of commodity, stock, exchange rate, futures, and new financial instruments' markets to be estimated and mitigated. These vicissitudes may include almost anything: shifts in the geography and timing of demand; political conditions in producing countries; climate shifts; and other longer-term changes that fall outside the parameters of "rational choice." We used to assimilate some of this kind of risk management to the many functions of government, valuing it

---

[5] In fact, the journals devoted to risk date largely from the 1990s: 1964 the *Journal of Risk and Insurance;* 1981 *Risk Analysis,* an official publication of the Society for Risk Analysis; 1997 *Risk Management and Insurance Review;* 1998 *Journal of Risk Research;* 1999 the *Journal of Risk Finance.*

by paying taxes to cover it, and holding officials accountable for its application to any and all "problems arising." But over the past twenty-five years risk management has become more and more independent of government control, extricated from institutions for collective deliberation, and located in the private corporate sphere.[6]

This much is well-known (in outline), but what does it mean for our analysis of popular or "peopled" economies (Löfving 2005) in the present and future? In my review of our social science literatures, I find that risk turns up with varied referents: as the human condition, as modern sociological principle (Beck 1992), as moral challenge (Douglas 1992), and as various other not-quite-consonant ideas. We have not fully assimilated what risk has actually become as a *gainful commodity*. Beck's seminal book of 1986 looked at "the hazardous side effects to the growth of wealth" (Beck 1992: 20), but grasps only at a conceptual level that mitigation will become a commodity with a price. In a later book, Beck (1999) reviews the "eight major points" of his sociological concept of risk and the risk society, none of which grapples with the burgeoning growth of risk management for sale in markets. Neither does the wider social science literature (as judged by the entries in the *International Encyclopedia of the Social and Behavioral Sciences*; Thrift 2001; Yearley 2001) pay much attention to risk instruments as commodities with prices. Latour's (2005) new introduction to actor network theory is organized around uncertainty, but neither the index nor the chapter titles include finance or risk, or markets, profit and prices. Zaloom (2004, 2005) and Maurer (2006) stand out for taking the profit of risk management in their stride as they move into the specific cultures that make the price of risk mitigation plausible and livable.

In the professional finance literature, by contrast, risk instruments are indeed noted to be sources of new *profit* as well as of enormous intellectual satisfaction and perhaps (even) increased general welfare. In his history of the mastery of risk, Bernstein concludes that "all of them (famous forebears in probability theory) have transformed the perception of risk from chance of loss into opportunity for gain ..." (1996: 337). But Bernstein himself leaves ambiguous whether he means collective "gain" through the eventual mitigation of shared or generalized risk or something more immediate and individual. Surely he includes the more immediate meaning: gain from the market sale of information about risk and of the control mechanisms to mitigate the projected scenarios. Within the financial world, the profitability of novel risk management instruments is surely utterly taken for granted. This is one way in which money is made.[7] But the public has yet to catch up in this case. The newspapers try to inform us:

---

[6] A publication of the American Petroleum Institute that explains crude oil markets points out how recent is the institution of futures markets in oil (*Lexecon* 2006).

[7] See, for example, the history of SPDRs invented in the late 1990s: Standard & Poor's Depositary Receipts (pronounced "spiders")... Typical volume for the SPDR is over 42 million shares per day ... (Wikipedia). If one puts SPDRs into Google over 28,000 entries appear. These are not small phenomena.

"the company (Enron) came to symbolize the transition to a world where practically anything can be traded, from weather predictions to broadband Internet connections to forecasts involving the housing market ... Enron pioneered ... the trading of commodities that had never been traded before." To his credit, the journalist keeps returning to one chorus: "At their best, new markets can provide efficient new forms of insurance, enabling people or businesses to transfer risks they cannot control – for a fee, of course" or "at a price." (Berenson 2006: 1, 4)

I like this passage for two implications. First, like the sociologists, it recognizes that risk is "transferred" not eliminated, so we may ask some classic anthropological questions that are rooted in social and semiotic thinking: What is "risk" as a transacted "thing?" From whom and to whom is it transferred? Since mitigation can only ever be partial, where is the excess located in relation to a theory of ownership? (Maurer 1999). But, second, there are two intellectual icebergs partially hidden in the above passage. The first is the implication that the original object – risk – is already out there to be disembedded from a shared social matrix, transformed into a definition, and linked to an insurance strategy, in order to be revalued for sale on the market. Second, and relatedly, there is a conflation of fee and price that is intriguing, given our classic concepts for the functions of money. Fees and prices are considered by Polanyi and a long list of writers on money as analytically separate: fees as "payment" and price as "exchange" (Polanyi 1977). Money as exchange is for "the acquisition ... of desired goods" (1977: 104), whereas money given in payment "is the discharge of an obligation by handing over quantified units" (1977: 105). The former reflects market forces; the latter social relations. To claim that neither category is stable and that their relationship is reflexive is certainly to move beyond the analytical categories that derive from "the first modernity" (Beck 1999). But moving too fast over the process itself of mutual imbrication misses the price moment, when *both* may be explicitly at play at the same time and where both bring specific conditions and consequences into "reality." We do buy a commodity (an insured product) at a price, but we cannot choose what modes of insurance it accrues nor whether to buy it (the insurance component); hence the concept of "fee."

Given the ambiguities, and perhaps blindspots, in new social theory, would it help to apply Polanyi's concept of "fictitious commodity," to lend to risk mitigation some qualities commensurate with its stated importance? Polanyi's entire argument for the world-historic disembedding of "the self-regulating market" from the social matrix in the nineteenth century and its subsequent restructuring centers on the fate of the fictitious commodities of land, labor, and money, which he differentiates from simple commodities:

None of them is produced for sale. The commodity description of labor, land, and money is entirely fictitious. Nevertheless it is with the help of this fiction that the actual markets for labor, land, and money are organized; their demand and supply are real magnitudes ... But no society could stand the effects of such crude fictions ... unless its human and natural substance as well as its business organization was protected against the ravages of this satanic mill. (2001: 76–77)

Social history in the nineteenth century was thus the result of a double movement: the extension of the market organization in respect to genuine commodities was accompanied by its restriction in respect to fictitious ones. (2001: 79)

Polanyi is making three different arguments here, each of which may be relevant. First, he endorses the classical categories of the factors of capitalist production – land, labor, and capital – and their establishment as commodities as the defining characteristic of the historical event of capitalist transition. Second, he refers fictitiousness to the *ongoing* historical battle between society and the disembedded economy. Fictitious commodities *remain* recognizably fictitious because of the continuing inability of the "genuine" commodity form to contain all their attributes. Labor is irretrievably embedded in people and thereby in hunger, anger, mockery, and the collective capacity for all kinds of sociality. Land may degrade, subside, and flood. And money is never fully instrumentalized (Maurer 2006). De Angelis (1999) picks up the *continuing* quality of fictitiousness in Polanyi's terms to argue that Marxian "primitive accumulation" is a continuing process rather than a historical event:

Another way to put it would be through Karl Polanyi's concept of "double movement" (Polanyi 1944). In Polanyi's terms, the continuous element of Marx's primitive accumulation could be identified in those social processes or sets of strategies aimed at dismantling those institutions that protect society's from the market. The crucial element of continuity in the reformulation of Marx's theory of primitive accumulation arises therefore once we acknowledge the other movement of society ... Therefore, the current neoliberal project, which in various ways targets the social commons created in the post war period, set itself as a modern form of enclosure, dubbed by some as "new enclosures."

We could argue that it is precisely collective insurance, from the state to local sociality, that currently constitutes the most important and most lucrative commons that is being privatized and commoditized.

Third, there is another implication of fictitiousness that is particularly important for an anthropology of prices, and perhaps better indicated by Marx through the concept of fetishism than by anything Polanyi developed. As means of production, the fictitious commodities are a condition of *all subsequent actions and transactions*. At the same time as being "factors of production," land, labor, and capital are also the selected framing devices to define returns in a conventional manner as rent, wages, and profits.[8] As many have

---

[8] There is an interesting commentary by Joan Robinson (1962), that profit has never been adequately theorized or measured. However, it is reported, thanks to the corporate tax provisions. I remember a social conversation with a business school professor who related the two conditions: that the tax law determines how profits are measured, which results in murkily inaccurate representation of the profitability of American business as seen from an economics perspective.

pointed out, including Leslie White in anthropology, there are other options for calculating efficiency than reducing it to the use of land, labor, and capital, including energy and information. Beck argues that "we must conceive of *relations of definition* (with respect to risk) analogous to Karl Marx's *relations of production*" (1999: 149, original emphasis).

The configuration of risk has not yet been shaken down into a public culture or set of narratives in any of these senses, although the accounts given by its advocates suggest that it certainly deserves to be. The uneven advance of financial instruments in the world (Thrift 2001) poses familiar political disjunctures and consequent moral ambiguities with respect to those defined outside them altogether. For example, one passing CNN comment after the tsunami of 2004 was that "fortunately most of these people do not have insurance; otherwise the whole industry would collapse." Of course, those who lack private insurance are also those for whom their states have limited capacity for collective insurance, as well. Hence philanthropy. For those living within a developed risk/price regime, the implications of the mode of insurance for day-to-day living are more obscure. Industry advocacy of risk instruments is phrased entirely in terms of the benefits for everyone. For example, for the oil industry, "Consumers benefit because holding down producers' risks encourages investment in future supplies" (*Lexecon* 2006: 16). Beck, however, sees the identification of dangers and their parsing into risk and other cognates such as "hazard" as creating "a *bottomless barrel of demands, unsatisfiable, infinite, self-reproducible*"... they are "the insatiable demands long sought by economists" (Beck 1992: 23, original emphasis). That is, particular markets are so permeated by risk technologies that we would not even know how to unearth what they cost exactly as an added element to the components of the "cost of living" in a risky world or as producing remnants that are "defined out" and thereby fall to our aggregated philanthropic effort. The breakdowns in price and cost-of-living figures, however, come from a different era of stable definitions, and – in this case – definitions which have always rendered aspects of financial costs and benefits particularly difficult to discern. In household budget studies, for example, the interest on a mortgage appears under "housing," not "finance." The difficulty of "seeing" finance and risk mitigation is largely attributable to the traditional-customary nature of our categories of price composition, even while the exposure of the compositional process itself seems like a radical shift in public accountability for price levels.

Finance in comparative perspective

Does it matter that we can't see the price implications of changing financial instruments? We may detect the insertion of payments into prices when they directly affect us, or the public at large, when they become issues in the press.

We can look at the phone bill, the insurance bill, and other itemized accounts that do a conventional breakdown for us. Or we can read the cost-of-living statistics and wonder where certain costs are counted (interest on college loans; fees and interest on credit card debt?). And we can continue to study markets and prices in Africa where formal financial instruments only intermittently offer comparative and analytical insights. One of the analytical paradoxes we face is that the places Bohannan and Dalton (1962) characterized as "peripheral markets" may well be more competitive and self-regulated than the payment-permeated systems now growing up in the West. But we are grossly naïve about the full range of components that a new ethnography of price composition could reveal, in all the varied market matrices of the twenty-first century world. What people sense without knowing – or simply do not know but are connected to – are all elements of consciousness and consequence, and they must be analyzed.

Polanyi, following Marx (Halperin 1984), set up categories for comparative analysis between capitalism and other economic forms. He lived long enough to see some varied forms arise *within* capitalism, largely around the economy–society relationship. The expansion of risk instruments as commodities seems to be creating yet other possibilities in the relationship between monetary valuation in price regimes and forms of sociality. Before figuring out how powerful they might be and making sweeping claims, we need first to locate the actual ways in which risk instruments intervene in the world and the terms under which they are understood, exploited, circumvented, analogized, and so on. I am not yet able to think forward in time, as Marx and Polanyi did, because it would take the kind of knowledge of the financial sector that they built up about labor, wages, and political dynamics over a lifetime of empirical study. Theirs were studies of practice, not only of principle. But I can think back to how finance has figured in studies of issues that have been important to anthropologists in the past, and can ask about the implications of concepts that conceal it. In a re-analysis of budget studies, I started along a critical track with respect to financial costs by examining the conventional categories of data-gathering and analysis (Guyer 2004; Udry and Woo 2007).

There are two implications of this work. One is the implication for a comparative understanding of diffused financial costs as their own component of the price of things in economies where financial instruments are available, as opposed to those where they are not (like the middle- and working-classes in England in the 1930s; in Africa and other "soft currency" economies in the present). We cannot expect prices to be composed similarly across this spectrum, either in people's consciousness or in the consequences. The other implication is temporal. As financial commitments play out, the purchasers who thought of themselves as "buying a policy" on a human actuarial timeframe may become fee-payers living according to strict entailments, for a price, and on pain of monetary sanction. Indeed, the idea of "making payments," as distinct from "paying prices," is far more widespread than it used to be: the service contract, cable TV, consumer debt, penalties for late repayment, transfer costs for bank transactions, and so on. One senses that these small fees, based on limitations and cutting corners, are proliferating in some contexts, appearing in many forms in what are otherwise referred to as "markets."[9] And they may be becoming less and less recognizable, either in the record or in the popular conscience as the price of something that is recognizable.

Final thoughts

There does seem to be widespread tacit acceptance of the idea of the self-regulating market, with price as a mediator of supply and demand in some impersonal sense, and of the idea that this harmonizes with customary configurations that are livable. But with greater emphasis on price and markets, as at present, payments creep in as ever more crucial components of the price of staying in the business of living. Making these price components explicit would constitute a new kind of pragmatic and moral economy. On closer inspection, however, the traditional character of price may conceal its most novel components. So has the moral focus of this new economy taken shape yet? People are being weaned of any "redistributive" expectation. Philanthropy revives and reshapes a morality of "community" and "reciprocity." But is there some other emergent social form or process on which our moral compass and analytical lens should be focused?

An anthropology of value that fails to address prices is unsatisfactory, and so are studies of risk and reflexive categories that don't take into account the composition, levels, conditions, and consequences of price. Price is a major cultural as well as political-economic phenomenon. I have tried here to illustrate key features of this phenomenon that ethnography, adapting classic theory, could open up much further, as one potential avenue for new theory and analysis in economic anthropology. I agree with Beck (1999) and Latour (1993) that we may be in the foothills of a brave new world, for which past social theory is a limited guide. One of its features, however, is clearly monetization and the components of price: water in drought-prone areas of Africa; insurance against a downturn in housing prices in the United States; a trick with a trafficked Colombian prostitute in Tokyo; a nugget of cobalt dug up by a child laborer in Congo; a portfolio of financial assets; a hedge against exchange-rate fluctuations; and the cost of environmental protections. Everything costs. But customary approaches to price components through a model of "supply and demand

---

[9] The line between extortion and earnings is necessarily blurred here; criminal actions are fairly easy and common, like the one penny that a colleague said was being taken from his Barclays bank account as some kind of fee that turned out to be a fraud.

plus tax" no longer offer a satisfactory popular explanation, nor should they for the categories of anthropological analysis. There is a space here to take a closer look at the categories and their implications for revelation, concealment, and moral commentary in the twenty-first century. Thompson exemplified this for the eighteenth century and Polanyi did the same when he looked back at the nineteenth century and forward to the second half of the twentieth.

12   Illusions of freedom: Polanyi and the third sector[1]

Catherine Alexander

Introduction

This chapter is concerned with understanding the recent prominence of the third sector in British public policy and the light such an analysis sheds over neoliberalism's current form. Through two ethnographic studies of community recycling schemes I examine the divergence between the public rhetoric of freeing society from statist intervention and the practice of entangling third-sector groups into contractual relationships with the state. I suggest that not only do market principles mould how government now operates, but that the autonomy of the third sector is being eroded as it becomes little more than an instrument of the state, providing "public" services of welfare and environmental concern while internalizing the risks of operation. Polanyi helps us to locate and understand the process of treating "the economy" as something quite separate from human relations. What the ethnography here indicates is that, in the guise of re-invigorating social institutions as extensions of household values, the reach of market principles has, in fact, expanded to shape both state and society. The good citizen is now defined by an ability and desire to engage in the mainstream market as producer and consumer. The nature of the good state is more ambiguous.

In brief, my argument is this. The question of welfare is central to understanding changing relationships between society, the state, and the economy. Although implicit in *The Great Transformation*, shifts in managing the alleviation of poverty and in understanding its causes are pivotal to the upheavals Polanyi describes. In its broadest sense, welfare[2] is concerned with the margins and cracks within a given social system where individuals are excluded from

---

[1] I use the term "third sector" specifically because of its rising centrality in Britain: in 2006, the Office of the Third Sector was established as part of the Cabinet Office at the center of government.

[2] I take "welfare" to embrace charity and philanthropy, other than where I specifically distinguish between the three. As a brief indication of the differences: "charity" has religious connotations; "philanthropy" indicates private, secular activity; "welfare," at least to modern ears, suggests the intervention of the state into this arena. In practice, the terms are often used interchangeably.

dominant systems of exchange, whether reciprocity, redistribution, or the market. In a sense, welfare is a form of second-line redistribution.

A glance back over the various forms that welfare has taken, both before and after the early nineteenth century, shows that it has always been provided by a mixture of local and central state institutions, religious, or philanthropic organizations and individuals, albeit in markedly different configurations at various times. The current emphasis on commoditizing social and environmental care is unique; Polanyi charts the first emergence of this abstract notion of an economy.

He points to the moment when mercantilism – the coalescence of state and economy – shifted to a liberal doctrine of laissez-faire capitalism founded on the belief that the economy had an independent existence which state intervention only served to hinder. In line with this, contemporary neoliberal rhetoric claims that the institutions, services, and scope of the state should be retracted in favor of an autonomous market and civil society. Thus, this reasoning runs, civil society in the form of the third sector itself provides flexible, tailored, innovative responses to the welfare requirements of the less securely placed members of society; a Keynesian welfare state merely encumbers civil society with regulative bureaucracy.

Alongside these moves, anxieties about social instability have also resulted in an emphasis on the ability of the third sector to foster social cohesion, providing the trust in a community of strangers that the state no longer credibly supports. The values of the family and household, typically seen to be incarnated by women, are linked by extension to community-based schemes. The third sector is thus given the role of morally legitimating a market society while having to perform in line with commercial operations in order to win state grants.

My ethnography adds further layers to this reshaping of relations between state and society. Acting as a redistributive agent between those who have excess objects and the needy, this unequal exchange relationship is massaged by the community recycling schemes into one of apparent equality by attaching token prices to the objects passed on. The community recycling schemes assert that purchase has dignity, as opposed to the humiliation of being a recipient unable to reciprocate; and this suggests that the clients themselves are being reformed into citizens. In this frame, citizenship depends on the ability to participate in market exchange, thereby giving a new twist to the idea of the "consumer citizen," a term first used to denote the reciprocal relationship of a collective state providing services to its citizens in return for labor (Webb and Webb 1921).

The exchange of items mediated by these community recycling schemes is thus seen as being productive. Donors, voluntary workers, and recipients are all conceptually refashioned into good citizens through the work and objects of exchange. The responses and resistance of those on whom this transformative magic is being worked indicates, however, that the freedom and equality of third-sector citizens is as illusory as it was when freedom was first seen as isolation from social relations.

Polanyi's *Great Transformation* is structured around a number of related themes and debates. First, 1834 is identified as the point when a free labor force emerged, enabling economic relations to appear in England that were both divorced from local social milieux and unregulated by external institutions. This shift in labor relations was a direct consequence of the Poor Law reforms of that year revoking the Speenhamland System or allowances-in-aid-of-wages. Speenhamland had buffered the rural waged poor against grain price fluctuations, but caused downward pressure on wages and inhibited movement in search of better remuneration. Thereafter laborers were "free" to move.

From this epochal point, the argument flows backward and forward in time to emphasize the historical and ethnological abnormality of this move and the profoundly dislocating effects of the separation of economy and society in ideology, policy and practice. Before, as Max Weber observed, economic action was merely a special form of social life (quoted in Granovetter 1985: 481): allocation was effected through mechanisms of reciprocity or redistribution that were part and parcel of existing social roles and relations. After 1834, the working class, forced to confront a reserve army of labor that included the chronically unemployed, was exposed to savage social unrest that ultimately gave rise to fascism. Unfettered market exchange, in other words, produces material gain for the few but wastes human potential at both the level of individuals and the nation.[3] For Polanyi (1957a), severing the economy from social life is unnatural and hence profoundly immoral, producing the lapidary anthropological maxim that "the human economy is embedded and enmeshed in institutions."

One key opposition drives Polanyi's analysis forward: the antinomy that prompted the debate of the 1960s between formalist accounts of economic life and the substantivist emphasis on the connectedness of social phenomena (Plattner 1989: 1–4; Isaac 2005). Formal economy is the result of liberal policies based on the abstract notion of a maximizing, autonomous individual. As has been frequently observed, however, actually existing market forms of exchange are rarely unregulated and never pure, at least not in the north European states of the nineteenth-century liberal revolution (Galbraith 1987: 209). Polanyi, it might be added, appears to take the model for real, juxtaposing a condition of complete market separation with a stereotype of feudal

---

[3] Polanyi's language was borrowed from the movement for National Efficiency, prompted by statistics on ill-health and rural distress released after the Boer war. An effective welfare state was seen as a means of resolving the problem of such wasted potential. This meant direct intervention by the state into what had hitherto been seen as the private, separate realm of the household.

society that was itself quite unstable.[4] A similar relationship between reductive abstraction and complex social practice continues to dog debates on market, society, and welfare today. Polanyi's analysis of embedded versus disembedded relations points to this slippage between rhetoric and practice, but also shows how assumptions concerning welfare may serve as mobilizing tropes.

This argument is developed through three sections. The first offers a brief history of welfare provision in England, showing how both funding sources and the object and means of welfare are continually changing. The second provides ethnographies of two community recycling schemes. The last part considers how far the third sector represents a domain independent of state and market, given that organizations have to simulate the values and practices of commercial firms in order to win government support, and what light these "voluntary" schemes throw on ideas of citizenship and freedom. My conclusions consider the third sector as a product of both market failure and state failure.

A brief history of English welfare

Welfare provision has always been a mixture of aid from the state, churches, private organizations, and individuals (Mayo 1994; Cunningham and Innes 1998). More specifically, the history of welfare shows: first, shifting sources of funds and of arrangements for their allocation; second, changeable views of the object of such benefits; and, third, a variable gender component. All three themes are linked to broader economic changes and are still salient to the current debate on social justice and welfare. The main aim has always been the alleviation of poverty and its effects, but this has become hazier of late, when welfare structures and processes have been made to embrace environmental concerns.

The first main shift in provision was a move from ecclesiastical to secular control, with the church continuing to distribute alms while the state and local secular bodies increasingly took responsibility for collecting funds. Recognizing the inadequacy of local funding, a national poor tax was raised in 1576 to be administered locally, financed through central taxation but depending "on volunteers for its operation" (Cunningham 1998: 2). The first major Act, passed in 1536,[5] instructed each parish to undertake weekly voluntary collections for the relief of their "impotent poor," understood as those who relied on wage labor outside the feudal relationship and were willing but unable to work because of age or disability. There were also the able-bodied who were

---

[4] Geremek's (1994) historical overview of poverty in Europe shows not just its constancy, but how the poor have variously been treated by more secure classes: as an object of revulsion, a means to salvation, or a potential source of revolt.

[5] Often referred to as the Henrician Poor Law, its full title was the Act for the Punishment of Sturdy Vagabonds and Beggars.

willing to work, but unable to find it. These were "entitled" to the outdoor relief that became so scandalously severe in its application that the Poor Laws were eventually ended. A third category distinguished between those who were poor through no fault of their own and those who could work, but chose not to. The freewheeling trickster, who fleeced the unwary and virtuous, was already intrinsic to a value system that had begun to separate the deserving from the undeserving poor long before the Victorians made the distinction common-place (Cunningham 1998: 1–3). In this way an appreciation of productive labor fed off condemnation of merely verbal conjuration of value.

The late-eighteenth and nineteenth centuries saw key transformations in the idea of welfare. A new emphasis on individual donor–recipient relations entailed visits to the poor in their homes, usually by women. This normative focus on the family as the core social unit also led to attempts to control it and thereby produce an ideal family that was tractable to factory discipline (Donzelot 1997). Such interventions were driven by the Enlightenment credo of progress, which underscored the rehabilitation of the poor. A politics of charity had Catholic and Protestant missions competing for the souls of the poor; the continuing competitiveness of charities for both funding and clients was a notable feature of our research in 2006.

In the latter part of the nineteenth century, poverty came to be understood differently, just as responses to it became more formalized. It had been accepted earlier that women and individuals at key lifecycle junctures (children and the elderly) were more susceptible to hardship. The advent of industrialization and of a relatively unregulated market economy brought with it an increasing appreciation that poverty was also structural, caused by the need to keep profits up and by a new category of urban poor created by the market. One reaction to the misery caused by Polanyi's great transformation was an expansion of urban charitable and philanthropic institutions directed toward the mitigation of suf-fering. Just as state responses to poverty were deemed inadequate and private provision was encouraged in the late-nineteenth century so, fifty years later, the welfare state emerged out of recognition that private management of welfare was defective. The pendulum continues to swing.

Welfare state

Prompted by the sheer scale of urban poverty highlighted in a series of high-profile publications at the end of the nineteenth century (e.g. Mearns 1883; Booth 1890), and exacerbated by the economic depression of the 1880s, pri-vate philanthropy came to be seen as inadequate and the state began to take center stage in welfare provision from the 1908 Pensions Act onward. The emergence of state-controlled welfare provision at the start of the twentieth century and its consolidation after the Second World War were both responses to economic crises that threatened political stability, rather than a rethinking of social and economic structures. In both cases, too, if we follow Polanyi's line, these social catastrophes were caused by the atomizing effects of the free market. For Kirkman Gray (1908), the principal contribution of nineteenth-century philanthropy was to demonstrate, through its ultimate failure, the need for a radical reconceptualization of social structure. David Owen (1965: 505) later neatly suggested that the welfare state was nothing more than "a homeopathic preventative of socialism."

Private and voluntary actions and associations became "the junior partner in the welfare firm" (Owen 1965: 545). William Beveridge's (1948) enthusiasm for voluntary work was the beginning of contract – rather than status-based relations between the state and philanthropy (Briggs 1973: 509). Voluntary action appears here as a conscience to ice the cake of economic realism. Only at the end of the twentieth century did the third sector come to be seen as an essential plank in public-sector economics, with all its multiple forms, practices, and values contained under one rubric.

The end of Fordist mass industry, full employment, and state welfare from the 1970s on was, in its way, a second great transformation. The elderly machinery and infrastructure, which had once spearheaded the industrial revolution, were liquidated in the great sell-offs of the 1980s. With the global reorganization of capital and industry, unemployment became chronic and the welfare state was increasingly unable to cope with post-Fordist pauperism. The neoliberal move was to dismantle the state welfare safety net, in the process "rediscovering" the third sector as a means of addressing the resulting gap (Etzioni 1988, 1993; Levitt 1973).

Although renaming the various non-profit organizations and movements as a "third sector" suggested an alternative to state and market, connections between all three domains have since been tightened through various forms of privatization. Another way of seeing this is as the externalization of risk from government to society and individuals in a market model. State assets and services, in particular in the growth areas of welfare and environment, are being divested to both the private (market) and third sectors. Environmental justice is now increasingly taking center stage, sometimes in place of social justice, sometimes as an adjunct to it, and sometimes as the very foundation of equity.

The oscillation between central and local provision, state and private responsibility for welfare is a recurrent theme; so, too, is the resuscitation of old remedies for new causes of inequality. Contemporary efforts to foster community, understood through locality rather than networks of affiliation and kin, evoke Beatrice Webb's solution to the economic devastation of post-war Britain:

The whole theory of the mutual obligation between the individual and the state, which I find myself working out in my poor law scheme, is taken straight out of the nobler aspect of the mediaeval manor. (1948: 385)

Gender

The idea of women as both recipients of welfare and the ideal donor provides a key to understanding how welfare and environmental concerns are addressed and, by extension, broader changes in economic history.

The late-eighteenth and nineteenth centuries saw a distinct gendering of private welfare (Cunningham 1998: 11). Both the spiritual aspect of charity and the secular characteristics of philanthropy drew on what were perceived as the feminine virtues of care, love, and domesticity. It was a respectable activity for middle-class women otherwise largely confined to the home, for "woman's virtuosity lay in her containment, like the plant in the pot" (Davidoff and Hall 1987: 191). In effect, as Prochaska (1980, 1988) notes, this was merely extending the proper concerns and values of the household into the streets, slums, and byways of the city. The nineteenth-century philanthropist, Josephine Butler, explicitly contrasted "masculine" state-controlled welfare systems with the more feminine parochial service; and several feminist critiques of the welfare state (e.g. McIntosh 2004; Pateman 2004) suggest that it merely replicated dominant ideologies, excluding women, whether as recipients or donors, from full civic personhood. Feminist analysts of post-socialism, such as Watson (2000), Einhorn (1993) and Einhorn and Sever (2003), have made a similar point for the states of the former Soviet bloc and their response to poverty. Women are still held to be crucial to recovering a lost social integrity, rooted in family and home but extendable into the city's streets. They also increasingly have to bear the double burden of domestic care and principal wage earner.

Manuals such as *Household Administration,* published in 1910, explicitly take up this theme in linking care of the home to industrial efficiency and thence beyond the threshold. In defense of this rational approach to running the house, one of the editors (Schiff) explains:

Scientific training in Household Administration can alone save the sorely taxed housewife of today ... It is only by being a mistress of her craft ... that she can make sufficient time to devote herself to ... those ever-growing outside duties which the 20th century is imposing upon her in the shape of public and social work ... [T]he help and advice of scientifically trained women are absolutely necessary in the management of hospitals, the administration of the Poor Law and the general solution of social problems. (Ravenhill and Schiff 1910: 14–15)

In the same volume Alkinson (1910: 129) cites the Webbs as noting that the essential difference between businesses and households is that the former are run for profit, the latter for comfort; the former are concerned with exchange values, the latter with use values. The distinction between household and market is commonplace in economic anthropology (see Gudeman, Chapter 2, and Gregory, Chapter 8, in this volume). What is notable here is the emphasis on extending domestic values of solidarity and social reproduction, honed through science, into the moral and social vacuum beyond. This anticipates the clash of values when inimical principles associated with household and market meet on common ground in the third sector initiatives described below.

Broadly speaking, welfare was often directed toward women while, on the other side, middle-class women continued to provide voluntary labor, whether in visiting the homes of the deserving poor and raising money in the late-nineteenth century (Prochaska 1980) or, in the late-twentieth century, staffing the administrative and fund-raising side of charitable ventures.

Recent economic developments, however, are affecting the gender composition of the voluntary labor force in quite new ways. More women are entering the growing services sector, though usually in low-paid, part-time, short-term contract work; while unemployed men, especially in regions once dominated by smokestack industries, are turning to the voluntary sector. Nevertheless, this sector is still dominated by women in terms of numbers, if not seniority.[6] In the community recycling schemes we worked with there was a distinct gendered division of labor: women took office jobs and served clients with second-hand clothes. The collection and distribution of food or bulky goods (furniture or white goods) was managed and operated by men. In our three examples, the community recycling scheme was run by men.

Labor supply in these community recycling schemes was a constant headache, other than for faith-based organizations, which drew on a reserve of female voluntary labor from associated faith groups. The traditional feminization of voluntary labor reflects the standard account of housework (England 1993): simultaneously valorized and marginalized, it lends to the voluntary sector and unremunerated labor the ethos of an extended family, but (self) exploitation is often masked by the discourse of care.

Community recycling schemes

The third sector is far from being homogeneous. At a minimum, there is a clear separation between organizations that operate a system for beneficiaries and cooperative, flatter structures where mutual interests bind the group together. This parallels the distinction between philanthropy and mutual aid (Deakin 1995). The latter may be seen as a model for a kind of participatory democracy. The community recycling schemes we worked with acted *on* rather than *with* any discernible community; as such they belong to the former category and furthermore were closely entangled with both the state and the market.

---

[6] Sixty-six percent of workers are women Wilding *et al.* 2004: 119) with over 80 percent (23,500) of new jobs created by the voluntary sector during 1998–2000 being taken by women (Wilding *et al.* 2003: 13). Seventy-one percent of trustees are aged over 45, 95 percent of board members are white, male trustees dominate organizations with large incomes (Cornforth 2001: 11–13).

Rising interest in community recycling schemes was prompted by the 1999 EU Landfill Directive,[7] which, in turn, led to the Household Waste Recycling Act (2003), setting recycling targets for English local authorities. Failure to achieve the targets will result in severe financial penalties devolved to local authorities. So far, statistics suggest that targets are unlikely to be met. The Department for Environment, Food and Rural Affairs (DEFRA) therefore encouraged local authorities to form partnerships with community recycling schemes with a view to "educating the public, encouraging participation and involving communities" (DEFRA 2006). The belief is that, since they are in and of the people, community recycling schemes can provide the missing link between the state and its citizens.

One problem is the instability of many community recycling schemes. Start-up or capital funding is relatively easy to secure, continuation funding less so. According to a London local government officer in 2004:

The public's lost trust in government; community groups are a better way of getting in touch with people. The problem is that we can't provide funding for more than two years without going through a formal tendering process mandated by government – and most community groups don't know how to compete. Even if they're successful, they then lose their credibility in the eyes of the public who just see them as an extension of the Council.

This was confirmed by another local authority officer, who also pointed to the conflict between pressure on local authorities to form alliances with community groups and the demands of public accountability. He was legally unable to contract with any organization that could not demonstrate a three-year history of financial viability and a turnover in considerable excess of the contract value. Moreover, the costs and benefits of such contracts often fall in different places and in different timeframes, so that one local authority department effectively subsidizes another. Further, quantification is a perennial difficulty: it is difficult to say precisely what items and how many are diverted from landfill. Few local authorities or indeed community recycling schemes possess weighbridges. Proxies must therefore be used to calculate what the local authority is getting for its money. It is impossible to track and cost every exchange, and the benefits are so diffuse that they are impossible to quantify for a neat balance sheet. The following section details the difficulties two community recycling schemes had in securing and maintaining funding for their operations.

FRAME

FRAME is a charitable organization, based in a city in southern England, which acts as an umbrella for a number of recycling operations. Originating

---

[7] The directive requires that, by 2010, the UK reduces the amount of biodegradable waste going to landfill by 75 percent of 1995 levels.

in, and still directed by the local Methodist church, it is headed by Malcolm, a part-time evangelical preacher. In line with the founding Methodist mission, FRAME's principal aim is to alleviate the effects of poverty; more than this, as Malcolm insists, "We exist to give people their dignity back, and dignity means *choice*. Dignity means *ownership*." This mantra underpinned a plan for a quasi "shop" where clients could choose items of furniture they wanted in exchange for a voucher, produced by FRAME, to a nominal value of £50. The items would be priced with the limits of the vouchers in mind. The vouchers could be supplemented by cash but could not be redeemed for money either wholly or in part.

When first established in the 1990s, FRAME ran a furniture-recycling enterprise, FREE, which collected unwanted items from donors, stored the furniture in a warehouse on-site[8] and later distributed it to "customers" as the clients are also known. As the only such local organization FRAME had a continuous stream of donated items. Recipients were located through an extensive referral system, with over sixty organizations – from the police to Church visitors – logged on a database who contacted FRAME whenever they encountered someone in need of basic furniture. In short order, either a "basic pack" would be dispatched or the one item of furniture desperately needed. If clients were in a condition of extreme poverty, the function of delivered items was all that mattered; style and quality were irrelevant. This response to a condition of bare life was rather removed from "choice."

FRAME also operated a "Basics Bank" to provide clients with a set of clothes and shoes on presentation of a voucher. Again, recipients were largely identified by referral agents. At a meeting held with these agents in 2005, Malcolm announced that, without formal financial support, this operation would have to close. The referral agents revealed at this time that processing claims for public welfare by statutory bodies often took so long that they handed out Basic Bank vouchers as one way of addressing immediate needs. FRAME was thus absorbing these institutions' costs but the transfers went unmarked; senior managers of these bodies were largely unaware of FRAME's existence, and there was no record of how many people were benefiting from this stop-gap measure.

Most of FRAME's office staff are female volunteers from the Methodist Church, many of whom said they felt they were "working for God," a calling that was perhaps reinforced by their attachment to Malcolm. Malcolm is less popular in the warehouses where the workers, all men, tend to talk rather of the "management's" distance from the coalface and the anxieties caused by fluctuations in staffing levels caused by FRAME's erratic funding. The warehouse workers were a combination of volunteers, paid staff, and occasionally

---

[8] The local authority charged a nominal rent for the warehouse. Furniture that could not be re-used was "disposed of" free of charge, with neighborhood wardens turning a blind eye to what was often fly-tipping.

a reluctant recruit from a Community Service Order (CSO) or Youth Enablement Scheme.

Although FRAME aimed to re-skill the chronically unemployed or recently released prisoners – a local organization for placing volunteers said that FRAME had "worked wonders" in this regard – there was no sign of this during our fieldwork. Rather, some volunteers stayed on as paid staff, while others, both paid and voluntary, expressed no desire to reenter formal employment preferring, in the words of Tony, a van driver, "to stay outside the rat-race." Others, suffering from psychiatric or other illnesses, were unable to find full-time paid work. Ian, the warehouse volunteer coordinator, complained that his work was done for free while others were paid for the same effort. There were also periodic flare-ups when paid workers were asked to move between schemes. On being told that he had to move to FREE, Graeme, a paid van driver, refused to go, "I speaks my mind, and them up there doesn't like that," he said, but he had already had a final written warning and so Malcolm sacked him on the spot. This generated much heated discussion in the warehouse; the volunteers, Community Service Order recruits and enabled youths took his side with talk of solidarity and strikes, though in the end nothing happened.

Staffing and management problems aside, the core difficulty was funding the various ventures. FRAME always seemed to be on the edge of collapse, despite the rosy picture painted in its annual reports. Malcolm resisted external commercial advice as being contrary to the ethos of his venture, but had not tried to secure long-term funding and was unsure how to tap into EU or other grants by exploiting what he saw as the multiple benefits offered by FRAME – retraining in driving skills, food hygiene, first aid, warehousing, rehabilitation, health and safety, quite apart from providing clothing and furniture to the local needy.

The lack of funding resulted in Malcolm's ultimatum to the local Social Services that FREE would be closed within the week unless money was forthcoming. A cheque for £90,000 was drawn and sent the following day. The continuing problem was to demonstrate that FRAME absorbed some costs of the local authorities and thereby avoid the rollercoaster of one-off grants and reliance on the dribble of donated money.

Provide

"Provide" was established as an independent furniture re-use charity in London in the early 1990s, but floundered for lack of funds, lack of coordination, and an inadequate supply of labor and stock. In 2002, it was taken over by the not-for-profit agency of a Housing Association, which provides advice and repairs to social housing stock. The current director, John Marks, was seconded from the agency.

Provide was a quite different operation from FRAME, specializing in the collection and redistribution of bulky goods rather than addressing diverse social needs, although its manifesto mentioned "social concerns." John cultivated contacts with various local authorities and maintained close links with the social housing sector, frequently gaining contracts to refurbish "voids:" empty blocked-off flats. A secondary operation cleared the flats of any existing contents, passing on usable items to the venture's recycling arm, and disposed of the rest in local council landfill at a concessionary rate. Voids were usually refurbished with cheap furniture acquired wholesale from contacts. Trade was brisk: the turnover of families and individuals being moved out of bed and breakfasts is high; the volume of "decants" needing accommodation is similarly growing as regeneration programs aimed at "sink estates"[9] follow a systematic agenda of demolition and rebuild. The other key difference between the two community recycling schemes was the difficulty John had in maintaining labor levels for Provide.

In 2005, Provide's annual turnover was nearly £500,000. The main sources of income were from one-off and recurrent contracts with local local authorities. There were two kinds of contract: either clearing and refurbishing flats or collecting bulky waste from householders, keeping re-usable items for redistribution, and disposing of the remainder to landfill at a concessionary rate offered by the local authority. The refurbishment contracts provided new and second-hand donated furniture to clients moving from temporary to permanent social housing. These contracts were the backbone of the organization, providing a constant flow of local authority money to pay for fuel, collections, staff, and so forth. The new furniture, often acquired at reduced prices, smoothed over the erratic supplies from donors. Unlike FRAME, Provide was in competition with other re-use schemes for donated items. In a curious inversion of the idea of the "free" market as inherently unstable and in need of moderation, here, redistribution of one-off donations had to be buffered by traded goods.

The second kind of contract, collecting bulky waste from householders, was intended to supplement donated items to Provide and to save money for the local authority. Landfill costs are high. The local authority rerouted calls from its bulky waste collection department to Provide if items sounded reusable. Provide collected all the furniture, selected some for the warehouse or housing to be refurbished, and sent the rest to landfill at no cost to themselves. In this way, the local authority diverted bulky waste from landfill, thus saving disposal costs, and avoided punitive penalties of not meeting nationally set household recycling targets.

But one problem, in common with many community recycling schemes, was that few items collected or donated were appropriate for re-use. Provide's published figures suggested that 45 percent of donated items were re-used. Our

---

[9] "Sink" estates is a common term for British housing estates, often built in the 1960s and 1970s with a high degree of social deprivation, poverty, and poorly maintained housing.

own observation, confirmed by the drivers and warehouse workers, was that 10–25 percent were re-used. Drivers sometimes took away more items from the donor than had originally been agreed; these were not formally logged and were usually thrown straight on the council skip. FRAME's drivers also told us that, even after telephone screening, many items they collect cannot be re-used. Identifying throughput of reused items was thus not straightforward.

The first catch therefore was how to measure transactions. The items were neither sold nor exchanged or bartered, so a money figure is inadequate for representing total stock flow. In quality and style the items varied from cumbersome 1930s wardrobes fitting neither small flats nor the taste of most clients, to flatpack furniture that satisfied an IKEA aesthetic, but often collapsed in the process of reconstruction. Since landfill charges are based only on weight, this is how the value added of contracts was calculated: by the landfill cost averted of a given weight of furniture. But community recycling schemes had to rely on proxies. Costs are also calculated in terms of penalty avoidance for end-of-life disposal, rather than in terms of the benefits to recipients when their life is extended. "Diversion" from landfill is also a temporary measure: many recipients planned to return their donations to Provide or to throw them out when they were able to afford something more to their own taste.

Illusions of freedom

How does Polanyi's emphasis on the market as a realm independent of social relations square with this account of life in the three sectors of Britain's economy today? Use of the name, "the third sector," suggests that groups and actions within it are outside the state and the market. Being "outside" may variously mean the pursuit of aims other than profit or forms of social cohesion that rely neither on market transactions nor on the government. In fact, the values and practices of each sector are intertwined. The continuing social life of objects, after the initial moment of purchase for consumption, offers a window into the kind of relations that are imagined, formed, broken, and re-made in the course of donation, collection, and allocation. These relations, in turn, hinge on the complex interplay of ethical ideas concerning work, alienation, gift, and just desert.

The neat division suggested by the three-sector model is informed by the neoliberal myth of devolution and independence from the state, while in practice regulative control is tightened. Neoliberal governance concerns the nominal privatization (separation or seclusion in this reading) of all aspects of life. This ranges from restructuring economic enterprises and decentralizing power to the inculcation of self-monitoring techniques, which at once outsource the business of government to the governed (Cruickshank 1999) and do so in a manner that is tractable to market interests. This drive does not simply favor market principles to increase wealth, but also promotes the *virtues* of solitariness as personal self-reliance (Carrier 1997) through finite and hence "transparent" transactions. Transparency offers visible proof that each action has extracted the maximum benefit in a just environment although, as the burgeoning literature on audit shows (Strathern 2000), recording mechanisms often create rather than reflect particular forms of action and sociality. Further, the full effects of any given process are infinite and may only be measured through artificial containment (Alexander 2005).

In the rhetoric of international aid agencies such as USAID, an unregulated, "free" market and private property are an essential precursor to democracy. Thus, power in this diffuse form is put at the service of a market ideal, while the market is cast as the *sine qua non* of political freedom. The poverty and instability that has resulted in the former Soviet bloc, not to mention Africa, would seem to suggest otherwise. Equally, market principles and values have seeped into government administration itself. Again, this is generally cast in terms of maximizing the efficiency of public services and thus of providing the best and most cost-effective service for the public (Alexander 2001).

In Britain, "internal markets" have been introduced, compelling departments to sell their services to each other and to the public, or to outsource services through private finance initiatives or public private partnerships,[10] or as more conventional fixed-term contracts. In consequence, the operating timeframe of public-sector departments has been shortened and there is less, rather than more, "joined-up" government. The arch liberal Ludwig von Mises (1944), who castigated the excessive intervention of state bureaucracy into market affairs, also held that state administrations cannot embrace market operations because their long-term goals are fundamentally different from those of commercial bureaucracies focused on short-term profits.

As the studies reported above show, many such organizations rely on public funding,[11] which, since it is guided by the market principle, is increasingly short-term, dedicated to start-up funding with the aim that they must become self-sufficient. Employment within these groups was therefore precarious, as the community recycling schemes stumbled from one short-term contract to another. Continuation funding was made more problematic by the fragmentation of central administrations into rival "cost centers." Without the use of imaginative proxies and surrogates, it was impossible for Provide or FRAME to demonstrate precisely how much material had been diverted from landfill

---

[10] These are two methods of the state contracting services or asset construction for a long but finite period to the private sector. The supposed advantages are the injections of private money into public service provision and the transference of risk. In effect it is a method of long-term borrowing that is not recorded as such.

[11] Amin, Cameron, and Hudson (2002) note that 3 percent of the social enterprises they studied were wholly self-reliant; 67 percent were completely dependent on government funding.

and exactly what the cost savings were to the local department funding the contract. Their actions also alleviated "bed-blocking" for local hospitals by providing temporary accommodation for the homeless and providing them with skills training, thus effectively taking on other departments' costs. These services do not complement those of the state, as in former configurations of the welfare mixed economy, but replace them.

The formal institutional context reveals a contradictory plurality of values and practices. While local authorities attach importance to the alleged ability of community recycling schemes to connect to local people, this can only be harnessed through formal contracts. The more successful community recycling schemes undoubtedly have close links with councils, related third-sector schemes, and commercial enterprises; but their direct relations with "the people" are tenuous. As tracing the objects and labor incorporated in the process suggests, the role of the community recycling schemes tends more to be a mediating and transformative one between those who have more than they want (not need) and those who are impoverished.

The second life of objects

People gave to a community recycling scheme for a range of reasons. Donated objects were rarely seen to be past their useful or sentimental span. Rather, life events, principally a change of kin relations, often resulted in an excess of things that forced divesting rather than throwing them away. Thus death or a break-up or children moving away frequently resulted in minor explosions of objects that perhaps entangled too much history for comfort, or simply took up too much space.[12] Again, moving home, often because of such changes, generated objects for which no recipient could be found close to home, but which were deemed too good for throwing out. Reasons for giving to a community recycling scheme, as opposed to the local authority collection service, were various. Most donors spoke of wanting such things "to go to a good cause," "to help the poor," "for someone else to be able to use it," or "to help the environment." Some also mentioned that the community recycling scheme was quicker than the council to collect bulky goods and would haul out stuff from inside the house rather than make the householder leave it in the road. There was little exchange in these rapid collections and almost no continuing relationship, whether mediated by objects or not. There was no direct connection between donor and recipient as in the material donations made by nineteenth-century philanthropists.

---

[12] Contrary to our expectations, none of the donors we spoke to had got rid of an item because they wanted a change.

Nevertheless, both donors and the community recycling schemes firmly spoke of these items as "gifts," which generated a measure of awkwardness. Prospective donations were first screened by office staff on the telephone in order to weed out unusable items and then by the drivers, who had their own ideas of what was appropriate and of what recipients deserved. Rejection of an offer invariably caused outrage, "But it's a *gift*! I'm giving it to you for free! Why won't you take it?" or "It's been good enough for me, why isn't it good enough for the people you're giving it to?" Although the donation was usually made as an altruistic act, the moral shock of rejection evoked refusal to participate in the obligations of gift exchange.

The reciprocal relations of the gift (Gregory 1982) are clearly missing here. But then it was scarcely a "commodity situation" (Appadurai 1986: 13) either: these items were not intended for money exchange. The new phase of their life was predicated on use value, not exchange value, recalling the contrast between households and businesses. The offer of unwanted furniture has an element of altruism in it, but it has closer affinity with Parry's (1986) model of asymmetrical giving. In this case, however, the gift relationship entails an abstract body such as the state as guarantor of exchange (see Titmuss 1971). Titmuss also noted that the act of donation (in his case, of blood), when not purely pragmatic, could be seen as a reciprocal act, "giving back" to a society that has favored some over others. The ultimate recipients, however, are in no position to reciprocate. For many, receiving these items marked a condition of desperation and they spoke of looking forward to when they could, in turn, rid themselves of these items and buy furniture that suited an anticipated "lifestyle."

After disposal, the objects were placed in a state of limbo. The specific social relations that they had embodied for the donors, whether with positive or negative connotations, were curtailed. Entering the warehouses, they were again picked over, thrown away, or cleaned up, and given prices within the range of the vouchers. At this point, warehouse staff, in particular at FRAME, would often take home odd items to which they had taken a fancy, as a perk of the job. There was no sense of theft here since the items did not belong to anyone.

Placing the anonymous, priced items in a shop transformed them into quasi-commodities. As Malcolm said, the aim was for the clients to achieve dignity through a market transaction-based choice and ownership. In all the community recycling schemes that we worked with staff referred to redistributing goods through vouchers or token prices as removing the stigma of the charitable gift: this, they said, made it more like proper shopping. By calling recipients "clients" or "customers" an asymmetrical relationship is transformed into one of apparent equality. Even so, moral discourse, in the offices of FRAME in particular, centered on notions of need and desert. "Giving" items away in the tradition of Victorian self-help philanthropists, it was said, would breed dependency and, recalling the older distinction between sturdy vagabonds and the deserving poor, would render the recipients unsuitable. Sorting through furniture in the warehouse also drew a distinction between luxury items and those that met basic needs, with different price-setting criteria for each. The former were priced beyond the voucher limit or sold elsewhere for what they could make "in the market." In other words, the illusion of self-sufficiency helped to construct the dignity of a consumer-citizen able to participate in market consumption through anonymous commercial transactions. Though much of the furniture did make a substantial difference to recipients who had nothing, few colluded in this fantasy of free-market exchange, either referring to them as "handouts" or as rubbish that they had been given and promptly binned, turning instead to friends for gifts and loans – with whom a more sustained relationship was possible. The illusion of free engagement with the market and the wider social collective was largely not upheld by those whom the redistribution system was supposedly liberating.

Work and the third sector

From the time when the poor were first classified as work-shy or impotent to New Labour's "welfare to work" policy, work has been intrinsic to how welfare is understood and practiced. Work in its various forms also meshes the third sector with state and market. This is work as the desire and ability to engage in wage labor, in contrast with the rootless wanderers, who were punished under the Henrician Poor Law, and the helpless, whose incapacity to work deserved compassion. For work, in contemporary political cant on both sides of the Atlantic, has become the watchword tempering the gift of welfare (Shersow 2005). But this is work as waged labor. Work is more than that. It both denotes the transformative labor of man on material, and the life project of Work, which enables and defines personhood and participation in social life. Work is central to everything I have described above.

The use of the work ethic to locate the deserving poor is explicit in most private or state charitable ventures. A form of productive consumption is therefore taking place in the quasi-shops operated by the community recycling schemes, where mimicry of market exchange fosters the illusion of participation and choice as preconditions of free social being. Equally, many donors to the community recycling schemes participate in exchange with the abstractions of community or environment through material reciprocations of an immaterial form of wellbeing. Pure altruism is negated by the anger shown when donations are rejected or by the suspicion that donated items end up on landfill, which effectively denies reciprocity.

The schemes themselves approach the question of labor in a number of ways. In standard renditions of a firm's incomings and outgoings, labor would appear as an input, a cost of production. Such paid labor certainly exists in the voluntary sector, but there is also a significant proportion of volunteer and coerced labor. Much of this unwaged labor requires a high level of supervision.

The distinction between the three categories is blurred: some move between being paid and unpaid; other volunteers, sent to the community recycling scheme for short-term rehabilitation, end up staying on full-time, as opposed to moving back to the wage labor market, as intended. It is worth noting that aversion to entering the formal labor market through such jobs may, on occasion, take the pathological form of illness. Though described as "volunteers" by the community recycling schemes, the Community Service Orders made it clear that they were at the community recycling schemes for no other reason than serving a penalty. There were also distinctions between the voluntary workers: the office staff from the Methodist mission maintained their distance from the warehouse workers and drivers. There was limited movement between employment with the community recycling schemes and the odd paid job elsewhere. Labor was therefore both an input to the process, but also an output in that, theoretically, retrained, newly docile bodies and souls reentered the labor market. Thus people as well as furniture were being recycled through these schemes; the success rate for each was roughly equal.

Conclusion

These schemes were extremely fragile. Much warehouse discussion centered on the likelihood of projects collapsing, and with them, the employment of workers, paid or unpaid. Provide took over from a similar community recycling scheme that had collapsed, but was itself constantly under threat of having local authority grants pulled if the money did not seem to equate to the services provided to the contracting department. FRAME lurched from one one-off grant to another. Thus, although the voluntary labor supply of these third-sector community recycling schemes was affected by fluctuations in the local formal labor market, they themselves were just as unstable, offering no greater security. The ability to sustain social reproduction, which underlay the discourse of supporting local communities to do things for themselves, was thus hobbled from the start. As Amin, Cameron and Hudson (2002) note, the localities where the state emphasizes the need to build self-sustaining communities have often suffered most from the decay of both state infrastructure and industry, and are thus least able to "help themselves."

In addition, for all the stress on local community recycling schemes supporting government initiatives to rebuild local economies and meet EU household waste recycling targets, most recycling is done by multinational companies with secure long-term contracts of up to thirty years with local authorities or by groups of them who can tap into global markets for secondary materials. The community recycling schemes thus serve a flexible, niche market. Re-use of bulky goods, as opposed to pulping and recombining material, is labor-intensive and tends to be unprofitable in the conventional sense, especially when the community recycling schemes aim to provide work as well as to redistribute furniture.

These considerations indicate that the existence of the third sector, at least in its contemporary form illustrated by these community recycling schemes, is the effect of, or response to both market failure and state failure in Britain. The former may be understood in two ways. First, it occurs as instances where market exchange cannot or has yet to realize potential gains; this is illustrated by the paucity of commercial operations involved in extracting value from re-using objects. The second type of market failure is where exchange of commoditized labor and objects is an inefficient means for allocating public goods and services according to need. The numbers of paupers and formally unemployed today, as well as growing concern over social atomization, confirm this once again. The Labour Force Survey of the Office of National Statistics (2004) clearly shows that unemployment is highest for the young (aged sixteen to eighteen years), those over fifty, women, short-term contract workers, and, regionally, in the north east – thus demonstrating the structural elision between geography, gender, age, and poverty that is endlessly replicated from global- to micro-levels.

Such market failure is the classic Keynsian justification for state intervention in areas concerning the public interest. State failure is where the state equally does not effectively deliver public goods and services, classically defined as safety, education, and welfare, all of which are steadily being transformed either into marketized operations or handed to the third sector to take care of within contractual constraints. This is not straightforward state failure. Bauman (2004: 67–9), quoting Garland (2001: 75), suggests that yet another Great Transformation has taken place where a penal state has taken the place of a welfare state. By realigning itself in this way, and externalizing functions of care (and the risk of their operation) to the third sector, the accusation of state failure is side-stepped. In essence, then, not only is the state divesting itself of its familiar array of basic public services and assets, but the very ideas of what constitute the good state, the good citizen, and public assets are being radically changed.

The center-left economic imaginary, in Gibson-Graham's (2003) phrase, is that of market-based social parity and cohesion. This idea gains its potency from apparently twinning morality with pragmatism, rather than being a misalliance of fundamentally opposing principles. As is so often the case, however, "pragmatism" merely indicates acceptance of the status quo: sharply unequal allocation. The third sector, freighted with the morality of embeddedness, kin relations, and households, is also burdened with the task of restoring social equilibrium on a larger scale whilst shackled to short-term funding and uneven labor supplies. What is largely enacted is an illusion of equality and ersatz civic engagement.[13]

[13] I am grateful for Keith Hart's insightful advice; my thanks, too, to Chris Smaje.

13 Market and economy in environmental conservation in Jamaica

James G. Carrier

Karl Polanyi's position in economic anthropology is odd. His essay "The Economy as Instituted Process" (Polanyi 1957b), and the collection in which it appeared (Polanyi, Arensberg, and Pearson 1957), were central to the main intellectual dispute in the sub-discipline, the formalist–substantivist debate in the 1960s (see Isaac 2005; Wilk 1996: 3–13). At the same time, *The Great Transformation* (Polanyi 1944) has had little influence. There are good reasons for this imbalance. The essay speaks of orders and processes of the sort that anthropologists commonly see in their field research, while the book describes something rather different, changes in Britain and Europe over almost two centuries. The scope of these changes is alien to the more circumscribed focus of conventional anthropology, which makes the book less accessible than the essay.

Though perhaps less accessible, the book should be useful. The changes it describes revolve around a growing stress on the self-regulating market free from interference by the state, on the expansion of the market to areas of life hitherto outside of it, and on the medium of the market, money, as the measure of value and the motive for market actors. These are very much the neoliberalism that, for the past decade or two, has increasingly been the political-economic milieu of the people and situations that anthropologists study.

This milieu is pervasive, and its influence means that attention to economic beliefs, motives, institutions, and practices is necessary if we are to make sense of many of the things that we observe that are not, on the face of it, economic. As I hope to show in this chapter, even something that seems to be distant from economy and the self-regulating market, the spread of environmental conservation in Jamaica's coastal waters, cannot be understood without reference to the issues that Polanyi addressed. However, as I hope also to show, his book offers only a partial account of the spread of conservation in Jamaica. This partiality in itself is unlikely to surprise anyone. However, it is worth pursuing because it points to questions concerning the ways that we think about the changes he described.

The Great Transformation is helpful in pointing to the important spread of the idea and practices of the self-regulating market, and to the expansion of market relations in general. It is also helpful in pointing to some of their features and consequences. Equally, though, the general political–economic ideas and forces that concern Polanyi need to be located in the contexts in which they exist. It is in doing this that we can begin to understand their forms, successes, and failures in particular times and places, and thus what drives them. This sort of locating requires that we complement his institutional orientation with others that attend more to the orientations and situations of people who are part of that spread, whether as active advocates, passive participants, or reluctant sufferers.

We need this shift in attention because of the way that Polanyi analysed the subtitle included in later editions, "The Political and Economic Origins of Our Time." Dealing with events in England and Europe over almost two hundred years justifies the loose narrative structure that he used; tracing the emergence and consequences of the spread of the self-regulating market justifies attending mostly to the elements of that market and their interconnections. The result is a work that is almost teleological in its orientation, and that relies on historical sequence to connect the events and changes that concern it.

It is important to inquire into the political and economic origins of our time. However, doing so as Polanyi did slights the consideration of what models we might use to understand that sequence. Similarly, by allowing us to identify what turned out to be important, his retrospective approach eliminates the uncertainties that appear in situations when they are viewed without the benefit of hindsight. It is reasonable to be inspired by *The Great Transformation* as a description of broad processes and conditions, and to use it to think about the general trends apparent in concrete situations. However, we may find it difficult to relate those general trends to the situations that concern us. Many of us study events of relatively shallow history: environmental conservation in Jamaica and the Caribbean did not really get under way until the 1980s; many of us study events that have not reached outcomes that allow us to identify with confidence what our times actually are: conservation remains in flux in Jamaica and the region. The result is that *The Great Transformation* may inspire us to ask important questions, but may offer little help in finding answers.

My concern here is not reducible to the complaint of a field-working anthropologist who longs for thick description. Rather, it reflects a desire to make sense of events and processes as they unfold, to see where they come from and where they seem to be headed. This, in turn, means a desire for the analytical apparatus that allows us to understand the interplay among people's orientations, their situations and their actions, and the consequences of those actions. Polanyi is aware of the questions such an apparatus would allow us to address, as when he relates the origins of the Speenhamland system to the political structure of rural England and the desire of county squires to maintain their positions (e.g. Polanyi 2001: 173–4). However, his retrospective orientation means that he has little need for such an apparatus, and he devotes little attention to it.

Desire for this sort of apparatus is not uniquely anthropological. For instance, Weber's *Protestant Ethic and the Spirit of Capitalism* (1904–05) is an extended deployment of such an apparatus, to explain why ascetic Protestants tended to act in the ways they did and what the consequences tended to be. Before Weber, Marx devoted significant attention to such an apparatus as well. This sort of apparatus points to factors that are contingent from Polanyi's perspective, in the sense that they are the context in any particular place and time of the expansion of the market that concerns him. These contingent factors are what shape people's interpretations of their situations, the actions that they take, and the result of those actions; in some cases extending the reach of the market or making it more self-regulating, in others not doing so. If, then, we are to move beyond a general description of historical changes in the reach of the market, we need to pay attention to how and why it expands its scope in one situation or fails to do so in another. To do this, we need to locate that market in its context.

Environmental conservation in Jamaica

As I said, environmental conservation has a shallow history in Jamaica, with substantial advocacy developing only in the 1980s (Lundy 1999). The first two national parks were declared in 1991, and one of them had control over coastal waters, in Montego Bay. The second national park with oversight of coastal waters was declared in 1998, in Negril. Montego Bay is a city of about 100,000 and is the largest tourist destination in the country, with a few under 420,000 arrivals in 2003, while Negril is a town of about 20,000 people and is the third-largest destination, with about 275,000 visitors in 2003 (Bakker and Phillip 2005). In both places the coastal environment is degraded, and people advocated the creation of these parks in order to protect it. However, conservation in these two places, and in Jamaica generally, is not simply a matter of biology and environmental science. It is also a matter of political economy. Both Jamaica's natural and its political–economic environment are important.

On Jamaica's north, and especially north-west, coast there is only a narrow coastal shallow, often less than 1 km wide, before the sea floor drops sharply into the Cayman Trench. As a result of increasing pressures of various sorts, marine life along that coast has declined markedly over the past few decades. Fishers have had to work harder and travel further, and still they are not bringing ashore the catch that they did ten years ago. Similarly, the coral along the coast is under threat, which is worrisome because coral is an indicator of the state of the waters, an important part of the inshore ecology and a protective barrier against storms. In Montego Bay, the director of the marine park said that about three-quarters of the coral is dead; in Negril, senior park staff say about half the coral is dead. The coral that is alive appears to be recovering more slowly from natural events, especially hurricanes, than healthy coral would (see generally Aiken n.d.; Aiken and Haughton 1987). Although there is some debate about the causes of this state of affairs, efforts to deal with it are fairly uniform: establish marine protected areas and restrict disturbances of sea life, primarily the inshore, artisanal fishing that is common around the island (Haley and Clayton 2003).

Just as the country's coastal waters are in difficulty, so is its economy. As both a British colony and an independent country, Jamaica has relied on exports of primary products to rich countries in a market system beyond its influence. Initially, its exports were agricultural, produced in large plantations purchased with overseas capital using commodity labor, first through slavery, and after 1834, through wages. Because its economy was focused on exports, Jamaica did not develop a significant industrial or agricultural sector aimed at the domestic market (this resembles another British colony in the Caribbean, Belize, described in Wilk 2006: Chapter 5). Historically its main export was sugar. At one point, Jamaica was the leading sugar producer in the British empire, but the repatriation of profits by plantation owners and the attendant lack of investment meant that its competitive position deteriorated from the middle of the nineteenth century onward. Its other main agricultural export has been bananas, but both these crops are now threatened with near extinction by the end of the preferential treatment that is part of the Lomé convention (see generally Ahmed 2001). Its other main export has been bauxite, sent to North American aluminium companies. This began early in the 1950s, and Jamaica quickly became one of the biggest sources of bauxite in the world. However, its position has declined since then, though bauxite and alumina are still Jamaica's largest export commodity and the second-largest source of foreign exchange income (after tourism).

This reliance on foreign markets had important consequences in the last quarter of the twentieth century. As Jamaica relies on imported oil for almost all its energy, the sharp rise in oil prices in 1974 harmed the country. Late in the 1970s the government approached the International Monetary Fund (IMF), which required structural adjustment as a condition for its loans (Payne 1994: chapters 4–5). The result was a decline in government revenue, an increasing proportion of which went to service debt, and a reduction of trade barriers, which weakened the Jamaican economy and the tax revenue that it could generate. Together, these increased the demand for foreign exchange to pay for imports and to service debt.

With the declining importance of its primary products, and with structural adjustment ending the country's inward-looking development programs based on import substitution, the government had only one obvious way to generate that foreign exchange: an expansion of tourism. This was timely, for tourism was being advocated as a development strategy through the economic expansion it would generate, based on the comparative economic advantage of countries like Jamaica, their sun, sand, and sea (for a critical account of this view of tourism, see Brohman 1996).

In this situation, there was little support for the idea that protecting the environment should be a matter of public action, which is to say state action. Rather, marine conservation in Jamaica, as in much of the Caribbean, has a trajectory that resembles what Polanyi described in *The Great Transformation*. As I will show, conservation efforts have tended to extend the reach of the market and convert land and labor into commodities, although this has been an uneven process with uncertain results. However, these tendencies are not in any simple way consequences of an adherence to the model of the self-regulating market, even though market advocates are part of the story of coastal conservation, not least the IMF. Rather, in many ways these were the consequence of the circumstances in which environmental activists had to operate. Thus, while Polanyi's work may point to the overall direction of what has been happening concerning the conservation of the coastal waters, we need to attend to the context in which moves toward market extension occur. I will describe those first in terms of land (in this case, the sea) and then in terms of labor.

Land

In opposition to Adam Smith's famous assertion of an innate human "propensity to truck, barter, and exchange one thing for another" (1976: 17), Polanyi made it clear that market systems, which include a commodity market in land, are not spontaneous generations of humanity. Rather, they are political achievements realized through the state. This is illustrated in the marine protected areas that concern me, which reflect Jamaica's political–economic circumstances and policies. To see how this is so, it is necessary to sketch the background of those marine protected areas.

In Montego Bay a handful of people became concerned for the condition of the coastal waters early in the 1970s, as happened in Negril toward the end of that decade. The details of this emergence were a consequence of the histories and positions of specific individuals (described in Carrier 2003b: 12–18), but in both places leading environmental advocates were expatriates in the tourism industry. As their early concerns developed into local conservation organizations and political advocacy in the 1980s, they confronted the constellation of constraints and interests that influenced the development of environmental protection systems in the country.

Central to this constellation was the government of Jamaica. In its straitened circumstances it was unlikely to support conservation on environmental or social grounds, whether it wanted to or not. It simply did not have the money. Instead, the only argument likely to have a reasonable chance of success was an economic one, that conservation would increase government revenues while imposing no significant drain on the budget.

This was the strategy pursued by advocates of a marine protected area in Montego Bay, and it shaped a report that they produced for the Organization of American States (OAS), describing possible sites for the first marine national park in the country. That report linked conservation and tourism, suggested that conservation would attract tourists and so increase Jamaica's tourism revenue, and stressed the commercial potential of marine protected areas, which would reduce their costs to government. The report noted:

… marine parks can be pretty much self-supporting through a number of activities: snorkeling, SCUBA diving, glass bottom boat tours arranged for a fee. Usually the marine park organization will leave most of these activities to commercial diver operators and watersport centers. In that case, however, substantial revenues may be obtained from concessions. (O'Callaghan, Woodley, and Aiken 1988: 37)

The strategy worked. As I said, the Montego Bay park was declared in 1991 and Negril was declared in 1998.

This approach signaled two important and related shifts concerning the environment. One was the linking of conservation and tourism, especially with regard to the coastal waters. This is reflected in government policy, which has sought to increase the country's attractiveness for tourists by presenting an environmentalist image (see Jamaica 2003), visible in Blue Flag certification for beaches (www.blueflag.org) and Green Globe certification for hotels (www.greenglobe.com). Each is based primarily on the environmental state and practices of potential recipients, and by early 2005 there were twenty-nine Green Globe hotels and four Blue Flag beaches (this was only the first year of Blue Flag operation in Jamaica). Whatever the environmental merits of these programs, they were presented in commercial terms. Those in the tourism sector commonly said that they would increase tourism by Europeans, who are supposed to be more concerned with the environment than the North Americans who predominate among tourists.

The second shift concerning the environment was the transformation of the coastal waters from a Jamaican perspective. Hitherto they had been a resource that people could draw on when their efforts to get by failed. They were something like a national "family land," to which people had rights based on their group membership, as kin in the case of family land or as Jamaicans in the case of coastal waters, and on their need (Carrier 2003a: 222). In a sense, the coastal waters were a commons, more open than land would be. It is not only that boundaries are difficult to mark in any but the shallowest waters, making assertion of territoriality harder than would be the case on land. In addition, it is not really possible to improve the waters in a way that one could, for instance, clear brush and plant crops on land. And, of course, most of what Jamaicans drew from the waters was fish, which could not be fenced and respected no boundaries.

The approach of the environmentalists who linked conservation and tourism turned all this on its head, by converting those waters into a commercial resource. The coastal waters, at least in these parks, became something that people would have to pay to visit. Maps identified the boundaries, marker buoys sub-divided the waters and rangers were charged with enforcement. In effect, the approach enclosed the commons (e.g. Dixon *et al.* 2001: Chapter 3).

This policy did not simply turn the coastal waters into fictitious commodities. It also changed the operation of marine protected areas and the duties of managers, whose goal ceased to be environmental management and became commercially successful management. Income becomes of central importance (as illustrated for the Caribbean in Esteban *et al.* 2002: 13–14, 17–18). Indeed, at times the success and failure of marine protected areas appears to be reduced to profit and loss. For instance, in the Caribbean two marine protected areas have long been seen as exemplars of successful conservation, Saba and Bonnaire, in the Netherlands Antilles (see Scura and van't Hof 1993). While their success is partly environmental, the aspect that often attracts attention is their ability to set, charge, and retain access fees from tourist-divers.

This commercialization of conservation strengthened a tendency that was implicit in the orientation of early activists. That was to see a healthy environment as one that would attract tourists, illustrated by the continuing interest of the management at the Montego Bay park in finding out what made a "good dive," one that tourist-divers would be willing to pay for. This has been occurring throughout the region, as indicated by what is effectively market research, studies that assess different species of fish (e.g. Rudd and Tupper 2002) or other features of the environment (e.g. Avila-Foucat and Eugenio-Martin 2004) in terms of the likelihood that tourists will pay to see them. This view of the surroundings predominated among members of the board that oversaw the Negril park. For most of them, a good environment is one that would attract tourists and so help Negril prosper (Carrier 2005), and also the tourism businesses with which they were involved.

This conjunction of tourism and conservation did not just reflect the predilections of many activists. In addition, it was urged by the bodies that supported the establishment of these parks (see Carrier 2003a: 216–22). The Montego Bay park received early funding through a United States Agency for International Development (USAID) program called DEMO (Development of Environmental Management Organizations), concerned with "capacity building." In practice this meant obliging park management to adopt a commercial orientation, which they complained about repeatedly as hindering their ability to get on with the more immediate problems facing the park. However, the USAID pressure was effective. Of the five action plans in the park's 1998 management plan (Montego Bay Marine Park 1998), the longest is the fifth, "Financial sustainability." The Negril park received substantial European Union money in 1995 and 1999, also to be spent on making it commercially successful:

The project aims at protecting the coral reef ecosystem and at achieving long-term financial sustainability of the Negril Marine Park and Protected Area through income generating measures. The project will contribute to the overall objectives of the Jamaican government to stabilize its economy by maintaining and increasing foreign exchange earnings through tourism, while at the same time protecting the fragile coastal environment of Negril, including the entire coral reef ecosystem. (EU 2002)

And, like the Montego Bay park's management plan, the Negril park plan focuses on revenue (Negril Marine Park 1997).

In this process of market expansion, the state was initially reluctant to the point of being a hindrance. However, with the encouragement of the USAID (which occupied the top floor of the relevant ministry building and was intensely engaged in "capacity building" in the ministry), early in the 1990s the Natural Resources Conservation Department, a government agency, was transformed into the Natural Resources Conservation Authority, a quasi-autonomous organization. The justification for this change was summarized by some environmental activists in Jamaica (Goreau *et al.* 1997: 2093; see also Lundy 1999: 94–5):

The Natural Resources Conservation Authority (NRCA) … recognizes that officials in the capital are less able than locally-based organizations to identify local problems, propose solutions, or implement them. Central control over environmental policy has historically resulted in decisions favoring short-term financial interests of individuals and institutions which are well connected in the capital. Decision-making is often protracted and may not address local concerns. Residents of the area feel increasingly dispossessed and powerless to control access to resources or halt degradation from development that adversely affects their quality of life, causing increasing alienation from the political process. NRCA has decided to increase the power of local communities to decide which forms of development, conservation, and environmental management best meet their long term needs. (Goreau *et al.* 1997)

This view echoed the growing global stress on participatory or community conservation, part of a rhetoric of "empowering" local people (see Christie and White 1997). In Jamaican resort towns, however, the only people who were empowered turned out to be those associated with tourism and concerned with the profitability of their businesses. Moreover, the environmentalism that these parks embodied was attractive to larger hotels and the mass tourism sector more generally. Espousing environmentalism helped protect them from criticisms that they were despoiling Jamaica for their own profit (Sommer and

Carrier 2006). Furthermore, and unlike most other people in these towns, those in the mass tourism sector had the financial and other resources to organize and press home their views.

The events I have described, culminating in the establishment of national parks at Montego Bay and Negril, expanded and intensified the reach of the market in Jamaica. However, these events, and the marketization that they foster, may be understood only in terms of the contexts that shaped them in the past and continue to shape them.

The most important contextual factor probably has been the country's reliance on the sale of primary products to overseas markets, an unstable position made worse by the structural adjustment the country suffered in the 1980s. The result was the absence of significant public money for conservation. Also important was the fact that formative activists in both towns were associated with the tourism sector, and that the two parks remain oriented toward tourism. The result was conservation dominated by people and companies which exploited the coastal waters for profit and which saw conservation as a way to secure that exploitation. In the absence of these contextual factors, coastal conservation might have looked very different. Establishing marine parks for conservation in the absence of tourism might have dispossessed those who used the pertinent parts of the coastal waters, but would be unlikely to have turned those waters into a commodity.

Contextual factors of a different sort continue to shape these parks and the marketization that they represent. Particularly in Montego Bay, but also in Negril, local fishers ignore park regulations and occasionally threaten park staff. The parks are in financial trouble as well. When the money they received from overseas bodies has run out, the parks have foundered. In 2004 the bankruptcy of the Negril park was forestalled by last-minute, emergency support from a Jamaican environmental organization; in 2005 the Montego Bay park ceased paying its staff, including its executive director. Both parks had shut previously when money had run out.

Labor

As was the case with land, marine conservation appears to extend the reach of the market and encourage the development of a fictitious commodity, labor. As was the case with land, the situation with labor is complicated, and the emergence of commodity labor depends upon contingent, contextual factors that are not encompassed in Polanyi's model.

One such factor was a change in development policies around the start of the twenty-first century, which was fortuitous in relation to the growth of conservation in Jamaica. That was a reorientation toward "pro-poor" development (e.g. Ashley *et al.* 2006), which appeared in the main overseas development bodies that were concerned with the Caribbean: the USAID, the Canadian International Development Agency, the European Union, and the UK Department for International Development. Pro-poor development seeks to benefit especially the poorer members of society, who are to be helped in a particular way. That is, by increasing their ability to be market actors, typically as petty entrepreneurs or as members of small associations such as producer cooperatives.

This shift to pro-poor development followed a change that had taken place five or ten years before in programs intended to conserve biodiversity, the appearance of the "enterprise-oriented" approach. This is exemplified in the large Biodiversity Support Program, which ran in the 1990s and was funded by the United States government and a number of large conservation organizations (see Biodiversity Support Program 1999). That approach assumed that people would be more likely to protect local biodiversity if they could make money from it without destroying it. The most obvious example of this is ecotourism.

Pro-poor development and enterprise-oriented conservation complement each other and appeared to address two linked problems that conservation projects in poorer countries commonly faced. One was being seen to be equitable to those displaced by those projects, the other was securing local support for those projects. Together, pro-poor development and enterprise-oriented conservation offered a way around these problems. Those who were displaced could find alternative livelihoods in the tourism that conservation projects would generate. This would help lift them out of poverty, while giving them an economic interest in the success of the project. Displaced fishers, for instance, might become guides to take tourists through environmentally attractive areas like mangrove swamps, knowledgeable boatmen might take tourists to sites for catch-and-release fishing or become water-taxi operators to take tourists to dive sites. This reorientation of policy would result in an expansion and intensification of the market, and so accord with Polanyi's ideas. People whose activities have been peripheral, often to the point of invisibility, in market terms would be brought into recognizable market relationships.

It is not clear, however, that this would be the self-regulating market that concerned Polanyi. One sign of this is attempts to define the tourism sector in ways that turn out to benefit powerful firms. This definition is important because it shapes the allocation of government support as part of its economic development policies. Large tourism businesses are included in this definition. Small hotels and operators are on the margins, often criticized both by large businesses and by quasi-government bodies like the Tourism Product Development Company for what is said to be their inefficiencies and backward practices. The typical criticism of small hoteliers, for instance, is that they have not progressed from the "old days," and still think that all they have to do is open their doors and people will come. Petty traders are excluded, as being disruptive, irresponsible, and presenting a bad image of the country to tourists. These are the people whom the Prime Minister, in a budget debate in 1985, referred to as "touts, pimps, hustlers, and drug pushers" (in Chambers and Airey 2001: 111). Viewed dispassionately, petty traders and small hoteliers are as much in the tourism sector as multinational resort companies, and in a self-regulating market they would be free to compete with each other. However, government programs skewed this market, offering support for some, indifference to others, and hostility to the rest.

The logic of the OAS report described above points to another reason why the conjunction of pro-poor development and enterprise-oriented conservation is unlikely to work in Jamaica, or in most parts of the Caribbean. Recall that it argued that fees charged to tourists would fund parks. This means that a park would be remunerative, and hence justifiable, only in places with significant tourist demand. Because such places already have significant tourism, there would be no room for new entrants in the sector unless the creation of the park led to more tourists and hence more commercial opportunities. This has not happened in Montego Bay or Negril. Furthermore, and reflecting the prevailing definition of the sector, the government continues to encourage large-scale tourism dominated by regional, European, or North American firms running all-inclusive hotels. Such firms are reluctant to deal with small entrepreneurs, who they see as difficult and unreliable. As a result of these factors, the tourism associated with these parks does not provide the market opportunities envisaged in pro-poor development and enterprise-oriented conservation.

Where the logic of the OAS report is not followed, where environmental protection precedes the emergence of substantial tourism, things may work differently. An example of this is Hol Chan, a marine protected area near San Pedro, in Belize. Tourists began to go there in the 1970s and 1980s, and hired local fishers to ferry them to dive sites. This became an important source of income for fishers, who were fairly readily persuaded to curtail their fishing and support the establishment of Hol Chan. This case looks like a success for pro-poor development and enterprise-oriented conservation. However, this does not mean the expansion of a free market. This became obvious during a minor incident in 1997, when the Montego Bay park organized a meeting with local fishers to discuss alternative livelihoods. Among others, they invited a few San Pedro former fishers to tell about the success of their new entrepreneurial activities. Informally, over a meal after a day of formal talks and presentations, the San Pedro visitors asked local fishers why there were so many whites in tourism in Montego Bay. Asked what they meant, the visitors said that they excluded outsiders, and especially whites, from their activities. Those who had tried to enter the business found that their boats became damaged, their petrol became fouled, all in a series of most unfortunate incidents that led them to abandon their efforts.

However, in Montego Bay and Negril significant tourism preceded conservation, so that the only opportunity that tourism is likely to provide to those displaced by the parks is wage employment in the service sector. In Polanyi's terms, this would mean the expansion of labor as a fictitious commodity. However, yet another contextual factor has meant that this rarely occurs. In Jamaica, and throughout the Caribbean, people of the sort displaced by environmental conservation dislike wage work. This does not spring from a preference for non-market transactions, such as those of a gift economy or patron–client system. In fact, there is a long history of involvement in market transactions in the region (Olwig 1993: 48–50), "higglering" or petty trading being an obvious example (see Katzin 1971). Such transactions are valued positively, which is just what makes wage work unattractive.

Both the positive valuation of market transactions and the negative valuation of wage work reflect the importance of autonomy, a complex value that takes many forms and is widely reported in the Caribbean. Put simply, there is a desire, particularly but not exclusively among men, for relationships that are fluid and equal rather than structured and hierarchical. In such relationships, people are evaluated in terms of their ability to respond imaginatively and amusingly to their immediate situation.[1] This is associated with a dislike of the sort of durable subordination that is found in wage work and especially in the personal subordination that characterizes service jobs in tourism. The strength of this dislike is apparent to, and worrisome for, those seeking to promote tourism in the region. They complain that Caribbeans are reluctant to take on service jobs, because they equate "service" with "servitude."[2]

This valuing of autonomy takes various forms. One, common among men in Jamaica and throughout the region, is the pursuit of a variety of economic activities at the same time (classically Comitas 1964; e.g., Browne 2004). One reason for this is economic insecurity, but that is not the only explanation. One part-time fisher in Montego Bay illustrated this. He worked half-time as a driver for a transport company, and during a recent period of illness had been unable to work. Even so, his employer gave him half his normal pay. Clearly, this was a desirable employer. However, the fisher turned down the employer's offer to work full-time, explaining that he would rather be able to work at his own choosing than be tied to a single boss.

---

[1] The classic statement is Wilson's (1973) work on reputation and respectability, and an extended historical treatment is in Olwig (1993). This valuation appears also in work on the performance of identity (Abrahams 1983), the realm of transience and immediacy (Miller 1994a) and the adventure (Wardle 1999) (see also Austin 1983; Besson 1993).

[2] How pervasive this worry is can be illustrated by a brief Google search in April 2005, which found it in statements by the president of the Barbados Hotel and Tourist Association, the Trinidad and Tobago Chamber of Commerce, the Guyana National Development Strategy, the newsletter of the Inter-American Development Bank, the Institute for Hotel and Tourism of the University of the West Indies at Mona, and the Chief Minister of Montserrat.

It appears as well in the way fishers relate to each other. They are not a community in any reasonable sense. People in Negril fished from the same beach, had a common work environment and skills, and in some cases were joined by personal friendships. However, the closest they came to a common identity is something like a loose working-class consciousness. This meant that they were reluctant to cooperate in a common enterprise, and indeed they distrusted each other: it was generally assumed that another fisher would steal the fish from your traps given the opportunity. It is perhaps best to see these fishers as a set of independent petty entrepreneurs who happened to carry out their activities from the same place, the Negril fishing beach.[3]

One attraction of fishing in the region is its association with autonomy. Richard Price (1966) observes that fishing and fishers are much more salient in the region that would be justified by a dispassionate evaluation. He explains this by linking fishing to the escape from the rigours of slavery. Under the old slave-plantation system fishing slaves were able to trade some of their catch on their own account in local markets, and so secure a degree of independence from their owners. While this is an historical association, it is important to recognize that the cultural memory of slavery remains a lively force in the Caribbean (e.g. Austin-Broos 1997; Nettleford 1998). In the contemporary Caribbean, this marks fishing as an escape from subordination. David Griffith and Manuel Valdés Pizzini (2002) say that many of the fishers in Puerto Rico that they studied value fishing because it allows them to avoid the subordination associated with wage labor. The same is the case for many in Jamaica, whether fishing is a central part of their subsistence or only an occasional activity. The sea is a realm where one is free from the constraints that others impose. What you catch is the result of the sea and your own effort: no other person is involved.

Another fisher described this attraction of autonomy in a different way. He was talking about what happens when a person makes, say, a fishing lure and sells it to a visiting tourist-fisher. As he explained it, payment means something different from what it does in a self-regulating market. The amount the tourist gives is the expression of the buyer's assessment of the value of the lure and the person who made it. The better and more energetic and imaginative the maker, the more the lure will fetch. Like fishing, what you get is the result of the customer and your own effort: no other person is involved.

As with land, so with labor. The events I have described point in the direction that Polanyi describes, as dispossessed fishers look to become the petty entrepreneurs of pro-poor development and enterprise-oriented conservation or the wage workers of an expanded tourism sector. However, if we are to understand why movement in that direction takes place or fails to do so, we need to place the overall thrust that Polanyi describes in its context. The conjunction

---

[3] This view comes from Andrew Garner, who did the field research on fishers in Negril.

of conservation and tourism in Jamaica has shaped the economic options that are available to those dispossessed by these parks. Petty entrepreneurism turns out to be foreclosed. All that was left was routine service jobs in tourism. However, the value of autonomy that fishing represents to most people in Jamaica meant that these jobs were unattractive.

Conclusion

I have pointed to the importance of economic factors for understanding what might seem distinctly non-economic, environmental conservation in Jamaica's coastal waters. Those who joined conservation with tourism expected that environmental protection would lead in directions described in *The Great Transformation*. The creation of marine parks in Montego Bay and Negril enclosed most of the waters in those places, with park regulations limiting all sorts of fishing and banning some, so dispossessing those who had fished there. Those waters became something very close to commodities. They were treated as assets to be exploited through attracting fee-paying tourists, thereby generating revenue for these parks. In addition, the combination of conservation and tourism would lead to the conversion of petty artisanal fishers into market actors who would support conservation and the income it would generate. And even if the pro-poor vision of small-scale market actors was not realised, these displaced people would secure jobs in the expanded tourism sector.

I have described these processes in term of the Jamaican context in which they occurred. However, they are more general than that, particularly so in the case of the conversion of land into a commodity. The conjunction of conservation and commerce is not restricted to Jamaica (e.g. Drumm 2003), or even to poorer countries. For instance, national park managers in Canada are admonished to think of themselves as providers of a tourist attraction, take a businesslike stance, assess market demand, and seek to serve it. If they fail, their revenues and futures are in peril (Eagles 2002). This conjunction occurs with commerce other than tourism, illustrated by the spread of transferable fishing quotas in the last quarter of the twentieth century (e.g. Helgason and Pálsson 1997). Here, too, the justification was marine conservation, in this case cod stocks that were said to be threatened by overfishing, and here, too, the result was to restrict access to those who were prepared to pay for it.

Noting that the sort of events that I have described for Jamaica occur more commonly does not, however, mean that we can understand what is happening without attention to local context. A failure to attend to context would leave us only with a grand march of the market, which would not encourage us to see why that march occurs or why it is more successful in some places and times rather than others. After all, the conjunction of tourism and conservation in Jamaica occurred for different reasons than it did in Canada, just as the commercialization of the waters occurred for different reasons than it did in the North Atlantic. The parts of the surroundings that these different systems are meant to protect signify different things; the consequences of commercialization and protection differ in these places.

This stress on local context is, of course, congenial to anthropologists, whose professional lives commonly revolve around close attention to a circumscribed place and set of people. There is, however, more to my stress on context than disciplinary habit. Attending to that context allows us to see the mechanisms, orientations, and motives that shape the processes and outcomes that we observe, when they operate and when they do not.

There are a range of existing attempts to get at those mechanisms, orientations, and motives, and I have mentioned the two people whose attempts are most famous, Marx and Weber, both of whom describe these factors and the ways that they constrain and motivate people. For Marx, the competitive nature of capitalism, together with the changing composition of capital that is related to it, compels firms to extend their reach if they are to survive. The result is that "the bourgeoisie ... compels all nations, on pain of extinction, to adopt the bourgeois mode of production; it compels them ... to become bourgeois themselves. In a word, it creates a world after its own image" (Marx and Engels 1848: Part I). For Weber, modern capitalism is, above all, rational, and only those who embrace that rationality can survive in competition with rational capitalists. This rationality requires, first, "the appropriation of all physical means of production ... as disposable property;" second, "freedom of the market, that is, the absence of irrational limitations on trading in the market;" and third, "free labor. Persons must be present who are not only legally in the position, but are also economically compelled, to sell their labor on the market without restriction" (Weber 1982: 276–7).

I do not refer to these two writers because they have explained in a definitive way the nature, origin, and expansion of capitalist market rationality that concerned Polanyi; I am not historian enough to know if they have. Rather, I refer to them because they have asked the right questions: What is that rationality? How and why does it expand? Answers to these questions, or at least the information that would allow the beginning of answers, come from attention to the context in which people operate, the factors that motivate them and the results, intended or otherwise, of their actions.

This brings us back to where we began, Polanyi's odd position in economic anthropology. I suggested that one reason for this is that his "Economy as Instituted Process" deals with a level that is congenial to anthropologists, while *The Great Transformation* does not. I have argued that this level is attractive because it allows us to address the question of what leads people to think and act as they do. It is at this level that we can see the interplay of the key institutional forces that feature in *The Great Transformation* and the other factors that shape both the context in which those institutional forces operate and the outcome of their operation.

This interplay is important. As I have noted, it is essential if we are to make sense of the emergence and consequences of environmental conservation in Jamaica's coastal waters. As I have also noted, it is essential if we are to understand why and how that emergence and those consequences resemble and differ from analogous events, whether in Canadian parks or North Atlantic fisheries. It is in these resemblances and differences that we can begin to understand the nature of the big institutional forces at work. Through that understanding we can begin to see the reasons for their operations, histories, and changes, and the ways that people may start to affect them.

Acknowledgements

This relies on research carried out or overseen under a grant from the Overseas Development Administration/Department for International Development, "Ecological and social impacts in planning Caribbean marine-reserves" (1997– 2000, project number R6783; the field researcher was Lucy F. Robertson), and a grant from the Economic and Social Research Council, "Conflict in environmental conservation: a Jamaican study" (2004–5, RES 000 23 0396; the field researchers were myself, Andrew Garner, Monica Lorenzo Pugholm, and Gunilla Sommer). The comments from workshop participants, especially Johnny Parry, stimulated me to think more imaginatively about this material; a provocative interchange with Keith Hart helped clarify my thinking. I am grateful for both.

14　Embedded socialism? Land, labor, and money in eastern Xinjiang

Chris Hann

Introduction

"Nineteenth century civilization has collapsed," declares Karl Polanyi in the opening sentence of *The Great Transformation*. His ensuing analysis focuses on the emergence of the self-regulating market as a world-historical aberration, contrasting both with the great agrarian empires and with the non-literate societies studied by anthropologists. Yet the work remains full of ambiguity: did Polanyi mean the "self-regulating" as a realistic descriptor or did he mean the *idea* of such a market? It is in any case a very Eurocentric narrative. It is concerned in particular with Britain, where Polanyi conceived his study of "the political and economic origins of our time" in the late 1930s.

"Our time" today is quite different. It is tempting now to proclaim the collapse of twentieth-century civilization, but this collapse demands a more complex explanation than the Polanyi prototype. Such an account would need to address, first, the attrition of that "embedded liberalism" (Harvey 2005a, following Ruggie 1982) which came to characterize the advanced capitalist countries in the decades after Polanyi's dramatic indictment of pre-welfare state "disembedding." As Keith Hart and I point out in our Introduction to this volume, this metaphor has been a continuous source of confusion. I distinguish here between general moral embedding and political embedding. Polanyi shows in his *magnum opus* that the conditions for the catastrophic existential moral and social disruption of human communities in industrial communities were the work of the capitalist state. New forms of political embedding were and remain indispensable to "market society," but this aspect has been played down by advocates of neoliberalism who mistake an ideology of free markets for the institutional reality. Second, an account of our present moment in history needs to consider the significance of socialism in the civilization of the past century, and to deal with the fact that, although the Marxist–Leninist regimes of the Soviet bloc collapsed around 1990, two decades later some of the world's most remarkable economic performances are being notched up by countries which claim not to have abandoned socialism.

In this chapter I address this latter agenda. I argue that the tools supplied by Polanyi may be adapted for understanding socialism, both its demise in some places and its persistence in others. This requires a departure from his relentless emphasis on the rise and fall of the self-regulating market. Polanyi is at pains to argue that barter and market exchange are qualitatively different from the basic principles of comparative economic systems that he identifies in Chapter 4 of *The Great Transformation*. There are three such principles. Reciprocity is exemplified by moiety polities and by trading systems such as the Melanesian *kula*, as documented by Malinowski (1922). Redistribution, by contrast, depends on political centricity and is well illustrated in the chiefdoms of the Northwest coast, famous in the anthropological literature for their potlatch rituals. The third principle identified by Polanyi is the one he calls "householding;" this is the Greek *oeconomia*, and it is exemplified by the self-reliance (autarky) of peasant farmers all over the world. This principle disappears in his later work and did not become part of the substantivist canon (see Gregory, Chapter 8 in this volume). Only the market, argues Polanyi in *The Great Transformation*, is underpinned by a unique motivation that has the potential to lead to general disembedding, that is, the detachment of the economy from social relations (Polanyi 1944: 56–7). On the other hand, Polanyi never denies that markets and "voluntaristic" exchange are to be found as "accessories" in all kinds of economic system; he acknowledges that markets are an essential condition for consumer freedom in modern industrial societies.

I propose a reworking of this schema in order to explore China's "actually existing socialism."[1] Polanyi's abhorrence of nineteenth-century liberalism was driven by the social consequences he observed in the Europe of his day, not only in Austria and Britain in the interwar decades but also, and perhaps above all, during his formative years in Hungary before the First World War. Massive dislocation had destroyed the integrity of traditional communities and paved the way for Fascism. The main cause of this great transformation was the expansion of capitalist markets, and in particular the conversion of land, labor, and money into "fictitious commodities," thereby eclipsing the three general principles which had hitherto predominated. But what if, instead of attributing to market exchange the unique explanatory status it has for Polanyi, we simply place it alongside reciprocity, redistribution, and householding as a fourth general principle? This would open up the possibility that generalized moral disembedding, that is, the dislocation of the evolved institutions which have hitherto ensured that the economy is "absorbed," "submerged," or "enmeshed" in a social totality (these alternative metaphors are used more or less interchangeably

---

[1] This chapter is not concerned with debates about whether China might better be classified as state capitalist or as neoliberal "with Chinese characteristics," the phrasing suggested by Harvey (2005a: Chapter 5). Here I follow Frank Pieke (forthcoming), who holds that the vast majority of citizens of the People's Republic of China understand their country to be socialist, accept the term "reform era," and are far from rejecting the fundamental tenets of the national ideology. Pieke himself suggests the term "neo-socialist."

by Polanyi) may have causes other than market fundamentalism. It is hard to imagine that a sudden upsurge in reciprocity could have farreaching deleterious consequences for the cohesion of society. An enforced shift to economic autarky in an era of political instability would be more likely to have such effects. But the most pertinent principle for our case is, of course, that of redistribution. I shall argue that Marxist–Leninist–Maoist socialism promoted a non-market disembedding of the economy from social relations, with social consequences no less devastating than the market-driven processes analyzed by Polanyi. In a second step I shall suggest that "reform socialism," that is, modifications of collectivist central planning which re-introduce the principle of the market, can be consistent with a renewal of moral embeddedness, analogous to the embedded liberalism of the Keynesian generation in the West.

There is some irony in applying Polanyian concepts in this way. Karl Polanyi was very familiar with the writings of Marx and also with the academic and policy-oriented debates in the interwar decades in which socialists played a prominent role. There is no doubt that he was deeply sympathetic to socialist ideals.[2] However, although the catastrophic consequences of Soviet collectivization were already known in the 1930s, Polanyi did not engage closely with the realities. Instead he contented himself in *The Great Transformation* with the assertion that the Soviet experience was "inapplicable" to Western countries (2001: 243). Toward the end of his life he returned to Hungary, the country in which he grew up, and he apparently endorsed the efforts of János Kádár's regime to build a socialist society in the wake of the repression of the 1956 revolution (Litván 1990: 36–7). In 1968, four years after Polanyi's death, Hungary embarked on a path of "market socialism," comparable with that followed by China since the late 1970s. I shall return briefly to the comparative analysis of what I shall term "reform socialism" in the concluding section of this chapter. But first, in the following sections, I present an ethnographic case study based on recent fieldwork in eastern Xinjiang.[3]

---

[2] See Halperin 1984. By equating Marxism with economic determinism, George Dalton and other substantivist followers of Polanyi sought to absolve him of this error, which was of course highly fraught politically when the Cold War was at its peak (see also Isaac 2005). In *The Great Transformation* he wrote: "From the point of view of the community as a whole, socialism is merely, the continuation of that endeavor to make society a distinctively human relationship of persons which in Western Europe was always associated with Christian traditions" (2001: 242).

[3] The project "Feudalism, Socialism, and the Present Mixed Economy in Eastern Xinjiang" is organized by the Max Planck Institute for Social Anthropology. It is being undertaken jointly with Dr. Ildikó Bellér-Hann, in cooperation with Professor Arslan Abdulla and other Uyghur colleagues at Xinjiang University, Urumchi. I am grateful to Busarem Imin for research assistance in 2007. Fieldwork in rural Qumul was spread over nine months in 2006–2007, of which ten weeks were spent in the mountain villages that form the main focus of this chapter. For the rest of the time I lived in a quite different settlement adjacent to the modern city of Qumul (Chinese: Hami). Bellér-Hann is preparing publications on local history and representations of the pre-socialist period. We intend to address many facets of the socialist era more fully in future papers.

Feudalism

According to the official socialist historiography propagated after 1949, which was mediated by Soviet scholarship and based ultimately on the materialist philosophy of history of Marx and Engels, presocialist Xinjiang, like most of the rest of China, was a feudal society. In *The Great Transformation* Karl Polanyi followed Richard Thurnwald in taking a broad definition of feudalism. Although he held the forms of vassalage which developed in Western Europe during the Middle Ages to be a particularly significant example, feudalism was understood as a generic term for all types of stratified society between slavery and capitalism.[4] Before looking more closely at the feudal mode of production in eastern Xinjiang, it is necessary to introduce the region and the characteristics of the settlements which will be the main focus of this discussion.

The territory, known historically as Eastern Turkestan and since 1955 as the Xinjiang Uyghur Autonomous Region, is roughly three times the size of France (Millward and Perdue 2004: 29). Only in recent centuries has it been effectively incorporated into the Chinese state, though links may be traced back all the way to the Han dynasty. The largest "indigenous" group is the Uyghur, who presently number almost ten million. The second-largest group is the Han Chinese, most of them recent migrants. Other significant minorities include Kazaks, Kirgiz, and Hui (also known as Tungans, i.e. Chinese Muslims). Before the middle of the twentieth century the Uyghur were commonly known to Western travelers as Turki. They were the dominant group in the oases of the Tarim basin. In terms of language, religion, and most other social characteristics they closely resembled other Turkic populations of Central Asia, notably the people we know today as Uzbeks. In the presocialist era it seems clear that throughout this vast region oasis-specific identities (Bukhara, Kashgar, Turfan, and so on) were for most purposes more significant than ethno-national identities.[5]

Most of these oases were long-established settlements along the network of trade routes known as the Silk Road, which even after the opening up of the sea routes remained a major conduit for the transfer of goods and ideas between East and West. But, as Polanyi pointed out, such long-distance trade had little relevance for the formation of competitive markets. The movement of merchandise along the Silk Road was largely insulated from local trade between town and countryside. Following the incorporation of Eastern Turkestan into the Qing empire in the middle of the eighteenth century, Han and Hui (Chinese Muslim) merchants promoted new forms of commercial penetration; but these new groups remained highly segregated from the local Muslim population and

---

[4] Eric Wolf coined the term "tributary mode of production" in order to escape from this Eurocentrism (1982: 79–88).

[5] On the continued significance of oasis-specific identities see Rudelson (1997). The theme of ethnic relations is an extremely important and sensitive one in contemporary Xinjiang, but it is too complex to be treated in this chapter. (See Starr 2004, Bellér-Hann *et al.* 2007.)

their market activities were regulated by an "ethnic policy" in Beijing that functioned to protect locals against the imperial power (Millward 1998).

Qumul, located between Turfan and Dunhuang (Gansu Province), is Xinjiang's most easterly gateway city. Between the end of the seventeenth century and 1930 the Qumul Khanate was ruled by a local dynasty known as the Wangs, who combined the principles of Muslim theocracy with a *realpolitik* based on loyalty to the Qing powerholders in Beijing and their provincial representatives, who gradually consolidated their capital in Urumchi. Between 1931 and 1949 power was exercised by Chinese warlords, though descendants of the Wangs retained much of their prestige and landholdings at the center of the oasis.

While Han and Hui dominated in the "new city," the Uyghur population of the Qumul oasis lived in the so-called Muslim City (*Huicheng*) and in villages nearby endowed with a similar climate and water supply. But over the centuries Uyghurs also migrated into the foothills of the eastern Tian Shan, where they developed a transhumant economy and interacted with Kazak pastoralists during the summer months in the high pastures. One such Uyghur mountain settlement was Qizilyar, established by migrants from the lowlands in the late-nineteenth century next to the older village of Qoray.[6] Most households sold some animals annually and used this cash to acquire what they needed from the bazaars in the city, 50–60 km away.[7]

In the absence of integrating market mechanisms, the presocialist agrarian economy of the Qumul periphery may be categorized in terms of the three basic principles indentified by Polanyi. "Redistribution" primarily took the form of taxation by the Wangs, who could require the villagers of Qizilyar and Qoray to carry out "corvée" labor tasks as well as to deliver some of their animals annually to the *dorga*, a local man who represented the government in Qoray. Political relations were not always harmonious: Qoray villagers were active in violent peasant protests at the end of the Qing era and again following the death of the last Wang.[8] Other forms of redistribution had nothing to do with the political hierarchy. Thus the giving of alms was prescribed by Islam, and

---

[6] At the time of my fieldwork in 2006–2007, Qizilyar had about seventy households (all Uyghur) and Qoray some 250 (including a handful of Kazak families). The pre-socialist numbers were much smaller.

[7] Sometimes it was necessary to buy in wheat, since yields in the mountain villages were poor compared with the oasis center; at the higher elevations only barley could be grown.

[8] It seems that the main factors motivating the major rebellion that took place in 1931 were the stiff tax demands of the authorities in Urumchi, who incorporated the Khanate of Qumul into the province following the death of the Khan in 1930. Another significant factor was Uyghur resentment over land encroachment by Han settlers (Forbes 1986: 42–8). Nowadays few inhabitants of Qumul, urban or rural, have any clear opinion about the Wangs; the history of this dynasty is not taught in local schools. While some consider their rule to have been exploitative (the official ideology of the Communist Party), rather more informants say that they were good rulers, in particular because they observed Islamic injunctions to help the poor.

food was regularly redistributed to those in need at collective rituals. Arguably this is better classified as a form of "reciprocity" in Polanyi's typology. The two villages did not resemble moieties, but the movement of women at marriage allowed families to conduct more or less continuous exchanges both within and between villages.[9] Another significant form of reciprocity was that practiced through labor cooperation. However, the most important economic principle in presocialist Xinjiang was that of "householding." In some cases the household was a multiple family unit and, in wealthy families, brothers typically divided responsibility for animal breeding and field tasks. But for the great majority the basic unit of production and consumption was the nuclear family. The degree of autarky was high and money was of little significance. Taxes were paid in kind, and marital payments consisted primarily of animals and fabrics.[10] Land and labor were allocated primarily through the patriarchal power of the household head.

Maoism

From the early 1950s the evolved political and moral economies were both subjected to massive external intervention. The Qumul Wangs, who had lost their political power two decades before, were now divested of their remaining economic power; several members of the dynasty were executed in 1953. Adapting the class labels used in the Soviet Union a generation earlier, the new socialist authorities quickly eliminated the old landlord elite (not significant in the mountain villages) and the institution of the *dorga*.[11] They initially promoted the "voluntary" formation of mutual aid groups; poor families with plentiful labor were encouraged to cooperate with families that held a large acreage and owned the means to farm it (tools and draught animals). Within a few years it was decided, in Xinjiang as in the rest of the country, to implement policies even more radical than those pursued in Soviet collectivization. The Great Leap Forward of 1958 brought a whole array of settlements into

[9] First-cousin marriages were common in this era. Even the weddings of less prosperous families were occasions to invite the entire village (in the case of Qizilyar) or at least the *mahalla* (in the case of Qoray).

[10] Money was, of course, more conspicuous in the major oases of Xinjiang. The historical record for the Qing era suggests a picture consistent with the Polanyian model of "special-purpose" monies, with coins of various provenance enjoying varying degrees of acceptance and convertability; for a discussion of local *pul* and its relation to the "silver lifeline" from the imperial center see Millward 1998: Chapter 2. Value was occasionally measured in terms of other goods, such as tea; moneylending, pawnbroking, and banking were strongly associated with ethnic minorities, including the Han Chinese (Bellér-Hann 2008: 97–100). The nominal fiduciary unity of the Qing was systematically broken up by the Warlords who held power after 1911 and maintained four separate paper currencies to facilitate their policies of rapacious exploitation (Forbes 1986: 28–32).

[11] In Qizilyar two villagers were identified as rich peasants and harshly treated. One was beaten so badly that he later lost his sight in consequence.

the new structure of the People's Commune (though economic management remained largely under the control of the brigade (*da dui*), often corresponding to a natural village). Until 1961 consumption, too, was organized in the brigade's central canteens. For the last fifteen years of Mao's life (1961–1976) households were again able to prepare their own food at home, but supplies were hardly sufficient for survival and mortality rates were high. Political turmoil peaked again after 1966 during the early years of the Cultural Revolution. The Red Guards destroyed many mosques, among them that of Qizilyar. But even where the mosque survived, religious life was severely attenuated; not only were all religious gatherings outside mosques prohibited but villagers no longer had any food available to support established patterns of domestic ritual and collective celebrations. Marriage ceremonies and betrothal gifts were also severely curtailed.

Land was actually farmed by the production team (*xiao dui*) in a complex division of labor. Women were required to spend far more time in the fields than they had previously. Male tasks involved more specialization, for example in stockbreeding, field crops, or transportation. The modernization of agriculture in capitalist conditions has often proved compatible with the principle of householding, where it has been closely linked to increased production for the market and the domination of money. By contrast, in Maoist China the mechanism for rewarding labor was based (as in the Soviet Union and eastern Europe) not on money but on work points. Their disciplinary function was the same: the points translated into subsistence entitlements and households that did not earn enough were liable to go hungry. Women were allocated fewer points for the same long working day on the grounds that their inferior strength rendered them less productive. Looking back, people stress the physical hardship, for example when they were required to blaze new roads across the mountains, or to convert barren hillsides to arable fields through terracing. They became alienated, both in the sense that their work was no longer focused on their own fields, and because their expenditure of labor was not under their own control but rather that of the brigadier, who was in turn subject to the dictates of higher party officials. The continuous propaganda campaigns seem to have had effects that were opposite to those intended: villagers particularly resented being required to spend many evenings at political meetings, where they were harangued by a new elite of Communist Party members.

Maoist ideology could be said to have raised the principle of *oekonomia* to the level of the state: the entire Chinese people was encouraged to pursue policies of self-reliance.[12] But the peasant household ceased to operate as such, little scope remained to negotiate reciprocity between households, and the market principle was suppressed entirely. The dominance of a principle of political centricity was

---

[12] This is not to deny that significant regional redistribution continued even in this era. Since the early 1990s Chinese policies to develop the Western regions have revived earlier patterns of macro-level redistribution.

comparable to the market's dominance in the era of liberal capitalism as outlined by Karl Polanyi in *The Great Transformation*. The major difference was that, whereas in nineteenth century Britain the idealogy of laissez-faire in reality underpinned by state policies, generated a strong counter movement, the ideology and realities of Maoism left little room for adulteration. I suggest that we view the case of China under Mao as a variant of the "great transformation," as a general moral disembedding induced by political coercion rather than the market, which was just as devastating for the previous balance of social relations. Despite some infrastructural improvements – in roads and in irrigation – the material indicators of performance in this morally disembedded economy were consistently negative; hunger and malnutrition were constant threats. Of course, as with capitalism there were some "winners:" those who joined the Party and prospered as cadres and teachers were often of poor peasant background, but they paid a high price for their upward mobility. Unlike the European elites who profited from the moral disembedding of market capitalism, the new Uyghur socialist elites were obliged to sever their links to their moral community, notably in the previously central domain of religion.[13]

The reform era

The reform processes launched in Beijing in 1979 reached Xinjiang a few years later. Decentralization to the household led immediately to increased production, with valued spinoffs for community life generally. The new system of egalitarian smallholdings was generally able to resolve the problems of food shortage (except in the most densely populated districts of the south). Crop yields benefited from some of the investments of the socialist period, notably in the irrigation network.[14] Grain surpluses allowed for a revival of traditional patterns of hospitality, lifecycle rituals, and communal events suppressed in the Maoist years. The state continued to practice some redistribution in accordance with its "five guarantees" policy.[15] This was now supplemented by a renewal of Islamic alms-giving. Although the household now became the basic unit of production and consumption, households cooperated with each other on a voluntary

---

[13] In practice some officials found ways to circumvent these ideological expectations; yet even at village level it was difficult for teachers and state officials to maintain active membership of the mosque community. For Communist Party members it was impossible and to this day they are able to attend the mosque only at the feasts of Ramadan and Sacrifice, which are classified by the authorities as "cultural" rather than religious holidays.

[14] On the other hand many of those "improvements," such as new mountain roads, soon fell into irreparable decay.

[15] The five guarantees are: food, clothing, housing, healthcare, and a funeral. As everywhere in China, medical expenses remain a major worry for many households, but in the villages investigated here there has been a significant improvement in recent years, thanks not only to the construction of a new hospital in this rural township but also to a new insurance scheme which, for the payment of a modest premium per person, provides for the reimbursement of a substantial proportion of the costs of treating more serious illnesses at any of the hospitals of the oasis center.

basis, especially at peak periods. This was universally preferred to the previous factory-style division of labor. Women were once again more emphatically associated with the home, but they joined the men in the fields at peak periods. The men of Qizilyar built themselves a new mosque and its *imams* have participated in the pilgrimage to Mecca (with the financial assistance of their communities).

Although little grain is imported to or exported from these villages nowadays, the animal stock has expanded considerably.[16] Animals are generally sold to middlemen who come from the town throughout the year in modern vans and trucks. The pace of modernization has accelerated in recent years. The main road from Qizilyar to the oasis center has an asphalt surface and there is a daily bus service. A reliable link to the provincial electricity grid has existed since 2003. As a result almost every house is now equipped with a television and many also own refrigerators and other modern utilities, including motorcycles. The next major infrastructural investment will be the installation of a piped water network and water pumps throughout the settlement; the benefits will be felt especially by women. Agricultural production, too, is being gradually transformed, thanks above all to the availability of affordable small-scale tractors, which have greatly eased the physical burden of ploughing and sowing. Households which do not own a tractor usually hire the services of a neighbor. A close kinsman may be charged less than a stranger, but he is nonetheless expected to pay; this demonstrates the increasing significance of money in the local economy (some villagers say that in the case of their kin they charge only for "fuel expenses").

The trends of the reform era are well illustrated in social engineering schemes of the kind that Qizilyar experienced in the 1990s. Following years of preparation, in 1997 twenty Qizilyar households, mostly married couples with young children, received state support to help them set up new households in a desert "model village" that had been equipped with the latest irrigation technologies. The idea was that these families would use the land allocated to them for growing cash crops (overwhelmingly cotton). A decade later most of them were doing exactly this, supplemented by grapes and other fruit production. They were allowed to retain their lands in the mountain village, more than 70 km away, and most have continued to cultivate these plots for subsistence purposes. To do so they depend on occasional help from kin still resident in Qizilyar (mainly to irrigate their fields during the growing season), and they sometimes reside with kin when they return to the village for the peak summer

---

[16] Pressure on pastureland has become a serious problem, recognized as such by the authorities, though they have not so far been able to devise effective solutions. Households have in recent years been able to increase the size of their herds through buying in cheap fodder from the town. Excessive grazing in the summer months has had highly detrimental effects and it has become necessary to bring the animals back to the valley settlements much earlier than was formerly the case.

activities. These kin often offered help in the autumn with cotton picking in the new settlement. Some migrants offered cash to their kin, but they also provided other forms of support as a result of their better access to the city with its rapidly developing market, medical, and educational institutions. Thus the expansion of cash-cropping did not lead to a decline in subsistence-oriented activity or to a weakening of kin relations. A large mosque has been built in the new settlement and the first burials took place recently; but some insist on being buried alongside their ancestors in the mountain village.

My general argument here is that, after the decades of dislocation under Mao, in the reform era villages such as Qizilyar have reestablished themselves as moral communities. This community is thoroughly imbued with Islam. Most men attend the village's rebuilt mosque regularly. It is accepted that Communist Party members, along with teachers and other cadres who are not members, are not free to do so, but they are not thereby excluded from the networks of hospitality and gift-giving. Even these officials are in practice able to attend the service at the major feasts of Ramadan and Qurban, and they too will receive an Islamic funeral. Some families have prospered more than others in recent years. One sometimes hears negative comments about families thought to be showing excessive zeal in the pursuit of money. Those who have become wealthy through building up large herds are sometimes criticized for their lack of cultural sophistication. But differentiation in housing and consumption remains low. The renewed unity of this community is rendered visible at weddings and funerals, when virtually everyone stops whatever else they might be doing in order to participate in the collective rituals, which are again performed with strict gender divisions.

Let me now examine three aspects of this reembedded community more carefully. For Karl Polanyi, land, labor, and money were the prime examples of "fictitious commodities" (2001: Chapter 6). By this he meant to draw attention to the fundamental moral impropriety of treating nature and human beings like economic goods manufactured to satisfy a demand on the marketplace. In suggesting that these could be considered as the litmus tests of a capitalist disembedded economy, Polanyi overlooked or played down countless historical examples of markets for land, wage labor, and money. At the same time, as many economic anthropologists and sociologists have pointed out, noneconomic factors generally play a major role in all of these "markets", even in the most modern industrial and postindustrial economies. Bearing these points in mind, it is instructive to examine these particular "commodities" more carefully in the contemporary Chinese case.

Land

For villagers, the single most important change of the post-Mao era was the introduction of the "responsibility system," which restored a link between the household and a particular plot of land. This change was so important that the people of villages such as Qizilyar still refer to this moment as "the time when the land was given." Although the brigades and production teams were dissolved, the land was not distributed as private property. Rather, households exercised only use rights over an acreage determined in egalitarian fashion by the number of members. These use-rights were later extended into leases of thirty years, and in practice many villages came to consider their plots as "ours." Formal ownership is vested in the village, as represented through its (nominally) elected committee. Implementation has varied across the country and within regions. In some parts of Xinjiang no adjustment has been made to the original allocations, so that the balance of deaths and births has had a sharp impact not only on the labor supply available to the household but also on its ability to sustain itself from the land allocated to it. In the Tian Shan villages investigated, however, regular minor alterations have been implemented every few years by the village headman.[17]

The present arrangements for land, in Qizilyar as elsewhere in China, are neither egalitarian nor efficient. Although allocation is adjusted here to take care of household composition, the fact that the resettled families have been allowed to retain their holdings in their community of origin is a major source of structural inequality. The land-tenure system is inefficient in that it clearly inhibits optimum utilization of the fields from the economist's point of view. It would be more rational, especially since tractors became plentiful, to consolidate the present patchwork. In theory a land market would allow for better use of the existing machine park and perhaps even, following *remembrement*, for the introduction of combine-harvesters, leading to enormous savings in unpaid family labor as well as increased output if the existing network of tracks and paths can be converted to farmland. Needless to say there is no demand whatsoever for such a reform. Villagers seem content (some are perhaps even proud) that they harvest and thresh in family groups, perform the appropriate rituals at the end, and then consume throughout the year the grain which they themselves have produced on their plots.

According to some analysts (e.g. Pei 2006), this suboptimal economic performance reflects the "trap" facing China as a whole. It is argued that it was possible to maintain high growth rates in the early decades of the reform era only because the baseline was so low, and that for progress to be sustained a rigorous specification of property rights, backed up by legal enforcement, is essential (Nee 1989, 1996). It is indeed well documented that corrupt authorities have regularly taken advantage of poorly specified rights to appropriate farmland in periurban locations (Pieke 2005). But others have argued

---

[17] The land of a woman who married outside the community can sometimes be exchanged for the land of a woman from that settlement who marries in.

that measures to avert abuse of this kind need not have to take the form of strengthening private property. For example, Peter Ho (2005) has argued persuasively for the merits of localized common property solutions. For the time being, at any rate in settlements such as Qizilyar, the authorities' refusal to allow farmland to become a "fictitious commodity" in Polanyi's sense may be viewed as the kernel of a more general policy to maintain a balance of economic principles in rural areas.

Labor

The most visible form of work undertaken in these mountain villages is the production of wheat and other crops (notably beans and maize) in irrigated fields. As noted, mechanization has proceeded apace in recent years, but harvesting is still carried out by hand, often with the help of visiting family members from the city. Labor cooperation in the fields with other households has become rare in recent years. However, mutual aid remains extremely important in housebuilding and in the preparations for ritual performances.

The livestock sector, the main source of cash income for most villagers, is characterized by a variety of practices. Most Qizilyar households look after their own animals in private pens close to their homes during the winter months; they often cooperate informally, for example for local grazing of goat herds, and no money changes hands. During the rest of the year, groups of households, usually neighbors, contract with a herdsman (often a young neighbor), who takes the animals to graze either in the nearby "winter pastures" (*kishlaq*) or in the summer to the more distant higher mountains (*yaylaq*). The herdsman receives a cash payment per animal per month. This payment is relatively low and this job is regarded as difficult, even though the herdsman is usually supported by members of his family, who may rotate with him as well as taking him the provisions he needs. Two households in Qizilyar and a larger number in Qoray migrate temporarily as family units to the *yaylaq*. In addition to taking in the animals of others, these families have built up substantial herds of their own; they have contracted with the state to acquire exclusive access to additional pastures and become wealthy; but even they will send some family members back to the village at the peaks for work in the wheat fields.

Apart from the embroidery practiced by a few women, there are few other possibilities to earn cash in the villages.[18] However, labor-market opportunities outside the villages have increased in recent years. Uyghurs who acquire

---

[18]   In the few cases where no family labor is available, it is possible to hire young men as day laborers for fieldwork. Excluded from consideration in this discussion are the numerous villagers on the state's payroll, including teachers and officials ranging from senior cadres working full-time at the level of the township to part-time officials charged with implementation at *mähällä* level of family planning policies.

only a smattering of Chinese in the course of their village education are poorly equipped to join the country's vast "floating" migrant population. Some do, however, make use of kin links in Qumul or in the provincial capital Urumchi to escape from farming, at least temporarily, for example by taking jobs as apprentices in restaurants or ateliers. Others seek seasonal work as day laborers in Qumul's vast state-owned vineyards and cotton fields. The private sector has grown very rapidly in the latter branch, where the price has fluctuated greatly in recent years. The government no longer insulates producers from volatile markets; this provides the most striking evidence of the incorporation of this remote region into the global economy.

Some Qumul villages still mobilize labor for communal tasks along the lines followed in the Maoist years (*halis ämgäk*). This is especially important in the lowlands for opening up new areas of the surrounding desert for cultivation. This "corvée" labor has largely disappeared in the mountain villages. However, the villagers of Qizilyar were mobilized over several years to plant a protective screen of trees alongside the main road leading down to Qumul. For this work they were paid piece rates: a strong, hard worker could earn four or five times as much as a weaker individual for whom the effort of digging holes in the barren ground was extremely demanding physically.

Money

I often had the impression that younger men of the village were grateful for almost any opportunity to earn cash. Some complained that for much of the year they had little to keep them busy on their farms. In contrast to the case of land, where the very idea of commodification seems unthinkable, in the case of labor there was a widespread wish to experience *more* of the market principle.[19] Money was essential not only to purchase the fridges and motorbikes mentioned above, but also for the celebration of the basic life-cycle rituals. Marriage is by far the most expensive, though other occasions ("cradle ceremony," circumcision, funeral) may also involve substantial outgoings, depending on the status of the family. The *toyluq* paid for a bride began to rise as soon as the land was decentralized and at the time of fieldwork was well over 10,000 *Yuan* (1,000 *Euros*) for a first marriage. It varies significantly according to the status of the families concerned. Much of the excited gossip surrounding marital alliances

---

[19] In this context it was sometimes pointed out that local public works, such as the construction of new commune offices, bridges, or the rebuilding of private houses through state aid following storm damage, are invariably undertaken by gangs of Han Chinese from outside the region. This practice was sometimes criticized, but it was also acknowledged that few Uyghurs would be willing to carry out such tasks for very low remuneration and in very unpleasant physical conditions in which female and male workers shared the same temporary accomodation.

has come to revolve around the cash amount of the *toyluq*, in a manner that was not characteristic of the Maoist era (when payments were leveled down to minimal levels) or of the pre-1949 situation (when payments also varied greatly, but money was not the dominant medium).

This is consistent with the evidence for changing patterns of marital payments in other parts of China (Yan 2005) and indicative of the increasing domination of money in Chinese reform socialism generally. However, it is important to enter a few provisos. It is not the case that money has entirely displaced other goods to function as a medium of exchange in lubricating the market for women. Cloth, silk, and other items are still given. It is emphasized that the cash payment is not retained by the bride's parents but is used to cover wedding expenses and to purchase consumer goods for the new couple, which are displayed at the wedding feast. Monetary donations to the *imam* for his ritual services are nowadays criticized by both Muslim reformers and the secular authorities (Waite 2003). However, they are not entirely new. The annual hospitality extended by the mosque community at the ritual known as *Sara* (which nowadays consists basically in the performance of a *Mavlud*) requires a substantial contribution from all members of the community. Those who cannot afford to give cash will contribute in kind or in some other way and this will be noted accordingly by the community's accountant. It is customary to make a token payment of one *Yuan* to each guest on this occasion, to thank him for attending.[20] This illustrates the persistence of very old local ideas about reciprocity and hospitality rather than a new fetishization of money *per se* (see Bellér-Hann 2008).

Conclusion

The seventy households of Qizilyar can hardly be depicted as a microcosm of the People's Republic. Nonetheless, the mix of economic principles observable in some eastern Tian Shan villages does correspond to the mix at the national level. The principle of the market has expanded greatly, but it is modified by redistribution undertaken both by the state and by kin and neighbors in accordance with Islamic precepts. I have drawn attention to ambivalence concerning the "fictitious commodities." The market principle has made greater inroads in the case of labor than it has with land, which here is seldom farmed by

---

[20] *Sara* is not known in Qizilyar or Qoray and I observed this ritual in another community close to the oasis center. Money was much scarcer in the mountain villages. I was struck here by how very reluctant people of all social groups were to accept the modest cash sum (20 *Yuan*) which I distributed in return for their cooperation in completing a short household survey. I usually had to insist that it was my obligation to hand over this "German money," and that if the household did not wish to keep it, it would be proper for them to pass it on to a deserving neighbor as charity.

anyone other than the designated holder of the use rights. Although "general-purpose" money has extended its reach into new spheres, it has not entirely supplanted traditional forms of transfer, let alone displaced values. Villages such as Qizilyar have again become highly autarkic units in which most work is unpaid and subject to the patriarchal structures of the household. Many younger people would welcome better opportunities to participate in the labor market at regional and national levels, but their remote location and Uyghur ethnicity are a handicap.

Although Karl Polanyi's ideal type of redistribution would seem highly relevant to Marxist–Leninist–Maoist socialism, the most influential anthropological accounts of this form of social organization have made little or no use of his work (Humphrey 1983; Verdery 1996).[21] In any case, these studies were based on forms of socialist practice that differ considerably from the reformed models introduced in Hungary after 1968 and in China a decade or so later. In this chapter I have drawn on Polanyi to develop a new framework that would allow us to include these reform variants. Specifically, I have suggested an alternative way to operationalize the central Polanyi metaphor of embeddedness. If the market principle is neither privileged nor demonized but simply set alongside the other "forms of integration" (see Polanyi 1957b, by which time their number had been reduced to three through the elimination of householding; Gregory, Chapter 8 in this volume), we may conclude that a disruptive Great Transformation might equally be the result of a sudden exaggerated emphasis on one of the other forms.

In the countryside of Xinjiang the dramatic implementation of a new form of redistribution after 1949 wrought havoc with social relations, leading to economic disasters and the undermining of the previous basis of the moral community, which was grounded in religion. In the reform era a new balance has been struck. The household is once again the key unit of production and consumption. The market principle has greatly expanded its reach, but labor, land, and money have not been reduced to the status of fictitious commodities, either as defined in Polanyi's "ideal type" or as found in practice in contemporary capitalist economies. China's continuing ambivalence is an anomalous irritation to many critics, from neoliberal property-rights theorists to those who still romanticize the lost collectivism of the Maoist era. But we could see this as a balancing act, as a socialist equivalent of the welfare state, the "embedded liberalism" which prevailed in the West in the decades following the Second World War. I think that Polanyi would have approved of this embedded socialism. He would hope that the Chinese variant will continue to evolve in this

---

[21] The position is different in sociology: see Beckert, chapter 3, and Steiner, chapter 4, in this volume. See also Szelenyi 1983, 1991. This chapter may be read as the belated resumption of a dialogue with Ivan Szelenyi, whose comments (1991: 238) on my own earlier readings of Polanyi I only discovered when preparing this chapter.

direction, and that it will last longer than the ephemeral example of "market socialism" in Hungary and even the postwar welfare state in Western Europe.

Acknowledgements

I am grateful to Ildikó Bellér-Hann, Keith Hart, Frank Pieke, Yongjun Zhao, and my Uyghur colleagues at the Max Planck Institute Ayxe Eli, Sawut Pawan, and Äsäd Sulaiman for their comments on earlier drafts of this chapter.

15   Afterword: learning from Polanyi 2

Don Robotham

The essays in this important collection pose the central issues facing the field of economic anthropology today. After the triumph of formalism in the debate with the substantivists, the question became whether any such subfield could continue to exist at all. This collection shows that a theoretically coherent field called economic anthropology is not only possible but vitally necessary and that its revival is underway. What will give this revived discipline coherence and what are some of the issues that it will have to confront? The classical work of Polanyi, shorn of the restrictions placed on it by Dalton (Isaac 2005), offers a point of departure for answering these questions, but many issues remain unresolved.

Taken as a whole, these essays suggest a tentative convergence between aspects of economic anthropology, economic sociology, and the new institutional economics. This synthesis is by no means unproblematic, and indeed several of the papers (Gudeman, in Chapter 2, and Beckert, in Chapter 3) argue that a considerable number of obstacles have to be overcome. In the end, reconciliation may not be possible, given the fundamentally individualistic and rationalist assumptions of the new institutional economics (see Gudeman's critique of Landa above). Notwithstanding these reservations, we may discern the outlines of what such a synthesis might look like. To focus on purely economic structures, mechanisms, and actions is properly the domain of the discipline of economics. All the contributors here seem to agree that we must also study the broader context – institutions, structures, customs, traditions, and so on – in which the economy is in some sense "embedded." The study of the economy in relation to this broader "structure," "culture," "repertoire," "institutional complex," or "political framework" creates a space where the disciplines of economic sociology, economic anthropology, political economy, and, indeed, institutional economics converge. In substance this is a Weberian view, rooted in nineteenth-century institutionalism.

This rationale for the field is entirely different from those put forward by the substantivists, at least by those of the Dalton school. The authors of this volume clearly do not accept that a separate subfield of economic anthropology is necessary on the grounds that the economies studied by anthropologists are qualitatively different from the capitalist type. Economies may well differ qualitatively one from another, but that particular justification for economic anthropology was always questionable. The notion that we needed a different subdiscipline to study "primitive," "archaic," or "precapitalist" economies because they functioned in a radically different manner from their capitalist equivalents never could stand serious scrutiny. Why only one subdiscipline? Why not a separate one for each "socio-economic formation" – an "archaic economics" and a "feudal economics" *ad infinitum*? There must be some universal or at least general features underlying all economic life for it to be studied at all, however these may be configured by historical circumstances, geography, institutions, culture, politics, and so forth. The dominant position taken in this volume is that all economies are composed of the same elements – "exchange" and "base," or the economy *per se* and the institutional context in which it is "embedded" – and that these have been, are, and may be arranged differently with radically differing outcomes.

Given this definition of the field, the question of what "embedding" means becomes critical. Various schools have different approaches to this inherently vague and slippery term. Some in the not-so-new institutionalism, following Granovetter (see Beckert, in Chapter 3) and the overall influence of neoclassical economics, have a "thin" notion of embeddedness. Often they identify and study in the economy only networks or economic institutions that reduce transaction costs (corporations, for example), without considering the broader social, cultural, political, or legal context of the economy as a whole. If the institutional framework of this broader context is addressed, it is presented as the product of individual rational calculation or state regulation (rationally calculating legislators) which, while not directed to benefit any individual economic actor or action, seeks to shore up the edifice that makes rational maximization possible in the first place. Beckert's suggestion that "embeddedness" should be seen as arising from the need to resolve three main "coordination problems" is an example of this instrumental perspective, an expression of a prevailing methodological individualism in which social, cultural, and political forces seldom appear in their own right.

The rationalist approach to institutions is one tendency coming from the economics side. From the side of an anthropology deeply influenced by anti-capitalism of one form or another, the tendency is to see the institutional framework as "base," as a source of "mutuality" and "trust," even of "necessity" (Gudeman, in Chapter 2) or as the foundation for "human economies" (Graeber, in Chapter 7). This "thick" version of embeddedness does not see the institutional framework as facilitating or arising from self-seeking calculation, but rather represents it as its very antithesis. It is made up of non-rationalist elements expressing values that are ends in themselves. It is *Gemeinschaft* – community – struggling to constrain the alienating forces of "contingency" (opportunism?) unleashed by general-purpose money. To this line of think-ing, the role of "embeddedness" is precisely to curb the worst excesses of the market economy and of capitalist modernity. Sociology, if the work of Zukin and DiMaggio (1990) is anything to go by, sits somewhere between these two viewpoints. It makes an effort to specify areas and types of embeddedness, allowing for different forms to have diverse outcomes that need to be studied empirically in each case.

The authors here, with the partial exception of Guyer (in Chapter 11), also tend to reject a social constructivist or relativist approach to the study of eco-nomic life which in recent decades has gained ground in both sociology and anthropology. By this I mean the relativist view, derived from post-structural-ism, which would restrict the subject matter of anthropology to the study of collective (and individual) perceptions, ideas, representations, and discourses. Its proponents argue that one never can gain access to an unvarnished reality "out there," even assuming that such may actually exist. This approach, notably in the work of Knorr Cetina, reads like a revival of a bleak version of sym-bolic interactionism, but without the rationalist calculating actor at the center of the network of interaction (Knorr Cetina and Bruegger 2002). Instead, these vacant "post-social" actors have their intersubjectivity defined by relations with objects and are as much constituted by microstructures and objects as they con-stitute them (Knorr Cetina and Bruegger 2000). Here we have traveled very far from classical notions of a masterful *Homo economicus* coolly weighing the options before choosing the path of maximization, usually in a Scrooge-like bourgeois manner. Indeed, these are not self-confident "actors" at all.

Steiner's contribution (in Chapter 4), echoing Callon's notion of "framing," adds the idea of "cognitive embeddedness" of the economy, a particularly French adaptation of the concept that would have surprised Polanyi. In gen-eral, however, this intellectualist interpretation – the notion of the economy as a "model" or a series of "microstructures" and of economic anthropology or sociology as the study of how various actors "enact" these "models" of the economy (or have it enacted on them) – gives way here to the idea that all models are constructed of certain common elements – "base" and "exchange" or "mutuality" and "market" – that actually exist in reality. The related post-structuralist notion of economic action as drawing on an "assemblage" of "rep-ertoires" which are "performed" pragmatically by actors in given situations likewise finds little representation in this collection, although there are echoes of it in Guyer's essay (Chapter 11; see also Maurer 2006).

Gudeman and Servet (in Chapters 2 and 5) seem to converge on the view that the reciprocal and the self-serving should not be conceived of as either present or absent in a particular economy, *tout court*. These two "value realms" are vari-ably present in different economies or even entangled in particular transactions in the same economy. The task of the economic anthropologist then becomes to tease these two different elements out. Guyer uses another terminology to make a similar point. She argues that one is dealing not with pure situations in which prices are either the result of rationalist calculation or the fruit of sentiment. Rather, what we have here are "composites" that are constituted situationally. In other words, Guyer, too, is a realist analyzing an economy which is "out there." "Base" and "market exchange" are mixed in various proportions and with a variety of outcomes, but not in a rigid schematic manner – the situation is fluid, as her account of the drama of petroleum price composition at the pump in Nigeria in 1997 demonstrates vividly in her chapter.

This notion of the need for economic anthropologists to understand the fluidity and interpenetration of different types of economic activity (Gudeman's dialectic) is another important contribution of this collection, one consistent with much of the new work in the anthropology of finance. Gregory's intriguing essay (Chapter 8) takes the point much further when he argues for an approach that appreciates the contradictory nature of economic and social phenomena. "Householding," he insists, is not simply autarkic as conceived in Polanyi's earlier work, but also non-autarkic. Some economic processes are institutionalized but others are not. "Brotherhood" and "estrangement" go hand in hand – in fact one is the necessary condition for the other. It is this fluidity that the different models of the economy capture.

Variation in modeling may likewise be seen in the history of economic theory, since different paradigms – the Physiocratic, Ricardian, and Marxist models, for example – arise because they capture more or less adequately certain features of reality at the time. Thus there is an anthropology of economic knowledge contained here as well. For the time being though, we should note these authors' apparent consensus on realism and against social constructivism, and if my inference is correct, this in itself is an important contribution.

This idea of fluidity extending to contradiction – that there is no pure economy of mutuality and no pure economy of exchange – as put forward in the chapters of Gudeman, Beckert, Servet, Guyer, and Gregory, makes it difficult even to conceive of a "Great Transformation." If trust and exchange are variously mixed in any concrete case, how does Polanyi's entire historical perspective hold up? Maurer recently raised this question when he wondered whether "money's homogenizing effects were as complete as once believed" (Maurer 2006). Likewise Carrier (in Chapter 13), in his discussion of the specifics of environmental conservation efforts in Jamaica, shows that a rigid and schematic application of Polanyi's periodization simply does not work. His essay issues a timely warning against overly structuralist applications of Polanyi's categories which ignore the subjectivities of specific situations. Some of the most recent work in the anthropology of finance has this idea as a pervasive theme: what had hitherto been regarded as the acme of callous

self-enrichment – trading on the stock market – turns out to be not primarily about calculation at all (Zaloom 2003). Knorr Cetina and Bruegger, as
Maurer (2006) points out, also discover social reciprocity in financial
"microstructures."

It is one thing, however, to argue that no pure situations of "mutuality" or
"market" actually exist, that general-purpose money does not instantly dissolve
non-market norms, or that the notion of the all-knowing bourgeois rational
man is a worse than useless myth, and quite another to assert that Polanyi's
historic narrative breaks down in its fundamentals. This story of an era of Free
Trade in the nineteenth century, dominated by Britain as the workshop of the
world, long predated Polanyi and was not original to him. In this sense it is not
Polanyi's narrative at all. Likewise the idea that this era came to an end with
the Great Depression and, in the case of Britain, the abandonment of the gold
standard in September 1931, is beyond debate. It is equally obvious that the
era of social democracy which encroached on the "rights of capital" to make
extensive social provision came to an end with the collapse of Bretton Woods
after 1971. The modified periodization suggested by Hart (in Chapter 6) does
not challenge this framework of history. Without it the entire politics of the
past and indeed the recent present, including the current debates for and against
neoliberal globalization, make no sense. Yet Carrier is right that we must be
able to see how and where local histories connect or do not connect to this
larger narrative.

What Polanyi brought to the table was not this periodization *per se* but the
way he drew out the social and cultural implications of transformations that
had already been well established in historiography. He went on to use this
periodization to develop a theory of the universal place of market relations
in the social and cultural systems of humanity and of the role this relationship has played in human history. Notwithstanding all the qualifications made
by various authors, this general historical theory still stands in its essentials
(Maurer 2006).

This leads us to the question Beckert (in Chapter 3) raises of whether a modern capitalist economy is fundamentally different from precapitalist economies
– whether this entire terminology of "capitalist" and "precapitalist" ("primitive," "archaic," "historical," "stone-age," "mercantile," and so on) is valid. The
distinction is so deeply entrenched in history, anthropology, and, to a lesser
extent, sociology that it is hard to see how it can be challenged. Yet the majority
of neoclassical economists do challenge it – arguing that the differences are of
degree, not fundamental and qualitative (even though Frank Knight maintained
in his critique of Herskovits that without the presence of impersonal institutions and a labor market, neoclassical economics could not be applied; this
remains a crucial question in so far as economic anthropology is in dialogue
with economics, as Hart and Hann point out in Chapter 1).

In the more extreme forms of neoclassical analysis (e.g. Becker on the family or Landa on the *kula ring*, see Gudeman, in Chapter 2), the presence or absence of a modern capitalist economy is not essential for the theory to be generally applicable (Gregory, in Chapter 8). Moreover, the development of a method and paradigm applicable to all forms of economy does not assume that all forms are therefore qualitatively the same. The method and paradigm may be specifically historical, for example, explicitly assuming profound distinctions between types of economy, while applying a general approach. This is the point made by Gregory in his distinction between "universalist" and "generalist" approaches. The former pursues an abstract generality immune to the specifics of time and space, while a generalist understands how the application of abstract concepts necessarily differs in historically concrete situations. This is particularly clear in the work of Adam Smith and the classical economists who, despite the famous affirmation of a universal human tendency "to truck, barter, and exchange," outlined a grand historical narrative of four stages of human development – hunting and gathering, pastoralism, agriculture, and the modern manufacturing era, which built on earlier Scottish philosophers. Indeed, we might argue that institutional economics is significant precisely in this respect: it allows the universal methodology of neoclassical economics to be upheld at a general level, while recognizing substantial differences of institutional context within which the economy is entrenched. Heath Pearson (2000) already made this point in discussing how generalization in economics can allow for the presence not just of *Homo economicus*, but of also *Homo paleoeconomicus*.

Isaac (2005) has pointed out that Dalton's version of Polanyi departed sharply from the original in so far as his substantivist position restricted economic anthropology and the issue of embeddedness to non-capitalist societies. None of the essays here takes this position. On the contrary, all take for granted that Polanyi's aspiration to "embed" the modern capitalist economy was substantially achieved in the postwar social democratic settlement. This brings us to the fundamental political issue. Polanyi was motivated by what one could loosely call a social democratic outlook: leftist, but not unambiguously Marxist or communist. It is important to recognize this because today's debates about neoliberal globalization are motivated by a similar rejection of the social, economic, and political consequences of free market capitalism. All talk of the need to "embed" the market and to recognize the importance of "institutions," "trust," and the like is a critique of the received wisdom that upholds the status quo. This was always what the debate was about – in Polanyi's time, then in the formalist–substantivist debate of the 1960s, not to mention French Structural Marxism, world systems, and dependency theory in the 1970s. So this point cannot be ignored.

There are so many positions on this issue – from rejecting the capitalist system in its entirety to the search for palliative reforms – that it is not surprising that the vague metaphor of embedding has been seized upon and given far more weight than it was ever intended to carry by Polanyi himself (Beckert, in Chapter 3). What can it possibly mean, this "embed"? A kind of "Third Way" of the kind touted by Anthony Giddens or Tony Blair? Or does it depart completely from the "Anglo-Saxon" model? Can it embrace the French "Social Model," Scandinavian Social Democracy, and the "21st Century Socialism" of Hugo Chávez? Might it also be applied to centrally planned state socialism or to some combination of market and plan? Is "embeddedness" a cognitive aspect of the *conscience collective*, an objective institutional fact or some combination of the two – one the result of the other? The ambiguity of the term reflects the ambivalence of different authors toward this crucial political issue. By applying it in new ways to distinguish the Maoist and Reform periods of Chinese socialism, Hann (in Chapter 14) widens the range of application still further. Yet as the infatuation with economic neoliberalism wanes, what an embedded economy actually is remains unclear.

Polanyi is not much help here, since he shared the vagueness of most *Kapitalismuskritik*, then and now. He had a typical Central European abhorrence of economic liberalism. His thought was pervaded by this "hatred" (his wife's word, not mine) of economic liberalism and his yearning for another, less alienated, less materialistic society – for *Gemeinschaft*, in other words. He was not too clear on what this alternative could be, except in so far as he was attracted to Guild Socialism. Polanyi's wife argues, in the book put together by Kari Polanyi Levitt, that *The Great Transformation* was worked out (if not written) by 1940 and was shaped primarily by Polanyi's personal experience of the English class system, after coming to teach for the Workers Education Association there from 1933 (Duczynska Polanyi 2006).

This critique of capitalist modernity is, of course, an old story in Western social science, especially in its German variant. I was therefore struck by the absence of reference here to the work of Tönnies or to the deep similarities between Polanyi's thought and that of Weber – down to the common fascination with Tolstoy and Dostoyevsky in the Weber Circle in Heidelberg. The big difference between Polanyi and Weber, however, is that Weber, who understood the failings of modern capitalism, saw no escape from this rationalization of modern life. The "forms" of modernity were fixed. Alienation and "disembedding" were existential burdens that one must learn to bear. As far as Weber was concerned, the triumph of instrumental rationality was not just inescapable, but also, to some degree, desirable. It was certainly not possible for general-purpose money to be "embedded" by some political fiat emanating from the state. That way lay inflation and ruin. Weber agreed with Knapp that the state had a role to play, but he also agreed with von Mises that the value of money was established impersonally by global market forces, and not by the

Canute-like pronouncements of Finance Ministers, even of the most powerful states (Roth 2003). In other words, the iron cage had disembedded us for good. Nineteenth-century individualistic liberalism was no longer feasible in its classical form – its pietistic ethic having culminated in a calculating, secular, bureaucratic machine inspired by "the philosophy of money" (Simmel 1900).

This rise of bureaucratic capitalism and the necessary collapse of old-style liberalism, as far as Weber and Simmel were concerned, was the real "Great Transformation." Under these circumstances, the most one could do was to promote competition between bureaucracies in civil society (trades unions versus corporations) and hope that a skilful deployment of charisma and democracy by plebiscite would preserve a modicum of personal freedom. Hence the peculiarly authoritarian quality of Weber's bureaucratic liberalism. Polanyi missed entirely the rise of bureaucratic capitalism from the late nineteenth century (see Hart, in Chapter 6). Hence his inability to envisage the form social democracy took after the war in the leading capitalist countries and his apparent endorsement of Hungarian central planning shortly before his death (Nagy 1994).

For Weber, rationality, including the purely formal kind, was a vehicle not only for economic liberalism but also for liberal politics, the liberal public sphere, and liberal culture in general. The peculiar antinomy of a bitter rejection of liberal economics combined with a steadfast affirmation of liberal politics and culture – a common recipe on the Left in the United States and Britain – was out of the question for Weber. In its original form of the protestant ethic, the free market was the source of many of the freedoms and values that Weber and other political liberals held dear. In other words, Polanyi's wholesale rejection of economic liberalism was foreign to Weber's (and Simmel's) way of thinking. Although deeply influenced by anticapitalism, like so many of that generation and background, Weber was no romantic. In fact, as is well-known, he was highly skeptical of all attempts to regulate the market, believing that this would end in a bureaucratic nightmare. In that sense, Weber's thought is closer to that of Hayek and von Mises than to Polanyi (Roth 2003). They may have shared common Central and Eastern European intellectual traditions, but ideas such as "embedding" the market economy, from Weber's point of view, were hopelessly impractical.

This issue goes beyond pointing out historical parallels and genealogies. The dominant attitude expressed by the essays in this volume seems to me inadequate on this point. Without accepting Cook's famous assault (Cook 1966), an insufficient appreciation of the market is palpable here. Several authors do make the often-forgotten point that Polanyi's critique was not directed against *all* forms of market relations, but against markets in land, labor, and money in particular. The last is immediately relevant to current debates about monetarism, inflation targeting, floating versus fixed exchange rates, and the exchange controls imposed by states. While some authors tolerate the market as an inescapable requirement of modernity, they generally do not see it as a source of positive values or social relationships. More often, the extension of market relations is portrayed as the insidious undermining of an otherwise wholesome "base." Is it permissible to ask if these "bases" are or were all that wholesome (see Gregory, in Chapter 8)? Have the market and division of labor brought no economic, social, cultural, and political benefits? Is there nothing to be said in favor of breaking down communal insularity and narrow "identities" of one sort or another and of constituting sociality on a broader basis? Does liberalism in that broad sense have no virtues? Is everything from Petty, Bacon, and Hobbes (not to mention Locke, Smith, Bentham, Ricardo, and Mill) just one long nightmare of "possessive individualism"? A litany of "English cant"? Are the arguments concerning the value of "multiple identities" of contemporaries such as Sen (a political and cultural liberal of a classical stamp) simply to be dismissed (Sen 2006)?

At stake here is, first, the connection between economic liberalism (the market) and political and cultural liberalism or cosmopolitanism. From Adam Smith's *Moral Sentiments*, it has been argued that the extension of market relations brings with it not only utilitarian attitudes and self-seeking relationships, but also the broader sympathies of society, civic culture, and humanity they help to create (Smith 1759). Indeed, this is perhaps the central meaning of enlightenment humanism and of its contemporary expression as cosmopolitanism. Even if this cosmopolitanism is largely formal and its humanism attempts to reduce issues of exploitation and oppression to an abstract concern with "rights," it is not entirely without content, especially when compared with other forms of economy and society. The question should be how to give this hollow cosmopolitanism substantive content as a lived concrete reality experienced globally by all.

But there is a second, even more important issue arising from the first. This is the claim that an extension of capitalist relations, in addition to its materialistic achievements, creates the foundation for an alternative universal sociality containing the potential to overcome the alienation and exploitation of capitalist society itself. In other words, without a further extension of market relations, a solution to the alienation and exploitation created by capitalist modernity is hard to conceive. This dialectical perspective – "without capitalism, no socialism" – goes against the main drift of the essays presented here.

This point – that capitalism, in the course of exploiting and oppressing, also emancipates us from parochialisms and relations of personal dependence – is crucial (see Hart, in Chapter 6). The idea that the obverse of the market's individualism is a much greater expansion of the social sphere was taken up most clearly by Durkheim with his notion of organic solidarity and later in the work of Habermas (Habermas 1991). It is critical to how we understand Mauss's work, as when Steiner and Hart observe above that Mauss, after studying the early Soviet economy, concluded it was impossible to eliminate market relations, a point that remains of the greatest importance in theory and politics. If, as Hart (2007a) maintains, Mauss was a cooperative socialist for whom the labor market was not just a source of alienation, but also dialectically a vital engine of a broader sociality, then it is not possible to recruit Mauss to the antimarket elements of the Polanyi tradition. This Maussian perspective is missing from the work of Polanyi and of many economic anthropologists strongly influenced by him. I suspect that this is largely because they focus on the sphere of exchange (where individualistic consumption rules) rather than on the sphere of production, which is where the expansion of sociality most clearly manifests itself. This relatively uncritical attitude to past economic formations and a failure to see any merit in the expansion of capitalist relations (including the labor market) justifies pinning the label "nostalgic" on Polanyi's thought and on many of those who follow him.

Thus Gudeman (in Chapter 2) argues that the problems for mutuality arise from contradictions between "necessity" and "contingency," between the "base" and "exchange." In this scenario "exchange" and "contingency" are the root of all evil. But what if the contradictions are within the "base" itself and the problem is one of conflicting "necessities?" What if "brotherhood" takes contradictory forms – not only the practice of "giving" and "sharing" but also that of "taking" (embezzlement, theft, fraud, estrangement, personal violence including murder)? This issue is raised most tellingly in Gregory's contribution (Chapter 8), but also in Parry's (Chapter 10) from a rather different angle.

Parry, while rightly rejecting Burawoy's and Halperin's claim that Polanyi was a Marxist, sets out to show, by way of an ethnography of a particular stratum of the Indian working class (contract labor) how a counter-movement to the depredations of the market concretely arose. His penetrating account of labor, class, and political relationships in a community dominated by an Indian steel plant may be taken as an example of a rather unattractive case of "embedding" – the fruit of Nehruvian social democracy in postwar India, before state-centered economic development gave way to the current phase of deregulation and neoliberalism. Parry presents this Indian case of "embedding" as a particularly unlovely process, but one nonetheless that enhances the growth of broader solidarities and an "unusually cosmopolitan world" in the wider context of Indian society. Spittler (in Chapter 9) makes a similar point when he criticizes Polanyi's neglect of the work experience, in contrast to Malinowski, Thurnwald, and a long German tradition that extended to the rest of Europe and North America, for example in Braverman's well-known work (Braverman 1998). He rightly points out that the workplace is much more than the locus of exploitation; it is also a source of self-assurance, cooperation, and political solidarity.

As a corrective to this optimism, Alexander (in Chapter 12) warns economic anthropologists not to be seduced by notions that civil society can effectively address market-driven impoverishment. This form of what we might call "embedding-lite," so characteristic of Britain's New Labour, represents in fact a further disembedding from the social nexus and the commoditization of charity. This is yet another case of *faux* community – the type of "agency" routinely manufactured by the media and the advertising industry. Anthropologists ought not to be so naïve as to claim to detect "reciprocity" and "trust" beneath every microstructural stone, while the self-seeking nature of social relationships is cynically concealed behind all sorts of bonhomie.

The broader issue is whether the economic problems of our era may be addressed through a simple choice of restraining or unleashing market relations. Might feasible solutions require both – constraining them in many respects but expanding them in others? Are there no "necessities" hidden deep within "contingency?" Is this not the salient lesson of Gregory's contribution and of Hart's seminal work on the informal economy of Frafra immigrants in the Nima neighborhood of Accra (Hart 1988)? Seen in this light, it is interesting to evaluate the contradictory impact of the extension of market relations in China – the gigantic social transformations taking place there, including record reductions in poverty and even more dramatic increases in inequality (see Hann, in Chapter 14). Given the likelihood of a similar extension of market relations in Cuba after Fidel Castro, it is noteworthy that, so far, not one of the new leftist regimes in Latin America (including Venezuela) has taken wholesale steps to encroach on capitalist property relations or even seriously to restrict the market. If what "21st century socialism" (Chávez's slogan) means is public education, free healthcare, and antipoverty programs, plus a larger economic role for the state, then this form of "embedding" is not only compatible with the market at the national and international level, but actually requires its expansion for continued prosperity.

The crisis of neoliberalism conceals a crisis of the anticapitalist critique of modernity. This critique actually contains two moments: a desire to constrain the role of the market and a realization of the need to expand the sphere of exchange, nationally and globally, albeit under political supervision. No wonder that many in the West are now looking anxiously at the Chinese example as a possible model. As many have pointed out, Polanyi was no career academic, but a public intellectual deeply committed to improving the human condition. The issue therefore becomes: does the amelioration or abolition of exploitation, poverty, alienation, and insecurity at national and global levels require *both* a "reversal" (or curbing) of the Great Transformation in a nonmarket direction *and* a broader extension of market relations under the supervision of the state and international political organizations?

The dialectic of "market" and "society" goes deeper than Polanyi perceived and we need to interrogate his emphasis on the "market" as the central analytical concept for economic anthropology or economics. This is linked to Polanyi's labeling of the contemporary economy as "industrial capitalism," an extraordinary misnomer. Despite his concern about the encroachment of money into social life, his approach neglected finance capital. Hart's work on money, informatics, and the role of the state redresses this balance (Hart 2000 and in Chapter 6; see also Graeber, Chapter 7). But some further thought could profitably be given to critiquing the label "industrial capitalism" for what has emerged since the nineteenth century, especially given the vast foreign exchange imbalances, the dollar crisis, the dominance of the big banks, and the modern British economy's dependence on financial services – a "national economy," that is, "an enormous hedge fund," according to the *Financial Times* (Wolf 2006). Polanyi understood how the problems caused by the gold standard, fixed exchange rates, and a focus on curbing inflation at the expense of social provisioning arose to some degree from the requirements of Free Trade. He did not grasp the decisive role played by international finance, the repatriation of profits, and debt repayments. As Gregory (in Chapter 8) points out, Polanyi understood "money-making" as "a species of exchange," but that was an inadequate perspective even in his own times (Hilferding 1910). Finance capitalism, a phenomenon of the late-nineteenth and early-twentieth centuries, has lately become a central focus of anthropological research (Maurer 2005a); but it is doubtful that this research will throw light on the questions which interest Hart – where is capitalism heading and what alternatives to capitalist modernity are feasible?

It is equally true that a focus on markets diverts attention from the growth of large transnational corporations whose monopolistic behavior is the very antithesis of liberalism, as Weber clearly saw. Polanyi has nothing to say about this, precisely because he sees the need to control the market as the central issue. He does not understand the ubiquity of the market as deriving from private ownership of the means of production. That form of "embedding" in which the "market" is dominated by corporate monopolies and a large portion of international "trade" consists of interfirm transfers is beyond his purview. The dynamics of capitalist economy and alienation from capitalist modernity proceed apace whether the market is embedded or free. Indeed, one lesson from the collapse of both state socialism and social democracy is that, for different reasons, those forms of "embedding" could not and did not last. It remains to consider what realistic alternatives exist in the current state of affairs. Polanyi's heritage should be part of the search for new answers, but not without critical examination of its premises.

Bibliography

Abrahams, R.D. 1983. *The Man of Words in the West Indies: Performance and the Emergence of Creole Culture.* Baltimore, MD: Johns Hopkins University Press.

Adloff, F. and Mau, S. 2006. "Giving social ties: reciprocity in modern society." *Archives Européennes de Sociologie* **XLVII**: 93–123.

Aglietta, M. and Orléan, A. (eds.). 1992. *La violence de la monnaie.* Paris: PUF.

(eds.). 1995. *Souveraineté, légitimité de la monnaie.* Paris: Association d'Économie Financière (Cahiers finance, éthique, confiance).

(eds.). 1998. *La monnaie souveraine.* Paris: Odile Jacob.

Ahmed, B. 2001. "The impact of globalization on the Caribbean sugar and banana industries." *Society for Caribbean Studies Annual Conference Papers* 2. (Available online at: www. scsonline.freeserve.co.uk/olvol2.html)

Aiken, K.A. n. d. *Fisheries and Marine Conservation.* MS. (Available online at: www. reefrelief. org/jamaica_body_3.html)

Aiken, K.A. and Haughton, M.H. 1987. "Regulating fishing effort: the Jamaican experience." *Proceedings of the Annual Gulf and Caribbean Institute* **40**: 139–50.

Akin, D. and Robbins, J. 1999. *Money and Modernity: State and Local Currencies in Melanesia.* Pittsburg, PA: University of Pittsburg Press.

Alexander, C. 2001. "Legal and binding: time, change and long term transactions." *Journal of the Royal Anthropological Institute* 7 (3): 467–85.

2005. "Value: economic valuations and environmental policy." In J. Carrier (ed.), *A Handbook of Economic Anthropology,* pp. 455–72. Cheltenham: Edward Elgar.

Allard, J., Davidson, C., and Matthaei, J. (eds.). 2008. *Solidarity Economy: Building Alternatives for People and Planet* (Papers and reports from the U.S. Social Forum 2007). Chicago, IL: Change Maker Publications.

Amin, A., Cameron, A. and Hudson, R. 2002. *Placing the Social Economy.* London: Routledge.

Aoki, M. 2001. "Community norms and embeddedness: a game-theoretic approach." In A. Masahiko and Y. Hayami (eds.), *Communities and Markets in Economic Development,* pp. 96–125. Oxford: Oxford University Press.

Aoki, M. and Hayamai, Y. 2001. "Introduction: communities and markets in economic development." In M. Aoki and Y. Hayami (eds.), *Communities and Markets in Economic Development,* pp. xv–xxiv. Oxford: Oxford University Press.

AP. 2004. "$60 million to say 'I do'." (Available online at: www.msnbc.msn.com/id/5297284).

Appadurai, A. (ed.). 1986. *The Social Life of Things: Commodities in Cultural Perspective.* Cambridge: Cambridge University Press.

Arendt, H. 1958. *The Human Condition.* Chicago, IL: University of Chicago Press.

Arrighi, G. 1994. *The Long Twentieth Century.* New York, NY: Verso.

Arrow, K. J. 1990. "Kenneth J. Arrow." In R. Swedberg, *Economics and Sociology: Redefining their Boundaries: Conversations with Economists and Sociologists,* pp. 133–51. Princeton, NJ: Princeton University Press.

Asbury, H. [1927] 2001. *Gangs of New York: An Informal History of the Underworld.* New York, NY: Basic Books.

Ashley, C., Goodwin, H., McNab, D., Scott, M. and Chaves, L. *Making Tourism Count for the Local Economy in the Caribbean: Guidelines for Good Practice.* London: Pro-Poor Tourism Partnership and the Caribbean Tourism Organization.

Atkinson, M. 1910. "The economic relations of the household." In A. Ravenhill and C. Shiff (eds.), *Household Administration: Its Place in the Higher Education of Women,* pp. 121–206. London: Grant Richards Ltd.

Austin, D. J. 1983. "Culture and ideology in the English-speaking Caribbean: a view from Jamaica." *American Ethnologist* **10**: 223–40.

Austin-Broos, D. J. 1997. *Jamaica Genesis: Religion and the Politics of Moral Orders.* Chicago, IL: University of Chicago Press.

Avila-Foucat, V. S. and Eugenio-Martin, J. L. 2004. *Modeling Potential Repetition of a Visit to Value Environmental Quality Change of a Single Site.* Presented at the tenth biennial conference of the International Association for the Study of Common Property. Oaxaca, Mexico, 9–13 August.

Babb, S. 2001. *Managing Mexico. Economists from Nationalism to Neoliberalism.* Oxford and Princeton, NJ: Princeton University Press.

Bagnasco, A. and Sabel, C. F. (eds.). 1995. *Small and Medium-Size Enterprises.* London: Pinter.

Baker, W. 1984. "The social structure of a national securities market." *American Journal of Sociology* **89**: 775–811.

Bakker, M. and Phillip, S. 2005. *Travel and Tourism – Jamaica – February 2005.* London: Mintel International Group Ltd.

Balmuth, M. S. 1975. "The critical moment: the transition from currency to coinage in the eastern Mediterranean." *World Archaeology* **6**: 293–9.

Barber, B. 1995. "All economies are 'embedded': the career of a concept, and beyond." *Social Research* **62**: 387–413.

Barley, S. R., and Orr, J. E. 1997. "Introduction." In S. R. Barley and J. E. Orr (eds.), *Between Craft and Science,* pp. 1–19. Ithaca, NY: Cornell University Press.

Baum, G. 1996. *Karl Polanyi on Ethics and Economics.* Montreal: McGill-Queen's University Press.

Bauman, Z. 2004. *Wasted Lives: Modernity and its Outcasts.* Cambridge: Polity Press.

Baumol, W. J, Blinder, A. S. and Wolff, E. N. 2003. *Downsizing in America.* New York, NY: Russell Sage Foundation.

Beals, R. L. 1975. *The Peasant Marketing System of Oaxaca, Mexico.* Berkeley, CA: University of California Press.

Beck, K. 1994. "Die kulturelle Dimension der Hirtenarbeit in den nordkordofanischen Hirtengesellschaften." In M. S. Laubscher and B. Turner (eds.), *Völkerkundetagung 1991,* pp. 157–176. München: Anacon.

286   Bibliography

1996. "Islam, Arbeitsethik und Lebensführung." In K. Beck, and G. Spittler (eds.), *Arbeit in Afrika*, pp. 161–78. Münster: Lit.

Beck, U. 1992. *Risk Society. Towards a New Modernity*. London: Sage.

1999. *World Risk Society*. Cambridge: Polity Press.

Becker, G. S. 1981. *A Treatise on the Family*. Cambridge, MA: Harvard University Press.

1993. "Nobel lecture: the economic way of looking at behavior." *Journal of Political Economy* **101** (3): 385–409.

1996. *Accounting for Tastes*. Cambridge, MA: Harvard University Press.

Beckert, J. 1996. "What is sociological about economic sociology? Uncertainty and the embeddedness of economic action." *Theory and Society* **25**: 803–40.

2002a. *Beyond the Market: The Social Foundations of Economic Efficiency*. Princeton, NJ: Princeton University Press.

2002b. "Von Fröschen, Unternehmensstrategien und anderen Totems. Die soziologische Herausforderung der ökonomischen Institutionentheorie." In A. Maurer and M. Schmid (eds.), *Neuer Institutionalismus. Zur soziologischen Erklärung von Organisation, Moral und Vertrauen*, pp. 133–47. Frankfurt: Campus.

2003. "Economic sociology and embeddedness: how shall we conceptualize economic action?" *Journal of Economic Issues* **37**: 769–87.

2005. "Soziologische Netzwerkanalyse." In D. Käsler (ed.), *Aktuelle Theorien der Soziologie. Von Shmuel N. Eisenstadt bis zur Postmoderne*, pp. 286–312. München: Beck.

2006a. "Interpenetration versus embeddedness. The premature dismissal of Talcott Parsons in the new economic sociology." *American Journal of Economics and Sociology* **65**: 161–88.

2006b. "Was tun? Die emotionale Konstruktion von Zuversicht bei Entscheidungen unter Ungewissheit." In A. Scherzberg (ed.), *Kluges Entscheiden. Disziplinäre Grundlagen und interdisziplinäre Verknüpfungen*, pp. 123–41. Tübingen: Mohr Siebeck.

Beckert, J and Zafirovski, M. (eds.). 2006. *International Encyclopedia of Economic Sociology*. London: Routledge.

Bellér-Hann, I. 2008. *Community Matters in Xinjiang, 1880–1949; Towards an Historical anthropology of the Uyghur*. Leiden: Brill.

Bellér-Hann, I., Cesáro, M., Harris, R. and Smith Finley, J. (eds.) 2007. *Situating the Uyghurs between China and Central Asia*. Aldershot: Ashgate.

Benham, W. G. 1924. *Benham's Book of Quotations*. London: Ward, Lock & Co.

Berenson, A. 2006. "The other legacy of Enron." *New York Times*, May 28.

Berghoff, H. 2005. "Markterschließung und Risikomanagement." *Vierteljahrschrift für Sozial- und Wirtschaftsgeschichte* **92**: 141–62.

Berndt, R. 1951. "Ceremonial exchange in western Arnhem Land." *Southwestern Journal of Anthropology* **7**: 156–76.

Bernstein, H. and Byres, T. J. 2001. "From peasant studies to agrarian change." *Journal of Agrarian Change* **1** (1): 1–56.

Bernstein, P. L. 1996. *Against the Gods. The Remarkable Story of Risk*. New York, NY: John Wiley.

Besnard, P. [1986] 2003. "L'impérialisme sociologique face à l'histoire." In P. Besnard, *Études durkheimiennes*, pp. 299–310. Genève: Droz.

Besnard, P. 1987. *L'anomie. Ses usages et ses foncions dans la discipline sociologique depuis Durkheim*. Paris: Presses Universitaires de France.

Besson, J. 1993. "Reputation and respectability reconsidered: a new perspective on Afro-Caribbean peasant women." In J. Momsen (ed.), *Women and Change in the Caribbean: a Pan-Caribbean Perspective*, pp. 15–37. London: James Currey.

Beveridge, W. 1948. *Voluntary Action: A Report on Methods of Social Advance*. London: Allen & Unwin.

Biodiversity Support Program. 1999. *Biodiversity Conservation Network 1999 Annual Report: Final Report*. Washington, DC: Biodiversity Support Program.

Blanc, J. 2004. "Karl Polanyi et les monnaies modernes: un réexamen." In G. Lazuech and P. Moulevrier (eds.), *Contributions à une sociologie des conduites économiques*, pp. 51–66. Paris: L'Harmattan.

Blanc, J. (ed.). 2006. *Rapport exclusion et liens financiers 2005–2006*. Paris: Economica.

Bloch, M. 1961. *Feudal Society*. (2 Vols). Chicago, IL: University of Chicago Press.

Block, F. 2001. "Introduction." In K. Polanyi, *The Great Transformation*, pp. xviii–xxviii. Boston, MA: Beacon Press.

2003. "Karl Polanyi and the writing of 'The Great Transformation'." *Theory and Society* **32** (3): 275–306.

Block, F. and Sommers, M. 1984. "Beyond the economistic fallacy: the holistic social science of Karl Polanyi." In T. Skocpol (ed.), *Vision and Method in Historical Sociology*, pp. 47–84. Cambridge: Cambridge University Press.

Blyth, M. 2002. *Great Transformations. Economic Ideas and Institutional Change in the Twentieth Century*. Cambridge: Cambridge University Press.

Bohannan, P. and Dalton, G. (eds.). 1962. *Markets in Africa: Eight Subsistence Economies in Transition*. Evanston, IL: Northwestern University Press.

Boltanski L. and Thévenot, L. 1991. *De la justification. Les économies de la grandeur*. Paris: Gallimard.

Booth, W. [1890] 1970. *In Darkest England, and the Way Out*. 6th ed. London: C. Knight.

Born, G. 1996. "(Im)materiality and sociality: the dynamics of intellectual property in a computer software research culture." *Social Anthropology* **4** (2): 101–16.

Bottom, B. 1988. *Shadow of Shame: How the Mafia Got Away with the Murder of Donald Mackay*. Melbourne: Sun Books.

Bourdieu, P. 1963. *Travail et travailleurs en Algérie. Etude sociologique*. Paris: Mouton.

1989. *La noblesse d'état. Grandes écoles et esprit de corps*. Paris: Minuit.

2000. *Les structures sociales de l'économie*. Paris: Seuil.

Bowker, G.C., and Leigh Star, S. 2000. *Sorting Things Out. Classification and its Consequences*. Cambridge: MIT Press.

Braudel, F. [1979] 1985. *Civilization and Capitalism, 15th–18th Century*. London: Fontana.

Braverman, H. 1998. *Labor and Monopoly Capital: The Degradation of Work in the Twentieth Century*. New York, NY: Monthly Review Press.

Breman, J. 1999. "The study of industrial labour in post-colonial India – the formal sector: An introductory review." In J. Parry, J. Breman, and K. Kapadia (eds), *The Worlds of Indian Industrial Labour*, pp. 1–41. New Delhi: Sage Publications.

Briggs, A. 1973. "The welfare state." In P. Wiener (ed.), *The Dictionary of the History of Ideas: Studies of Selected Pivotal Ideas,* pp. 509–11. Vol. 4. New York, NY: Charles Scribner's Sons.

Brohman, J. 1996. "New directions in tourism for Third World development." *Annals of Tourism Research* **23**: 48–70.

Browne, K. 2004. *Creole Economics.* Austin, TX: University of Texas Press.

Bücher, K. 1896. *Arbeit und Rhythmus.* Leipzig: Teubner.

   1904. *Industrial Evolution,* trans. S. Morley Wickett. New York, NY: Holt.

Bugra, A. and Agartan, K. (eds.). 2007. *Reading Karl Polanyi for the Twenty-first Century: Market Economy as a Political Project.* New York, NY: Palgrave MacMillan.

Burawoy, M. 1979. *Manufacturing Consent. Changes in the Labor Process under Monopoloy Capitalism.* Chicago, IL: University of Chicago Press.

Burawoy, M. 2003. "For a sociological Marxism: The complementary convergence of Antonio Gramsci and Karl Polanyi." *Politics and Society* **31**(1): 1–69.

Burt, R. 1992. *Structural Holes: The Social Structure of Competition.* Cambridge, MA: Harvard.

Caillé, A. 1986. *Splendeurs et misères des sciences sociales. Esquisses d'une mythologie.* Genève: Droz.

   2000. *Anthropologie du don. Le tiers paradigme.* Paris: Desclée de Brouwer.

   2005. *Dé-penser l'économique. Contre le fatalisme.* Paris: La Découverte.

Callon, M. 1998a. "Introduction: The embeddedness of economic markets in economics." In M. Callon (ed.), *The Laws of the Markets,* pp. 1–57. Oxford: Blackwell.

   1998b. "An essay on framing and overflowing: economic externalities revisited by sociology." In M. Callon (ed.), *The Laws of the Markets,* pp. 244–269. Oxford: Blackwell.

Callon, M. 1999. "Actor-network theory – the market test." In J. Law, and J. Hassard (eds.), *Actor Network Theory and After,* pp. 181–95. Oxford: Blackwell.

Callon, M. (ed.). 1998. *The Laws of the Markets.* Oxford: Blackwell.

Callon, M, Méadel, C. and Rabeharisoa, V. 2002. "The economy of qualities." *Eonomy and Society* **31**: 194–217.

Callon, M and Muniesa, F. 2003. "Les marchés économiques comme dispositifs collectifs de calcul." *Réseaux* **122**: 1–45.

Carrier, J. G. 2003a. "Biography, ecology, political economy: seascape and conflict in Jamaica." In A. Strathern, and P. J. Stewart (eds.), *Landscape, Memory and History,* pp. 210–28. London: Pluto Press.

   2003b. "Mind, gaze and engagement: understanding the environment." *Journal of Material Culture* **8**: 5–23.

   2005. *Conserving What? Understandings of the Environment among Conservationists in Jamaica.* MS.

Carrier, J. G. (ed.). 1997. *Meanings of the Market: The Free Market in Western Culture.* Oxford: Berg Publishers.

Carrier, J. G. (ed.). 2005. *A Handbook of Economic Anthropology.* Cheltenham: Edward Elgar.

Carrithers, M. and Humphrey, C. (eds.). 1991. *The Assembly of Listeners: Jains in Society.* Cambridge: Cambridge University Press.

Carsten, J. 1989. "Cooking money: gender and the symbolic transformation of means of exchange in a Malay fishing community." In J. Parry and M. Bloch (eds.), *Money and the Morality of Exchange,* pp. 117–41. Cambridge: Cambridge University Press.

Cela, P. 1997. *Le tre forme dello scambio. Reciprocità, politica, mercato, a partire da Karl Polanyi.* Milano: Il Mulino.

Chamberlin, E. 1933. *The Theory of Monopolistic Competition.* Cambridge: Cambridge University Press.

Chambers, D. and Airy, D. 2001. "Tourism policy in Jamaica: a tale of two governments." *Current Issues in Tourism* 4 (2–4): 94–120.

Chatterjee, P. 1986. *Nationalist Thought and the Colonial World: A Derivative Discourse?* London: Zed Books.

Chayanov, A. V. [1925] 1966. *The Theory of Peasant Economy.* Homewood, IL: Irwin.

Christie, P. and White, A. T. 1997. "Trends in development of coastal area management in tropical countries: from central to community orientation." *Coastal Management* **25**: 155–81.

Clancier P., Joannès, F., Rouillard, P. and Tenu, A. (eds.). 2005. *Autour de Polanyi: Vocabulaires, théories et modalités des échanges.* Paris: De Boccard.

Coase, R. H. 1988. *The Firm, the Market and the Law.* Chicago, IL: Chicago University Press.

Comaroff, J. and Comaroff, J. L. (eds.). 2001. *Millennial Capitalism and the Culture of Neoliberalism.* Durham, NC: Duke University Press.

Comitas, L. 1964. "Occupational multiplicity in rural Jamaica." In L. Comitas and D. Lowenthal (eds.), *Work and Family Life: West Indian Perspectives*, pp. 157–73. Garden City, NY: Anchor Press.

Commons, J. 1934. *Institutional Economics: Its Place in Political Economy.* New Brunswick, NJ: Transaction.

Community Economies Collective. 2001. "Imagining and enacting noncapitalist futures." *Socialist Review* **28** (3–4): 93–135.

Comte, A. [1830–42] 1975. *Cours de philosophie positive.* Paris: Hermann.

[1851–3] 1890. *Système de politique positive.* Paris: Rue Monsieur le Prince.

[1891] 2002. *Catéchisme positiviste.* Paris: Flammarion.

Cook, S. 1966. "The obsolete 'anti-market' mentality: a critique of the substantive approach to economic anthropology." *American Anthropologist* **68** (2): 323–45.

Cornforth, C. 2001. *Recent Trends in Charity Governance and Trusteeship.* Guide to Board Development. London: NCVO Publications.

Cruickshank, B. 1999. *The Will to Empower: Democratic Citizens and Others.* Ithaca, NY: Cornell University Press.

Crump, T. 1981. *The Phenomenon of Money.* London: Routledge.

Cunningham, H. 1998. "Introduction." In H. Cunningham and J. Innes (eds.), *Charity, Philanthropy and Reform: From the 1690s to 1850*, pp. 1–14. Basingstoke: Macmillan Press.

Cunningham, H. and Innes, J. (eds.). 1998. *Charity, Philanthropy and Reform from 1690–1850.* Basingstoke: Macmillan Press.

Dalton, G. 1968. "Introduction." In K. Polanyi, *Primitive, Archaic and Modern Economies*, pp. ix–liv. New York: Anchor Books.

1981. "Comment on 'Symposium: Economic anthropology and history: the work of Karl Polanyi'." *Research in Economic Anthropology* **3**: 69–93.

Dalton, G and Köcke, J. 1983. "The work of the Polanyi group: past, present, and future." In S. Ortiz (ed.), *Economic Anthropology: Topics and Theories*, pp. 21–50. Lanham, MD: University Press of America.

Das, A., and Pandey, D. n.d. *Contract Workers in India: Emerging Economic and Social Issues.* (Available online at: www.kli.re.kr/iira2004/pro/papers/AshisDas&Pandey.pdf)

Davidoff, L. and Hall, C. 1987. *Family Fortunes: Men and Women of the English Middle Class, 1750–1850.* London: Taylor & Francis.

Davidson, A. 2006. "Analyst: Blame investors for high gas prices. Business Section. *National Public Radio* (USA). August 24.

Davis, J. 1992a. *Exchange.* Minneapolis, MN: University of Minnesota Press.

1992b. "Trade in Kufra (Libya)." In R. Dilley (ed.), *Contesting Markets; Analyses of Ideology, Discourse and Practice*, pp. 115–27. Edinburgh: Edinburgh University Press.

Davy, G. 1922. *La foi jurée. Étude sociologique du problème du contrat et la formation du lien contractuel.* Bibliothèque de philosophie contemporaine. Travaux de l'Année sociologique. Paris: Alcan.

de Angelis, M. 1999. *Marx's Theory of Primitive Accumulation: A Suggested Reinterpretation.* (Available online at: http://homepages.uel.ac.uk/M.DeAngelis/PRIMACCA.htm)

Deakin, N. 1995. "The perils of partnership: the voluntary sector and the state 1945–1992." In J. Davis Smith, C. Rochester, and R. Hedley (eds.), *Introduction to the Voluntary Sector*, pp. 40–65. London: Routledge.

DEFRA. 2006. *Review of England's Waste Strategy: A Consultation Document.* London: DEFRA.

Delamotte, E. (ed.). 2004. *Du partage au marché: Regards croisés sur la circulation des savoirs.* Lille: Presses Universitaires du Septentrion.

Descola, P. 2005. *Par-delà nature et culture.* Paris: Gallimard.

Dezalay, Y. and Garth, B. 2002. *The Internationalization of Palace Wars: Lawyers, Economists and the Transformation of Latin American States.* Chicago, IL: Chicago University Press.

2006. "Les usages nationaux d'une science 'globale'" *Sociologie du travail* **48** (3): 308–29.

DiMaggio, P. and Louch, H. 1998. "Socially embedded consumer transactions: for what kinds of purchases do people most often use networks?" *American Sociological Review* **63**: 619–37.

Dixon, J., Hamilton, K., Pagiola, S. and Lisa Segnestam, L. 2001. *Tourism and the Environment in the Caribbean: An Economic Framework.* (Paper 80) Washington, DC: Environment Department, World Bank.

Dobbin, F. 2001. *How Institutional Economics is Killing Microeconomics.* Princeton, NJ: Princeton University Press.

2004. "The sociological view of the economy." In F. Dobbin (ed.), *The New Economic Sociology. A Reader*, pp. 1–46. Princeton, NJ: Princeton University Press.

Donzelot, J. 1997. *Policing the Family.* Baltimore, MD: The Johns Hopkins University Press.

Dore, R. 1986. *Flexible Rigidities.* Stanford, CA: Stanford University Press.

Douglas, M. 1992. *Risk and Blame. Essays in Culture Theory.* London: Routledge.

Douglas, M. and Isherwood, B. 1979. *The World of Goods: Towards an Anthropology of Consumption.* London: Routledge.

Drucker, P. and Heizer, R. 1967. *To Make My Good Name: A Re-examination of the Southern Kwakiutl Potlatch.* Berkeley, CA: University of California Press.

Drumm, A. 2003. *Sustainably Financing Protected Areas: Applications for Success – Tourism-Based Revenue Generation Mechanisms.* Presented at the World Parks Congress. Durban, September.

Duczynska Polanyi, I. 2006. "I first met Karl Polanyi in 1920 ..." In K. McRobbie and K. Polanyi Levitt (eds.), *Karl Polanyi in Vienna: The Contemporary Significance of the Great Transformation*, pp. 302–15. Montreal: Black Rose Books.

Dumont, L. 1950–51. "Kinship and alliance among the Pramalai Kallar." *The Eastern Anthropologist* **4** (1): 3–26.

    1967. *Homo hierarchicus*. Paris: Gallimard

    1977. *Homo aequalis I. Genèse et épanouissement de l'idéologie économique*. Paris: Gallimard.

    1983. "Préface." In K. Polanyi, *La Grande Transformation*, pp. i-xx. Paris: Gallimard.

Durkheim, É. [1893] 2007. *De la division du travail social*. Paris: Presses Universitaires de France.

    [1895–6] 1971. *Le socialisme. Sa définition, ses débuts, la doctrine saint-simonienne*. Paris: Presses Universitaires de France.

    [1897] 1976. *Le suicide. Essai de sociologie*. Paris: Presses Universitaires de France.

    [1905] 1969. *L'évolution pédagogique en France*. Paris: Presses Universitaires de France.

    [1912] 1968. *Les formes élémentaires de la vie religieuse*. Paris: Presses Universitaires de France.

Duval, J. 2004. *Critique de la raison journalistique. Les transformations de la presse économique en France*. Paris: Seuil.

Eagles, P.F.J. 2002. "Trends in park tourism: economics, finance and management. *Journal of Sustainable Tourism* **10**: 132–53.

Einaudi, L. 1953. "The theory of imaginary money from Charlemagne to the French Revolution." In F.C. Lane and J.C. Riemersma (eds.), *Enterprise and Secular Change*, pp. 229–61. London: Allen & Unwin.

Einhorn, B. 1993. *Cinderella Goes to Market: Gender, Citizenship, and Women's Movements in East Central Europe*. New York: Verso.

Einhorn, B and C. Sever, C. 2003. "Gender and civil society in Central and Eastern Europe." *International Feminist Journal of Politics* **5** (2): 163–90.

Einzig, P. 1949. *Primitive Money in its Ethnological, Historical, and Ethnographic Aspects*. New York, NY: Pergamon Press.

England, P. 2003. "Separative and soluble selves: dichotomous thinking in economics." In M. Ferber, and J. Nelson (eds.), *Feminist Economics Today: Beyond Economic Man*, pp. 33–59. Chicago, IL: University of Chicago Press.

Epstein, G. 2005. *Financialization and the World Economy*. Cheltenham: Edward Elgar.

Esping-Andersen, G. [1990] 1999. *Les trois mondes de l'état providence. Essai sur le capitalisme moderne*. Paris: Presses Universitaires de France.

Esteban, N., Garaway, G., Oxenford, H., Anderson, W. and McConney, P. 2002. *Project Workshop: Institutional Arrangements for Caribbean MPAs and Opportunities for Pro-Poor Management*. London: MRAG Ltd.

Etzioni, A. 1988. *The Moral Dimension: Toward a New Economics*. New York, NY: The Free Press.

    1993. *The Spirit of Community: Rights, Responsibilities and the Communitarian Agenda*. New York, NY: Crown Publishers, Inc.

EU. 2002. "The European Commission's Delegation to Jamaica, Belize, the Bahamas, Turks and Caicos Is. and the Cayman Is." *The EU and Jamaica*. (Available online at: www.deljam. cec.eu.int/ en/ jamaica/ projects/ environment/ negril.htm)

Faccarello, G. and Steiner, P. 2008. "French *Philosophie économique* (1690–1830): sensationism, interest and the legislator." *European Journal of the History of Economic Thought* **15**(1): 1–23.

Fajans, J. 1997. *They Make Themselves: Work and Play Among the Baining of Papua New Guinea*. Chicago, IL: University of Chicago Press.

Fél, E. and Hofer, T. 1972. *Bäuerliche Denkweise in Wirtschaft und Haushalt*. Göttingen: Otto Schwartz.

Fél, E. and Hofer, T. 1974. *Geräte der Átányer Bauern*. Budapest: Akadémiai Kiadó.

Ferguson, N. 2001. *The Cash Nexus: Money and Power in the Modern World*. New York, NY: Basic Books.

Ferry, E. E. 2005. *Not Ours Alone*. New York, NY: Columbia University Press.

Finley, M. I. 1974. *The Ancient Economy*. Berkeley, CA: University of California Press.

  1981. *Economy and Society in Ancient Greece*. New York, NY: Penguin.

Firth, R. 1972. "Methodological issues in economic anthropology." *Man* **7**(3): 467–75.

Fligstein, N. 2001. *The Architecture of Markets*. Princeton, NJ: Princeton University Press.

Forbes, A. D. W. 1986. *Warlords and Muslims in Chinese Central Asia: A Political History of Republican Sinkiang 1911–1949*. Cambridge: Cambridge University Press.

Foucault, M. [1978] 2004. *Sécurité, territoire, population*. Paris: Gallimard-Seuil.

Fourcade, M. 2006. "The construction of a global profession: the transnationalization of economics." *American Journal of Sociology* **112**: 145–94.

Fourcade-Gourinchas, M. and Babb, S. 2002. "The rebirth of the liberal creed: paths to neoliberalism in four countries." *American Journal of Sociology* **108** (3): 533–79.

Fourquet, F. 1980. *Les comptes de la puissance. Histoire de la comptabilité nationale et du Plan*. Paris: Encres.

Fortes, M. 1969. *Kinship and the Social Order*. Chicago, IL: Aldine.

Foster, R. 1999. "In God we trust? The legitimacy of Melanesian currencies." In D. Akin and J. Robbins, (eds.), *Money and Modernity*, pp. 214–31. Pittsburgh, PA: University of Pittsburgh Press.

Fournier, M. [1994] 2006. *Marcel Mauss: A Biography*. Princeton, NJ: University Press.

Frankenberg, R. 1967. "Economic anthropology: one anthropologist's view." In R. Firth (ed.), *Themes in Economic Anthropology*, pp. 47–90. London: Tavistock.

Friedman, J. and C. Chase-Dunn (eds.). 2005. *Hegemonic Decline; Present and Past*. Boulder, CO: Paradigm.

Friedman, M. 1953. *Essays in Positive Economics*. Chicago, IL: University of Chicago Press.

Friedmann, G. 1950. *Où va le travail humain?* Paris: Gallimard.

Fukuyama, F. 1995. *Trust*. New York, NY: The Free Press.

Fusfeld, D. J. 1994 "Karl Polanyi's lectures on general economic history; a student remembers." In K. McRobbie (ed.), *Humanity, Society and Commitment: On Karl Polanyi*, pp. 1–6. Montreal: Black Rose Books.

Galbraith, J. K. 1987. *A History of Economics: The Past as the Present*. Harmondsworth: Penguin.

Galey, J.-C. 1983. "Creditors, kings and death: determinations and implications of bondage in Tehri-Gathwal (Indian Himalayas)." In C. Malamoud (ed.), *Debts and Debtors*, pp. 67–124. London: Vikas.

Gambetta, D. 1988a. "Can we trust trust?" In D. Gambetta (ed.), *Trust. Making and Breaking Cooperative Relations*, pp. 213–37. New York, NY: Basil Blackwell.

Gambetta, D. (ed.) 1988b. *Trust. Making and Breaking Cooperative Relations*. New York, NY: Basil Blackwell.

Gardiner, G. 2004. "The primacy of trade debts in the development of money." In L. Randall Wray (ed.), *Credit and State Theories of Money: The Contributions of A. Mitchell Innes*, pp. 128–72. Cheltenham: Edward Elgar.

Garland, D. 2001. *The Culture of Control: Crime and Social Order in Contemporary Society*. Oxford: Oxford University Press.

Geertz, C. 1963. *Peddlers and Princes: Social Development and Economic Change in Two Indonesian Towns*. Chicago, IL: University of Chicago Press.

1973. "Deep play: notes on a Balinese cockfight. In C. Geertz, *The Interpretation of Cultures*. New York, NY: Basic Books.

Gell, A. 1982. "The market wheel: symbolic aspects of an Indian tribal market." *Man* **17** (3): 470–91.

Gellner, E. 1983. *Nations and Nationalism*. Oxford: Blackwell.

Gemici, K. 2008. "Karl Polanyi and the antinomies of embeddedness." *Socio-Economic Review* **6**: 5–33.

Geremek, B. 1994. *Poverty: A History*. Oxford: Blackwell Publishers.

Gibson-Graham, J. K. 2003. "Enabling ethical economies: co-operativism and class. *Critical Sociology* **29** (2): 123–61.

Giddens, A. 1973. *The Class Structure of the Advanced Societies*. London: Hutchison.

1990. *The Consequences of Modernity*. Cambridge: Polity Press.

Gislain, J.-J. and Steiner, P. 1995. *La sociologie économique (1890–1920): Durkheim, Pareto, Schumpeter, Simiand, Veblen et Weber*. Paris: Presses Universitaires de France.

Gleason, J. T. 2000. *Risk. The New Management Imperative in Finance*. Princeton, NJ: Bloomberg Press.

Godbout, J. and Caillé, A. 1998. *The World of the Gift*. Montreal: McGill-Queen's University Press.

Godbout, J. and Caillé, A. 2000. *L'Esprit du don*. Paris: La Découverte.

Goody, J. 2004. *Capitalism and Modernity: The Great Debate*. Cambridge: Polity.

Goreau, T. J., Daley, L., Ciappara, S., Brown, J., Bourke, S. and Thacker, K. 1997. "Community-based whole-watershed and coastal zone management in Jamaica." *Proceedings of the Eighth International Coral Reef Symposium* **2**: 2093–6.

Graeber, D. 1996. "Beads and money: notes toward a theory of wealth and power." *American Ethnologist* **23** (1): 4–24.

1997. "Manners, deference and private property: the generalization of avoidance in early modern Europe." *Comparative Studies in Society and History* **39** (4): 694–728.

2001. *Toward an Anthropological Theory of Value: The False Coin of Our Own Dreams*. New York, NY: Palgrave.

2004. *Fragments of an Anarchist Anthropology*. Chicago, IL: University of Chicago Press.

2005. "Turning modes of production inside out: or, why capitalism is a transformation of slavery." *Critique of Anthropology* **26** (1): 61–81.

2006a. "Beyond Power/Knowledge: An Exploration of the Relation of Power, Ignorance, and Stupidity." Malinowski Memorial Lecture, LSE, London.

(Available online at: www.lse.ac.uk/collections/LSEPublicLecturesAndEvents/
events/2006/20060328tl456z001.htm)

2006b. "Fetishism and social creativity, or retishes are gods in process of construction. *Anthropological Theory* **5** (4): 407–38.

Gramsci, A. [1929–34] 1971. *Selections from the Prison Notebooks* (edited and translated by Q. Hoare and G. Nowell Smith). London: Lawrence & Wishart.

Granovetter, M. 1973. "The strength of weak ties." *American Journal of Sociology* **78**:
1360–80.

1985. "Economic action and social structure: the problem of embeddedness."
American Journal of Sociology **91** (3): 481–510.

1990. "The old and the new economic sociology: a history and an agenda." In R.
Friedland and A. F. Robertson (eds.), *Beyond the Marketplace. Rethinking Economy
and Society*, pp. 89–112. New York, NY: Aldine de Gruyter.

[1974] 1995. *Getting a Job: A Study of Contacts and Careers,* 2nd ed. Cambridge,
MA: Harvard University Press.

2005. "The impact of social structure on economic outcomes." *Journal of Economic
Perspectives* **19**: 33–50.

Gray, K. 1908. (ed. by E. Gray and B. Hutchins). *Philanthropy and the State, or, Social
Politics*. London: P. S. King & Son.

Gregory, C. 1982. *Gifts and Commodities*. London: Academic Press.

1997. *Savage Money. The Anthropology and Politics of Commodity Exchange.*
Amsterdam: Harwood Academic Publishers.

Greif, A. 1993. "Contract enforceability and economic institutions in early trade: the
Maghribi Traders coalition." *American Economic Review* **83** (3): 525–48.

1994. "Cultural beliefs and the organization of society: a historical and theoretical
reflection on collectivist and individualist societies." *Journal of Political Economy*
102 (5): 912–50.

2001. "Impersonal exchange and the origin of markets: from the community
responsibility system to individual legal responsibility in pre-modern Europe."
In A. Masahiko and Y. Hayami (eds.), *Communities and Markets in Economic
Development*, pp. 3–41. Oxford: Oxford University Press.

Grendi, E. 1978. *Polanyi. Dall'antropologia economica alla microanalisa storica.*
Milano: Etas Libri.

Grierson, P. 1977. *The Origins of Money*. London: Athlone Press.

1978. "The origins of money." *Research in Economic Anthropology* **1**: 1–35.

Griffith, D. and Pizzini, M. V. 2002. *Fishers at Work, Workers at Sea: A Puerto Rican
Journey through Labor and Refuge*. Philadelphia, PA: Temple University Press.

Gudeman, S. 1986. *Economics as Culture: Models and Metaphors of Livelihood.*
London: Routledge & Kegan Paul.

1992. "Remodeling the house of economics: culture and innovation." *American
Ethnologist* **19**(1): 141–54.

2001. *The Anthropology of Economy: Community, Market, and Culture*. Malden,
MA: Blackwell.

2005. "Realism, relativism and reason: what is economic anthropology all about?"
In S. Löfving (ed.), *Peopled Economies: Conversations with Stephen Gudeman*,
pp. 111–55. Uppsala: Uppsala University.

2006. Trade's Reason. *Working Paper* 81. Halle/ Saale: Max Planck Institute for
Social Anthropology.

2008. *Economy's Tension: The Dialectics of Community and Market*. Oxford: Berghahn Books.

2009a. "The persuasions of economics." In S. Gudeman (ed.), *Economic Persuasions*, pp. 94–121. New York, NY: Berghahn Books.

Gudeman, S. (ed.) 2009b. *Economic Persuasions*. New York, NY: Berghahn Books.

Guérin, I. 2003. *Femmes et économie solidaire*. Paris: La Découverte.

Guseva, A. and Rona-Tas, A. 2001. "Uncertainty, risk, and trust: Russian and American credit markets compared." *American Sociological Review* **66**: 623–46.

Guyer, J. I. 1994. *Money Matters: Instability, Values and Social Payments in the Modern History of West African Communities*. London: Heinemann.

1999. "Comparisons and equivalencies in Africa and Melanesia." In D. Akin and J. Robbins (eds.), *Money and Modernity: State and Local Currencies in Melanesia*, pp. 232–45. Pittsburgh, PA: University of Pittsburgh Press.

2000. "Rationality or reasoning? Comment on Heath Pearson's 'Homo Economicus goes native, 1859–1945'." *History of Political Economy* **32** (4): 1011–15.

2004. *Marginal Gains. Monetary Transactions in Atlantic Africa*. Chicago, IL: Chicago University Press.

Guyer, J. I. (ed.). 1987. *Feeding African Cities. Studies in Regional Social History*. Manchester: Manchester University Press.

(ed.) 2002. *Money Struggles and City Life: Devaluation in Ibadan and other Urban Centres of Southern Nigeria, 1986–1996*. London: Heinemann.

Guyer, J. I. and E. Stiansen. 2000. *Credit, Currencies and Culture: African Financial Institutions in Historical Perspective*. Uppsala: Nordic Africa Institute.

Guyer, J. I., Denzer, L. R. and Agbaje, A. 2002. "Introduction: the Nigerian popular economy; strategies toward a study." In J.I. Guyer (ed.), *Money Struggles and City Life: Devaluation in Ibadan and Other Urban Centres of Southern Nigeria, 1986–1996*, pp. xvii–xlv. London: Heinemann.

Guyer, J. I. with Denzer, L. R. (2009). "The craving for intelligibility. Speech and silence on the economy under structural adjustment and military rule in Nigeria." In S. Gudeman (ed.), *Economic Persuasions. Studies in Rhetoric and Culture*. Vol. 4. New York, NY: Berghahn Books.

Habermas, J. 1968. "Arbeit und Interaktion." *Technik und Wissenschaft als 'Ideologie*,' pp. 9–47. Frankfurt: Edition Suhrkamp.

1984. *The Theory of Communicative Action, Vol. 1 Reason and the Rationalization of Society*. London: Heinemann Education.

1991. *The Structural Transformation of the Public Sphere: An Inquiry into a Category of Bourgeois Society*. Cambridge, MA: MIT Press.

Hahn, E. 1908. *Die Entstehung der wirtschaftlichen Arbeit*. Heidelberg: Winter.

Halbwachs, M. [1912] 1972. *La classe ouvrière et les niveaux de vie. Recherches sur la hiérarchie des besoins dans les sociétés industrielles*. Paris: Gordon and Breach.

Halbwachs, M. 1933. *L'évolution des besoins dans les classes ouvrières*. Paris: Alcan.

Haley, M. and Clayton, A. 2003. "The role of NGOs in environmental policy failures in a developing country: the mismanagement of Jamaica's coral reefs." *Environmental Values* **12**: 29–54.

Halperin, R. 1984. "Polanyi, Marx, and the institutional paradigm in economic anthropology." *Research in Economic Anthropology* **6**: 245–72.

Hamilton, G. G. and Biggart, N. W. 1992. "Market, culture, and authority: a comparative analysis of management and organization in the Far East. In M. Granovetter and R. Swedberg (eds.), *The Sociology of Economic Life*, pp. 181–221. Boulder, CO: Westview Press.

Hann, C. 1992. "Radical functionalism: the life and work of Karl Polanyi." *Dialectical Anthropology* **17**: 141–66.

Hann, C. and Hart, K. forthcoming. *Economic Anthropology: A Short History*. Cambridge: Polity.

Harriss-White, B. and Gooptu, N. 2000. "Mapping India's world of unorganized labour." In L. Panitch, and C. Leys (eds.), *Working Classes, Global Relations: Socialist Register 2001*, pp. 89–118. London: Merlin Press.

Hart, K. 1973. "Informal income opportunities and urban employment in Ghana." *Journal of Modern African Studies* **11** (1): 61–89.

1986. "Heads or tails? Two sides of the coin." *Man* **21** (3): 637–56.

1988. "Kinship, contract, and trust: the economic organization of migrants in an African city slum." In D. Gambetta (ed.), *Trust. Making and Breaking Cooperative Relations*, pp. 176–93. New York, NY: Basil Blackwell.

2000. *The Memory Bank: Money in an Unequal World*. London: Profile Books. (Republished in 2001 as *Money in an Unequal World: Keith Hart and His Memory Bank*. New York, NY: Texere.)

2004. "Formal bureaucracy and the emergent forms of the informal economy." Paper presented at the EGDI-WIDER conference "Unlocking Human Potential – Linking the Informal and Formal Sectors," September 17–18, Helsinki. (Available online at: www.thememorybank.co.uk/papers/emergent-forms/).

2005. *The Hit Man's Dilemma: Or Business, Personal and Impersonal*. Chicago, IL: Prickly Paradigm Press.

2006. "Bureaucratic form and the informal economy." In B. Guha-Khasnobis, R. Kanbur, and E. Ostrom (eds.), *Linking the Formal and Informal Economy: Concepts and Policies*, pp. 28–47. Oxford: Oxford University Press.

2007a. "Marcel Mauss: in pursuit of the whole. A review essay." *Comparative Studies in Society and History* **49** (2): 473–85.

2007b. "Money is always personal and impersonal." *Anthropology Today* **23** (5): 11–16.

2009. "The persuasive power of money." In S. Gudeman (ed.), *Economic Persuasions*. New York: Berghahn Books.

Harvey, D. 2005a. *A Brief History of Neoliberalism*. Oxford: Oxford University Press.

2005b. *The New Imperialism*. Oxford: Oxford University Press.

Hayek, F. A. von. 1960. *The Constitution of Liberty*. London: Routledge & Kegan Paul.

Healy, K. 2006. *Last Best Gifts: Altruism and the Market for Human Blood and Organs*. Chicago, IL: University of Chicago Press.

Hegel, G. W. F. [1821] 1967. *The Philosophy of Right*. Oxford: Oxford University Press.

Heidegger, M. [1950] 2000. *Das Ding. Vorträge und Aufsätze*, pp. 165–87. Frankfurt: Klostermann.

Heilbron, J. 2000. "Economic sociology in France." *European Societies* **3** (1): 41–67.

Helgason, A. and Pálsson, G. 1997. "Contested commodities: the moral landscape of modernist regimes." *Journal of the Royal Anthropological Institute* **3** (3): 451–71.

Helleiner, E. 2000. "Globalization and haute finance – déja vu?" In K. McRobbie and K, Polanyi Levitt (eds.), *Karl Polanyi in Vienna: The Contemporary Significance of The Great Transformation*, pp. 12–31. Montreal: Black Rose Books.

Henry, J. F. 2004. "The social origins of money: the case of Egypt." In R. Wray (ed.), *Credit and State Theories of Money*, pp. 79–98. Cheltenham: Edward Elgar.

Henwood, D. 2003. *After the New Economy*. New York, NY: The New Press.

Herman, G. M. 1997. "Gift or commodity: what changes hands in the U.S. garage sale?" *American Ethnologist* **24** (4): 910–30.

Heuzé, G. 1990. "Workers' struggles and indigenous Fordism in India." In M. Holmström (ed.), *Work for Wages in South Asia*, pp. 173–89. New Delhi: Manohar.

Hilferding, R. [1910] 1981. *Finance Capital: A Study of the Latest Phase of Capitalist Development*. London: Routledge & Kegan Paul.

Ho, P. 2005. *Institutions in Transition; Land Ownership, Property Rights, and Social Conflict in China*. Oxford: Oxford University Press.

Hobsbawm, E. 1994. *Age of Extremes: The Short Twentieth Century, 1914–91*. New York, NY: Vintage.

Hodgson, G. M. 2008. "Review essay: prospects for economic sociology." *Philosophy of the Social Sciences* **38**, 133–49.

Hohensee, J. 2003. "God's oil country." *Die Zeit*, March 20, 2003: 78.

Hollis, M. 1998. *Trust Within Reason*. Cambridge: Cambridge University Press.

Holmström, M. 1984. *Industry and Inequality: The Social Anthropology of Indian Labour*. Cambridge: Cambridge University Press.

Horkheimer, M. and Adorno, T. W. 2002. *Dialectic of Enlightenment*. New York, NY: Continuum Publishing.

Hornborg, A. 2005. "Resisting the black hole of neo-classical formalism in economic anthropology." In S. Löfving (ed.), *Peopled Economies: Conversations with Stephen Gudeman*, pp. 63–80. Uppsala: Interface.

Hudson, M. 2002. "Reconstructuring the origins of interest-bearing debt and the logic of clean slates." In M. Hudson, and M. van de Mieroop (eds.), *Debt and Economic Renewal in the Ancient Near East*, pp. 7–58. Bethesda, MD: CDL.

2003. "The creditary/monetarist debate in historical perspective." In S. Bell and E Nell (eds.), *The State, the Market, and Euro: Chartalism versus Metallism in the Theory of Money*, pp. 39–76. Cheltenham: Elgar Press.

2004. "The archeology of money: debt vs. barter theories of money." In R. Wray (ed.), *Credit and State Theories of Money*, pp. 99–127. Cheltenham: Edward Elgar.

Humphrey, C. 1983. *Karl Marx Collective: Economy, Society and Religion in a Siberian Collective Farm*. Cambridge: Cambridge University Press.

2002. "Rituals of death as a context for understanding personal property in socialist Mongolia." *Journal of the Royal Anthropological Institute* **8** (1): 65–87.

Ianni, F. A. J. and Reuss-Ianni, E. 1972. *A Family Business: Kinship and Social Control in Organized Crime*. New York, NY: Russell Sage.

Inden, R. B., and Nicholas, R. W. 1977. *Kinship in Bengali Culture*. Chicago, IL: Chicago University Press.

Ingham, G. 2000. "'Babylonian madness:' on the historical and sociological origins of money." In J. Smithin (ed.), *What is Money?*, pp. 16–41. New York, NY: Routledge.

    2004. *The Nature of Money*. Cambridge: Polity Press.

Innes, A. M. 1913. "What is money?" *Banking Law Journal* (May): 377–408.

    1914. "The credit theory of money." *Banking Law Journal* (January): 151–68.

Innes, J. 1998. "State, church and voluntarism in European welfare, 1690–1850." In H. Cunningham and J. Innes (eds.), *Charity, Philanthropy and Reform from 1690–1850*, pp. 15–65. Basingstoke: Macmillan.

Isaac, B. L. 2005. "Karl Polanyi." In J. G. Carrier (ed.), *Handbook of Economic Anthropology*, pp. 14–25. Cheltenham: Edward Elgar.

Jamaica. 2003. *Sustainable Tourism Master Plan*. Kingston: Ministry of Tourism and Sport. (Available online at: www.jsdnp.org.jm/Tourism%20Master%20Plan. PDF)

Jevons, W. S. [1871] 1970. *Theory of Political Economy*. Harmondsworth: Penguin.

    1875. *Money and the Mechanism of Exchange*. New York, NY: Appleton and Company.

Joas, H. 1992. *Die Kreativität des Handelns*. Frankfurt: Suhrkamp.

Jones, G. S. 1976. *Outcast London*. Harmondsworth: Penguin.

Joseph, M. 2002. *Against the Romance of Community*. Minneapolis, MN: University of Minnesota Press.

Kanappan, S. 1959. "The Tata steel strike: some dilemmas of industrial relations in a developing economy." *Journal of Political Economy* **67**(5): 489–507.

Kant, I. [1798] 2006. *Anthropology from a Pragmatic Point of View*. Cambridge: Cambridge University Press.

Katzin, M. F. [1960] 1971. "The business of higglering in Jamaica." In M. M. Horowitz (ed.), *People and Cultures of the Caribbean*, pp. 340–81. New York, NY: Natural History Press.

Kasmir, S. 1996. *The Myth of Mondragon*. Albany, NY: State University of New York Press.

Kaufmann, J.-C. 1997. *Le coeur à l'ouvrage. Théorie de l'action ménagère*. Paris: Nathan.

Keane, J. 2003. *Global Civil Society?* Cambridge: Cambridge University Press.

Keynes, J. M. 1930. *A Treatise on Money* (2 vols). London: Macmillan.

    1936. *The General Theory of Employment, Interest and Money*. London: Macmillan.

Khilnani, S. 1997. *The Idea of India*. Harmondsworth: Penguin.

Kildea, G. 1983. *Celso and Cora*, (video). Sydney: Australian Film Commission.

Knapp, G. F. 1928. *The State Theory of Money*. London: MacMillan.

Knight, F. H. [1921] 1985. *Risk, Uncertainty, and Profit*. Chicago, IL: University of Chicago Press.

Knorr-Cetina, K. and Bruegger, U. 2000. "The market as an object of attachment: exploring postsocial relations in financial markets." *Canadian Journal of Sociology* **25** (2): 141–68.

    2002. "Global microstructures: the virtual societies of financial markets." *American Journal of Sociology* **107** (4): 905–50.

Kocak, Ö. 2003. *Social Orders of Exchange: Effects and Origins of Social Order in Exchange Markets*. (Ph.D. thesis). Stanford, CA: Stanford University.

Kolakowski, L. 1981. *Main Currents in Marxism: Its Origins, Growth and Dissolution.* Vol. 3. Oxford: Oxford University Press.

Kollock, P. 1994. "The emergence of exchange structures: an experimental study of uncertainty, commitment, and trust." *American Journal of Sociology* **100**: 313–45.

Krippner, G. 2001. "The elusive market: embeddedness and the paradigm of economic sociology." *Theory and Society* **30**: 775–810.

Krippner, G. and Alvarez, A. 2007. "Embeddedness and the intellectual projects of economic sociology." *Annual Review of Sociology* **33**: 219–40.

Krippner, G., Granovetter, M., Block, F., Biggart, N., Beamish, T. and Hsing, Y. 2004. "Polanyi symposium: a conversation on embeddedness." *Socio-Economic Review* **2**: 109–35.

Krishna Moorthy, K. 1984. *Engineering Change: India's Iron and Steel.* Madras: Technology Books.

Kurke, L. 2001. *Coins, Bodies, Games, and Gold: The Politics of Meaning in Archaic Greece.* Princeton, NJ: Princeton University Press.

Landa, J. T. 1994. *Trust, Ethnicity, and Identity.* Ann Arbor, MI: University of Michigan Press.

Latouche, S. 2004. *Survivre au développement: De la colonization de l'imaginaire économique à la construction d'une société alternative.* Paris: Mille et une nuits.

2005. *L'occidentalisation du monde.* Paris: La Découverte.

Latour, B. 1993. *Nous n'avons jamais été modernes. Essai d'anthropologie symétrique.* Paris: La Découverte.

2005. *Reassembling the Social: An Introduction to Actor-Network-Theory.* Oxford: Oxford University Press.

Latsis, S. 1972. "Situational determinism in economics." *British Journal of Philosophy of Science* **23**: 207–45.

Laville, J.-L. n.d. "Towards a theory of plural economy: in the footsteps of Mauss and Polanyi." Available online at www.rethinkingeconomics.org.uk/web/w/www_26_en.aspx.

Laville, J.-L. and Cattani, A. D. 2006. *Dictionnaire de l'autre économie.* Paris: Gallimard.

Lawrence, T. B. and Phillips, N. 2004. "From Moby Dick to Free Willy: macro-cultural discourse and institutional entrepreneurship in emerging institutional fields." *Organization* **11**: 689–711.

Leach, E. 1954. *Political Systems of Highland Burma: A Study of Kachin Social Structure.* London: Bell.

Leach, E and Leach, J. W. (eds.). 1983. *The Kula: New Perspectives on Massim Exchange.* Cambridge: Cambridge University Press.

Lebaron, F. 2000. *La croyance économique: Les économistes entre science et politique.* Paris: Seuil.

2006. *Ordre monétaire ou chaos social: La BCE et la révolution néolibérale.* Bellecombes: Editions du Croquant.

Lemon, A. 1998. "Your eyes are green like dollars: counterfeit cash, national substance, and currency apartheid in 1990s Russia." *Cultural Anthropology* **13** (1): 22–55.

Lerner, G. 1983. "Women and slavery." *Slavery and Abolition: A Journal of Comparative Studies* **4** (3): 173–98.

1986. "The origin of prostitution in ancient Mesopotamia." *Signs* **11** (2): 236–54.

Lévi-Strauss, C. [1949] 1969. *The Elementary Structures of Kinship.* Eyre & Spottiswoode.

[1951] 2004. "Préface." In M. Mauss, *Sociologie et anthropologie de Marcel Mauss,* pp. IX–LII. Paris: Presses Universitaires de France.

1963. *Structural Anthropology.* Garden City: Doubleday.

Levitt, T. 1973. *The Third Sector.* New York, NY: Amacom.

Lévy-Bruhl, L. 1923. *Primitive Mentality.* London: Allen & Unwin.

Lewis, W. A. 1978. *The Evolution of the International Economic Order.* Princeton, NJ: Princeton University Press.

Lexecon. (K. Grant, D. Ownby, and S. R. Peterson [eds.]). 2006. *A Primer in Gasoline Prices. For the American Petroleum Institute.* Policy Analysis Study.

Lin, N., Cook, K. and Burt, R. S. (eds.). 2001. *Social Capital. Theory and Research.* New York, NY: de Gruyter.

Lind, C. 1994. "How Karl Polanyi's moral economy can help religious and other social critics." In K. McRobbie (ed.), *Humanity, Society and Commitment: On Karl Polanyi,* pp. 143–61. Montreal: Black Rose Books.

LiPuma, E. and Lee, B. 2004. *Financial Derivatives and the Globalization of Risk.* Durham, NC: Duke University Press.

Litván, G. 1990. "Karl Polanyi in Hungarian politics (1914–1964)." In K. Polanyi-Levitt (ed.), *The Life and Work of Karl Polanyi: A Celebration,* pp. 30–37. Montreal: Black Rose Books.

Löfving, S. (ed.). 2005. *Peopled Economies. Conversations with Stephen Gudeman.* Uppsala: Interface.

Lorenz, E. H. 1988. "Neither friends nor strangers: informal networks of subcontracting in French industry." In D. Gambetta (ed.), *Trust: Making and Breaking Cooperative Relations,* pp. 194–210. New York, NY: Basil Blackwell.

Lundy, P. 1999. "Fragmented community action or new social movement? A study of environmentalism in Jamaica." *International Sociology* 14: 83–102.

MacIntosh, M. K. 1988. "Money lending on the periphery of London, 1300–1600." *Albion* 20 (4): 557–71.

MacIver, R. M. 1944 "Foreword." In K. Polanyi, *The Great Transformation,* pp. ix–xii. New York: Farrar and Rinehart.

MacKenzie, D. 2006. "Is economics performative? Option theory and the construction of derivatives markets." *Journal of the History of Economic Thought* 28 (1): 29–56.

MacKenzie, D. and Millo, Y. 2003. "Constructing a market, performing theory: the historical sociology of a financial derivatives exchange." *American Journal of Sociology* 109 (1): 107–45.

Malamoud, C. 1983. "The theology of debt in Brahmanism." In C. Malamoud (ed.), *Debts and Debtors,* pp. 21–40. London: Vikas.

1988. *Lien de vie, noeud mortel. Les représentations de la dette en Chine, au Japon et dans le monde indien.* Paris: EHESS.

1998. "Le paiement des actes rituals dans l'Inde védique." In M. Aglietta and A. Orlean (eds.), *La monnaie souveraine,* pp. 35–54. Paris: Editions Odile Jacob.

Malinowski, B. 1912. "The economic aspect of the Intichiuma ceremonies." *Festskrift tillegnad Edvard Westermarck,* pp. 81–108, Helsingfors: Sinelli.

1921. "The primitive economics of the Trobriand islanders." *Economic Journal* 31(121): 1–16.

[1922] 1961. *Argonauts of the Western Pacific: An Account of Native Enterprise and Adventure in the Archipelagos of Melanesian New Guinea.* London: Routledge.

1925. "Labour and primitive economics." *Nature* **116**: 926–30.

[1935] 1965. *Coral Gardens and their Magic: A Study of the Methods of Tilling the Soil and of Agricultural Rites in the Trobriand Islands.* Indiana University Press.

Marshall, A. 1890. *Principles of Economics.* London: Macmillan.

Marx, K. [1857] 1986. *Outline of the Critique of Political Economy. Collected Works,* vol. 28. London: Lawrence & Wishart.

[1858] 1965. *Pre-Capitalist Economic Formations.* New York: International Publishers.

[1867–1894] 1970. *Capital: The Critique of Political Economy,* 3 Vols. London: Lawrence & Wishart.

Marx, K and Engels, F. [1848] 1995. *The Manifesto of the Communist Party.* Harmondsworth: Penguin.

Maurer, B. 1999. "Forget Locke? From proprietor to risk-bearer in new logics of finance." *Public Culture* **11**(2): 365–85.

2005. "Finance." In J. Carrier (ed.), *Handbook of Economic Anthropology,* pp. 176–93. Cheltenham: Edward Elgar.

2006. "The anthropology of money." *Annual Review of Anthropology.,***35**: 15–36. .

Mauss, M. 1924. "Essai sur le don. Forme et raison de l'échange dans les sociétés archaïques." *Annee sociologique* **1** (2): 30–186.

[1924] 1990. *The Gift: The Form and Reason for Exchange in Archaic Societies.* New York, NY: Norton.

1925. "Sur un texte de Posidonius. Le suicide, contre-prestation supreme." *Revue Celtique* **42**: 324–29. [*Oeuvres* 1968–69, III: 52–57.]

[1938] 1980. "Une catégorie de l'esprit humain: la notion de personne, celle de 'moi.'" In M. Mauss, *Sociologie et anthropologie.* Paris: Presses Universitaires de France.

1947. *Manuel d'ethnographie.* Paris: Payot.

1997. *Écrits politiques* (Marcel Fournier ed). Paris: Fayard.

Mayo, M. 1994. *Communities and Caring: The Mixed Economy of Welfare.* London: Macmillan Press.

McIntosh, M. 2004. "Feminism and social policy." In F. Pierson and F. Castles (eds.), *The Welfare State Reader,* pp. 119–32. Cambridge: Polity Press.

McRobbie, K. 1994a. "From the class struggle to the 'clean spring'." In K. McRobbie (ed.), *Humanity, Society and Commitment: On Karl Polanyi,* pp. 45–80. Montreal: Black Rose Books.

2000 "Literature and *The Great Transformation.*" In K. McRobbie and K. Polanyi Levitt (eds.), *Karl Polanyi in Vienna: The Contemporary Significance of The Great Transformation,* pp. 85–106. Montreal: Black Rose Books.

McRobbie, K. (ed.), 1994b *Humanity, Society and Commitment; On Karl Polanyi,* Montreal: Black Rose Books.

McRobbie, K and Polanyi Levitt, K. 2000 (eds.). *Karl Polanyi in Vienna: The Contemporary Significance of The Great Transformation.* Montreal: Black Rose Books.

Mearns, A. [1883] 1970. *The Bitter Cry of Outcast London: An Inquiry into the Condition of the Abject Poor.* London: Frank Cass & Co.

Meillassoux, C . 1971. *The Development of Indigenous Trade and Markets in West Africa.* London: Oxford University Press.

Menger, C. [1871] 1981. *Principles of Economics*. New York, NY: New York University Press.

1892. "On the origins of money." *Economic Journal* **2** (6): 239–55.

Middleton, J. 2003. "Merchants: an essay in historical ethnography." *Journal of the Royal Anthropological Institute* **9** (3): 509–26.

Mieroop, M. van de. 2002. "A history of Near Eastern debt?". In M. Hudson and M. van de Mieroop (eds.) *Debt and Economic Renewal in the Ancient Near East*. Bethesda, MD: CDL Press.

Milkman, R., and Townsley, E. 1993. "Gender and the economy." In N. Smelser and R. Swedberg (eds.), *The Handbook of Economic Sociology*, pp. 600–19. Princeton, NJ: Princeton University Press.

Miller, D. 1994. *Modernity: An Ethnographic Approach; Dualism and Mass Consumption in Trinidad*. Oxford: Berg.

1998. *A Theory of Shopping*. Ithaca, NY: Cornell University Press.

Millward, J.A. 1998. *Beyond the Pass; Economy, Ethnicity and Empire in Qing Central Asia, 1759–1864*. Stanford, CA: Stanford University Press.

Millward, J.A. and Perdue, P.C. 2004. "Political and cultural history of the Xinjiang region through the late nineteenth century." In S.F. Starr (ed.). *Xinjiang; China's Muslim borderland*, pp. 27–62. Armonk, NY: M. E. Sharpe.

Mintz, S.W. 1961. "Pratik: Haitian personal economic relationships." In Symposium: *Patterns of Land Utilization and Other Papers*, pp. 54–63. Seattle, WA: American Ethnological Society.

Mises, L. von 1944. *Bureaucracy*. New York: Libertarian Press.

Mitchell, T. 1998. "Fixing the economy." *Cultural Studies* **12** (1): 82–101.

Mizruchi, M. and Stearns, L. 2001. "Getting deals done: the use of social networks in bank decision-making." *American Sociological Review* **66**: 647–71.

Möllering, G. 2006. *Trust: Reason, Routine, Reflexivity*. Oxford: Elsevier.

Montego Bay Marine Park. 1998. Management Plan. (Computer file).

Montgomery, J.D. 1991. "Social networks and labor market outcomes: toward an economic analysis." *American Economic Review* **81**: 1408–18.

Moor, K. 1989. *Crims in Grass Castles: The Trimbole Affair*. Apollo Bay: Pascoe.

Mueller, F.M. (ed.). 1979. *The Laws of Manu. Sacred Books of the East*. Delhi: Motilal Banarsidass.

Mumford, L. 1966. *The Myth of the Machine: Technics and Human Development*. New York, NY: Harcourt Brace Jovanovich.

Munn, N. 1977. "The spatiotemporal transformations of Gawan canoes." *Journal de la Société des Océanistes* **33** (54–55): 39–53.

1986. *The Fame of Gawa: A Symbolic Study of Value Transformation in a Massim (Papua New Guinea) Society*. Cambridge: Cambridge University Press.

Myers, C.A. and S. Kannappan. [1958] 1970. *Industrial Relations in India*. London: Asia Publishing House.

Myrdal, G. 1968. *Asian Drama: An Enquiry into the Poverty of Nations*. (2nd vol.). Harmondsworth: Penguin.

Nagy, E. 1994. "After brotherhood's Golden Age: Karl and Michael Polanyi." In K. McRobbie (ed.), *Humanity, Society and Commitment: On Karl Polanyi*, pp. 81–122. Montreal: Black Rose Books.

Neale, W. 1994. "Exposure and protection: the double movement in the economic history of rural India." In C.M. Duncan, and D.W. Tandy (eds.), *From Political*

Economy to Anthropology: Situating Economic Life in Past Societies, pp. 149–69. Montreal: Black Rose Books.

Nee, V. 1989. "Peasant entrepreneurship and the politics of regulation in China." In V. Nee and D. Stark (eds.), *Remaking the Economic Institutions of Socialism; China and Eastern Europe*, pp. 169–207. Stanford, CA: Stanford University Press.

1996. "The emergence of a market society; changing mechanisms of stratification in China." *American Sociological Review* **54** (5): 663–81.

Negril Marine Park. 1997. *Management Plan*. (Computer file).

Nelson, B. 1969. *The Idea of Usury: From Tribal Brotherhood to Universal Otherhood*. Chicago, IL: Chicago University Press.

Nettleford, R. M. [1970] 1998. *Mirror, Mirror: Identity, Race and Protest in Jamaica*. Kingston: LMH Publishing Ltd.

North, P. 2006. *Alternative Currency Movements as a Challenge to Globalisation? A Case Study of Manchester's Local Currency Networks*. Aldershot: Ashgate.

O'Callaghan, P. A., Woodley, J. and Aiken, K. 1988. *Montego Bay Marine Park: Project Proposal for the Development of Montego Bay Marine Park, Jamaica*. (Typescript).

Office for National Statistics, Social and Vital Statistics Division. 2004. *Labour Market Statistics First Release, Three Months to December 2004*. London: HMSO.

Olwig, K. F. 1993. *Global Culture, Island Identity: Continuity and Change in the Afro-Caribbean Community of Nevis*. Amsterdam: Harwood Academic.

Orr, J. E. 1996. *Talking about Machines: Ethnography of a Modern Job*. Ithaca, NY: Cornell University Press.

Ostrom, E. (ed.). 2002. *The Drama of the Commons*. Washington, WA: National Academy Press.

Owen, D. 1965. *English Philanthropy 1660–1960*. London: Oxford University Press.

Pahl, J. 2000. "Couples and their money: patterns of accounting and accountability in the domestic economy." *Accounting and Accountability Journal* **13** (4): 502–17.

Pålsson Syll, L. "The pitfalls of postmodern economics: remarks on a provocative project." In S. Löfving (ed.), *Peopled Economies: Conversations with Stephen Gudeman*, pp. 81–110. Uppsala: Interface.

Panoff, M. 1977. « Energie et vertu: Le travail et ses représentations en Nouvelle Bretagne." *L'Homme* **17** (2–3): 7–21.

Parry, J. 1986. "The gift, the Indian gift and the 'Indian gift'." *Man* **21** (3): 453–73.

1999a. "Lords of labour: working and shirking in Bhilai." *Contributions to Indian Sociology* (N.S.) **33** (1, 2): 107–40.

1999b. "Two cheers for reservation: the Satnamis and the steel plant." In R. Guha, and J. P. Parry (eds.), *Institutions and Inequalities: Essays in Honour of André Béteille*, pp. 129–69. New Delhi: Oxford University Press.

2001. "Ankalu's errant wife – sex, marriage and industry in contemporary Chhattisgarh." *Modern Asian Studies* **35** (4): 783–820.

2003. "Nehru's dream and the village 'waiting room': long distance labour migrants to a central Indian steel town." *Contributions to Indian Sociology* **37** (1, 2): 217–49.

2005. "Changing childhoods in industrial Chhattisgarh." In R. Chopra, and P. Jeffery (eds.), *Educational Regimes in Contemporary India*, pp 276–98. New Delhi and London: Sage.

2008a. "Cosmopolitan values in a central Indian steel town." In P. Werbner (ed), *Anthropology and the New Cosmopolitanism: Rooted, Feminist and Vernacular Perspectives*, pp. 325–43. Oxford: Berg.

2008b. "The sacrifices of modernity in a Soviet-built steel town in central India." In F. Pine, and J. de Pina-Cabral (eds.), *On the Margins of Religion*, pp. 233–62. Oxford: Berghahn.

n.d. "The 'embourgeoisement' of a 'proletarian vanguard'." (unpublished ms).

Parry, J. and M. Bloch (eds.). 1989. *Money and the Morality of Exchange*. Cambridge: Cambridge University Press.

Parry, J., Breman, J. and Kapadia, K. (eds.). 1999. *The Worlds of Indian Industrial Labour*. London: Sage.

Parry, J. and C. Struempell. 2008. "On the desecration of Nehru's 'temples': Bhilai and Rourkela compared." *Economic and Political Weekly*, May 10, 2008, pp. 47–57.

Parsons, T. 1951. *The Social System*. Glencoe, NY: Free Press.

Parsons, T. and Smelser, N. [1956] 1984. *Economy and Society. A Study in the Integration of Economic and Social Theory*. London: Routledge.

Pateman, C. 2004. "The patriarchal welfare state." In F. Pierson, and F. Castles (eds.), *The Welfare State Reader*, pp. 133–50. Cambridge: Polity.

Payne, A. 1994. *Politics in Jamaica*. (Rev. ed.). London: Hurst.

Peacock, M. S. 2003. "State, money, catallaxy: underlaboring for a chartalist theory of money." *Journal of Post Keynesian Economics* **26** (2): 205–25.

Pearson, H. 2000. "*Homo economicus* goes native, 1859–1945: the rise and fall of primitive economics." *History of Political Economy* **32** (4): 932–89.

Pei, M. 2006. *China's Trapped Transition: The Limits of Developmental Autocracy*. Cambridge, MA: Harvard University Press.

Peterson, N. 1993. "Demand sharing: reciprocity and the pressure for generosity among foragers." *American Anthropologist* **95** (4): 860–74.

Phillips, K. and Bosman, J. 2006. "A failure to communicate? Big oil thinks it has a message, but it isn't reaching consumers." *New York Times*, May 3.

Pieke, F. 2005. "The politics of rural land use planning in China." In P. Ho (ed), *Developmental Dilemmas: Land Reform and Institutional Change in China*, pp. 89–117. London: Routledge Curzon.

forthcoming. *The Reinvention of the Party-State: The Training and Carreers of China's Political Elite*. Cambridge: Cambridge University Press.

Plattner, S. 1989. "Introduction." In S. Plattner (ed.), *Economic Anthropology*, pp. 1–20. Stanford, CA: Stanford University Press.

Polanyi, K. 1922. "Sozialistische Rechnungslegung." *Archiv für Sozialwissenschaft und Sozialpolitik* **49** (2): 377–420.

1924. "Die funktionelle Theorie der Gesellschaft und das Problem der sozialistischen Rechnungslegung." *Archiv für Sozialwissenschaft und Sozialpolitik* **52** (1): 218–28.

[1944] 2001. *The Great Transformation: The Political and Economic Origins of Our Time*. Boston, MA: Beacon Press.

[1947] 1968a. "Our obsolete market mentality." In G. Dalton (ed.), *Primitive, Archaic and Modern Economies. Essays of Karl Polanyi*, pp. 59–77. New York, NY: Anchor.

1957a. "Aristotle discovers the economy." In K. Polanyi, C.M. Arensberg, and H. W. Pearson (eds.), *Trade and Market in the Early Empires*, pp. 64–94. New York, NY: Free Press.

1957b. "The economy as an instituted Process." In K. Polanyi, C.M. Arensberg, and H.W. Pearson (eds.), *Trade and Market in the Early Empires: Economies in History and Theory*, pp. 243–70. New York, NY: Free Press.

1959. "Anthropology and economic theory." In M. Fried (ed.), *Readings in Anthropology*, Vol. 2, pp. 161–84. New York, NY: Crowell.

1966. *Dahomey and the Slave Trade: An Analysis of an Archaic Economy*. Seattle, WA: University of Washington Press.

[1957] 1968b. "The semantics of money uses." In G. Dalton (ed.), *Primitive, Archaic, and Modern Economies: Essays of Karl Polanyi*, pp. 175–203. New York, NY: Anchor.

1977. *The Livelihood of Man*. New York, NY: Academic Press.

Polanyi, K, Arensberg, C. M., and Pearson, H.W. (eds.). 1957. *Trade and Market in the Early Empires: Economies in History and Theory*. Glencoe, IL: The Free Press.

Polanyi, K. and Arensberg, C. [1957] 1975. *Les systèmes économiques dans l'histoire et dans la théorie*. Paris: Larousse.

Polanyi Levitt, K. (ed.). 1990. *The Life and Work of Karl Polanyi: A Celebration*. Montreal: Black Rose Books

Polanyi Levitt, K . 2005. "Les principaux concepts dans le travail de Karl Polanyi." In P. Clancier and M. Panoff, 1977. "Energie et vertu. Le travail et ses représentations en nouvelle Bretagne." *L'Homme* **17** (2–3). 7–21.

Portes, A. and Sensenbrenner, J. 1993. "Embeddedness and immigration: notes on the determinants of economic action." *American Journal of Sociology* **98**: 1320–50.

Prais, S.J. and Houthakker, H. S. 1955. *The Analysis of Family Budgets*. Cambridge: Cambridge University Press.

Price, R. 1966. "Caribbean fishing and fishermen: a historical sketch." *American Anthropologist* **68**: 1364–83.

1982. "Rethinking labour history: the importance of work." In J. Schneer, and J.E. Cronin (eds.), *Social Conflict and the Political Order in Modern Britain*, pp. 179–214. London: Croom Helm.

1983. "The labour process and labour history." *Social History* **VIII**: 57–75.

Prochaska, F. 1980. *Women and Philanthropy in Nineteenth-Century England*. Oxford: Clarendon Press.

1988. *The Voluntary Impulse: Philanthropy in Modern Britain*. London: Faber & Faber.

Quiggin, A. H. 1949. *A Survey of Primitive Money; The Beginning of Currency*. London: Methuen.

Ramaswamy, E.A. 1988. *Worker Consciousness and Trade Union Response*. Delhi: Oxford University Press.

1990. "Indian trade unionism: the crisis of leadership." In M. Holmström (ed.), *Work for Wages in South Asia*, pp. 160–72. New Delhi: Manohar.

Ramaswamy, U. 1983. *Work, Union and Community: Industrial Man in South India*. Delhi: Oxford University Press.

Rammert, W. and Schulz-Schaeffer, I. 2002. "Technik und Handeln. Wenn soziales Handeln sich auf menschliches Verhalten und technische Abläufe verteilt." In W. Rammert and I. Schulz–Schaeffer (eds.). *Können Maschinen handeln? Soziologische Beiträge zum Verhältnis von Mensch und Technik*, pp. 11–64. Frankfurt am Main: Campus.

Ravenhill A. and Schiff, C. (eds.). 1910. *Household Administration: Its Place in the Higher Education of Women*. London: Grant Richards Ltd.

Richards, A. I. 1939. *Land, Labour and Diet in Northern Rhodesia*. London: International African Institute.

Robbins, L. 1932. *The Nature and Significance of Economic Science*. London: Macmillan.

Robinson, J. 1933. *The Economics of Imperfect Competition*. London: MacMillan.

1962. *Economic Philosophy: An Essay on the Progress of Economic Thought*. Harmondsworth: Penguin.

Roitman, J. L. 2005. *Fiscal Disobedience: An Anthropology of Economic Regulation in Central Africa*. Princeton, NJ: Princeton University Press.

Rospabé, P. 1993. "Don archaïque et monnaie sauvage." *La Revue de M.A.U.S.S.: ce que donner veut dire: don et intérêt*, pp. 33–59. Paris: La Bibliothèque du Mauss.

1995. *La dette de vie: aux origines de la monnaie sauvage*. Paris: La Découverte.

Roth, G. 2003. "The near-death of liberal capitalism: perceptions from Weber to the Polanyi brothers." *Politics and Society* 31(2): 263–82.

Rudd, M. A. and Tupper, M. H. 2002. "The impact of Nassau grouper size and abundance on scuba diver site selection and MPA economics." *Coastal Management* 30: 133–51.

Rudelson, J. J. 1997. *Oasis Identities: Uyghur Nationalism along China's Silk Road*. New York, NY: Columbia University Press.

Rudolph, L. and Rudolph, S. 1987. *In Pursuit of Lakshmi: The Political Economy of the Indian State*. Chicago, IL: University Press.

Ruggie, J. G. 1982. "International regimes, transactions, and change: embedded liberalism in the postwar economic order." *International Organization* 36, 379–415.

Sahlins, M. 1972. *Stone Age Economics*. Chicago, IL: Aldine.

1976. *Culture and Practical Reason*. Chicago, IL: University of Chicago Press.

Saini, D. S. 1999. "Labour legislation and social justice: rhetoric and reality." *Economic and Political Weekly*, September 25.

Samuelson, P. A. 1948. *Economics: An Introductory Analysis*. New York, NY: McGraw Hill.

Schiff, C. 1911. "A brief historical sketch of woman's position in the family." In A. Ravenhill and C. Schiff (eds.), *Household Administration: Its Place in the Higher Education of Women*, pp. 11–33. London: Grant Richards Ltd.

Schneider, H. 1974. *Economic Man: The Anthropology of Economics*. New York, NY: Free Press.

Schumpeter, J. 1948. *Capitalism, Socialism and Democracy*. New York, NY: Harper Perennial.

1954. *History of Economic Analysis*. Oxford: Oxford University Press.

Scott, J. 1985. *Weapons of the Weak: Everyday Forms of Resistance*. New Haven, CT: Yale University Press.

Scura, L. F. and van't Hof, T. 1993. *The Ecology and Economics of Bonaire Marine Park*. (Divisional paper 1993–44.) Washington, DC: Environment Department, World Bank.

Seaford, R. 2004. *Money and the Early Greek Mind: Homer, Philosophy, Tragedy*. Cambridge: Cambridge University Press.

Sen, A. 2006. *Identity and Violence: The Illusion of Destiny*. New York, NY: W. W. Norton.

Servet, J.-M. 1998. "Demonétarisation et remonétarisation en Afrique-Occidentale et Équatoriale (XIXe-XXe siècles)." In M. Aglietta, and A. Orleans (eds.), *La monnaie souveraine*, pp. 289–324. Paris: Odile Jacob.

2001. "Le troc primitif, un mythe fondateur d'une approche économiste de la monnaie." *Revue numismatique* **157**: 15–32.

2004. "Karl Polanyi, au-delà de la démonomanie du marché." In E. Delamotte (ed.), *Du partage au marché. Regards croisés sur la circulation des savoirs*, pp. 315–32. Lille: Presses Universitaires du Septentrion.

2005. "Actualité des hypothèses polanyiennes de distinction entre place de marché et port de commerce et sur les cloisonnements monétaires dans les sociétés contemporaines." In P. Clancier, F. Joannès, P. Rouillard and A. Tenu (eds.), *Autour de Polanyi: Vocabulaires, théories et modalités des échange*, pp. 83–96, Paris: De Boccard.

2007. "Le marché, une évidence à revisiter. Parties vivantes et en débat dans l'oeuvre de Karl Polanyi." In Richard Sobel (ed.). *Penser la marchandisation du monde avec Karl Polanyi*, pp. 131–55. Paris/Lille: L'Harmattan.

Servet, J.-M, Maucourant, J., and Tiran, A. (eds.) 1998. *La modernité de Karl Polanyi*. Paris: L'Harmattan.

Servet, J.-M. and Bayon, D. (eds.) 1999. *Une économie sans argent. Les systèmes d'échange local*. Paris: Seuil.

Shersow, S. 2005. *The Work and the Gift*. Chicago, IL: Chicago University Press.

Sigaud, L. 2002. "The vicissitudes of *The Gift*." *Social Anthropology* **10** (3): 335–58.

Silver, M. 1992. *Taking Ancient Mythology Economically*. Leiden: Brill.

Simiand, F. 1907. *Le salaire, des ouvriers des mines de charbon en France. Contribution à la théorie économique de salaire*. Paris: Cornély.

1932. *Le salaire, l'évolution sociale et la monnaie*. Paris: Alcan.

[1912] 2006a. "La méthode positive en sciences économiques." In F. Simiand, *Critique sociologique de l'économie*, pp. 29–143. Paris: Presses Universitaires de France.

[1934] 2006b. "La monnaie, réalité sociale." In: F. Simiand, *Critique sociologique de l'économie*, pp. 215–79. Paris: Presses Universitaires de France.

Simmel, G. [1900] 1978. *The Philosophy of Money*. London: Routledge.

Singh S. 1997. *Marriage Money: The Social Shaping of Money in Marriage and Banking*. London: Allen & Unwin.

Smelser, N. and Swedberg, R. (eds.). 2005. *Handbook of Economic Sociology*. New York and Princeton: Russell Sage Foundation and Princeton University Press.

Smith, A. [1759] 2002. *The Theory of Moral Sentiments,* Cambridge Texts in the History of Philosophy. Cambridge: Cambridge University Press.

[1776] 1976 . *An Inquiry into the Nature and Causes of the Wealth of Nations*. Chicago, IL: University of Chicago Press.

Sombart, W. 1902–1927. *Moderner Kapitalismus*. (3 Vols.). München/Leipzig: Duncker & Humblot.

Sommer, G. and Carrier, J. G. 2006. *Tourism and its Others: Tourists, Traders and Fishers in Jamaica*. MS.

Spittler, G. 1978. *Herrschaft über Bauern. Die Ausbreitung staatlicher Herrschaft und einer islamisch-urbanen Kultur in Gobir (Niger)*. Frankfurt: Campus..

1998 *Hirtenarbeit: Die Welt der Kamelhirten und Ziegenhirtinnen von Timia*. Köln: Köppe.

2003. "Work – transformation of objects or interaction with subjects?" In B. Benzing and B. Herrmann (eds.), *Exploitation and Overexploitation in Societies Past and Present*, pp. 327–38. Münster und Hamburg: Lit.

2008a. *Founders of the Anthropology of Work – German Social Scientists of the 19th and Early 20th Centuries and the First Ethnographers*. Berlin: Lit.

2008b. "Caravaneers, shopkeepers and consumers – the appropriation of goods among the Kel Ewey Tuareg in Niger." In H. P. Hahn (ed.), *Consumption in Africa – Anthropological Approaches*, pp. 145–70. Berlin: Lit.

Srinivasan, N. R. 1984. *The History of Bhilai*. Bhilai: Public Relations Department, Bhilai Steel Plant.

Stanfield, J. R. 1986. *The Economic Thought of Karl Polanyi*. London: MacMillan.

Starr, S. F. (ed.). 2004. *Xinjiang: China's Muslim borderland*. Armonk, NY: M. E. Sharpe.

Steiner, P. 1998. *Sociologie de la connaissance économique. Essai sur les rationalisations de la connaissance économique (1750–1850)*. Paris: Presses Universitaires de France.

2001. "The sociology of economic knowledge." *European Journal of Social Theory* **4** (4): 443–58.

2002. "Encastrement et sociologie économique." In I. Huault (ed.), *La construction sociale de l'entreprise. Autour des travaux de Mark Granovetter*, pp. 29–50. Colombelles: Éditions EMS.

2004. "Le don d'organes: une affaire de famille?" *Annales. Histoire, Sciences Sociales* **59**: 255–83.

2005. *La sociologie économique*. Paris: La Découverte.

2005. *L'école durkheimienne et l'économie. Sociologie, réligion et connaissance*. Genève: Droz.

2008a. "La tradition française de critique sociologique de l'économie politique." *Revue d'Histoire des Sciences Humaines*, **17**: 63–84.

2008b. "Foucault and Weber and the history of the economic agent." *European Journal of the History of Economic Thought*, **15** (3): 503–27.

2009. "The economic theology of Herman Heinrich Gossen. The creator, human conduct and the maximization of utility." *European Journal of the History of Economic Thought*, forthcoming.

Steinkeller, P. 1981. "The renting of fields in early Mesopotamia and the development of the concept of "interest" in Sumeria". *Journal of the Economic and Social History of the Orient* **24**: 113–45.

Stiglitz, J. 2002. *Globalization and its Discontents*. New York, NY: Norton.

Strathern, M. (ed.). 2000. *Audit Cultures: Anthropological Studies in Accountability, Ethics and the Academy*. London: Routledge.

Streeck, W. 2007. *Wirtschaft und Moral. Facetten eines anscheinend unvermeidlichen Themas*. In W. Streeck and J. Beckert (eds.) *Moralische Voraussetzungen und Grenzen Wirtschaftlichen Handelns*, pp. 11–21. Forschungsbericht aus dem MPIFG. Cologne: Max Planck Institute for the Study of Societies.

Suchman, L. A. 1987. *Plans and Situated Actions: The Problem of Human-Machine Communication*. Cambridge: Cambridge University Press. (Republished in 2007 as *Human–Machine Configurations. Plans and Situated Actions*).

Swedberg, R. 1987. "Economic sociology: past and present." *Current Sociology* **35**: 1–221.

Szelenyi, I. 1983. *Urban Inequalities Under State Socialism*. Oxford: Oxford University Press.

1991 "Karl Polanyi and the theory of a socialist mixed economy." In M. Mendell and D. Salée (eds.), *The Legacy of Karl Polanyi; Market, State and Society at the End of the Twentieth Century*, pp. 231–48. London: Macmillan.

Tarot, C. 1999. *De Durkheim à Mauss: L'invention du symbolique. Sociologie et science des religions*. Paris: La Découverte.

Tax, S. 1953. *Penny Capitalism: A Guatemalan Indian Economy*. Washington, DC: US Government.

Testart, A. 2001. *L'esclave, la dette et le pouvoir. Études de sociologie comparative*. Paris: Errance.

2002. "The extent and significance of debt slavery." *Revue Française de Sociologie* **43** (Suppl.): 173–204.

The New Oxford Thesaurus of English. 2000. Oxford: Oxford University Press.

Théret, B. 1999. "The socio-cultural dimensions of the currency: implications for the transition to the Euro." *Journal of Consumer Policy* **22**: 51–79.

Thompson, E.P. 1967. "Time, work-discipline, and industrial capitalism." *Past and Present* **38**: 65–97.

1971. "The moral economy of the English crowd in the eighteenth century." *Past and Present* **50**: 76–136.

Thrift, N. 2001. "Finance, Geography of" *International Encyclopedia of the Social and Behavioral Sciences*. Elsevier, vol. **8**: 5655–7.

Thurnwald, R. 1916. "Banaro society. Social organization and kinship system of a tribe in the interior of New Guinea." *Memoirs of the American Anthropological Association* **3** (4): 251–391.

1932a. *Economics of Primitive Communities*. Oxford: Oxford University Press.

1932b. *Werden, Wandel und Gestaltung der Wirtschaft im Lichte der Völkerforschung*. Berlin: Walter de Gruyter.

1935. *Black and White in East Africa. The Fabric of a New Civilization*. London: G. Routledge and Sons.

Timberg, T. 1978. *The Marwaris: From Traders to Industrialists*. Delhi: Vikas.

Titmuss, R. [1970] 1996. *The Gift Relationship. From Blood to Social Policy*. London: Allen & Unwin.

Tocqueville, A. de. [1856] 1951. *L'ancien régime et la révolution. Œuvres complètes, édition définitive*. vol.2, t.1, Paris: Gallimard.

Toobin, J. 2003. "End run at Enron." *The New Yorker* Oct: 48–55.

Trautmann, T.R. 1981. *Dravidian Kinship*. Cambridge: Cambridge University Press.

Trigilia, C. 2006. "Economic society." In J. Beckert and M. Zafirovski (eds.), *The International Encyclopedia of Economic Sociology*, pp. 192–206. London: Routledge.

Turner, T. 1979. "Anthropology and the politics of indigenous peoples' struggles." *Cambridge Anthropology* **5**: 1–43.

1984. *Value, Production and Exploitation in Non-Capitalist societies*. Unpublished essay based on a paper presented at the AAA 82nd Annual Meeting, Denver, Colorado. (To appear in T. Turner *Critique of Pure Culture*. New York, NY: Berg [forthcoming]).

1985. "Dual opposition, hierarchy and value: moiety structure and symbolic polarity in Central Brazil and elsewhere." In J.-C. Galey (ed.), *Différences, valeurs, hiérarchie: Textes offerts à Louis Dumont*, pp. 335–70. Paris: Editions de l'Ecole des Hautes Etudes en Sciences Sociales.

1987. *The Kayapo of Southeastern Para*. (Unpublished monograph prepared for CEDI, Povos Indigenas do Brasil, Vol. VIII, Sul do Para, Part II).

Udry, C. and Woo, H. 2007. "Households and the social organization of consumption in southern Ghana." *African Studies Review* **50** (2): 139–53.

Uzzi, B. 1999. "Embeddedness in the making of financial capital: how social relations and networks benefit firms seeking finance." *American Sociological Review* **64**: 481–505.

Vallat, D. 1999. *Exclusion et liens financiers de proximité*. Thesis. Université Lumière Lyon 2.

Veblen, T. [1899] 1973. *The Theory of the Leisure Class*. Boston, MA: Houghton Mifflin.

1904. *The Theory of Business Enterprise*. New York, NY: Charles Scribner.

Verdery, K. 1996. *What was Socialism, and What Comes Next?* Princeton, NJ: Princeton University Press.

Waite, E. 2003. "The impact of socialist rule on a muslim minority in China: Islam among the Uyghurs of Kashgar." Unpublished PhD Dissertation, University of Cambridge.

Walzer, M. 1983. *Spheres of Justice. A Defense of Pluralism and Equality*. New York, NY: Basic Books.

Wardle, H. 1999. "Jamaican adventures: Simmel, subjectivity and extraterritoriality in the Caribbean." *Journal of the Royal Anthropological Institute* **5**: 523–39.

2005. "A city of meanings: place and displacement in urban Jamaican self-framings." In J. Besson and K. F. Olwig (eds.), *Caribbean Narratives of Belonging: Fields of Relations, Sites of Identity, pp. 79–93*. London: Macmillan.

Warsh, D. 2006. *Knowledge and the Wealth of Nations*. New York, NY: Norton.

Watson, P. 2000. "Politics, policy and identity: EU eastern enlargement and East–West differences." *Journal of European Policy* **7** (3): 369–84.

Webb, B. 1948. *Our Partnership*. London: Longmans.

Webb, S. and Webb, B. 1921. *The Consumer's Co-operative Movement*. London: Longmans, Green and Co.

Weber F. 2004. *Séparation des scènes sociales et pratiques ordinaires du calcul économique*. Premier congrès national de sociologie économique de l'Association Française de Sociologie. Paris: Villetaneuse.

Weber, M. [1904–05] 1958. *The Protestant Ethic and the Spirit of Capitalism*. New York, NY: Charles Scribner's Sons.

[1904–05] 2003. *L'éthique protestante et l'esprit du capitalisme*. Paris: Gallimard.

[1922] 1978. *Economy and Society: An Outline of Interpretive Sociology*. 2 Vols. (eds. G. Roth and C. Wittich) Berkeley, CA: University of California Press.

[1927] 1961. *General Economic History: (A Penetrating Analysis of the Origins of Our Economic System and Its Relation to Ethics and Religion.)* New York, NY: Collier Books.

Weiner, A. 1976. *Women of Value, Men of Renown*. Austin, TX: University of Texas Press.

Weule, K. 1909. *Native Life in East Africa: The Result of an Ethnological Research Expedition*. London: Sir I. Pitman & Sons. (First published in German: "Negerleben in Ostafrika", Leipzig: Brockhaus. 1908.)

White, H. 1992. *Identity and Control*. Princeton, NJ: Princeton University Press.
  2002. *Markets from Networks: Socioeconomic Models of Production*. Princeton, NJ: Princeton University Press.
Whyte, W. F. 1999. "The Mondragon cooperatives in 1976 and 1998." *Industrial and Labor Relations Review* **52** (3): 487–81.
Whyte, W. F. and Whyte, K. K. 1988. *Making Mondragon*. Ithaca, NY: Industrial and Labor Relations Press.
Wilding, K., Collis, B., Lacey, M. and McCullough, G. 2003. *Futureskills 2003 – A Skills Foresight Research Report on the Voluntary Sector Paid Workforce*. London: NCVO Publications.
Wilding, K., Cullins, G., Jochum, V., and Wainwright, S. 2004. *UK Voluntary Sector Almanac*. London: NCVO Publications.
Wilk, R. 1996. *Economies and Cultures: Foundations of Economic Anthropology*. Boulder, CO: Westview Press.
  2006. *Home Cooking in the Global Village: Caribbean Food from Buccaneers to Ecotourists*. Oxford: Berg.
Williamson, O. 1985. *The Economic Institutions of Capitalism*. New York, NY: Free Press.
Wilson, P. J. 1973. *Crab Antics: The Social Anthropology of English-Speaking Negro Societies of the Caribbean*. New Haven, CT: Yale University Press.
Wolf, E. R. 1982. *Europe and the People without History*. Berkeley, CA: University of California Press.
Wolf, M. 2006. "How labour steered an entire economy going global. *Financial Times* September 17.
Woodward, P. M. 1979. *Report of the Royal Commission into Drug Trafficking*. Sydney: Government Printer.
Worsley, P. M. 1956. "The kinship system of the Tallensi: a revaluation." *Journal of the Royal Anthropological Institute* **86**: 37–75.
Wray, L. R. 1990. *Money and Credit in Capitalist Economies: The Endogenous Money Approach*. Aldershot: Edward Elgar.
  1998. *Understanding Modern Money: The Key to Full Employment and Price Stability*. Cheltenham: Edward Elgar.
  2004. *Credit and State Theories of Money: The Contribution of A. Mitchell Innes*. Cheltenham: Edward Elgar.
Yamamura, K. and Streeck, W. (eds.). 2003. *The End of Diversity*. Ithaca, NY: Cornell University Press.
Yan, Y. 2005. "The individual and transformation of bridewealth in rural north China." *Journal of the Royal Anthropological Institute* **11** (4): 637–58.
Yearley, S. 2001. "Risk, sociology and politics." *International Encyclopedia of the Social and Behavioral Sciences* **20**: 13,360–4.
Zaloom, C. 2003. "Ambiguous numbers: trading technologies and interpretation in financial markets." *American Ethnologist* **30** (2): 258–72.
  2004. "The productivity of risk." *Cultural Anthropology* **19** (3): 365–91.
  2005. "The discipline of speculators." In A. Ong and S. Collier (eds.), *Global Assemblages, Technology, Politics and Ethics as Anthropological Problems*, pp. 253–69. Oxford: Blackwell.

Zelizer, V. 1979. *Morals and Markets: The Development of Life Insurance in the United States*. New York, NY: Columbia University Press.

1994. *The Social Meaning of Money*. New York, NY: Basic Books.

Zinkin, T. 1966. *Challenges in India*. London: Chatto & Windus.

Zucker, L. 1986. "The production of trust: institutional sources of economic structure, 1840–1920." In B. Staw and L.L. Cummings (eds.), *Research in Organizational Behavior*, Vol. 7, pp. 53–111. Boulder, CO: JAI Press.

Zukin, S. and DiMaggio, P. 1990. "Introduction." In S. Zukin and P. DiMaggio (eds.), *Structures of Capital: The Social Organization of the Economy*, pp. 1–36. Cambridge: Cambridge University Press.

Index

abstraction, 79, 82, 85, 99–101, 108, 118, 121, 122, 224
accounting, 15, 18, 25, 34, 43, 46, 63, 67, 77, 83, 85, 87, 89, 94, 96, 99, 103, 110, 118, 123, 126, 145, 156, 163, 164, 167, 180, 212, 219, 228, 233, 240, 244, 252, 256, 275, 281
Accra, 20, 54, 152, 156, 282
advertising, 28, 29, 31, 211, 282
Africa, 15, 104, 105, 121, 124, 125, 134, 158, 206, 207, 218, 219, 234
age, 19, 25, 73, 91, 98, 127, 128, 130, 205, 224, 239, 276
agrarian civilizations, 1, 3, 5
agriculture, 12, 18, 31, 92, 135, 141–43, 157, 262, 277
aid, 181, 182, 223, 224, 228, 231, 234, 267
Alexander, C., 6, 16, 234, 282
alienation, 38, 100, 233, 247, 280–83
alms, 224, 260, 263
altruism, 18, 62, 93, 120, 128, 236, 237
anthropologists, 8, 12–14, 17, 34–36, 50, 56, 57, 60, 63, 76, 111, 131, 160, 171, 174, 203, 216, 217, 219, 273–76
Aristotle, 1, 2, 3, 5, 88, 93, 133, 135, 136
Arrow, K., 20
association, 92, 100, 104, 153, 252
Austen, J., 1
Australia, 22, 154, 155, 205
autarky, 15, 81, 135, 257, 258, 261
autonomy, 2, 75, 79, 81, 90, 115, 152, 177, 221, 251–53

barter, 2, 24, 27, 36, 41, 80, 85, 88, 95, 110, 121, 244, 257, 277
base, 12, 19, 25, 28, 47, 69, 273, 274, 280, 281
Bastar, 145, 148, 149, 151, 154, 156
Beck, U., 213–15, 217, 219
Becker, G., 17, 18, 20, 37, 142
Beckert, J., 14, 38, 43, 45, 48, 50, 52, 54, 60, 272, 273, 275, 276, 278

Bohannan, P., 2, 84, 218
Bourdieu, P., 22, 53, 70, 71
bridewealth (also bride-wealth), 121, 122, 124, 154, 203
brigade(s), 262, 266
Britain, 3, 5, 6, 16, 97, 106, 204, 207, 226, 233, 234, 239, 240, 256, 257, 276, 279, 282
brotherhood, 145–56, 158, 281
budget, 31, 206, 217, 218, 245, 250
bullion
    gold, silver, 107, 126, 127, 129
Burawoy, M., 15, 165, 166, 175, 177, 178, 202, 281
bureaucracy, 4, 6, 158, 190, 222, 234
business, 23, 24, 27, 96, 148, 149, 176, 182, 200, 209, 216, 219, 233, 250
buying and selling, 1, 23, 95, 121, 124, 125, 128

calculability, 20, 21, 29, 53, 78, 118, 125, 213, 273, 275, 276
Callon, M., 47, 70, 274
capital, capitalism, 3–6, 8, 19, 38, 91, 94, 103, 148–9, 155, 157, 177, 179, 180, 184, 199, 201, 203, 207, 209, 226, 243, 254, 276; *see also* finance capital, trading capital
Carrier, J. G., 16, 234, 244–46, 248, 275, 276
cash, 21, 23–25, 32, 99, 109, 110, 117, 126, 192, 230, 260, 264, 267–69
caste, 1, 47, 86, 145, 146, 148, 150, 151, 153, 154, 181–83, 190, 194
charity, 30, 115, 128, 155, 225, 227, 231, 282
Chartists, 9
Chhattisgarh, 181, 183–85, 187, 188, 195, 196, 199, 202
chiefdoms, 144, 257
children, 23, 30, 115, 121, 172, 182, 197, 201, 205, 225, 235, 264
China, 7, 8, 16, 92, 105, 126–30, 208, 210, 256–59, 262, 266, 269, 270, 282

church, 6, 224, 230
cities, 1, 98, 158
citizenship, 82, 116, 201, 206, 211, 222, 224
civil society, 9, 19, 92, 106, 176, 177, 201, 202, 222, 279, 282
civilization, 4, 13, 15, 92, 94, 97, 98, 256
class, 59, 65, 98, 112, 140, 141, 176, 177, 180, 184, 187, 197, 199, 202, 227, 228, 252, 261, 278
Clinton, W., 10
cognitive embeddedness, 43, 49, 56, 71
coinage, 87, 109, 117, 127, 261
Cold War, 8, 13, 60
Colombia, 23, 31, 219
commercialization, 84, 246, 254
commodification, 15, 44, 74, 75, 84, 176, 178, 268
commodities, 4, 5, 16, 41, 44, 45, 51, 58, 60, 77, 79, 81, 87, 91, 95, 99, 110, 121, 123–26, 150, 162, 204, 212–16, 218, 236, 244, 246, 253, 257, 265, 269, 270
communism, 114, 131, 213
communist, 2, 6, 12, 185–87, 277
community, 21, 24, 26, 28, 134, 157, 265
community currencies, 73, 84
community recycling schemes, 221, 222, 224, 228, 229, 233, 235, 236, 238, 239
comparative method, 55, 57, 160
competition, 26, 33, 45, 47, 50, 55, 78, 80, 89, 127, 161, 190, 232, 254, 279
composite (prices), 205, 207, 213
Comte, A., 61, 68, 71, 120
conceptual tool, 133–35
conservation, 11, 16, 75, 240–42, 244–53, 255, 275
consumption, 27, 30, 32, 70, 93, 112, 119, 130, 169–71, 207, 208, 210, 219, 221, 222, 237, 257, 269
consumer-citizen, 82, 109, 110, 221, 222, 237
contango, 210, 212
contingency, 28, 32, 37, 49, 274, 281, 282
contract, 18, 19, 22, 33–36, 82, 83, 93, 97, 153, 178, 180, 181, 183–85, 187, 188, 190–93, 195–202, 219, 226, 228, 229, 232, 234, 239, 267, 281
contractor, 183, 191, 192, 195, 199, 201
Cook, S., 43, 279
cooperation, 26, 45, 48–50, 54, 55, 93, 162, 165, 261, 267, 281
cooperative(s), 26, 93, 177, 197, 228, 249
coordination, 14, 40, 44, 45, 47–50, 52, 54, 55, 79, 231, 273
corporations, 28, 29, 32, 104, 176, 203, 214, 283
corvée labor, 260, 268
counter-hegemony, 175, 176, 202

craftsman, 119, 169, 227
creative destruction, 3, 104
credit cards, 20, 21, 27, 29, 48, 49, 82, 85, 86, 94, 96, 100, 107, 109, 111–13, 118, 125–30, 148–50, 155, 160, 166, 213, 215, 218
cultures, 14, 17, 29, 42, 45, 49, 101, 144, 171, 193, 202, 212, 213, 217, 272, 273, 279, 280
currencies, 5, 72, 84, 86, 90, 93, 99, 110, 121, 122, 130
custom, 80, 93, 112, 115, 212
customer ties, 29, 32, 46, 148, 156, 167, 230, 236

Dalton, G., 2, 218, 272, 277
debt, 8, 15, 27, 82, 107, 110–14, 116–30, 206, 209, 218, 219, 243, 283
democracy, 7, 9, 93, 102, 179, 228, 234, 279
liberal, 3
social, 3, 8, 13, 74, 103, 276, 279, 281, 283
dependency, 80, 117, 237, 277
development, 13, 33, 41, 44, 52–54, 57, 75, 76, 90, 112, 129, 143, 150, 154, 157, 160, 162, 170, 175, 179, 247, 277
development program(s), 98, 182, 243–44, 246, 248, 249, 281
dialectic, 2, 14, 17, 19, 20, 24–27, 31, 37, 50, 275, 282
differentiation, 47, 48, 52, 90, 173, 265
digital revolution of communications, 91
disembedded, 9, 17, 18, 19, 32, 37, 57, 103, 136, 215, 216, 224, 263, 265, 279
distribution, 5, 39, 48, 49, 65, 96, 135, 152, 205, 209, 228
division of labor, 39, 92, 95, 104, 142, 228, 262, 264, 280
donor(s), 225, 227, 233, 235
double movement, 5, 9, 14, 15, 51, 53, 58, 63–65, 75, 178, 193, 216
dual organization, 133, 144, 145
Duczynska, I., 6
Dumont, L., 73, 76, 84, 146, 147
Durkheim, E., 4, 6, 15, 38, 40, 50, 51, 53, 56, 58–62, 65, 66, 68, 70, 92, 100, 101, 104, 120, 280

economic anthropology, 4, 7, 12, 14, 16, 17, 42, 46, 49, 51, 60, 76, 219, 227, 254, 272, 274, 277, 283
economic life, 11, 12, 14, 69, 135, 140–42, 223, 273, 274
economic sociology, 14, 38–44, 48–53, 55, 56, 58, 59, 61, 67, 69, 272
economics, 1, 10, 12–14, 18, 20, 34, 39, 42, 50, 59, 60, 66, 67, 69, 70, 76, 77, 80, 83,

87–89, 99, 103, 134–35, 141, 142, 179, 226, 273, 276, 279
economists, 3, 7, 10, 12–14, 17–18, 29, 32–34, 40, 43, 52, 64–65, 67, 76, 78, 87–88, 99, 106, 110–11, 141, 203, 217, 276–77
economizing, 7, 31, 32, 33
eighteenth century, 64, 80, 88, 204, 220, 259
Einzig, P., 121
embedded liberalism, 39, 103, 256, 258, 270
embeddedness, 14, 17, 40–44, 46–55, 70, 161, 239, 258, 270, 273, 277, 278
empires, 104, 127, 129, 161, 256
employment, 51, 176, 180, 182–84, 188, 189, 191, 193, 201, 226, 231, 238, 251
Enron Corporation, 27
environment, 9, 19, 49, 74, 80, 167, 194, 226, 234, 235, 237, 242, 244–47, 252
equilibrium, 44, 57, 58, 206, 239
equivalence, 82, 89, 110, 212
ethnic groups, 2, 32, 35, 170
ethnicity, 26, 47, 180, 182, 183, 190, 193, 197, 270
ethnography, 11, 13, 15, 34, 104, 135, 139, 150, 153, 162, 207, 218, 219, 221, 222, 281
evolution, 12, 16, 73, 76, 80, 91, 92, 97, 140
exchange, 9, 11, 15, 19, 21, 22, 24, 25, 30, 32–36, 39–45, 47–52, 54, 55, 61–63, 70, 72, 74, 76–89, 92, 93, 96–98, 100, 101, 104, 107, 110, 114, 115, 117, 118, 121, 125–29, 131, 133, 134, 138, 146, 147, 154, 157, 158, 160, 164, 169, 170, 173, 204, 211–13, 215, 219, 222, 223, 227, 229, 230, 235–37, 239, 243, 244, 247, 257, 269, 273–75, 277, 279, 281–83
expedition, 161, 169, 170
exploitation, 38, 39, 112, 156, 162, 228, 248, 280–82
ExxonMobil, 209

factories, 12, 165, 166, 176, 186, 199, 200, 225, 264
family, the, 9, 24–26, 30, 100, 119, 133, 142, 148, 155, 222, 225, 227, 261, 267, 268
farmers, 10, 87, 98, 119, 165, 172, 173, 211, 257
fee(s), 215, 218, 245, 253
feudalism, 115, 130, 223, 224, 259, 273
fiction, 78, 79, 88, 215
fictitious commodities, 5, 6, 16, 41, 44, 51, 58, 60, 77–79, 87, 95, 162, 204, 206–7, 213, 215–17, 248, 251, 257, 265, 267, 269–70
fieldwork, 13, 15, 145, 152, 153, 158, 231, 258, 268
finance, 72–4, 76, 78, 81, 87, 88, 95, 118, 129–30, 207–10, 218, 234, 275, 283
financial markets, finance capital, 9, 59, 99, 103, 213–7, 283

financialization, 93, 104, 130
firms, 11, 26, 200, 224, 249, 250, 254
First World War, 5, 12, 98, 99, 176, 257
fishing, 243, 249, 250, 252, 253, 284
food-supply, 3, 19, 21–25, 36, 74, 92, 99, 114, 131, 171, 172, 203, 205, 206, 228, 231, 261–263
formality, 4, 7, 17, 18, 21, 27, 30, 32, 33, 35, 48, 54, 59, 60, 63, 64, 67, 70, 76, 117, 153, 158, 183, 191, 218, 229–31, 235, 238, 250, 279, 280
formalist–substantivist, 7, 13, 240, 277
Foucault, M., 63
framing, 21–23, 26, 222
free market, 93, 95, 226, 237, 250, 277, 279
freedom, 3, 5, 10, 45, 49–51, 62, 75, 80, 89, 93–95, 102, 103, 223, 224, 234, 254, 257, 279
friendship, 28, 54, 66, 153
funeral(s), 199, 265, 268
fungibility, 86
futures, 22, 98, 203, 209, 210, 213, 253

Gambetta, D., 54
game, 33, 76, 83, 127, 156, 164–66
Gellner, E., 5
gender, 19, 25, 36, 47, 82, 224, 228, 239, 265
General Electric, 30
Giddens, A., 54, 184, 278
gift, 28, 30, 34–36, 50, 56, 60–62, 70, 80, 93, 110, 112–16, 122, 124, 125, 131, 138, 155, 170, 205, 233, 236, 237, 251, 265
giving, 10, 30, 50, 56, 61, 62, 70, 88, 93, 99, 106, 116, 128, 131, 146, 153–56, 222, 235, 236, 249, 260, 263, 265, 281
global, 2, 3, 9, 10, 12, 13, 37, 39, 72, 74, 92, 94, 99, 101, 102, 104, 130, 146, 150, 158, 159, 193, 204, 211, 213, 226, 238, 239, 247, 268, 278, 282
globalization, 8, 9, 13, 72, 73, 75, 90–93, 103, 276, 277
goats, 125, 164, 168
God(s), 46, 86, 108, 156, 168, 230
Godbout, J., 50
gold standard, 4, 5, 57, 95, 96, 98, 104, 130, 158, 276, 283
goods and services, 9, 11, 18, 23, 74, 77, 79, 80, 83, 99, 111, 117, 239
Goody, J., 5
government(s), 6, 21, 47, 92, 106, 111, 126, 127, 129, 179, 180, 182, 185, 186, 189, 191, 193, 202, 204, 205, 208, 210, 211, 213, 214, 221, 224, 226, 229, 233, 234, 238, 243–45, 247, 249, 250, 260, 268
Graeber, D., 5, 9, 15, 47, 111, 113, 124, 273, 283

Gramsci, A., 15, 175–78, 182, 201, 202
Granovetter, M., 17, 40, 42, 43, 50, 52, 223, 273
Great Depression, 4, 74, 276
Gregory, C., 7, 15, 79, 98, 130, 143, 148, 150, 227, 236, 257, 270, 275, 277, 280–83
Gudeman, S., 14, 18, 19, 24, 47, 50, 172, 227, 272–75, 277, 281
guilds, 32, 47, 52
Guyer, J., 15, 206, 211, 218, 274, 275

Habermas, J., 38, 164, 165, 172, 280
Halbwachs, M., 56, 59, 60
Hann, C., 16, 47, 60, 94, 97, 99, 103, 276, 278
Hart, K., 15, 20, 47, 49, 97, 109, 110, 111, 153, 255, 256, 276, 281, 283
Hayek, F. A., 21, 74, 279
Hegel, G. W. F., 3, 6, 93, 98, 164
hegemony, 8, 15, 176, 177, 180, 185, 189, 191, 201, 202
herders, 164, 165, 170, 171, 173
hierarchy, 77, 81, 83, 84, 87–89, 115, 169, 189, 190, 260
history, 1, 5, 8, 10, 12, 14, 15, 18, 49, 56, 57, 62, 63, 65, 67, 71, 74, 75, 88, 91, 93, 94, 102, 104, 107–9, 112, 125, 126, 131, 133–35, 142, 144, 146, 159, 162, 163, 194, 198, 204, 205, 213, 214, 216, 224, 227, 229, 235, 241, 242, 251, 256, 259, 275
Homo economicus, 14, 37, 60, 62, 66, 71, 76, 141, 274, 277
householding, 5, 79, 133–35, 138, 143, 144, 146, 157, 158, 160, 257, 261, 262, 270
housework, 107, 169, 228
housing, 3, 102, 187, 190, 215, 217, 219, 231, 232, 265
human, 4, 6, 7, 11, 13, 14, 17, 30, 62, 63, 71, 74–77, 80, 84, 85, 88, 89, 91–95, 99–101, 103, 105, 107, 108, 110, 117, 120, 123–25, 127, 130, 135, 141, 142, 144, 161, 162, 166, 168, 213, 214, 216, 218, 221, 223, 244, 256, 265, 273, 276, 277, 282
human economy, 93, 94, 99, 125, 141, 144, 223
humanity, 4, 10, 12, 16, 76, 91, 92, 104, 109, 117, 244, 276, 280
Hungary, 6, 16, 257, 258, 271
hunting, 46, 161, 170, 207, 277

identity, 19, 21, 28, 29, 32, 35, 46, 62, 88, 100, 158, 162, 181, 182, 190, 201, 252
ideology, 9, 15, 29, 42, 49, 79, 89, 101, 103, 106, 120, 148, 176, 177, 205, 223, 256, 262

impersonal, 9, 10, 12, 18, 19, 24, 30, 33, 93, 99, 100, 101, 108, 109, 115, 124, 125, 127, 128, 131, 219, 276
income, 25, 29, 79, 86, 87, 148, 151, 187, 197, 201, 206, 209, 232, 243, 247, 250, 253, 267
India, 8, 15, 92, 105, 116, 127–29, 143, 145, 147, 149, 153–55, 158, 178–80, 182, 185, 201, 208, 281
individualism, 3, 7, 21, 24–26, 28, 33, 44, 75–77, 80, 83, 89, 90, 93, 95, 101, 102, 107, 110–13, 144–45, 167, 186, 190, 214, 223, 225, 226, 268, 273, 274
industrial capitalism, 6, 97, 178, 283
industrial estate, 182, 184, 187, 198–200, 202
industrial relations, 38, 179, 181, 188, 189
industrial revolution, 3, 10, 150, 226
inequality, 3, 7, 12, 51, 84, 91, 103, 104, 226, 266, 282
inflation, 39, 99, 184, 278, 279, 283
informal, 11, 20–22, 32, 35, 39, 49, 150–53, 158, 183, 184, 282
informal economy, 39, 49, 152–53, 158, 282
information, 17, 19, 20, 23, 26–28, 32, 35, 40, 42, 48, 49, 126, 166, 171, 190, 214, 217, 254
instituted process, 7, 144, 145, 148, 152, 153, 157, 158
institutional economics, 3, 15, 83, 277
institutions, 1, 2, 7, 9, 10, 11, 12, 15, 18, 32, 34, 35, 38, 40, 42, 49, 50, 51, 53, 54, 57, 67–69, 71, 76, 79–82, 88, 93, 102, 103, 107, 110, 112, 118, 126, 128–30, 144, 146, 148, 152, 153, 157, 176, 177, 201, 204, 207, 214, 216, 221–23, 225, 230, 240, 247, 257, 265, 272, 273, 276
insurance, 27, 46, 61, 93, 152, 203, 207, 209, 213, 215–19
intellectual property, 28, 47, 203
interdependence, 4, 5, 9, 82–84, 90, 101
internal markets, 80, 82, 234
Internet, 91, 92, 207, 215

Jamaica, 16, 240–45, 247, 248, 250–53, 255, 275

Kant, I., 101
Karl Polanyi Institute, 8(n), 134, 135, 157
Keynes, J. M., 3, 5, 8, 96, 102, 111
kindred, 145, 148, 150, 152
kinship, 2, 18, 21, 26, 28, 35, 36, 116, 133, 140, 143–45, 150, 151, 153, 155, 195
knowledge, 12, 27, 56, 60, 63, 64, 66, 68–71, 76, 78, 88, 95, 162, 163, 167, 168, 205, 218, 275
kula, 35, 36, 93, 104, 108, 169, 170, 257, 277

labor, 5, 9, 15, 29, 37, 41, 44, 73, 77, 89, 107, 161, 162, 179, 189, 193, 201, 216, 237, 238, 244, 248, 261, 268
laissez-faire, 9, 75, 176, 178, 179, 222
land, 25, 95, 141, 178, 204, 216, 244, 245, 253, 261, 266
Landa, J. T., 34–37, 272, 277
landlord(s), 98, 157, 178, 261
language, 34, 85, 97, 101, 123, 147, 153, 168, 259
Latour, B., 168, 212–14, 219
Laville, J.-L., 15, 90, 102
law, 47, 107, 109, 155, 157, 179, 183, 192, 193, 207
Leach, E., 131
left, 93, 171, 187, 239, 279
Lévi-Strauss, C., 144, 153, 167
Lévy-Bruhl, L., 116
liberal state, 4, 57, 95, 103
liberalism, 3, 9, 63, 74, 81, 257, 278–80, 283
liberalization, 189, 190, 193
lifecycle, 225, 263, 268
livelihood(s), 4, 10, 67, 70, 134, 142, 249, 250
loans, 20, 26, 119, 148, 218, 237, 243
local, 21, 32, 36, 41, 51, 72, 77, 83, 93, 101, 120, 146, 158, 222, 224, 238, 247, 249, 253
Lumpenproletariat, 150, 152

machines, 10, 11, 65, 105, 162, 164–67
macro-social, -sociology, 54, 55, 65, 66
mafia, 150, 155, 158
magic, 70, 163, 223
Malinowski, B., 34, 36, 60, 93, 95, 104, 133, 139, 141, 160–63, 169, 170, 172, 257, 281
management, 1, 3, 8, 9, 29, 52, 99, 102, 166, 179, 180, 184, 186, 188–91, 192, 200–2, 210, 225, 231
Marcuse, H., 164
marginal utility, marginalist economics, 2, 22, 47, 141
marine park, 242, 245, 247, 248, 253
market agreements, 21, 22, 27
market capitalism, 8, 9, 263, 277
market expansion/extension, 15, 16, 247
market fundamentalism, 3, 8, 9, 103, 258
market mentality, 56, 63, 67, 68, 70
market model(s), 8, 34, 37, 226
market principle, 2, 16, 93, 221, 234, 263, 268–70
market socialism, 6, 258, 271
market system, 36, 56–59, 65, 67–70, 72–74, 77–79, 81, 87, 95, 125, 148, 162, 243, 244
market, world, 2, 8, 11, 78, 92, 94, 104, 190
marketization, 51, 70, 248

marketplace(s), 21, 23, 36, 70, 78, 82, 83, 87–89, 265
marriage, 22, 121, 125, 142, 151, 154, 261, 262, 268
Marshall, A., 10
Marwari, 148–150
Marx, K., 1, 2, 4, 6, 10, 15, 16, 40, 53, 74, 78, 84, 85, 91, 93, 97, 108–10, 124, 134, 139, 140–42, 159, 162, 164–66, 172, 184, 204, 207, 216, 218, 242, 254, 258
Marxism, 175, 177, 194, 277
Maurer, B., 214, 215, 216, 274, 275, 276, 283
Mauss, M., 4, 6, 15, 34, 36, 50, 56, 60–63, 71, 91–93, 95, 101, 102, 104, 110, 112–16, 124, 128, 141, 281
maximize, -ation, 44, 50, 273, 274
medieval, 1, 2, 33, 52, 115, 129, 138
Meillassoux, C., 170
Melanesia, 121, 122, 135, 172
Menger, K., 7
merchants, 2, 129, 143, 148, 149, 151, 259
method(s), methodology, 2, 12, 59, 66, 75, 134, 138, 142, 143, 160, 165, 166, 212, 277
micro-society, 65, 66, 68, 83
micro-structure(s), 274, 276, 282
migration, 54, 150, 153, 169, 171
mind, 2, 12, 63, 66, 68, 71, 179, 201, 211
mines, 129, 185, 186, 194, 195, 197
mixed economy, 6, 182, 235
modernity, 50, 52, 84, 88, 201, 213, 274, 278, 280, 282, 283
modernization, 18, 52, 53, 55, 262, 264
moiety, 23, 144, 145, 152–54, 257
monetization, 125, 154, 219
money, 1, 2, 4–6, 10, 11, 14, 15, 24–26, 30–32, 41, 44, 46, 60, 72–90, 91–105, 106–30, 145, 146, 150, 154, 161, 170, 171, 184, 193, 211, 212, 215, 216, 228, 240, 257, 261–79
money-making, 11, 133, 136, 138, 142–46, 283
moral economy, 16, 205, 207, 212, 219
morality, 21, 83, 99, 120, 125, 155, 205, 219, 239
mutuality, 14, 17, 18, 20–37, 274–76, 281
mystification, 20, 28, 32, 78, 103
myth, 36, 76, 83, 88, 89, 95, 106, 121, 145, 233, 276

national capitalism, 6, 98, 99, 103, 104
national park(s), 242, 245, 248, 253
nations, nationalism, 2, 4, 8, 19, 25, 57, 62, 254
nation-state, 5, 6, 9, 51, 120
nature, 11, 58, 74, 79, 84, 95, 144, 160, 164, 166, 168, 172, 209, 254, 255, 265

nature, human, 2, 10, 139, 141
necessity, 63, 85, 95, 273, 281
needs, 3, 4, 13, 31, 90, 114, 158, 165, 169, 171, 230, 232, 237
neoliberalism, 6, 39, 73, 76, 99, 103, 105, 106, 221, 240, 256, 278, 281, 282
networks, 1, 9, 21, 26, 42, 43, 48, 52–55, 92, 101, 111, 126, 128, 150, 211, 226, 265
new institutional economics, 40, 272
Nigeria, 15, 171, 206, 210, 211, 275
nineteenth century, 4, 5, 16, 46–48, 58, 59, 64, 65, 74, 75, 84, 94, 97, 98, 103, 104, 120, 134, 136, 160, 162, 176, 179, 215, 216, 220, 222, 225, 228, 243, 256, 260, 276, 279, 283
non-instituted process, 150, 152, 153, 157, 158
non-market, 52, 134, 135, 138, 142, 153, 158, 212, 251, 258, 276
norms, 18, 21, 32, 34, 35, 42, 48, 73, 84, 85, 117, 164, 171, 276

oasis, 171, 259, 260, 264
obligation, 148
obligation(s), 17, 22, 24, 33, 35, 36, 37, 62, 82, 87, 93, 107, 110–20, 125, 130, 153, 154, 215, 236
Oeconomia, 60
oil (petrol), 47, 92, 99, 207–12, 217, 243
order, 9–12, 33, 43, 44, 51, 69, 72, 83, 86–88, 144, 177, 179, 199, 200, 202, 238
ownership, 22, 80, 215, 230, 236, 266, 283

Panama, 24
Parry, J., 8, 15, 99, 182–84, 189, 195, 236, 255, 281
party, 6, 54, 82, 115, 179, 184–87, 190, 262, 263, 265
pay, 21, 24, 181, 186, 187, 189, 192, 194, 251
payment, 28, 77, 80, 82, 84, 85, 96, 97, 101, 110, 118, 123, 126, 127, 197, 204, 208, 209, 211, 212, 215, 219, 252, 267, 269
peace, 4, 5, 21, 72, 95, 126, 185
peasant proprietor, 141–43
performance, 97, 108, 162, 163, 174, 256, 263, 266, 267, 269
person, person-thing, personal, 19, 25, 101, 190, 200
philanthropy, 217, 219, 225–28
philosophy, 128, 152, 259, 279
planning, 4, 103, 178, 179, 181, 193, 255, 258, 279
Polanyi, K., 1–9, 13–17, 19, 36–38, 40–44, 49–53, 55–68, 70–82, 84–97, 99, 102, 103, 105, 106, 107, 121, 122, 132–48, 153, 157–62, 166, 169, 170, 172, 175–78, 180,

193, 202–7, 212–26, 233, 240, 241, 242, 244, 248, 249, 251, 252, 254, 256–61, 265, 267, 270, 272, 274–82
Polanyi Levitt, K., 278
police, 98, 157, 188, 191, 195, 196, 199, 200, 202, 211, 230
political economy, 5, 10, 11, 19, 58, 59, 63–68, 71, 82, 92, 105, 205, 242, 272
politics, 42, 49, 77, 92, 95, 102, 103, 107, 146, 158, 180, 189, 197, 201, 273, 276, 279, 281
possession, 28, 89, 96, 99
poverty, 3, 7, 221, 224, 225, 227, 230, 234, 239, 249, 282
power, 1, 2, 4, 5, 6, 9, 10, 12, 14, 26, 34, 48, 52, 65, 68, 74, 75, 86, 89, 92, 95, 96, 101, 102, 108, 121, 122, 124, 132, 138, 149, 163, 172, 176, 177, 180, 185, 188, 195, 233, 234, 260
pre-capitalist, 172, 212, 273, 276
pre-industrial, 2, 3, 7, 17, 44, 54, 96
price(s)
    setting, 15, 17, 22, 26, 31, 47, 58, 67, 83, 118, 138, 202, 203, 206, 207, 208, 210–12, 217–19, 237, 275
primary product(s), 243, 248
primitive societies, 5, 13, 56, 161
primordial debt, 118, 120, 121, 125
private property, 19, 75, 76, 80, 81, 182, 234, 266, 267
private sector, 178, 180, 185, 187, 193, 268
production, 2, 10, 16–18, 26, 31, 54, 72–74, 76, 77, 79, 81, 85, 87–89, 92, 98, 99, 103, 125, 130, 135, 136, 155, 157, 165, 188, 190–92, 194, 196, 199, 204, 209–11, 216, 238, 254, 259, 261–64, 267, 270, 281, 283
production team(s), 28, 262, 266
profit, 1, 7, 23, 24, 27–30, 60, 62–64, 102, 135, 156, 169, 193, 207, 216
property, 1, 5, 25, 28, 78, 80, 116, 141, 150, 154, 254
pro-poor development, 249, 250, 252
Protestant(s), 225, 242, 279
provisioning, 5, 7, 283
public interest, 3, 14, 102, 239

rational, 4, 7, 12, 17, 18, 33, 34, 36, 37, 39, 43, 50, 52, 62, 63, 66, 76, 78, 163, 174, 213, 254, 276, 278, 279
rationalization, 52, 163, 173, 278
recipient(s), 115, 152, 222, 225, 227, 230, 233, 235, 236, 237, 245
reciprocity, 5, 17, 18, 23, 28, 36, 37, 41, 50, 60, 61, 62, 73, 79–81, 84, 90, 102, 107, 115, 117, 131, 133–35, 138, 142, 153, 161,

219, 222, 223, 237, 257, 258, 261, 262, 269, 276, 282

recycling (schemes), 16, 222, 228, 229, 232–39

redistribution, 5, 6, 16, 17, 18, 41, 60–62, 79, 80, 107, 115, 133–35, 138, 142, 153, 161, 205, 222–23, 231, 232, 237, 257, 258, 260, 263, 269, 270

reform socialism, 6, 16, 258, 269

regulation, 2, 3, 22, 27, 33, 39, 41, 47, 48, 72, 94, 104, 111, 179, 193, 248, 253, 273

religion, 61, 62, 63, 64, 66, 83, 92, 100, 107, 127, 128, 140, 149, 153, 163, 181–83, 259, 263, 270

revolution, 6, 11, 64, 66, 91–94, 97, 98, 103, 119, 157, 177, 179, 201, 223, 258, 262

revolutionary, 93, 176, 195, 197, 199

rights (and duties), 89, 111, 116

risk, 16, 18, 21, 27, 33, 48, 54, 91, 92, 148, 188, 190, 192, 207, 213–19, 226, 239

ritual(s), 36, 85, 86, 108, 118, 154, 155, 257, 261–63, 265–69

Robotham, D., 7, 16, 104

sacrifice, 70, 108, 118, 195

Sahlins, M., 147, 151, 152

Samuelson, P. A., 110

savings (thrift), 31, 32, 99, 171, 235, 266

scarcity, 12, 67, 88, 89, 203

school, 40, 56, 59, 62, 71, 182, 184, 189, 197, 201, 205, 272, 273

Schumpeter, J., 3, 12, 74

science, 10, 65, 76, 163, 228

Second World War, 1, 4, 16, 69, 74, 85, 92, 179, 225

self-interest, 2, 20, 37, 83, 88, 93, 150, 151

self-regulating market, 1, 3, 4, 9, 15, 44, 50, 51, 72, 81, 95, 97, 103, 106, 107, 132, 136, 138, 142–44, 158, 162, 178, 206, 219, 240, 241, 244, 249, 250, 252, 256

self-reliance, 234, 257, 262

self-sufficiency, 1, 3, 11

Servet, J.-M., 9, 15, 88, 102, 178, 274, 275

sharing, 21–23, 143, 146–53, 155, 156, 281

shopping, 30, 31, 236

Simiand, F., 56, 59, 60, 67

slave (-ery), 2, 11, 84, 113–17, 123–25, 127, 129, 140, 243, 252, 259

slums, 54, 152, 153, 227

social groups, 59, 75, 87, 88

social integration, 38, 44, 51, 60

social relations, ties, bonds, 41–43, 54, 55, 74, 75, 78, 80, 85, 88, 124, 131, 132, 136, 141, 158, 160, 215, 223, 233, 236, 257, 258, 263, 270

social reproduction, 155, 228, 238

social sciences, 34, 39, 58, 62, 65, 68, 136

social theory, 3, 38, 51, 53, 215, 219

social whole, 83, 90, 146

socialism, 3, 6, 16, 65, 73, 77, 81, 90, 226, 227, 256, 257, 258, 270, 278, 280, 282, 283

society, 1–13, 19, 41, 51, 55–62, 64–68, 71, 72, 75, 77, 78, 80, 84, 85, 87, 89, 91–93, 95, 96, 100–4, 107, 108, 111, 114, 117, 120, 130, 131, 133, 138, 145, 146, 159, 160–62, 175, 176, 178, 179, 184, 214, 216, 221–24, 226, 236, 249, 258, 259, 280

sociology, 34, 38, 39, 40, 50, 52, 57, 60–64, 68, 69, 71, 274, 276

solidarity, 51, 58, 73, 81, 82, 83, 89, 90, 102, 201, 227, 231, 280, 281

Soviet Union, 92, 182, 261, 262

Spain, 26, 91

Speenhamland, 6, 177, 178, 223, 241

Spittler, G., 15, 163, 164, 170, 173, 281

Steiner, P., 14, 15, 50, 60, 68, 70, 71, 274, 281

strike, 104, 179, 185, 186, 189, 190, 194–99, 210, 231

structural adjustment, 72, 75, 243, 248

structure, 11, 20, 23, 26, 33, 35, 40, 42, 43, 47, 50, 51, 53, 87, 103, 119, 129, 146, 149, 152, 153, 158, 211, 224, 226, 241, 262, 272

subjectivity, 12, 37, 45, 46

subsistence, 25, 63, 67, 169, 252, 262, 264

Suchman, L., 166, 167

sugar, 23, 24, 243

suicide, 24, 58

survival, 4, 7, 12, 262

taking, 24, 146, 150, 151, 156, 281

taxation, 18, 87, 119, 224, 260

techniques

technology, 110, 128, 163, 168

The Great Transformation, 1, 4, 8, 13, 15–17, 40, 41, 43, 50, 51, 55, 57, 59, 60, 62–67, 72, 75–77, 79, 80–85, 91, 94, 104–6, 133, 134, 158, 160, 162, 170, 176, 177, 203, 213, 221, 240, 241, 244, 253, 254, 256–59

the markets, 3, 70, 92, 99, 148, 209

the poor, 112, 126, 150, 152, 162, 225, 235, 237

the state, 2, 3, 8, 9, 33, 34, 47, 74, 79, 81, 99, 102, 107, 110, 111, 117, 118, 121, 127, 130, 146, 153, 155, 157, 175–80, 183–86, 191, 201–3, 216, 221, 222, 224–26, 228, 229, 233, 235, 236, 238–40, 244, 247, 262, 267, 269, 278, 282

the time, 7, 13, 52, 128, 181, 190, 210, 266, 275

third sector, 221, 222, 224, 226, 228, 233, 237, 239

Thompson, E. P., 172, 204, 212, 220

Thurnwald, R., 60, 95, 133, 139, 160–63, 170, 172, 259, 281

Titmuss, R., 236

totality

total social fact, 78, 108, 111, 119, 131, 257

tourism, 244–53

trade, 11, 18–24, 26, 29–31, 34, 36, 37, 48, 75, 80, 82, 84, 96, 99, 104, 110, 124, 127, 129, 151, 157, 158, 161, 169, 170, 232, 243, 252, 259

international, 5, 83, 97, 259

trading capital, 148, 151

tradition, 3, 5, 12, 15, 57, 61, 71, 101, 106, 134, 155, 156, 162, 166, 175, 212, 236, 279, 281

transaction, 2, 17, 21–23, 54, 78, 82–86, 88, 89, 108, 109, 110, 115–17, 121, 122, 125, 126, 128, 129, 131, 146, 150, 152, 206, 219, 233, 234, 236, 237, 251, 273, 274

transaction costs, 18, 32–34, 36, 54, 80

transport, 36, 97, 104, 169, 171, 187, 197, 209, 211, 251

trust, 20, 21, 27, 48, 54, 55, 126, 129, 148, 153, 222, 273, 275, 277, 282

Tuareg (Kel Ewey), 164, 168, 170–1

twentieth century, 4, 6, 12, 52, 59, 63, 69, 91, 94, 102, 143, 162, 167, 204, 225, 226, 228, 243, 253, 259

uncertainty, 26, 32, 34, 45, 46, 50, 213, 214

unemployment, 39, 75, 99, 226, 239

unions, 9, 177, 179, 180, 184–89, 191, 192, 194, 196, 197, 199–202, 279

United States, 25, 29, 30, 46, 76, 98, 105, 112, 167, 177, 219, 249, 279

universal, 7, 10, 12–14, 63, 67, 74, 76, 80, 85–87, 91, 92, 98–101, 105, 128, 139, 141, 142, 166, 179, 277, 280

untouchable(s), 86, 181, 184, 190

utilitarianism, 9, 17, 34, 89, 139

utopia

utopian, 1, 4, 65, 67, 78, 82, 93, 95, 111

value, 45, 46, 218, 251

value realm(s), 18, 19, 274

violence, 15, 20, 107, 112, 116, 124, 125, 127, 132, 150, 158, 196–99, 281

voluntary (sector), 228, 238

voluntary work, labor, 197, 222, 226, 228, 238

volunteer(s), 224, 230, 231, 238

wage laborers, 3, 108, 252

wage work, 16, 108, 135, 140, 157, 173, 237, 238, 251, 252, 265

wage(s), 24, 25, 29, 59, 61, 127, 157, 165, 177, 180, 181, 185, 187, 189, 191, 193, 194, 201, 216, 218, 223, 243

war, 4, 92, 96, 98, 104, 107, 113, 114, 116, 117, 176, 179, 186, 211, 279

Washington consensus, 72

waste, 229, 232, 238

wealth, 2, 3, 18, 19, 25, 37, 65, 78, 94, 100, 104, 112, 115–17, 121, 125, 150, 154, 155, 214, 234

Weber, M., 4, 6, 16, 38, 40, 45, 47, 51, 53, 60, 63, 74, 162, 163, 165, 172, 223, 242, 254, 278, 279, 283

welfare, 7, 8, 25, 26, 95, 190, 214, 221, 222, 224–28, 230, 235, 237, 239

welfare state, 226, 227, 239, 256, 270, 271

Weule, K., 162, 163

women, 2, 25, 124, 126, 131, 151, 164, 165, 169, 184, 192, 194, 196, 222, 225, 227, 228, 239, 261, 264, 267, 269

work, 160–66, 171–74, 177, 180, 213, 237

work as interaction, 160, 169

working class, 15, 162, 176–78, 180, 183–85, 197, 201, 202, 223, 281

world, 1–4, 10, 12, 13, 32, 69, 73, 76, 92, 94, 95, 98, 103, 109, 127, 129, 146, 152, 154, 176, 178, 217, 218

world economy, 11, 13, 96, 97, 98, 104, 129, 158

world history, 5, 13, 14, 15

world society, 15, 91, 92, 94, 97, 99, 105, 158

Xinjiang, 258–61, 263, 266, 270

Zaloom, C., 214, 276

Zelizer, V., 46, 99

Lightning Source UK Ltd.
Milton Keynes UK
UKOW050635260412

191478UK00001B/51/P